FROM G
CO   ...DATTON,
26.7.1777

"The necessity of procuring good intelligence is apparent & need not be further urged—All that remains for me to add is, that you keep the whole matter as Secret as possible. For upon Secrecy, Success depends in Most Enterprizes of the Kind, and for want of it, they are generally defeated, however well planned and promising a favorable issue.

> I am Sir
> Yr. Most Obed. Sev."

THE BALLANTINE ESPIONAGE/INTELLIGENCE LIBRARY

is the first cohesive collection of true chronicles of the greatest, most important, and most intriguing events in the history of international espionage and intelligence gathering. The series offers astonishing new information for the professional and an exciting introduction for the uninitiated. The books delve deeply into the people, events, and techniques of modern espionage—the puzzles, wiles, ruthlessness, romance, and secrets of this endlessly fascinating world.

Written by eyewitnesses or experts, they read "like fiction." But they are undeniably more powerful, because they are *true . . .*

THE SPY MASTERS OF ISRAEL

STEWART STEVEN

BALLANTINE BOOKS • NEW YORK

Library of Congress Catalog Card Number: 80-21497

ISBN 0-345-33927-4

This edition published by arrangement with Macmillan, Inc.

Printed in Canada
First Ballantine Books Edition: February 1982
Seventh Printing: May 1986

In Memory of
Jadwiga Sobieniewska

Contents

Preface

IN *Tinker, Tailor, Soldier, Spy,* John le Carré argued that secret services are the only real expression of a nation's subconscious. It is a stunning phrase which I have chewed over many times during the writing of this book. It is not necessary to go all the way with John le Carré to realize that the history of an intelligence service must also be the history of the nation it serves, viewed, as it were, from the perspective of the servants' hall. The secrets of the "family," how they behave towards each other and the outside world, are often a more accurate and certainly more interesting reflection of the kind of people they are than is the public image they adopt for their friends. No book about an intelligence service can ever hope to tell the whole story. Every nation has secrets which it will clasp to its breast forever more. Suffice to say that I have had access at a sufficiently senior level within the Israeli intelligence community to make this an insider's book without its being in any way an authorized book. No non-Israeli writer has ever been permitted so close. No Israeli writer with such access has ever been permitted to write about it.

In order to try to keep this book to a manageable length I have barely touched upon internal security or counterintelligence; instead I have concentrated upon the two most important arms of Israeli intelligence operations overseas: military intelligence and political, civilian intelligence.

All countries possess both political and military intelligence operations. Usually it is political intelligence which has the upper hand. In the Soviet Union, for example, the KGB has always ranked, both in prestige and power, above the army's GRU. In American the CIA has been considerably more important than the intelligence agencies of the armed forces.

In Israel, as this book will show, power has switched back and forward between the two in an internal struggle for supremacy which has never been satisfactorily resolved. It is this battle as much as the work done by the agencies I describe that is one of the principal themes of this book. Israel has never quite got right the relationship which should exist between its political leadership and the armed forces. Nowhere is this better illustrated than in the history of the Israeli intelligence service.

For obvious reasons I am unable to name many of my sources. Often I couldn't even if I wanted to. People were sent along to see me at my hotel in Herzliya who gave only first names (probably themselves phony) and whom I could trust only because I knew who had sent them. Others asked me not to name them for the good and sufficient reason that to do so could, at worst, physically endanger them and their families, and, at best, inconvenience them in their daily lives.

Of those I can name, I interviewed Boris Guriel, ex-head of the Political Department of the Foreign Ministry; Avraham Kidron, an early member of the intelligence community and subsequently a distinguished Israeli diplomat; Ehud Avriel, one of the founding fathers of Israeli intelligence; Isser Harel, ex-head of Mossad; General Meir Amit, ex-head of Mossad and Military Intelligence; General Yehoshaphat Harkabi, ex-head of Military Intelligence; General Chaim Herzog, ex-head of Military Intelligence; Wolfgang Lotz, an Israeli agent in Egypt in the fifties and sixties; Yehuda Tajar, an Israeli agent in Iraq in the fifties; Shaul Avigur, the spiritual father of modern Israeli intelligence; Victor Levy, an Egyptian Jew, imprisoned for his part in what became known as "the Lavon affair," and members of his team; Yaacov Karoz, a distinguished ex-deputy-head of Mossad; and Aluf Hareven, ex-aide to the chief of Military Intelligence, General Aharon Yariv. All in all I conducted well over a hundred interviews, most of them taped, and I managed to speak to virtually every figure of significance who has emerged in either political or military intelligence since the founding of the State of Israel.

I am particularly indebted to "Abraham," then a senior Mossad executive in Europe, and to his immediate superior "David," without whose active lobbying on my behalf I would not have got to first base in Israel. "Abraham," who has become a close personal friend, is living proof of the thesis that it is possible to work in what must sometimes be a somewhat unsavory trade and yet remain a man of the utmost integrity, always human and humane.

I also owe a debt of gratitude to my researcher in Israel. Eitan Haber is one of Israel's most distinguished military commentators. He is military-affairs correspondent for *Yediot Aharonot* and author or co-author of many books, including *Entebbe Rescue,* the best and most authoritative account of the raid on Entebbe. Eitan Haber constantly bombarded me with high-quality material I would not otherwise have obtained.

I am grateful, too, to Mrs. Penina Peri and Mr. Jo Morgenstern, who did massive translations for me from Hebrew into English and to Mrs. Heather Dyer, who typed and retyped the manuscript as well as a large number of tape-recorded interviews. I wish also to record my thanks to Pat Towers, who so brilliantly edited the final manuscript.

I wish also to pay tribute to my wife, Inka. Not only did she suffer with the book as much as I did, but she did a great deal of research on my behalf. I took her to most of my interviews, where she contributed a great deal. Abraham, who set one up for us, reported later that the gentleman in question had said: "I could deal with him; but I hadn't realized how clever she was until it was too late." My thanks, too, to George Greenfield, who just happens to be, in my view, the world's best and certainly most supportive literary agent. He suggested the subject and held my hand when things were at their bleakest.

Prologue

It was late afternoon, Sunday, June 7, 1981. Heat haze shimmered on the end of the massive runway at Israel's Etzion Air Base in the Sinai Desert. In the control tower a General of the Air Force stood by a special phone connected directly to the war room in Tel Aviv. Minutes earlier fourteen of the world's most advanced aerial war machines had been lifted out of their massive underground bunkers and now stood on the airfield apron, their pilots making last-minute checks for a mission that they had been told was crucial to the survival of the State of Israel. There were eight American-built F-16s, part of a consignment that had arrived in Israel in 1977. Now their designers would hardly be able to recognize them. The Israelis seldom buy weapon systems without considerably modifying them for their exact and peculiar needs. The F-16s came off the General Dynamics drawing board as fighters. The Israelis had turned them into fast, maneuverable, lethal bombers—capable of all the flair of a fighter but carrying the killing power of an aircraft twice its size. Now each plane was carrying 2,000 bombs, a total of sixteen tons of TNT, with impressive additional armaments of Sidewinder missiles under their wings. The F-15s were more conventionally armed with Sparrow and Sidewinder missiles but with extra fuel tanks to permit them to travel distances for which they had not originally been designed. Suddenly at 4:40 P.M. local time the phone rang in the control tower. The General picked it up and listened intently for the identification code and the message "Go." Calmly he replaced the receiver, nodded affirmatively to the Ground Command Controller, and Operation Babylon was underway.

It was some fourteen hours later that the world woke up to discover what the Israelis had done. With one hammer blow, on a bombing raid of quite awesome precision,

xlv *The Spymasters of Israel*

they had set back the nuclear program of Iraq, a country that had been one of its most bitter enemies, several years and, if the international community had anything to do with it, perhaps forever.

The bombers' target was El-Tuwaitha, or rather the Osirak reactor of the huge nuclear complex in El-Tuwaitha, only a few miles from Bagdad. There, French and Italian scientists and technicians had been laboring for years to establish an Arab nuclear potential that the Iraquis always claimed, when they spoke to Western governments, was required for solely peaceful purposes but, when talking to militant Arab friends, they hinted that it could eventually be used to destroy Israel once and for all. "The Iranian people should not fear the Iraqi nuclear reactor," said a Bagdad newspaper in September 1980, when the complex was damaged in an Iranian air raid. "It is not intended to be used against Iran but against the Zionist enemy."

So the F-15s with the F-16s flying support, following a brilliantly conceived flight plan that took them clear of hostile radar stations and listening posts, swept in. The lead plane put a pair of video-guided "Smart" bombs straight through the vast dome of the nuclear reactor. With stunning accuracy, the following aircraft came in low and deposited their bomb loads into the crater, creating a raging inferno as first the atomic shield literally melted and then the reactor core, the heart of the whole system, disintegrated and crumbled into the cooling pool below.

Almost three hours after take-off, mission completed, all fourteen planes touched down successfully in Israel. Operation Babylon was over.

To the world at large, this brutal take-out of the Iraqi French-built Tammuz reactor was yet another example of the unacceptable use of Israeli muscle; a display of the kind of arrogance that the nation's critics have come to expect of this tiny country, with its minimal resources, that has yet so unexpectedly and so extraordinarily become the military superpower of the region.

Few of these were prepared to listen to Prime Minister Begin's defense of Israeli action—namely that Iraq, once the reactor was switched on—and this was due anytime—would be in a position to produce weapons-grade fuel for an atomic weapon that would put the whole of the State of Israel at risk. "There will never be another holocaust in the history of the Jewish people," he said theatrically. "Never again, never again."

It was the Prime Minister's emotional use of language that persuaded even normally sober commentators and politicians to assume the attack on Osirak was but a spectacular election-winning stunt, a demonstration not of Israeli power but of Begin's determination to win at all costs an election that was running perilously close. That is, of course, a preposterous notion, which, apart from any other consideration, fails to take into account the considerable non-Party nonpolitical influence in Israel of both its armed forces and its intelligence community.

And it was the latter, men operating deep within the shadows who, from 1975 on, had been warning their politicians and the leaders of the Western world of the increasing likelihood that Iraq was using its vast oil wealth to build an atomic weapon, that Iraq's President Saddam Hussein hoped would at one stroke give his country automatic leadership of the Arab world and the potential to blackmail Israel into acquiescent submission. This is not to say that the fact that Israel was in the middle of an election campaign did not have some influence on the decision to give the "Go" signal on June 7. The polls showed that Menachem Begin's early lead was slipping. Israel's military leaders, who had spent months seeking to persuade him to make the hard political choice to make the raid, were afraid that if he lost at the polls it would take longer than the July 1 deadline, when the reactor was expected on stream, to similarly persuade the dovish Labor Leader Shimon Peres that an attack was vital. If the attack came after July 1, an air assault would have unleashed a horrifying wave of radioactivity that would have killed thousands. That the Israelis were determined to avoid.

Israel had been exercising itself over the Iraqi bomb since September 1975, when President Hussein went to Paris to open the negotiations for the purchase of a French reactor to be built on the El-Tuwaitha site, 10.5 miles southwest of Bagdad. Statements by Iraqi politicians to their own press that the Arabs must have a nuclear capability against the Israelis were dismissed everywhere else but in Tel Aviv as Arab bombast, to be taken no more seriously than repeated Arab statements over the many years that the destruction of the "Zionist entity" was imminent.

But the Israelis, who live closer to the Arabs than do any of their critics, understand them much better too.

"The Americans and the Europeans," says one ex-Chief of Israeli Intelligence, "assume that when an Arab makes a statement that appears exaggerated or extreme, he doesn't really mean it. We know he does. He may not be able to execute his intentions, but he would if he could. So when an Arab country says that it wants to make an A-bomb, this is not mere rhetoric. Given the wherewithal, that country will make an A-bomb."

What made the Iraqi program so potentially dangerous was the huge amount of money available to the country through its oil wealth and the vast ambition of President Hussein to take over the leadership of the Arab world. The fact that Iraq had signed the Nuclear Non-proliferation Treaty and Israel had not was a factor that cut little ice in Tel Aviv but one that was to muddy the waters subsequently when Israel sought to warn the international community as to what was going on in Bagdad.

So it was in the beginning of 1976 that office space was prepared in the headquarters of Mossad, the political arm of the Israeli intelligence community, Tel Aviv's equivalent to the CIA, where a special task force was set up to monitor the Iraqi program. It had an anonymous, professional Mossad man at its head, an intelligence agent who had seen service on behalf of Israel in Europe and the Arab world, a superb linguist who could pass himself off as the national of at least four countries, and who was then regarded as one of the top half-dozen men in the intelligence field in the country. His deputy was a young nuclear scientist who had worked on Israel's atomic program, who had been educated at American universities, and a man unlikely to be swayed by any opinion unless it was scientifically soundly based.

The first task of this unit was to monitor the French nuclear-production facility at La Seyne-sur-Mer near Toulon. Members of Mossad attached to the agency's European offices were deployed so that a constant stream of information about the reactor-building program flowed through to Israel, and in the meantime the Israeli Embassy in Paris was provided with additional scientific officers so that on-the-spot assessments could be made on the material the agents were getting.

It was clear from the early returns, particularly from the political field, that the French Government honestly believed that the reactor they were building for the Iraqis could be used for only peaceful purposes. However, it also became clear that so aggressive had French selling become that ministers and officials, delighted with such a profitable order from oil-rich Iraq, had not looked too closely at the specifications. But by the end of 1978, the French Government and also the American Government were left in no doubt, as the result of the Israeli information gained exclusively by classic espionage techniques that the reactor, which was by now almost complete, could indeed be used to produce an awesome weapon in the wrong hands. Pressure was put on the French for them to renege on the order, but though they sought to persuade the Iraqis, unsuccessfully, to take delivery of another reactor type altogether, they said they could not break a contract that had been formalized at Head of State level. Instead, on April 5, 1979, three days before the reactor core was to be shipped to Bagdad, members of the French security services broke into the factory and laid explosive charges, sufficient to damage the reactor without destroying it, in the hope that this delay would give them time to persuade the Iraqis to change their minds. Unofficially the French hinted that Mossad was responsible for this act of sabotage, but then they could hardly let the world know that, working in concert with Mossad, they had deliberately damaged their own equipment at the behest of the Americans and the Israelis.

It was an extraordinary interlude in the secret world of espionage, a sport played at international level where not only does no one know the names of the players, no one knows the rules and, at the end of each game, no one is really clear as to the result. This truth was illustrated just over a year later, when on July 14, 1980, the Egyptian-born head of Iraq's nuclear program, Yahia El-Meshad, was killed at the Hotel Meridien in Paris.

Mossad was blamed, but the evidence suggests that El-Meshad was killed by the Iraqis themselves, having been suspected of supplying the Israelis with the blueprints of the nuclear program. For once again, cross and double-cross was to figure prominently in this affair. The

Israelis had obtained all the blueprints that had given them the lever to persuade American and French nuclear experts as to the lethal nature of the reactor the French were building. These blueprints fell into the hands of a French official who was closer to the Iraqis than his official function should have permitted. He handed a copy of their own blueprints back to the Iraqis, proving that they had been betrayed. Their investigations into the leak led directly to El-Meshad.

However, despite all of this, the French and the Italians who were supplying fuel and expertise felt their commitment to the Iraqis was such that if they could not persuade them to cancel or modify their order, then they had to go ahead. Having done so, they managed, it seems successfully, to persuade themselves that they would be able to monitor any diversion of enriched uranium by the Iraqis for bomb making or any plans for converting the reactor to plutonium production. France did its best to keep a tight grip on the amount of enriched uranium delivered, in order to prevent stockpiling that would permit the Iraqis to make a bomb, and at the same time tipped off the International Atomic Energy Agency inspectors to keep a careful watch for any reactor fuels coming from unauthorized sources and available on the international black market.

The Israelis, in turn, through the reactor task force office in Tel Aviv, also monitored the amount of fissionable material going to Iraq and, with agents actually inside the plant, kept a guarded but increasingly fearful eye on what they were seeing.

The trouble was that, for understandable enough reasons perhaps, the International Atomic Energy Agency was loathe to accept evidence from a country that had not signed the Nuclear Non-proliferation Treaty, which tended to finger a country that had.

"This was not deliberate," says an Israeli expert who had dealings with them, "but merely the manifestation of the perfectly human reaction of people prepared to believe a member of the club against the word of an outsider."

The fact is, and whatever their public references to the contrary, any country in the world who knows anything about the subject in and out of the Middle East, knew that not only was the Iraq Tammuz reactor ten times more powerful than any reactor anywhere in the world designed for the purposes for which this reactor was overtly designed, but Iraqi scientists had been buying black-market uranium.

Italy, Portugal, and Niger had signed an agreement with Brazil (not a signatory of the Non-proliferation Treaty) for supplies of uranium and an exchange of technology, and technical experts were ferrying back and forth between Sao Paolo, Bagdad, and Rawalpindi, where the Pakistanis were coming to the breakthrough point of manufacturing their own bomb.

By the middle of 1980, Mossad's special task force presented a thick report to Prime Minister Begin, which stated with no qualification whatsoever that the Iraqis were within eighteen months to two years of manufacturing the Moslem Bomb. Their recommendation: Take out the reactor field at El-Tuwaitha. Begin sent the report to President Carter, informing him that unless international measures were taken to stop Iraq, then Israel would feel free to operate on its own.

Carter agreed "to do something" and this commitment was taken on by the Reagan administration, but as talks between the Iraqis and the Americans become more and more bogged down by the constant denial of the Iraqis that there was anything to worry about, the Israelis knew they were on their own. Believing time was no longer on his side, Begin ordered the strike. With the classic precision of all such Israeli operations, possible because of the remarkable military work of Mossad and Israeli military intelligence in laying out the target for military plans down to the smallest detail, the bombers struck home with devastating effect.

Ever since Hiroshima, the world has talked about the problem of nonproliferation. This was the first time that a country about to go nuclear had been halted in its track, and it was military action and not negotiation that did it.

Considering the quite awesome nature of the Israeli raid, many will think it extraordinary that the political fallout on Israel had not been greater than it was. Despite the raid, a cease-fire was called in Lebanon; despite the raid, the Saudis produced a peace initiative that amounted to the nearest they had ever come to acknowledging the existence of the State of Israel; and the American Government, while it did temporarily hold up on the supply of

XX   The Spymasters of Israel

new aircraft for the Israelis, proved to be remarkably restrained in its condemnation of the Israelis.

"The fact is," as one senior Mossad official put it, "the whole world, not least other Arab countries, was secretly delighted with what the Israelis did. The French were getting off the hook, the Americans had one less problem with which to deal, and the Arab world knew that the overweaning ambition of Hussein had been once more held in check."

In many ways this raid, which used military means to round off one of the great espionage operations anywhere in the world since the end of World War Two, had all the hallmarks of a classic Israeli intelligence operation. A target was destroyed with awesome accuracy; the political repercussions had been precisely calculated, and the end result was to increase Israeli Security, at least in the short term, in order to give the prospects of peace a breathing space in the long term.

Technically, both in planning and preparation and then in final execution, it was yet another extraordinary illustration of the almost breathtaking ability of Israel to take up a military or an espionage commitment and carry it through to its conclusion with faultless timing and immaculate precision.

Shortly after President Carter's abortive and humiliating attempt to release the Iranian hostages, I talked through the operation with an ex-Head of Israeli Military Intelligence.

"Everything that went wrong with that raid was forseeable and should have been forseen. But the greatest failure was a failure in intelligence. The American helicopters actually set down a bus route. To us that is incredible. If that had been our operation, our men would have been set down on the ground weeks before, analyzed the terrain from every point of view, and if it had been found unsuitable as this clearly was, would have come up with a new landing strip. We have been successful because we leave nothing to chance. For we know that failure is always a poorer option than not trying in the first place. If the chances of failure are more than 25 percent we don't go."

If the Bagdad raid was a military success, an event in the political sphere of even greater importance occurred only a few years earlier.

When on September 18, 1978, before an incredulous world, President Anwar Sadat of Egypt and Prime Minister Menachem Begin of Israel embraced for the benefit of the television cameras to signify the successful conclusion of the Camp David summit, the Egyptian leader turned to Begin and, with all the mordant fatalism of Egyptian humor, said: "At least now you'll be able to come to my funeral." Replied Begin elliptically: "There will be no funeral." Only a very few who heard the remark understood its meaning.

President and Premier looked at each other with the shared smile of conspirators playing a secret game to an arcane rule book. What in fact they had produced was not merely a remarkable diplomatic triumph against formidable odds, but also one of the most extraordinary agreements in the history of that endlessly fascinating, frequently disturbing, and sometimes morbidly paranoic world of secret intelligence.

For the Israeli intelligence community this agreement, enshrined in one of the many closed codicils to the published agreement, was to prove the end of an era—an era in which Israeli intelligence had fought, frequently alone, against the combined might of the Arab intelligence services, the Palestinian resistance movement and the Russian KGB.

In the event, of course, tragedy was to strike, and Begin was forced to make that unhappy journey to Cairo for the funeral of his friend who had been struck down by the bullets of ruthless assassins. Yet, as he stood by the graveside, surrounded by his security men, Begin could comfort himself with the knowledge that it was not he who had let his friend down. Both knew when they signed the treaty that they could also be signing President Sadat's death warrant. Enemies would spring up throughout the Arab world, determined to cut him down; ruthless, determined men bent on killing the Camp David Treaty by slaying its author.

Begin pledged to Sadat the full protection of the Israeli Security Services. It would now become one of the additional functions of the Israelis' already overstretched secret services to infiltrate opposition groups to Sadat outside Egypt. For his part, Sadat was sure that his own security services would be able to protect him from fanatics in Egypt itself. We now know that he was wrong and paid the price for it with his life.

Yet Sadat's legacy of peace has, so far at least, survived him. That must be put into the balance against the brutal assassination made possible by the dereliction of duty of his own security people.

On the other hand, Anwar Sadat had every reason to respect the Israeli intelligence services. In July 1977, General Hacka Hofi, a tough, experienced ex-tank commander and head of Israel's CIA (known throughout the world as Mossad), called upon Israel's new Prime Minister, Menachem Begin, who had been in office less than a month after a sensational general election in which his party, the right-wing Likud, had finally—after thirty years of statehood—broken the Israeli Labor Party's stranglehold on government. Hofi brought with him a remarkable, detailed file of an operational plan set up by Colonel Muammar al-Qaddafi, President of Libya, that would use Palestinian hit men to assassinate President Sadat of Egypt.

This information had come from deep-cover agents that Hofi and his distinguished predecessors had established within the Palestinian Liberation Organization: men and women who had, over the years, provided the Israelis with the means time and time again to frustrate the world's largest, best-armed and most expertly officered and trained terrorist army. This was not the first time, of course, that Mossad's wide trawl had caught a fish that had little bearing upon the security of the state of Israel. The Israelis had no reason to love Sadat or to care a great deal about what happened to him. He had led his armies to war against them, and he had done nothing to suggest that he was anything but an implacable foe of the Jewish state. Nevertheless, Hofi proposed to do what Israeli governments had always done in similar circumstances in the past, and that was to pass along this information to the CIA, who, if they felt they could earn good-will by so doing, would pass it on to the Egyptian President as a piece of American intelligence. But Begin didn't agree. Let the Egyptians see that we have no quarrel with them. Pass the file to President Sadat with the compliments of the Israeli government. Within twenty-four hours, Hacka Hofi was on his way to Rabat, Morocco, for one of those remarkable meetings—which occur more often than we care to think in the secret world of intelligence men—to see, by prior appointment, the head of the Egyptian secret service, Kamal Ali. Whatever suspicions they may have entertained about Israeli motives, the Egyptians had to act; the Israeli dossier was too detailed not to be taken seriously. They quickly found they were right to do so. After a series of dawn raids on addresses in Cairo—provided by Mossad —Colonel Qaddafi's conspirators were arrested. After a few days in custody, his Palestinian mercenaries confessed to everything and produced arms caches and documents proving they were working on the orders of the President of Libya. Sadat responded immediately. He punished Qaddafi by launching a massive border raid into Libyan territory and thanked the Israelis by finally letting them learn that he had nursed for years a secret ambition, the belief that he could bring peace to his troubled region by agreeing to a nonbelligerency pact with his old enemies. So it was a secret intelligence operation that made President Sadat's historic mission to Tel Aviv possible, and it would be secret intelligence that would help keep the impetus of that journey through to Camp David and beyond to today, alive. Perhaps it was inevitable that this should be the case.

Nowhere has secret intelligence been played for higher stakes than it has, during the past thirty-five years, in the explosive region of the Middle East. The CIA and KGB have fought each other to protect and preserve the prestige of their nations. But the Israeli and the Arab intelligence services have been engaged in a struggle for life itself.

There have been five shooting wars (including the War of Attrition in 1969–1970) and numerous bloody military excursions between the Arabs and the Israelis since the first such strife in 1948. But for the respective intelligence agencies of each side, these wars were but mercifully brief reenactments, on a larger and more publicized stage, of the day-to-day realities of their lives, namely, the state of permanent war which existed between them. Not for a moment could either side afford to forget that; though there may have been periods when the armies retired to their barracks, hostilities never ceased.

These were intelligence agencies on a war footing—as deadly and as ruthless as any of those many agencies which the combatants in World War II employed to fight pitched battles of cunning and strategem, where plot and counterplot interwove to produce what Winston Churchill once described as "actual facts . . . in every respect equal to the most fantastic inventions of romance and melodrama."

"We are good at our task," recruits to the Israeli intelligence services are told during training, "because the alternative is too horrifying to contemplate."

Camp David was to have stunning significance as to how that war would be fought in future. For, almost unbelievably, it was agreed by secret treaty that the region's two most powerful intelligence agencies—the General Intelligence Directorate of Egypt and Mossad, the secret political-intelligence agency of Israel—would share information. Almost overnight the balance of power in the area switched dramatically.

Of course, Israeli intelligence, like the Israeli Army, had always been supreme in the region. Operating with few men and little money, it had usually managed at the worst to hold its ground, and at the best to enjoy a marginal superiority over its numerically powerful but usually politically divided opposition. But now, with the Israelis working hand in hand with the Egyptians, in one stunning stroke the Palestinian resistance movement had been weakened to an astonishing degree. Israel, in short, had won one of its greatest battles.

When the news of the Camp David agreement reached Palestinian leaders, they swore revenge. Anwar Sadat, as he later told associates, was put on so many hit lists that he could have papered his sitting room with them. Israel was to be the target of an unrelenting and remorseless campaign of terror. Egyptian and Israeli embassies and the airlines of both countries would suffer the consequences of their leaders' folly. Few commentators at the time believed that Sadat would long survive. Israel itself held its breath.

Yet since the signing of the Camp David agreement, Palestinian terror activity, remarkably and almost unbelievably, has been at a lower level than at any time since the Palestine resistance movement first became a reality in the early sixties. It is as if the genie has been put back into the bottle. How has this happened?

It was President Nasser who, in 1955, gave the Palestinians their first cohesive military structure. The Palestinian resistance meant nothing until Nasser devised the policy of using the Fedayeen to fight by proxy what he regarded as his war against the Israelis. He armed them, he trained them, he paid them, and his men officered them.

The Palestinians, of course, had moved a long way in the years that followed. They had sought and found new patrons in a conscious desire not to be beholden to any one country or interest. The Syrians, the Iraqis and the Russians played important roles in their development. Yet always, especially at times of crisis, it was to the Egyptians that the Palestinians were forced to turn. Of all of the Arab states, Egypt was the most stable; its intelligence services were not merely the largest and the most professional, it was the least corrupted by political intrigue, staffed with a corps of professional officers who owed their position to ability rather than patronage.

Those were the links between Palestinians and Egyptians which were suddenly slashed. It was a coup of almost unimaginable proportions for the Israeli intelligence community. The Israelis were able to pull it off only because their stature was such that, without a treaty of friendship between Mossad and the Egyptian General Intelligence Directorate, the Egyptians knew that all that had been achieved by Camp David would inevitably collapse. It was Mossad who could guarantee the life of the Egyptian President; it was Mossad who could monitor the activities of the rejectionist Arab states, and it was Mossad, working with the Egyptians, who would severely weaken the Palestinians as an effective terrorist organization.

For the Palestinians, though only now are they beginning to guess at its real significance, this Israel-Egyptian accord marks perhaps the greatest disaster in their history—greater even than the civil war in Jordan in 1970 and 1971, which led to the elimination of all Palestinian bases there and to the terrible suffering of the Palestinians during the Lebanese civil war beginning in 1975. During these two catastrophes, to be utterly cynical, the Palestinians merely lost men—soldiers who could soon be replaced on the battlefield as a new generation grew up to take their place. But the Israeli-Egyptian secret concordat on intelligence lost the Palestinians their ability to act.

There was little about the Palestine Liberation Organization that the Egyptians didn't know, since many PLO senior officials, both in the political and the military wings of the movement, were creatures of the Egyptians. The Israelis had, of course, for years successfully infiltrated many sections of the PLO. But now, with Egyptian cooperation, the Palestinians had virtually been eliminated as a serious threat.

The Palestinians reacted to these developments with a display of fratricidal hatred which can only be understood in the context of Camp David. The PLO organization in Iraq claimed that Yasser Arafat's Beirut headquarters had been so completely infiltrated and compromised that it was no longer capable of exercising the leadership necessary to launch a successful operation against a Zionist target.

Two PLO renegades—Abu Nidal (variously known as Sabri Khalil al Banna or Mazen Sabri al Banna) operating out of Baghdad, and Wadi Haddad from the South Yemen, both cold-blooded killers—ran attacks on PLO men in Paris, London and elsewhere in attempts to bomb their way to the leadership of radical Palestinian opinion. Their mistake was that, while it was true that the regular PLO had been penetrated to an unacceptable degree, so had the renegades. It didn't take long for the Israelis to get on their track and, with the operational ability which the Egyptians gave the Israelis, to use the PLO as their surrogates to discredit, almost totally, the dissident groups and their supporters.

In Damascus, Beirut and Baghdad, various Palestinian groups fought (and sometimes died) in squabbles which often went unpublicized. But all were monitored, and sometimes stirred up, by Mossad, the puppet-masters of a deadly game.

The remarkable hold the Israelis now had on the Palestinians was felt even as far away as America, and led directly to the resignation of the American ambassador to the United Nations, Andrew Young. On July 26, 1979, Andy Young went to the home of Abdalla Bishari, the Kuwaiti ambassador to the United Nations, where he met and talked to Zehdi Terzi, the official PLO observer at the United Nations. This meeting violated an agreement between President Carter and Prime Minister Begin that there would be no American recognition of the PLO, no meeting between American officials and PLO representatives.

Initially, when the news first broke, it was claimed that Terzi had only chanced to call on Bishari while Young was being entertained by his Kuwaiti colleague. This explanation proved to be less than the truth, as the Israelis, rather heavy-handedly, were quickly able to prove. They made it apparent to everyone that they knew precisely what had gone on at the meeting and how it had been arranged. They even appeared to have a transcript of part of the conversation.

Reactions in the American press and at the United Nations became understandably heated, even paranoic. Wild allegations that the Israelis had bugged the Kuwaiti ambassador became fact in American newspaper accounts. Senior U.N. officials from Kurt Waldheim, the Secretary General, down became convinced that the Israelis had "ears" everywhere.

The Israelis were secretly delighted at the furor. Certainly the reputation for omniscience could hardly do their intelligence service any harm. Success in intelligence, as in any other walk of life, breeds success. Agents can be persuaded to change sides; fear inhibits the opposition; potential friends agree to alliances. Everybody wants to walk with a winner.

But the truth behind the Andy Young affair was almost mundane. The Kuwaiti ambassador had simply dispatched a long diplomatic telegram the night of the meeting to his Foreign Office, detailing the conversation as precisely as he could and explaining the circumstances behind it. Immediately, the Kuwaitis, as was natural for them to do, made this telegram available to the infiltrated PLO, and within hours it was in the hands of Mossad in Tel Aviv. No one needed to bug the Kuwaiti Embassy, no one needed to break the ambassador's diplomatic code. Security had been broken the moment the Kuwaiti government decided to inform the PLO.

Today the Israeli intelligence community sits supreme in the Middle East. Its voice is ignored at peril. Months before the Shah fell, for instance, the Israelis were warning the Americans of the nature of the revolution they were ushering in by not more forcefully supporting

Pahlevi. The State Department—believing it was listening to the special pleading of a Jewish state that feared militant Islam—chose to disregard them. Moreover, the Israelis were able to warn the Saudis, through an intermediary, of an imminent attack upon the Holy Mosque at Mecca—only to be ignored. Never before have the Israelis been in a better position to influence the region in which they seek their precarious existence.

The Syrian and Palestinian missile crisis in the summer of 1981 amply illustrates this point. The Syrians did seek to alter the balance of power in the area by moving SAMs into a forward position, thus gravely weakening Israel's ability to maintain aerial surveillance of the "killing land," that area between the Lebanese border and Israel from which the Palestinians have sought to wreak such havoc over the years. What was generally overlooked, as the American mediator shuffled back and forth between Damascus and Jerusalem, was that though the Israeli side laid down a great deal of political flack, militarily it had always had the situation under complete control. Within hours of any troop movements or new missile emplacements, the Israelis were able to signal knowledge to the U.N. and the American mediator, either contemporaneously or, on at least three occasions, astonishingly before they took place. Israeli counter-thrusts were always precisely gauged to take out the target because they knew exactly where that target was. Even the air strike on the Headquarters of the PLO in Beirut on July 17, 1981, which inevitably cost the lives of innocent civilians, nevertheless caused in terms of modern warfare remarkably few casualties outside the target area. For so confident were the Israelis that their intelligence once again had it exactly right, their air-force bombers were equipped for the purpose with special light bombs in order to minimize nontarget fatalities.

Once again it was the Israeli intelligence community that made it possible. And it was because the Syrians and the PLO came to realize that the Israelis always had mastery, chiefly because of their uncanny ability in the field of intelligence, that they eventually agreed to a cease-fire, having made no military or political gains whatsoever.

Yet, as is true of any intelligence organization, Israeli intelligence has not had a history of unalloyed triumph. It has gone through trauma, even despair. It has faced, along with its many victories, spectacular defeats. If today Israel possesses one of the world's greatest and most successful intelligence operations, that is because it has proved it has the capacity to learn from its errors.

"Many men went before you," an instructor tells his pupils at the central school for intelligence in Tel Aviv. "It is your duty to ensure that many more men can follow in your footsteps. A few decades isn't long to build up a tradition. Learn from it."

The tradition, ordinary Israelis say, actually goes back to the Bible when Moses sent 12 men to ". . . spy out the land of Canaan . . . and see the land . . . and the people that dwelleth therein, whether they be strong or weak, few or many." From there, they say, a direct line can be drawn to a remarkable Jewish espionage service which operated in Palestine on behalf of the British during the First World War and then through to the activities of the Israeli intelligence services today.

The professionals actually involved disdain such romantic fancies. Their saga, they say, began during that period immediately before the Israeli State was founded. It was during those tumultuous times that their story, and this book, rightfully begins.

PART I

Uneasy Genesis

Chapter 1

A LIGHT POWDER OF FROST clung to the runway at Tel
Aviv airport—then no more than a collection of huts
alongside a bumpy runway—as the DC-4 of Swissair
Flight 442 hit into the thin early morning air, coughed as
if hesitant, and then soared up and away on its long journey to Paris.

The date was early February 1948. Israel had not yet
achieved full independence; that lay three months away
by vote of the United Nations. Yet the Jews were already
preparing themselves for the war against the Arabs they
all knew must come.

In the first-class compartment of the DC-4 sat a young
Syrian army officer, Captain Abdul-Aziz Kerine, on his
way, via Paris, to Prague as the accredited representative
of Syria's Minister of Defense Ahmad Charabati to purchase from the Czechs 10,000 rifles, which his country
would need for the avowed purpose of driving the Jews
into the sea.

A few seats behind Captain Kerine, by remarkable
coincidence, sat another passenger on a similar mission.
His Palestinian passport showed him to be George Uiber-
all, director of a Jewish firm with interests abroad. His
real name, however, was Ehud Avriel, the thirty-one-
year-old representative of one of the most secret organizations in Jewish Palestine, Rekhesh, the arms-procurement
agency for the Haganah, the underground army fighting
for independence from the British and survival against
the Arabs.

He, too, was on his way to Prague to purchase weapons for an armory which was all but empty. The Jews
were desperately short of guns, though it was not until
two months later, in April, that anyone bothered to make
a proper inventory of what fire power the Jewish underground army possessed to take with them into independ-

3

ence. All they had were 10,073 rifles, 190 submachine
guns, 186 Bren guns, 444 machine guns, 672 two-inch
mortars, and 96 three-inch mortars. They did not have a
single artillery piece or heavy machine gun, no antiaircraft guns or armored cars. Naturally, they had no tanks,
no air force or navy. Against that pathetic arsenal would
come an enemy equipped with the most modern weapons
that the world, and particularly the British, could then
provide.

Rekhesh, the organization, which Ehud Avriel then
represented, was only one of many clandestine estab-
lishments in pre-independence Israel that today lay claim
to being the real founding fathers of the modern Israeli
Secret Service. The country sometimes seemed awash
with undercover organizations, each more secretive than
the next. Apart from the Haganah itself, there was its
own secret-intelligence unit, called Sherut Yediot, or
Information Service, which came to be known as Shai.
Its members penetrated deep into the British administration, watched over dissident Jewish organizations, and
infiltrated the Arab population of Palestine. Then there
was the Palmach, an elite full-time military formation,
the strike arm of the Haganah, with its own secret service, the Arab section, which placed meticulously trained
young Jewish men to live and work as Arabs inside the
Arab townships. And Rekhesh, the overseas arms-
collection agency, had a twin organization which ran illegal immigrants into the country: Mossad le-Aliyah Bet,
or the Institute for Immigration "B," making a nice distinction between it and the officially permitted Immigration "A."

The particular stamp of any secret service has much to
do with a question of style. It is fair to suggest that the
remarkable clan of Rekhesh and Mossad le-Aliyah Bet,
more than any other organization of the period, helped
set the tone for what was to become the Israeli Secret
Service. Patrimony is disputed, but the daring, imagination and bravado of these two seems closest to what the
world now recognizes as the very special quality of the
Israeli service.

At the head of Rekhesh and Mossad was a magnificent
lion of a man, Shaul Avigur, one of the great founding
fathers of the state of Israel. Working out of two small
flats, one in Geneva and one not far from the Champs

Elysées in Paris, he ran what was, in effect, Israel's first overseas intelligence mission. Under Avigur a whole generation of Israeli secret agents learned their business. Those who worked for Mossad found themselves arranging escape routes, false passports, safe houses and the like, and chartering ships to take their charges to Palestine, all under the noses of the British Secret Service, then still regarded as the finest in the world. For Rekhesh, they learned how to set up dummy corporations, live under fake identities, and run a fully operational clandestine service hundreds and sometimes thousands of miles away from home. It was these men from Mossad and Rekhesh and the Arab section of the Palmach who would provide the backbone of Israeli intelligence during the fifties, sixties and seventies. Only now are the last of them retiring, men whose whole lives have been spent in an extraordinarily demanding clandestine hermitage where the demands have been heavy and the rewards few.

Shaul Avigur, the man in charge of Rekhesh and Mossad, was born in 1899 and came to Israel from his native Russia in 1912. Like the great majority of the early pioneers, he went straight to a kibbutz and might have remained a farmer if his best friend had not been killed in a skirmish with a band of Arab marauders. When he heard the news of his friend's death, Avigur put down his pickax, never to take it up again. Stubborn and irascible, totally dedicated to his job, Avigur proved to be a natural conspirator. (Golda Meir tells how when his daughter asked him to send her some Israeli newspapers in London, he wrote "Private and Confidential" on the wrapper.)

His commitment to the job was legendary. A member of his staff who had been working long hard hours and had promised his girl friend a day out reports how he went to Avigur to ask for time off.

"I've been working these eighteen-hour days . . ." he began.

Shaul Avigur nodded vigorously. "So have I," he said approvingly. "I'm sure we get far too much sleep. We really must do something about it."*

* One suspected that some of these stories were apocryphal until one met Avigur in his tiny flat on the kibbutz to which he returned upon his retirement. In the course of the inter-

The saga of Shaul Avigur's search for arms and matériel around the world would take another book to tell. His men learned their business as they went along. There was Yehuda Arazi who, after the war, in 1946 and 1947, using the code name "Alon" and wearing the uniform of a Polish airman, set up a headquarters on a farm outside Milan; there he established a military camp, requisitioning official Allied petrol to help run it, buying on the black market spare jeeps, trucks and weapons left behind as the Allied troops went home, and acting as the conduit for weapons brought in from other sources. Then there was the film crew who arrived with all the proper official authorizations from the Air Ministry at an airbase in southern England to make a war film for which they supposedly needed flying sequences. Permitted to use two old Bristol Beaufighters, they took off from the base with the entire "film company" on board and were not seen again until they turned up suitably disguised in southern Italy before flying to Israel the day of independence. In America a special organization was established to buy old military aircraft officially listed as scrap but which could be rebuilt by cannibalizing parts. Wherever arms brokers met, whether they operated legally or illegally, there were Rekhesh operatives, working under complex pseudonyms and prepared to pay rather more than the going price for the privilege of doing business.

But none of these exploits, as extraordinary as many of them were, matched for sheer bravado what became known as Operation Thief, the first genuine intelligence special operation launched by the new State of Israel. It all began in the months before independence with that February 1948 Swissair flight out of Tel Aviv carrying the two men, one a representative of Rekhesh, the other of Syria, who were each, unknown to the other, on their way to Czechoslovakia to arrange for the purchase of arms.

Traveling around to the various armament and munitions manufacturers of Czechoslovakia, Ehud Avriel, the undercover representative for Rekhesh, became aware

---

view, he paused, looking for the right word. Finally, in exasperation, he produced a key, went over to a heavy metal locker, unlocked it, opened it carefully, and took from an otherwise empty chest a dictionary.

that another man was following the same track, and he reported it. Careful inquiries established his identity. He was Captain Abdul-Aziz Kerine of the Syrian Army, dispatched by his government in order to equip the Syrian Army with the latest Czech matériel. Unlike Israel, the Arab countries, of course, had real armies and even air forces. Jordan, for example, had British officers and the finest of British equipment. Egypt had been provided with everything it needed from British Army matériel used during the desert war. (In every war between the Israelis and the Arabs, the Arabs have had the advantage in men and matériel. But in 1948 that disproportion was of an immensity which made the subsequent victory totally miraculous.)

By the standards of modern warfare, Kerine's purchases, Avriel discovered, had not been enormous; yet so poorly equipped was the Haganah that these additional arms could be decisive. Kerine had bought 6,000 rifles, 8,000,000 rounds of small-arms ammunition, as well as hand grenades and other explosives—enough to equip three good-sized infantry battalions, enough to overrun the ill-equipped northern Jewish settlements and open up the road for a full-scale assault through the plains of Galilee.

When Shaul Avigur reported the news to Ben-Gurion, the future Prime Minister of Israel didn't hesitate for a moment. Kerine's rifles were a real and potent threat to Israel's territorial integrity. These arms could tip the balance between winning or losing a war, between existence or nonexistence for Israel. Operation Thief was under way. Its purpose was to ensure by any means necessary that Kerine's shipment should never reach its destination. The arms had been loaded on an old tramp steamer, the SS *Lino*, of Italian registration, and the ship was already on the high seas.

Nobody really had much idea of how to head it off. Initially, a bizarre bombing force, a fleet of transport planes bought by the Haganah and sitting in Italy, was sent up to stop the ship. The planes included some Ansons and a few Curtiss C-46 Commandos, all under Panamanian registration. Since none of them had bomb doors, the plan was to fly at a low altitude and as soon as they saw the *Lino*, one of the crew members would simply roll a home-made bomb out of the open door. The probability that the bomb, once primed, would go off before anyone could get it out of the aircraft was evident to everyone, but this extraordinary bombing force actually did take off and began to scour the Adriatic for the ship.

An alternative plan had been put forward by a handsome young bushy-haired Haganah commander, Munya Mardor, who was in Europe working for Avigur. He argued that the *Lino* should be attacked at sea by a Rekhesh boat and either boarded and the whole ship seized or blown out of the water. That, too, was a fairly harebrained scheme with the built-in complication that none of the Rekhesh boats were bigger or very much faster than the *Lino,* as old and decrepit as she was; there was no guarantee that they would ever catch up with the Italian tramp steamer or, if they did, win the ensuing naval engagement. So, temporarily assigned to take charge of the *Lino* operation, Mardor had been outvoted. The Jews of Palestine, though they didn't then know it, had themselves an air force and that air force was already on a bombing mission. Any risk was acceptable. The *Lino* simply could not be permitted to reach its destination.

For three days the pilots for this motley force, Jewish World War II combat airmen of various nationalities, had combed the Adriatic without success. Shaul Avigur sat in Geneva anxiously gnawing at his knuckles, angrily sending the planes back up again after the telephoned report of each fruitless sortie. To all intents and purposes, the *Lino* had disappeared.

The mystery was cleared up on March 30th when Shaul Avigur cabled Mardor with information received from Yugoslavia that for unknown reasons the *Lino* had been ordered back to port. The next day Rekhesh operations in Yugoslavia cabled Mardor:

CRATE WITH FOODS FOR ISHMAELITES LEFT MORNING FIVE STOP NAME LINO STOP FLAG ITALIAN STOP SIX KNOTS CREW OF SEVEN SKIPPER VIZOLO PIETRO STOP IF WEATHER GOOD COURSE THROUGH OTRANTO STRAITS AND CYPRUS BUT IF BAD COURSE VIA CAPO SAPIENTZA AS ALSO IF ENGINE TROUBLE STOP DESTINATION BEIRUT.

The *Lino* was on its way again, and Avigur's air force prepared for take-off once more.

It was the weather which intervened this time. On April 1st a storm of such ferocity blew up that the pilots informed Mardor an air search had become impossible. Mardor, with some sense of relief, told Avigur that because of the reservations he had always had about the air raid, he himself had prepared an alternative plan. He had found and chartered a splendid yacht, lying at anchor off the coast of Italy, which was capable of speeds between fourteen and seventeen knots and thus of outrunning the *Lino*. Mardor had already organized a group of Haganah men in Italy as a boarding party.

The yacht was made ready for sailing, but even as it was casting off new information reached Mardor. The *Lino* had developed engine trouble. Its captain, realizing that the weather was turning very nasty indeed, put into Molfetta, a small port in southern Italy. Chance had come to the aid of the Israelis. With the *Lino* in harbor, a small group of dedicated professionals could blow it out of the water. It would be an operation requiring imagination and daring.

The imagination was provided by the young and beautiful Ada Sereni, widow of one of the greatest of the Haganah heroes, Enzio Sereni, who had been killed by the Germans in Dachau after being dropped by the British behind enemy lines in Italy. Now working for Shaul Avigur in Italy, she set up a simple but effective "disinformation" operation. Italy was in the grip of a bitterly contested general election, and wild charges were being swapped back and forth by the Christian Democrats and the Communists. Both sides seemed to believe the other was fomenting armed rebellion.

So Ada Sereni telephoned a friend on a Christian Democratic newspaper. "The Communists are landing arms," she said. "A ship has arrived in Molfetta loaded with rifles and ammunition." Within twelve hours that news was on the front page of every newspaper in the land. The government feared a Communist coup; the Communist newspapers immediately branded the accusations as provocations. The arms, they insisted, were for the right-wing parties, who planned to suppress the Communists by force. It was a brilliant stroke. The government, frightened of the Communists, but frightened also of its own supporters, had no alternative but to arrest poor Captain Pietro and his crew. On April 4th, the ship was towed out of Molfetta, taken to Bari, and placed in the military harbor under close observation. The target had been set up for the kill.

Munya Mardor was in charge of the operation to sink the *Lino* as it lay in the harbor. He had as his principal lieutenant Yosef Dror, who was already involved in the *Lino* affair. It was Dror who had built the percussion caps for the primitive bombs carried by Shaul Avigur's "bombers." Dror, one of the Palmach's top demolition men, recruited two more Palmach sappers to help.

It was clear that no time was to be lost. The captain of the ship would be telling the authorities the true story—that this cargo belonged to the Syrians, that the *Lino* itself had only put into an Italian port because of the weather and the condition of its engines. The Italian authorities would be eager to defuse the bitter political quarrel which had sprung up over the ship, and it would probably take no more than twenty-four hours for the captain's story to be confirmed and for the ship to be released. "Jossele," as Dror was known by his code name, together with two other Palmach sappers and a wireless operator, assembled in Gaeta, where they disguised a five-ton truck to look like a U.S. army crop-spraying vehicle. Ada Sereni's brilliant piece of black propaganda was now operating against them—in that whiplash effect characteristic of all such operations. Fearful of an armed uprising, the Italian police were taking every sort of precaution. Road blocks were being set up all over the country and vehicles searched for anything at all which could be termed suspicious. Jossele's cargo certainly would fit into that category. In the tank labeled DDT, he had put the explosives and everything else he needed to build his underwater mines. Concealed under tarpaulins were a wireless transmitter and receiver and a collapsible dinghy.

Meanwhile Mardor worked hard in Rome to submerge his identity as a Palestinian Jew; the last thing the Jews needed in these anxious weeks before independence was an international incident.

On the 6th of April, rumors began circulating among the Israelis that the British were applying pressure upon the Italians to release the ship. Whether true or not, the rumors added to the edge of panic which began to show itself. Jossele, who had arrived safely in Bari, wrote to a colleague in Rome:

> For God's sake, don't wait any longer. The bird's liable to fly off at any moment. The big wigs seem to have leaden bottoms, for they are devilishly slow to move. If anything at all can be done from a technical point of view, it had better be done no later than tomorrow evening. Otherwise we shall probably miss our chance. . . . History won't forgive us if we fail.

Mardor, presumably one of the "big wigs" Jossele was complaining about, left for Bari carrying a beautifully forged set of papers indicating that he was a Jewish refugee from occupied Europe. He drove down from Rome on the 7th, arriving on the morning of the 8th at the hostel for genuine refugees where Jossele and his team were staying. Jossele had already reconnoitered the harbor and had come up with a plan which had all of the merits as well as the drawbacks of utter simplicity.

Discovering a fisherman who hired out rowing boats, Jossele and his sappers proposed to hire one of the boats, pretending to be tour holiday-makers, then change into swimsuits when they were out of sight, row to the entrance of the harbor, avoiding the searchlight activity, and simply dive in, fix the mine, swim out, and row ashore again. The sense of urgency which produced this almost childlike plan of action was not entirely unjustified. As if to confirm every Israeli fear, a British naval destroyer had tied up in the harbor near the *Lino*. In retrospect, it is supremely unlikely that the British ship knew or cared about the history of the little Italian tramp steamer, but such was the suspicion with which the Palestinian Jews viewed the British at that time that any move by the British was interpreted in the worst possible light.

Mardor sent the following telegram to Avigur in Geneva:

GOODS NOW IN NEIGHBORHOOD OF SCOUNDRELS FAST SHIP [*i.e.*, the British destroyer] STOP ACCORDING TO DEE, BOOKS [*i.e.*, arms] WILL BE TAKEN OUT FROM LIBRARY TO FRESH AIR TODAY FOR INSPECTION AND COUNT STOP TRYING FIND THROUGH DEE IF THAT ONLY PURPOSE STOP HAVE DECIDED DEVOTE TIME TONIGHT TO

PRACTICAL PERUSAL [*i.e.,* sinking the ship] IF BOOKS
REMAIN IN LIBRARY.

Mardor did, in fact, have another half-plan in mind.
All that night when the British ship first appeared he,
Jossele and another senior Haganah man in Italy, Amon
Jonah, had pored over maps of the harbor. There appeared to be only one breach in its defenses—a small
opening in the harbor wall that led down to the rocky
beach below. At 6:00 A.M. they set out to inspect the
point of entry. It looked promising. The risks were still,
of course, formidable. Somehow they had to get a rubber
dinghy, men and equipment through the gap without
anyone seeing and reporting such obviously suspicious
activity to the authorities. If they could manage it, however, they would have direct access to the military harbor
and the ships within it. They decided to try that night.

The rest of the day Jossele and his sappers made their
mine. Jossele tested the explosive system by filling bottles
with sulphuric acid, stuffing them with varying layers of
papers, marking on each bottle the exact time it was
turned upside down and then noting the time when the
acid had seeped through the paper and onto the small
heap of potash he had placed beneath each upended
bottle. The mine itself was the inner tube of a motor-
cycle tire (and therefore waterproof) packed with TNT.
The detonators were put into rubber contraceptive sheaths,
fortuitously carried by one of the young sappers, who had
had other purposes in mind when he'd stuffed them into
his wallet; these, too, had the advantage of being water-
resistant.

Finally Jossele had worked out the exact timing on his
newspaper fuses, vital information because it would determine just how long the men had to fix the mine in place
and get safely away before the whole ship went up. The
bottles containing the acid, he explained to his colleagues,
would be fitted upside down to the inner tube. When the
acid ate through the paper, it would reach the potash in
which the three contraceptive detonators were embedded,
generating sufficient heat to touch off the detonators and
explode the TNT. It was simple but, in its own way,
brilliant.

If anything, nightfall came around far too quickly.
Nervously, the men ate an evening meal at the hostel. At

9:00 P.M., all the equipment—the rubber dinghy, the mine, and other paraphernalia—was loaded onto the truck, and they drove without incident to the Corso della Vittoria and the opening in the harbor sea wall.

The Corso was totally deserted when they arrived. The evening had that soft velvety hue which the Mediterranean throws off so effortlessly. What was alarming, however, was the degree of activity on the British destroyer. Its searchlight was sweeping the harbor, and sailors were busy on its decks. But there was no question of turning back. Quickly, the boat was lowered into the water and the Palmach sappers were rowing fast across the harbor, using other boats to shield them from the glare of the searchlight. The minutes, then the hours ticked by. At 4:00 A.M., the sappers returned, physically and mentally exhausted, said Munya Mardor later.

They had got to within yards of the *Lino* but had been unable to bridge the gap between the empty hulk behind which they had tied their boat and the *Lino* because of the British searchlight and the activity on both the destroyer and the tramp steamer. It was as if the Israelis had been expected. They had removed the detonators from the mine and abandoned it. There was no other way out.

The next night, at midnight, April 9th, they rowed out again to the ship with a new mine they had assembled on the same principle as the one they'd dumped. If anything, the activity on the British destroyer was greater than the night before. There were lights everywhere, orders being shouted, even a volley of rifle shots, which had the otherwise disciplined lookouts on the sea wall dashing frantically to see what they could.

At 1:30 A.M., as the sappers were crouched in their dinghy desperately looking for a chance to get through the incredible surveillance the *Lino* seemed to be under, the reason for the activity became clear. Majestically giving a blast on its siren, the destroyer let loose from its moorings, rocked gently in the sway, and then on half engines moved slowly out of the harbor and to sea. The British had gone. The *Lino* was now easy prey.

Immediately, Jossele and his men slipped out of their clothes and into the water. It took them only minutes to attach the mine and get back to the dinghy, though it seemed to take hours, especially as they could hear above them as they treaded water the footsteps of the Italian guards on deck. No one waited around for the explosion. Obviously, once the *Lino* went up, the whole area would be cordoned off. It was essential that the saboteurs should be well away.

At 4:00 A.M., the first drop of sulphuric acid touched the potash; seconds later, with an enormous roar, the mine exploded. It took less than ten minutes for the *Lino* to sink. By then, the men responsible were miles away on the road to Rome, to be told only on arrival that they had been successful. A group of Palestinian Jews had hit a target which could directly affect the security of the nation. It is the only kind of target the Israeli intelligence community has ever been interested in since.

The sinking of the *Lino* was not, however, the end of the affair. Colonel Fouad Mardam, quartermaster general of the Syrian Army, the man who had sent Captain Abdul-Aziz Kerine to Czechoslovakia in the first place, stormed in to see Premier Jamil Mardam.

"These weapons are vital for us," he said. "Yet by failing properly to notify the Italian government of their true ownership, they are at the bottom of Bari harbor, blown up by one or other of the Italian political factions. I demand that the Italian government be now informed about our legal claims, and also that we insist that they be lifted from the harbor and handed to us."

Jamil Mardam (no relation to Fouad Mardam) agreed. Fouad should go himself to supervise the salvage operation, the Premier said, and then charter a ship to bring the weapons safely to Damascus. Fouad Mardam arrived in Bari with the dredging operation well under way. One glance at the rifles, which had been well packed in thick grease, and he knew they were completely serviceable. Someone else, however, was watching the same salvage operation with considerably less enthusiasm.

The weeks had gone by since the *Lino* had gone down, and during that period the State of Israel had officially come into being. Ada Sereni was now working for the legally constituted secret service of a nation state recognized by the United Nations. But if her status and the status of the organization she was working for had changed, Israel's desperate needs had not. It was as urgent as ever that the *Lino*'s cargo should not reach Syria.

When Ada discovered that the weapons were being raised, she traveled to Bari in a state of some alarm. What she saw and heard there was deeply disturbing.

Colonel Mardam was organizing the raising of the weapons with great efficiency. Once out of the water, the rifles were being thoroughly cleaned under the supervision of an expert, then taken to be stored in the local warehouse. From her Italian contacts, Ada learned that the Italians, with the elections now well behind them and therefore considerably less neurotic on the subject, had accepted Mardam's ownership of the cargo and were cooperating with him in every way.

The Italians, Ada said in her cablé to Shaul Avigur, were taking no chances. Though nobody, not even Colonel Mardam, suspected that the Israelis had sunk the ship, the local authorities were manning a permanent around-the-clock guard on the weapons. They were determined that the Syrians should get them and equally determined that any dissident Italian political party should not. Effectively, that meant that any new attempt to sabotage the weapons would almost inevitably result in failure.

Avigur's reply was brief: If we cannot stop the shipment in Italy, we must stop it on the high seas. Operation Thief was in full flood again.

Colonel Mardam suspected nothing. His problem was not merely raising the weapons but transporting them to Syria. Since Syria itself had no merchant navy to speak of, chartering was the obvious step. But with a world shipping shortage, the kind of vessel Mardam was looking for was not easy to find. All his inquiries in Bari proved fruitless until the owner of his hotel suggested that there might be a shipping agency in Rome which could be of assistance.

The Menara Shipping Agency, when Colonel Mardam called upon it, was more than helpful. It had, said its managing director, the ideal ship, fairly old and battered but superbly seaworthy: the SS *Argiro*. Mardam needed no persuading. He paid over a million lire, and the 250-ton ex-navy corvette was his for the purpose of this voyage.

There were certain facts of which Mardam should have been aware. The manager of his hotel in Bari had been well paid by Ada Sereni to suggest the Menara

Shipping Agency to Mardam—a "commission," the manager had been told, for getting this important business for Menara. The Menara Shipping Agency itself had old ties with all those Israeli interests which before independence needed vessels for various purposes, from transporting immigrants and arms in through a British blockade to taking oranges out.

As for the captain of the *Argiro*, he discovered that two of his regular crewmen had suddenly gone sick. The two replacements he had been sent clearly knew their business, and he thought no more about it.

At the end of the first week in August, the *Argiro* set sail from Civitavecchia, Rome, for Bari, where under the supervision of Colonel Mardam the arms which had sunk to the bottom of the harbor with the *Lino* were loaded aboard. On the morning of August 19th, the *Argiro* slipped its moorings and made for the open sea on a course set for Alexandria. Mardam watched it go. His job was over. He cabled Damascus the good news and then boarded a plane for home.

The *Argiro*'s journey was not entirely uneventful. Hardly had the ship lost sight of land before its engines, which were under the charge of the new crewmen, broke down. As the ship lay wallowing in the Mediterranean swell, a fishing vessel drew alongside. On board were two men who informed the captain that they carried radio equipment and had been ordered to make contact with the *Argiro* by the Egyptian government, principally so that the *Argiro* could keep in radio contact with Alexandria. The captain accepted their story readily and invited them aboard.

The fate of the *Argiro* was sealed. There were now four members of Israeli intelligence aboard—the two sailors who had joined the ship originally in Bari and the two men who had come off the fishing boat. Along with their radio equipment, the latter also carried small arms and ammunition; within minutes the four men overpowered the small crew without incurring any casualties. Politely, they requested the captain to alter course for Tel Aviv, and then with the powerful radio set brought along for that purpose immediately informed headquarters in Israel.

In mid-passage, the *Argiro* was met by two Israeli corvettes, and the arms, crew and Israeli agents were transferred aboard. The *Argiro* was sunk without trace. A few hours later the corvettes reached Haifa. Israel's first "special operation" had come to an end—successfully, secretly, and without bloodshed.

Those Syrian arms had reached Haifa by an amalgam of force and cunning. The hand of Tel Aviv remained hidden during the crucial early stages. The captain, the crew, and the ship's owners were handsomely looked after. The affair would leave no undesirable aftermath. It was a classic of its kind.

Indeed, so clean had this operation been that the Israelis determined to keep it that way. When the Syrians discovered that they were not to get their precious arms after all, they turned with great fury on the hapless Colonel Mardam, who was accused of working hand in glove with the Israelis. By Christmas Fouad Mardam was sentenced to death. Uniquely—and by the harsher standards of today almost unbelievably—the Israeli intelligence services through the good offices of the French embassies in Tel Aviv and Damascus sent to the Syrians full details of Operation Thief, which, of course, totally exonerated the colonel from any involvement. He was simply a fly who had stumbled into a spider's web. Mardam's life was spared. Operation Thief was finally over.

Chapter 2

WHILE OPERATION THIEF was heading toward its successful conclusion, the new Israeli Secret Service was beginning its life clouded by scandal and error. In retrospect, this is perhaps hardly surprising. Israel is not the first newly independent country to discover that the very qualities required in the fight for independence become an embarrassment once that independence has been achieved. When the Israeli Secret Service was officially established out of the bones of the old pre-independence secret organizations, the same men who had lived such a

freebooting existence before the State was established
were put in charge of the new official secret agencies.
These men found hard to take the trammels and restric-
tions placed upon them by what was necessarily a bureaucratic structure, however loose, answerable both to
the rule of law and the *diktat* of government and Parliament. The truth, of course, was that no one either inside
or outside the Secret Service really understood the principles of democratic control established by the democracies (sometimes imperfectly) over their secret agencies,
and no one from the Prime Minister on down could com-
prehend the limits of executive authority which need to
be imposed upon an intelligence community if it is not to
become a state within a state, threatening the democratic
credentials of the nation as a whole.

The Israeli Secret Service officially came into being
on June 30, 1948, when a small group of men were summoned to a tiny conference room above a flower shop
at 85 Ben Yehuda Street, Tel Aviv. The plaque on the
door read "Veterans' Counseling Service." There was
nothing to distinguish this small suite of offices or the
house itself from any others in the area. Besides the
flower shop, there was a small café in the basement. Ordinary middle-class families lived on the first two floors,
and if they ever wondered why people called at the Veterans' Counseling Service at such strange hours of the
day and night, they were never heard to complain.

The Veterans' Counseling Service was the headquarters and cover of Shai, the official intelligence arm of the
Haganah.

Of all the Jewish organizations during the period before independence, Shai was the most secret. Its agents
operated everywhere—deep within the British administration and the police force, inside the Arab towns, and
even among Jewish groups hostile to what they regarded
as the soft line of the Haganah and its political arm,
Mapai, the Israeli Labor Party.

Shai had had many distinguished commanders, none
more so than the tall thin jug-eared, grey-haired ascetic
with the rank of full colonel in the new Israeli Army, Isser
Be'eri, who now addressed his colleagues.

Around the table sat Shai's section heads, men who
like Isser Be'eri were virtually unknown to the population
at large but who had been involved in nearly all the most

daring of the Haganah's operations. There was the young good-looking Benjamin Gibli, chief of Shai's Jerusalem District; Avraham Kidron, chief of the Northern District, a chunky incisively intelligent man with a crewcut who dreamed of being a diplomat; David Karon, chief of the Negev District, also a diplomat manqué; Boris Guriel, chief of the Political Department, whose spies had so successfully infiltrated the old British administration, a slight man a little older than the rest, an intellectual with a firm grasp of essentials; and Isser Harel, chief of the Tel Aviv District and what was known as the Jewish Department, which functioned to help control the right-wing dissident groups who refused to acknowledge the authority of the Haganah or its political leader, David Ben-Gurion, first Prime Minister of Israel.

Isser Be'eri had come from David Ben-Gurion's office that morning. The Prime Minister, he said, had asked him to reorganize Shai. There would be three divisions, he went on. The first would be the Bureau of Military Intelligence (Agaf Modiin—Information Bureau—abbreviated to Aman).* Attached to Military Intelligence would be the Department of Counterespionage (Ran). Military Intelligence was to be the senior arm of the community and would be headed by Isser Be'eri himself. The second division would be the Political Department of the Foreign Ministry, to be headed by Boris Guriel. Its function would be to collect intelligence relating to Israel and the Israelis on a worldwide scale. The third division would be the Department of Security (Shin Bet, a shortened version of Sherut Habitachon). Its director would be Isser Harel.

Guriel and Harel had already been told privately what their new roles would be. To everyone else this seemed yet another routine reorganization of the kind which had happened at regular intervals in the days before independence as Shai reacted from one crisis to the next. But they were wrong. For it was at this meeting that Shai ceased to exist. The modern Israeli secret intelligence services were born, and their often stormy history began.

Isser Be'eri himself had apparently come out of nowhere to head Shai when on February 6, 1948, he was

---

* Throughout this book, in order to avoid confusion, I will refer to Aman as "Military Intelligence," a term widely understood and employed by most countries of the world.

appointed by David Shaltiel, the ex-French Foreign Legionnaire who was taken from his own command of Shai to head the Jewish forces in the desperate battle for Jerusalem.

Be'eri had been a member of the Haganah since 1938, but had never been particularly active. He had impressed men like Shaltiel, however, with his sense of burning mission and his abhorrence—boldly stated—of the increasing degree of corruption which as head of a privately owned construction company he was ideally placed to see all around him. Some such corruption in Palestine, a land of many shortages, was natural. But much of it was not discouraged by the politicians. All of this offended Be'eri's sense of the rightness of things as much as it did men like David Shaltiel, who had brought Be'eri into Shai originally as an administrator, to make sure the organization did not become subject to what Shaltiel and others regarded as the possibility of political corruption.

But for all his spartan qualities, Isser Be'eri was the wrong man to head the new secret service. A good friend to his friends, an implacable adversary to his enemies, he was a zealot in an Old Testament sense, a magnificent and a dangerous man. Be'eri had a purity which was almost childlike. He found it impossible to accept the then-fashionable thesis that Israel needed to have its own burglars and prostitutes to consider itself a country like any other. He believed, with a kind of obverse racism, that Israel must represent the highest and most enduring values, and that those who could not live up to such standards should be crushed.

Regarded by his friends as one of the truly great men to shape Israel, to most of those Israelis today for whom the name Isser Be'eri has any meaning, he represents a dark and fateful chapter in the history of their country.

It did not take long to establish that Be'eri's appointment had been a terrible mistake. In December 1948, seven months after the founding of the State, Isser Be'eri, chief of Military Intelligence, effectively chief of the Israeli Secret Service, was brought before a secret court-martial in Tel Aviv. The charge: murder.

The victim was a wealthy, influential Arab named Ali Kassem. In the days before independence, he had played a somewhat ambiguous role in the affairs of Palestine. Jewish farmers in the area in which he lived, Sid-

ney Ali, a small village on the coast near Tel Aviv, had
been forced to pay protection money to him for many
years. Yet, at the same time, Kassem was helping the
Haganah. In July 1948, Ali Kassem suddenly disappeared. In September, his body, riddled with bullets, was
found at the foot of Mount Carmel. The police investigating the killing soon stumbled upon the fact that he
had been killed by the Secret Service. The matter could
easily have stopped there.

The police went to Be'eri and asked him if the killing
could be justified as State policy. (After all, Arabs and
Jews were being killed every day in the fighting on the
borders.) Be'eri, who had not himself ordered what
amounted to an assassination but who typically took
upon himself as head of the service any criticisms aimed
at his subordinates, declared simply: "Kassem was a
traitor, so we killed him."

It was nearly but not quite enough for the police.
Be'eri, of course, was not arrested, but the police did
send a report to the Attorney General, who in turn
passed it on to Prime Minister Ben-Gurion.

Ben-Gurion knew what the others did not, that Be'eri
was involved in at least one other potential scandal: that
scandal had been simmering for some time. Its origins
went back even farther than the Kassem case.

In the spring of 1946, the Palmach had planned an
operation against the British Navy, which was carrying
out a successful blockade of the coast preventing illegal
immigrants from entering the country. Palmach frogmen
had already attached magnetic mines to British coast
cutters in Jaffa harbor once and had blown them up.
Now the target was to be coast-guard cutters in Haifa.

On the evening of the raid, however, Shai radio interceptors, working from an underground station in Tel
Aviv, picked up British police messages warning of the
impending raid and instructing troops with machine guns
to move to the harbor to ambush the frogmen. Israel
Amir, then head of Shai, got a car and drove at high
speed the eighty miles to Haifa along the narrow coastal
road. There he was able to get hold of a motor boat and
headed out to sea to the position where he knew the commandos' support boat would be waiting to make the
strike. He managed to get there in time to call off the
operation.

In the end, thanks to the work of the radio interceptors, no damage was done. But that did not disguise the fact that quite obviously the operation had been betrayed. Be'eri believed he knew who the man was: Abba Hushi, a powerhouse of a man in David Ben-Gurion's Labor Party, the secretary of the Labor Council in Haifa, and as such the political czar of northern Palestine.

Hushi was a personal friend of Ben-Gurion and was frequently spoken of as a possible Prime Minister of Israel. He had got where he was by playing a complex game of end against the middle. He was, in short, an operator—the kind of man Isser Be'eri despised. Though Hushi had close contacts with the British and regarded operations of the Palmach type as unnecessarily interfering with business, the evidence was of a shadowy and dubious nature. But whether or not Hushi was guilty, the Palmach was convinced of his guilt. So was Isser Be'eri. All that was lacking was the proof.

In May 1948, almost exactly two years later, Jules Amster, an expansive, easygoing friend and a close aide of Abba Hushi, was arrested by military police as he was sitting drinking coffee with friends celebrating the establishment of the State of Israel.

He was not seen again until August 1st, when he returned to them, a man teetering on the edge of existence. His teeth had been knocked out; his legs were scarred; he had had to endure water tortures. Driven to the very limits of his sanity, he had tried to kill himself. The purpose of his illegal detention was to try to get from him a confession that Abba Hushi had betrayed the Palmach. That confession was never forthcoming. But Hushi's guilt appeared to have been established when Be'eri himself arrived at Ben-Gurion's office with two documents, cables, he said, found among the British papers in the Haifa telegraph office. Dating from April 1945, they purported to be top-secret British CID notifications to branches around the country and proved that Abba Hushi had been a traitor, a prime informant of the British.

By this time, however, doubts were beginning to set in about Be'eri, and the support Ben-Gurion had shown him earlier was evaporating fast. Those doubts were finally confirmed at the end of August, when the Haganah's top forger, the man who had constructed so many identities for so many Haganah officers on missions at home and abroad, admitted that he had forged the alleged British police cables on the orders of Isser Be'eri.

Abba Hushi was cleared. Isser Be'eri's career had come to an end. Now the floodgates were open. Almost immediately, a third appalling and unpardonable illegality came to light.

Grotesquely enough, this third incident had taken place on the very day that the Israeli Secret Service came into being, June 30, 1948, a few hours after Isser Be'eri formally wound up the affairs of Shai and established his three bureaus for intelligence and espionage.

The new era which Be'eri ushered in that morning was stained that very afternoon by a terrible crime committed on behalf of the new State. For it was on June 30th, in the blazing heat of an Israeli summer, that a young Israeli army officer, Captain Meir Toubianski, was convicted by a drumhead court martial of spying for Britain, found guilty, sentenced to death and, before the day was out, placed before a firing squad of soldiers of the Palmach and summarily executed.

The case against Meir Toubianski was fairly murky. At the beginning of June, during the siege of Jerusalem, it had become clear that the British-officered Arab Legion had access to high-grade military intelligence, which could only have come from behind the Jewish lines. For several nights, the Legion had bombarded an Israeli munitions plant, doing great damage to the factory. In the dead of night, under conditions of the highest secrecy, the equipment was moved to new premises. Within four hours, the new factory was again under enemy bombardment.

The chief of Shai's Jerusalem District, Colonel Benjamin Gibli, probably the most photogenic officer in the whole of the Haganah, a dashing, effervescent soldier whose brilliance was unquestioned, began his inquiries. The investigation led to the Jerusalem Electric Company, the only outside body which could have known of the new factory, since it had been asked to supply power the moment the machinery was installed.

The Jews, who had no reason to trust the British, believed that the predominantly British directors were in the employ of the British Secret Service. Gibli certainly was convinced of that. The British directors and employees of the company were feeding information, he believed, to the Arabs by telephone, which throughout the entire siege operated between the two sides without a hitch. But Gibli believed there also had to be an Israeli informer, and he suspected he had found his man in Israeli Army Captain Meir Toubianski, an ex-major in the Royal Engineers and a passionate anglophile.

On June 30th, Toubianski set out for Tel Aviv to visit his brother but was arrested on the way and brought before a field court-martial. His judges were men distinguished in the service of their country. Isser Be'eri, that day officially appointed head of Israeli Military Intelligence, was chairman; the other members were Benjamin Gibli, chief of the Jerusalem District; David Karon, chief of the Negev District; and Avraham Kidron, chief of the Northern District, later to become editor general of the Israeli Foreign Ministry and still later the Israeli ambassador in London.

They found Toubianski guilty of treason. A local Palmach squad commanded by a Captain Goldmann executed him on the spot.

If it hadn't been for Lena Toubianski, the young pretty wife of the dead man, that would have been the end of that. But Mrs. Toubianski was not going to let the matter rest so easily. After her husband disappeared on June 30th, Mrs. Toubianski had begun making inquiries. She feared he had been killed in the fighting in Jerusalem, but was puzzled that she had received no official confirmation. More confusing was the attitude of the military headquarters in Tel Aviv when she sought information. There she was roughly brushed aside. Cruelly, she only knew the truth when she read an account of the death of her husband as a spy in an Israeli newspaper on July 22nd. It was a terrible moment. She wrote a bitter letter to Ben-Gurion, faultless in its logic:

How did it happen that the most basic legal rights were denied my husband, who was a loyal ranking officer in the Haganah? If Toubianski ever had a trial, where did it take place and when? What law justified the verdict? Why was the condemned man given no opportunity to say farewell to his wife and his young son before he was executed? Even the vilest criminal has that privilege.

When he received this letter, Ben-Gurion ordered an immediate investigation, and on December 27th he replied to Mrs. Toubianski:

> I have no right to pass judgment on your late husband, but I had checked into his trial and have determined that it was not according to law. Consequently, I have ordered the Commander in Chief of the Army to review the records of the trial and to appoint a new military tribunal. The Government will continue to provide for your child's education whatever the verdict of the new trial. Neither you nor your son need feel the slightest guilt.

On July 1st, Lena Toubianski received the following letter from Ben-Gurion:

> I wish to inform you that I have just received a detailed report on the investigation conducted by the Military Prosecutor in compliance with the Commander in Chief's orders as to the trial and execution of your late husband. It has been established that Meir Toubianski was innocent. His death was a tragic mistake. In order to make such amends as are possible for this terrible miscarriage of justice, the Commander in Chief has decreed with my approval:
>
> 1. To restore to Meir Toubianski posthumously his rank of Captain;
> 2. To reinter his remains in a military cemetery with all due honours;
> 3. To pay you and your son appropriate damages.
>
> It isn't possible for me to convey to you the anguish that I and all others connected with the affair feel. Such a thing should never have happened. Those responsible will be handed over to justice.
>
> Your late husband, it is true, did make a mistake by sending his British boss a list without presupposing that it might fall into the wrong hands. He admitted his error and regretted it, but he had no wicked intent and no intention whatever of committing treason.

On July 7, 1949, Toubianski's remains were buried with full military honors; twelve days later, on the 19th, Isser

Be'eri, now a private citizen, was arrested and charged with his murder. Hammer blow after hammer blow had already rained upon Be'eri's head.

In November 1948, Be'eri had been suspended by Ben-Gurion pending investigation of the Ali Kassem case. In December of the same year, Attorney General Pinhas Rosen opened the case for the prosecution in the secret court-martial which Ben-Gurion had insisted should take place to decide the guilt or innocence of the head of the Israeli Secret Service. Be'eri's defense was simple: "My position as head of the Secret Service entitled me by definition to act outside the law and to use extra-legal methods. You have no right to try me according to regular procedures."

It was not a view accepted by the court. Be'eri was found guilty and dismissed from his post. In January 1949 the Abba Hushi forgery had come home to roost; this time Be'eri was stripped of his rank and dismissed from the Army. So it was that when he went to trial for the illegal execution of Captain Toubianski, he was plain Mr. Be'eri.

Surprisingly enough perhaps, in view of all this, there were those who were prepared to speak on behalf of Isser Be'eri, though others, like the charismatic Benjamin Gibli—who might have helped—were less than heroic in the witness box. Isser Be'eri did little to present a defense. On November 23, 1949, he was found guilty, but because of his record received only a token sentence: "One day from sunrise to sunset." On December 18th, even that was commuted by President Chaim Weizmann "in consideration of the loyal service that Isser Be'eri has rendered Israel."

He died on January 30, 1958, a broken man certainly (as one Israeli writer has put it) and bitter, too, but alone and friendless he was not. There are men who served under him who regard him as a Titan among men, who speak of him with affection and love. Set against that is the view of Isser Harel, who told the Israeli writer Michael Bar-Zohar that "Be'eri was a dangerous megalomaniac," and quotes Ben-Gurion in describing him as "a rascal without a shred of conscience."

There is, of course, an intrinsic fascination in trying to analyze these quite remarkable divergences of view which depict Be'eri as Jekyll and Hyde. The nature of his character becomes even more important when put in the context of the Israeli Secret Service. Isser Be'eri was, to all intents and purposes, the head of that service for almost six months, from the time it came into being as a legal entity until he was court-martialed as a result of the Ali Kassem case. To understand Isser Be'eri then, to understand what went wrong, is to understand something about the Israeli Secret Service today.

The whole of the Be'eri case is indeed as central to the ethos of the Israeli Secret Service as the Kim Philby affair was in a different way to Britain's SIS, the Secret Intelligence Service, or the peculiar and specific character of Allen Dulles to the development of the CIA.

At odds were two remarkable men—David Ben-Gurion, a bizarre and fascinating mixture of Old Testament prophet and Tammany Hall ward politician, a man of immense vision and at the same time a man of narrow party interest, and Isser Be'eri, who shared many of Ben-Gurion's virtues but despised the temporizing of politics and found himself in the situation of many who share that view who are ultimately forced to seek solutions for their problems in an even more coruscating arena than the political one.

Perhaps he saw himself in almost comic-book terms as a "righter of wrongs"; unquestionably, he was a man who was not prepared to see evil go unpunished. That is a dangerous belief; it is an impossible one for the head of a secret service. In his defense, his friends point out that the Israel of the late forties was a very different country from the Israel of today. The proper administration of justice in a newly independent country is difficult to achieve. The various departments lack investigators, lawyers, judges. The courts have no precedents from which to work; the police are unsure of their role. In Israel, all this was compounded by the fact that not only was the country newly independent, but it was also fighting for its very existence. Who could be found who would say that the way Be'eri behaved in such circumstances was unacceptable? In Israel—and the country can be grateful for this—there was such a man. No one, David Ben-Gurion declared, no matter what the circumstances, is ever above the law ... not even when the law is insufficient.

The State—or rather its elected political leaders—was there to define the crime and its punishment; that duty must be reserved to the State. If the State decided, for example, that no purpose was served by reopening the wounds of the years under the British, by seeking out collaborators, then that decision had to be observed. The concept was difficult for many in Israel to understand at that time. It is to the credit of David Ben-Gurion that his decision is completely understood today.

Many inexcusable things were done in the forties in the name of the State, as is apparent in the Abba Hushi and Ali Kassem affairs. In the former, Isser Be'eri behaved with the fanatical conviction of a man who believes that original sin must be tackled at its source. In the latter, it is clear that though Be'eri took direct and personal responsibility before the investigating authorities, he himself had nothing to do with what occurred. But in the Toubianski case, his responsibility was clearly immediate as the man who presided over the field court-martial; it was on Be'eri's direct orders that Toubianski was shot. Only a handful of people in Israel, however, know about the quite extraordinary drama that occurred behind the scenes during Be'eri's trial.

In the midst of the trial, the political branch of Israeli secret intelligence, based in the Foreign Ministry under Boris Guriel, picked up and deciphered a dispatch from the British Embassy in Tel Aviv to London signed by John Balfour, who was then the SIS resident in Israel and a legendary British agent who at one time during the war years had operated out of Greece in the guise of a Greek Orthodox monk.

What the British didn't know was that the Israeli Security Services were quite aware of Balfour's background and that he was no ordinary British diplomat. He was being carefully watched and his telegrams subjected to the most careful scrutiny. By that time the Israelis had already broken even the most secret British diplomatic ciphers.

One of those telegrams was potentially dynamite. It made plain that whatever Toubianski's motives, he *had* been helping the British Secret Service at the time of his arrest—whether wittingly or not. Boris Guriel received the intercept and stared at it long and hard, then sought out his political chief, Foreign Minister Moshe Sharett, but Sharett was in Jerusalem. The director general of the Foreign Ministry, Walter Eytan, was then in the Tel Aviv building, and Guriel went to him about his find and informed him that he was going to Haifa to tell Jacob Solomon, Be'eri's lawyer.

The next day Guriel saw Be'eri and without saying why asked permission to speak to his lawyer. Be'eri agreed, and Guriel met Solomon. Guriel told Solomon that he himself had been placed in an impossible position. Clearly, the document he had in his possession was a state secret, and he, Guriel, was the guardian of that secret. But it seemed to him that other considerations now applied. Solomon told him not to concern himself. The matter would be looked after. And it was. Be'eri refused to permit this evidence to be introduced, but news of what Guriel had done got back to Tel Aviv. When he arrived back at his desk the following morning, there was a message for him to see the minister immediately. Sharett was blazing.

Eytan bravely stood by Guriel and told the minister that he had encouraged Guriel to see Solomon. Both men's jobs hung by a thread. But Sharett couldn't act on his own. That same morning an intensely nervous Boris Guriel faced Ben-Gurion across his desk.

Ben-Gurion was surprisingly gentle. "Don't you realize," he said, "that secrets will flow across your desk all the time and that you simply cannot use them either to help your friends or pursue vendettas for any private purposes."

Guriel's reply was simple. He admitted that he was "technically wrong." But, he said, if he hadn't behaved as he had, he would have been no better than the German officer who all along had the information in his hand that would have proven the innocence of Dreyfus but who never spoke out. Guriel felt he had to act.

"I know about Isser Be'eri, and I know about Toubianski," said Ben-Gurion quietly, and Guriel was shown the door. He was one of the few men in Israel who was not surprised when Be'eri was released without serving even his token sentence.

Chapter 3

AFTER ISSER BE'ERI'S DOWNFALL, Military Intelligence passed into the capable hands of his deputy, Colonel Chaim Herzog, who had served as a senior intelligence officer with the British Army during World War II. This experience had already proved invaluable. Be'eri had been no soldier, and it was left to Herzog to turn Military Intelligence into a properly functioning unit, with its own organization and methods, its own green-and-white flag and *fleur-de-lys* cap badge.

After Herzog became chief of Military Intelligence, he developed the now famous training establishment and organized a real chain of command. Herzog's principal achievement was to integrate Military Intelligence with the Army and rid the service of the cowboy image it had under Isser Be'eri as the onetime undercover arm of an illegal freedom-fighting organization. Herzog turned it into a smoothly functioning modern machine, while educating the leaders of the new State on the overwhelming importance of intelligence to any military action. In the late forties, he managed to persuade Ben-Gurion to spend an entire day with Military Intelligence in order to observe what was being done and understand its potential for the future. Immensely impressed, the Prime Minister gave instructions that funds should be allotted to Herzog far beyond the budget the Army had agreed to. When the director general of Military Finance saw the new figure, he had a near seizure. It was Herzog who came to his rescue. "We'll take half that," he said, knowing that even that amount would do very nicely. It was a turning point: from that moment on the status of Military Intelligence was never really in doubt.

In April 1950, Chaim Herzog handed over Military Intelligence to his deputy, Colonel Benjamin Gibli. Gibli was something of an enigma. Be'eri's friends mistrusted him because of the testimony he had given at Be'eri's court-martial. Be'eri's enemies mistrusted him because he was one of Toubianski's judges, and at one stage very much a Be'eri acolyte. Yet no one could deny that few senior officers in the Israeli Army managed to pack quite so much glamor or charisma. Gibli was young, intelligent, shrewd, and popular among his men. True, there were small but insistent voices who had suggested he be passed over, but Ben-Gurion had ignored them all and appointed Gibli chief of Military Intelligence. Immediately, Gibli campaigned for changes.

Principally because Herzog had been a British army officer but also because of Israel's long British involvement pre-independence, Military Intelligence, like most of the defense establishment, was constructed upon the British model. In Britain the chief of Military Intelligence is on the staff of the chief of Operations. As such he has a colonel's rank. Gibli moved over to the American and French systems. In these countries Intelligence is an army branch in its own right and ranks alongside more traditional branches such as Operations and Quartermaster. This means that the chief of Intelligence gets a general's rank and, more importantly, has direct access to the Chief of Staff rather than, as in Britain, only to the chief of Operations. Gibli himself, as a chief of Intelligence, never made the rank of general, but every one of his successors got a generalship the day of his appointment.

As for Herzog, he was sent to Washington as the Israeli military attaché. On the face of it, Herzog's appointment was a curious one, an apparent demotion. And at least as odd was the presence in Washington of one of the most mysterious men in Israel, Reuben Shiloach, as minister at the embassy. Born in Jerusalem the son of a rabbi, Reuben Shiloach's brilliant, mercurial mind made him a natural behind-the-scenes adviser, first to the Zionist and then to the Israeli leadership. His instinctive flair for conspiracy was given a boost in the thirties when the political division of the Jewish Worker's Federation decided to send some of its most able young men to Arab countries in order to study the Arab question at first hand.

The most outstanding of them all was Reuben Shiloach, who was sent to Baghdad. He stayed three years, working as a teacher and, officially at least, as a journalist for the Palestine *Bulletin*. During that time he traveled the length and breadth of Iraq and learned to speak every Iraqi dialect including Kurdish.

In 1936, while still only twenty-six, he was appointed by the Jewish leadership in Jerusalem as liaison officer with the British. In 1939 he flew to London as one of the special counselors to Ben-Gurion and Chaim Weizmann at the Round Table Conference in St. James's Palace, and when World War II broke out he ran special operations behind enemy lines for the Jewish Agency and helped negotiate with the British in Cairo the formation of a special Jewish Commando Corps for acts of sabotage in occupied Europe.

Wherever any dirty work was to be done, there was Shiloach; he ranged from Bari, Italy, in 1943, when he negotiated with the British Secret Service the sending of Jewish self-defense units into the Balkans, to Minneapolis, Minnesota, in 1946, where he persuaded Jewish millionaires to set up dummy companies in order to purchase the latest arms-manufacturing machinery and smuggle it to Palestine. On several occasions during the War of Independence, he negotiated secretly with King Abdullah of Jordan. But in 1950 in Washington he appeared to have become an ordinary dull diplomat. It was perfectly true, of course, that America was of vital importance to the newly emerging country, desperately in need of money, arms, and moral support, and obviously the Israeli diplomatic team had to be impressive. Yet this did not quite explain why both Shiloach and Herzog were posted to Washington during a period of great danger to Israel, when on the face of it they would have been more useful at home.

In fact, few jobs were more important to the nation than the one Shiloach and Herzog were then involved with. The governments of Israel and the United States had agreed to exchange intelligence secrets. And most important of all as far as the Israelis were concerned, the Central Intelligence Agency along with the Federal Bureau of Investigation had undertaken to supply the Israelis with some top secret equipment, including the most advanced computers for cyptoanalysis, as well as to train selected Israeli officers in their use.

It was Shiloach and Herzog whose job it was to evaluate this matériel and take charge of the training program, and in effect run Israeli intelligence for a brief period from Washington. As far as the Israelis were concerned it was a vital time. The Soviet Union, which had helped the new State into being principally in order to get Britain out of the area, realized almost immediately that Israel, far from being a compliant customer of the Russians in the Middle East, was to become a pro-Western democratic country, while the Arab nations surrounding it, still in many cases colonies or near colonies, were ripe for Communist revolution. What is more, the Arab countries, not Israel, were where the oil was. Almost immediately then, the Soviet Union turned on Israel with great viciousness. KGB agents poured into the Soviet Embassy in Tel Aviv and worked against Israeli interests elsewhere in the world. As a result, at this the very height of the cold war, a community of interest began to exist between the Israelis and the Americans that was eventually to turn into an alliance which would grow into that special relationship upon which Israel has now relied for so long.

During these upheavals in Military Intelligence, the Political Department of the Foreign Ministry under its chief Boris Guriel was not left unscathed. Guriel was a strangely gentle man for what is, after all, a tough profession. He lacked the ruthlessness a successful chief of intelligence must have. That he went to the aid of Isser Be'eri with a state secret, while it was an act of great generosity, putting his own career on the line, was also an act of quite stupefying naivety. It was excusable only because the professionalism that would make such an act unthinkable today simply did not exist in the fledgling country.

Boris Guriel himself never quite knew why he was chosen to head the Political Department of Shai (whose function was to supervise the infiltration of the British presence in Palestine) or later appointed head of the Political Department of the Foreign Ministry. Certainly his years as a POW in German camps were no training ground, though he did develop an admiration for his fellow British prisoners and the British way of life. East European in culture and education, he found among the British soldiers a toughness and resilience which always dazzled him. At one point the Germans sought to separate Jewish prisoners from the rest, but a rough British regimental sergeant major made it absolutely plain to the Germans that while he himself "didn't much hold for Jews," as long as he was an RSM and as long as there were Jews under his charge they would be separated from the others over his dead body. It was an attitude which undoubtedly saved Guriel's and others' lives. All of us, Guriel told his colleagues later, are subject to irrational prejudices, but it takes a truly civilized man like the so-called "uneducated" sergeant major not to succumb to them.

Boris Guriel was in Jerusalem that fateful summer of 1948 when an urgent summons came from Foreign Minister Sharett in Tel Aviv. Sharett told Guriel that the Prime Minister had decided there should be a Political Department of the Foreign Ministry, and that Guriel was to head it.

Guriel was already well known to Ben-Gurion. Long before the State came into being, an Anglo-American commission of inquiry of both British and American parliamentarians and judges had come to Jerusalem in March 1946 to take evidence on the conflicting claims of the Jewish and Arab communities, and Guriel as head of the Political Department of Shai was put in charge of their welfare. They knew him only as the guide laid on by the Jewish Agency to provide for them whatever they wanted. Some of the commissioners, like the late Richard Crossman, became enormously friendly with the slight figure who every day met them with a ready smile and an apparently inexhaustible ability to smooth the most bumpy paths.

What they didn't know was that every night after Guriel left the commissioners at their hotel, he hurried over to Ben-Gurion's house in Tel Aviv. Step by step Guriel would go over the ground of the day, noting every shift of opinion as the commissioners took evidence. When a witness made a bad impression—and Guriel was quick to discover it—a new witness was produced the next day to correct the errors of the day before. When the commission made its report, published as a "blue book" by the British government on April 22, 1946, it gave little to the Jews but unquestionably less to the Arabs. The commissioners never knew that the unassuming friend they had all made in Jerusalem was the head of the country's most important secret-intelligence agency.

Guriel settled down to his new task as head of the Political Department with no great difficulty. He brought together a formidable team of men, who were subsequently to rise high in the ranks of the Israeli Foreign Ministry. These men tended to be intellectuals with a well-developed sense of adventure, of European background, perhaps a bit arrogant. In the view of some of their critics, they were not quite Israelis. In those years of hardship for Israel, when to be an Israeli was almost by definition to be someone who didn't own a suit of clothes, they tended to own complete wardrobes, to live well, to enjoy doing so, and they were ultimately to suffer the consequences.

Guriel's chief of operations was Arthur Ben Nathan, who rather audaciously assumed the straightforward cover name of "Arthur"; subsequently he became the Israeli ambassador in Bonn, and later was a most effective ambassador in Paris until 1975, when he was appointed a special adviser to the Minister of Defense.

Under Guriel, "Arthur" had style and panache, operating out of a splendid apartment in Paris from which he ran a highly successful espionage apparatus throughout Europe. His way of doing things offended many of the Israelis with whom he dealt, no one more than Shaul Avigur. The two men could not have been more diametrically opposite. "Arthur" was open and expansive, Avigur restrained and frugal. Insiders recall the time Boris and Avigur were in Paris together working hard on a delicate operation. After several days of intensive effort, Avigur proposed that they take time off to "relax and enjoy themselves." Delighted, Guriel, who enjoyed the high life himself, agreed. Avigur marched him to the Bois de Boulogne, hired two seats for fifty centimes, and spent the rest of the day watching Paris walk by. Arthur Ben Nathan, on the other hand, was likely to work out of the bar at the Crillon or the George V. He spent money lavishly, booked suites wherever he traveled, and encouraged his men to do the same.

In this, Ben Nathan had the absolute backing of Guriel. "If you want to know what important people are thinking, you've got to be where important people are congregating," Guriel told Ben-Gurion. Guriel taught the Political Department a simple lesson: It is, he would say, of little value to us to know that the Egyptian government has taken receipt of new weaponry if we do not also know what Egypt intends to do with it. It was political intelligence he was after.

Military Intelligence had a rather more hard-nosed approach to the trade. Guriel's views were regarded as little more than intellectual theorizing. Opposition to him became extremely vocal in May 1949 when Benjamin Gibli took over Military Intelligence and won over perhaps the greatest commander in chief the Israeli Army has ever had, Yigal Yadin. With Yadin (now a world-famous archaeologist and the Deputy Prime Minister of Israel) in opposition to him, Guriel's days were numbered.

Initially, the Political Department had under its aegis all special operations outside the borders of Israel. After enormous pressure by the Defense Ministry, this rule was modified in the autumn of 1949. The military were told that they could run special operations but only under the control of Boris Guriel and the Political Department. This stricture Military Intelligence completely ignored.

Boris Guriel and Arthur Ben Nathan were outraged, not out of bureaucratic pique but because all over the world Israeli agents working for rival agencies were beginning to trip over each other and because, by and large, Military Intelligence activity during that period was amateurish and badly conceived.

There is an example, famous within the profession but not generally known, of one fiasco which resulted from that amateurism. A breakthrough had occurred on a particular operation being handled by Ben Nathan. After months of slow and careful negotiation, he had come to Boris Guriel with a truly magnificent prize. Ben Nathan had arranged for an Israeli agent to go to Cairo as "Consul General for the Republic of San Salvador." The agent would be able to operate in the Egyptian capital with all the required legal papers and with full diplomatic immunity. It wasn't necessary to be head of an Israeli intelligence agency to realize what an opportunity this presented Israel and what a coup Ben Nathan had pulled off.

Though Guriel was having a rough time with Military Intelligence, so important was this project he had no hesitation in putting the full facts before Benjamin Gibli. Gibli immediately insisted that the job had to go to someone from Military Intelligence. Since a good deal of the intelligence available in Cairo would be of a military nature, Guriel agreed, though he did so with some foreboding.

Gibli picked for the job a man he regarded as one of his best—a man who spoke fluent Spanish and was even familiar with Latin America. The agent set off from Israel for Brussels, where the precious San Salvador diplomatic passport, made out in his cover name and purchased at great expense from the San Salvador Foreign Office, was waiting for him. The Egyptians had been told by the San Salvador authorities that the country's new consul general would be traveling in Europe and that once the "agrément" came through, he would complete the necessary formalities at the Egyptian Embassy in Brussels. Approval was obtained, and the Israeli officer, expensively suited, looking every inch a rich South American, walked into the office of the Egyptian consul. They had coffee and exchanged pleasantries.

"Well," said the Egyptian, unscrewing his fountain pen after half an hour or so, "down to business. Like all countries, we are consumed by bureaucracy. Forms to be filled in all the time . . . forms, forms. Now," he went on to the Israeli, at this point completely at ease, totally relaxed, "place of birth . . ."

"Haifa," said the Israeli.

An expensive magnificent game was over.

Largely because Foreign Minister Sharett was unable to stand up to the rampant military, Guriel found himself very much alone. Men like Walter Eytan sought to protect the Political Department's position, but Sharett refused to put up a fight.

Yadin and Gibli, determined to take over the operational capacity of the Political Department, poured scorn upon "Arthur and his playboys." At the same time, the head of the Department of Security (Shin Bet), the tough and ambitious Isser Harel, who was drawing close to Ben-Gurion, used his influence in order to diminish the status of the Political Department, which he regarded as a rival to his own branch. Finally, there was Reuben Shiloach, back from Washington full of new ideas, his mind sparking in every direction at once. The CIA, he told Ben-Gurion, was breaking new ground in espionage techniques. Israel, he said, needed a separate intelligence agency, an independent agency responsible only to the Prime Minister. It needed, in short, a CIA.

Though Guriel knew that the big guns were raised against him, he believed he had the support and backing of Ben-Gurion. But drastic remedies were being put forward, and Ben-Gurion, bowing to the pressure from all sides, established a select committee to advise him on what changes were needed in the intelligence establishment. He must have known that the committee's conclusion was very much preordained. Of the four men who served on the committee, only one, Walter Eytan, director general of the Foreign Ministry, could be regarded as impartial. General Yigal Yadin, the commander in chief, and Reuben Shiloach had staked out their positions within the government months earlier, and Sharett had long since abandoned Guriel in the face of such withering fire from influential quarters.

The committee's report produced no surprises. It was Walter Eytan, Guriel's only friend on the committee, who was given the task of telling Guriel.

"The Prime Minister," Eytan assured Guriel, "asked specifically what will happen to Boris. We replied that of course you will have a senior position inside the Foreign Ministry."

"I cannot accept that," said Guriel. "I will of course resign."

"But what will you do?" asked Walter Eytan.

"I can sell oranges in Tel Aviv," replied Guriel. "A very good business these days. What is more important is, what will Israel do?"

It was a good question.

The question was answered, formally, at least, the following day on September 1, 1951, when a directive from the Prime Minister went around to the heads of Government ministries in Tel Aviv and the top political leaders in the country.

A new agency was being formed whose function it would be to gather all intelligence from abroad and run all special operations deemed necessary. This organization would be called the Central Institute for Intelligence and Special Missions, to be known simply as Mossad, or "Institute," as was its great predecessor in charge of illegal immigration in the thirties and forties. Its director would be Reuben Shiloach. The Foreign Ministry's Political Department was to be abolished, and in its place a new Research Department established. Its role would be to act as a study and evaluation center for the use of the Foreign Minister. The director of Mossad would be responsible to the Prime Minister.

So it was that Mossad was born in the autumn of 1951. Denied a proper voice in the secret committee which brought Mossad into being, believing absolutely in the correctness of his own ideas, Guriel himself did resign after an emotional and angry scene with Sharett. His colleagues expressed their frustration in a remarkable way.

Many of Guriel's operatives in the field hurried back to Tel Aviv to discover what was happening; when the department heads learned, they resigned virtually en bloc. Indeed, of all the senior men, only one, Avraham Kidron, stayed on, but then, as was said bitterly at the time, "What would you expect of a man who sat on the Toubianski court-martial?"

The rebellion spread until virtually every agent in the field was involved. Not only did the men refuse to go on assignments or cooperate with Shiloach, they even refused to hand over current operations. The Israeli Secret Service, in short, was on strike.

Shiloach moved quickly. A commission was formed to seize the files of the now-dissolved Political Department. Orders went out that leaders of the revolt would be dismissed summarily from employment and the others given twenty-four hours to decide whether or not they were prepared to return immediately to work or face the consequences.

Most of the junior staff did return to their jobs, but the men at the top went into a voluntary wilderness. Most of them were forgiven within a comparatively brief time and eventually rose to high office within the Israeli Foreign Ministry. Boris Guriel, a name known today to few Israelis, now lives in Tel Aviv in quiet obscurity.

Guriel had to wait twenty-two years before events justified the stand he took back then. But the circumstances of his vindication then were such that he could take no pleasure from it. After the War of Yom Kippur, a commission including one of the men most responsible for removing Guriel from office, General Yadin, came to the conclusion that Israeli intelligence had failed on this occasion because it lacked political intelligence of any sophistication. The Research Department of the Foreign Ministry had been starved of funds and was taken seri-

ously by no one, not even the Foreign Minister; Mossad
had become merely a collection agency, with no research
facilities to evaluate its own intelligence. These were the
very dangers Boris Guriel had warned of, and he had resigned from the Foreign Ministry rather than be in any
way associated with politics he knew to be potentially
disastrous.

At the time of his resignation, Guriel's ideas were regarded as being somewhat academic. Instead, what
seemed to matter to Israeli intelligence were "special operations"—that fascinating, often crucial, but always
limited sphere of activity in which all intelligence agencies
glory. Perhaps because of Israel's military perception of
itself as a David confronting a Goliath, special operations
assumed a greater importance in Israel than they might
have elsewhere. And right through to this day, the argument over which agency will take ultimate responsibility
for special operations has never been properly resolved.

After long debate, a compromise was reached on the
formation of Mossad. It was agreed that the Military Intelligence should plan all "special ops" and should nominate the targets. Mossad, however, would have to give its
authorization before final approval could be had. The
actual operation would normally be carried out by military intelligence.

Mossad initially was a very small agency indeed, with
few top operatives. Those it did have tended to come
from the Department of Security, or Shin Bet (the equivalent of the U.S.'s FBI), which, under Isser Harel, had
built up a massive counterespionage expertise in order
to combat Communist infiltration, a very real menace in
the early days of the State. Harel had realized that in order to be effective against an adversary seeking to penetrate your governmental apparatus, it is vital that you
know as much about the art of penetration as he does.
Harel certainly had developed these techniques, and by a
combination of total dedication to his work, natural guile,
remarkable intuition, and ruthless energy had firmly
established Shin Bet as a well-run, efficient agency over
which there had not been a single breath of scandal since
its formation.

As a result of a disastrous operation in Iraq in 1951,
when it had become clear that various intelligence
branches were working at cross purposes, it was decided

that a coordinating committee should be established comprised of the heads of branches. The membership consisted of the chief of Mossad in the chair, the chief of Shin Bet, the chief of Military Intelligence, and the head of the Special Branch of the Israeli police force. It was a decision which was to bring Harel to the fore.

For very quickly, Isser Harel decided that Reuben Shiloach was not a man he could work for or with. Shiloach was incredibly disorganized, of that there could be no doubt. He had a mercurial mind which would leap at a subject with enormous enthusiasm and discuss it endlessly; a day later he might forget that it had ever arisen or brush it airily away. He was the kind of man who was a superb adviser but a hopeless administrator.

Within twelve months, it had become clear to everyone that the new Mossad, far from improving Israel's situation, had made the country more vulnerable than ever. Harel and Shiloach were constantly at each other's throats in meetings of the heads of branches and elsewhere, and the rows between the two men began to reach titanic proportions. Finally Harel threw down the gauntlet. "You are not a fit man to run this service!" he told Shiloach. Shiloach received little support from his own branch, who found him an impossible taskmaster. Indeed, few people within the espionage establishment could be found to support Shiloach. Those who might have had been thrown out with Guriel. So Shiloach was quite alone—a Cardinal Richelieu without any bishops. Eventually, on September 19, 1952, Shiloach acknowledged defeat and submitted his resignation to the Prime Minister.

An hour later, Ben-Gurion was on the phone to Isser Harel. "I want you to run Mossad," he told Harel.

For a brief period Shiloach stayed on as a kind of super chief, overseeing the work of all the intelligence branches and representing them to the Prime Minister and the Foreign Minister. This situation became even more intolerable to Harel and his friends than the earlier one. Shiloach, as brimful of ideas as ever, was not the sort of man to accept a sinecure. He dabbled in every department and fired off directives with boundless enthusiasm. When Shiloach protested that Harel was not following those instructions, he was told coldly that unless the instructions were sensible, Harel would not carry them out.

On February 8, 1953, tired and worn out (he had had

a motorcar accident the previous winter that had taken a physical toll), Shiloach wrote to Ben-Gurion asking to be relieved for "personal reasons" and making it quite plain that he and Isser Harel were irreconcilable; Harel played too rough for his liking.

Shiloach suggested another super chief to be named to replace him: Ehud Avriel, the man who had done so much to bring Czech arms into the country before independence. But, realizing that his own position was now unchallenged, Isser Harel resisted the proposal. He would not, he said, accept anyone between him and the Prime Minister.

So a few days after Shiloach's resignation Harel's position as head of Mossad was confirmed, and Harel was also given control of Shin Bet, with its head directly under him. Isser Harel had brushed aside all opposition and had finally reached the very top of the Israeli intelligence establishment. It was the start of a new era in which the Israeli Secret Service was to become one of the greatest in the world.

Chapter 4

THOUGH HE KNEW from gossip within the intelligence community that Reuben Shiloach had turned chaos into an art form, Isser Harel was not prepared for the extraordinary mess that he found when he arrived at Mossad headquarters in Tel Aviv to assume the directorship.

Mossad, when Isser Harel took it over on September 14, 1952, was little more than three small rooms, with a staff of only a dozen people, including a secretary to the director who was on the verge of a nervous breakdown —partly because she had not been paid for several months. The Mossad treasury was completely empty. Israel is not a rich country, and the demands upon its national budget are enormous. However important a department, nobody is going to give it money which it hasn't

first fought for. Reuben Shiloach, for all his many talents,
had never properly accounted for what he'd got, and he
failed totally in budgeting any of his operations. What to
some people might seem an endearing characteristic was
dangerous incompetence to Isser Harel. How can we organize anything at all, he exploded angrily, if we can't
first of all organize ourselves?

Isser Harel's first act as the new head of Mossad was to
track down "Akivah," the director of Mossad's finances
who was in Paris setting up a $2 million loan for the
nation. Akivah received a telegram recalling him immediately. He arrived triumphant at the success of his mission,
but was cut off mid-smile by an angry Harel. A witness
to the conversation remembers Harel's icy response to Akivah's glowing account of how he had achieved the loan.
"That's fine," Harel is reported as having said. "But in future, in between organizing multimillion dollar loans for
the Ministry of Finance, can you kindly concentrate sufficient of your mind to find enough money to pay the
wages of my secretary?"

Harel's next call was on the Prime Minister, David Ben-
Gurion. Isser Harel remembers to this day what he said.

"Prime Minister," he began, "there is an argument that
Israel should not have a political-intelligence agency at
all, that the whole thing should be left to the military. I,
as you know, believe that would be a mistake, and if I
have understood you correctly so do you. On the other
hand, I believe that if we continue to run political intelligence as it is currently being run, starved for money,
proper resources and manpower, the operations it conducts will inevitably come back to embarrass and humil-
iate Israel. So if the choice has to be between a political-
intelligence agency run as it is now or no secret-service
agency at all, then I would support the proposition that we
have *no organization at all*."

That afternoon the Mossad budget was increased ten-
fold. Isser Harel had been given the wherewithal to start
building. He wasted no time before doing so. Shin Bet,
the internal-security organization Harel had headed, continued to lose many of its top men to Mossad, and
Mossad moved into new premises to accommodate the
overflow. Operatives already abroad were brought back to
Israel and subjected to an intensive interrogation by
Harel. Those regarded as unsuitable for one reason or an-

other were dismissed; the rest were put through a full-scale retraining program before they were permitted back in the field.

When old hands, those who had worked for Israeli intelligence well before Independence and into the new era, complained that Harel was leaving large and sensitive areas completely uncovered while this process was going on, he told them what he had already told Ben-Gurion, and what he now described as the basis for his many successes: "I'd rather have no agents at all than a vast number of agents who don't know what they're doing."

It was an approach which was always to characterize Harel's work, and it grew not merely naturally out of his personality but as a direct result of his work as chief of Shin Bet. Harel was a security man, a super policeman pure and simple when he took over Mossad. As a counter-intelligence expert, he had watched and studied the activities of the CIA, MI-6 and the KGB. He knew the damage a blundering agent could do. He had learned the subtleties of the trade from close observation; he had learned from others' mistakes. A spy hunter turned spy starts with many advantages.

It would be difficult to imagine anyone who looked less like the conventional image of a spymaster than Isser Harel did when he took over Mossad. He was forty years old but looked fifty. He seemed to be almost round. He stands only about five foot two, and was then very much overweight (he has since trimmed down). He wore the clothes of a pedantic bank clerk.

First names are freely employed in Israel, but Isser Harel made sure that not only was he "Isser" to close colleagues but also to his driver and doorman. He worked an eighteen-hour day and expected others to follow suit. Those who disapproved of he froze out; those he liked he treated almost like sons. He was no intellectual like Guriel, not a great ideas man like Shiloach, not someone at ease in every situation. He had huge areas of ignorance and many prejudices. His education was limited. His knowledge of the world extremely sketchy. Yet he had that indefinable quality which permits some men to elicit from their subordinates a remarkable loyalty. To this day men who worked for Isser Harel, while they might reluctantly acknowledge that, like other men, he had his faults, still speak of him in terms close to adoration and still fight the battles he had with the Israeli establishment. For there was, of course, a concomitant to the almost mesmeric hold he had on his staff. As much as they worshiped him, he was hated and feared elsewhere. For Isser Harel was a ruthless man and those who sought to balk him were soon taught the error of their ways.

There can be no doubt, whatever his critics may have said, that it was this personality which did more than anything else to build up Mossad into the outstanding intelligence-collecting organization it is today.

An Israeli agent is on a civil-service pay scale. If he travels abroad or is away from home, his expenses are carefully scrutinized when he returns. He cannot tell his friends (or even his parents) what his job really is. All that leads to a sense of isolation; men draw into themselves, and the friends they have tend to be other professionals, the only people with whom they can talk freely. Any glamor the job may have wears off very quickly. It is a closed, often claustrophobic world in which they live.

So it was that Isser Harel's personal magnetism meant so much to the service. With nothing to offer his men in the way of rewards, not even glory, he would send them off on frequently uncomfortable, often dangerous missions. They would go, glad to have the opportunity to serve, because Isser had asked them to.

He worked out of a small, bare, unpretentious office, furnished only with a desk, chair and settee. Men knew they were about to be sent on a tough mission when he would get up from the desk and suggest they join him on the settee. "We've got this problem," Isser would begin, and never mind if the agent had promised his wife that morning that he would resign immediately and take up his father-in-law's offer of a directorship in the family firm, he would know as soon as Isser began talking that he would not be able to say no.

Harel is a man of puritanical honesty. No Mossad man would ever have dreamed of padding his expense account, because if Isser Harel ever discovered it, he would be fired. On one occasion, an agent living abroad was having an affair with a Christian woman. Mossad heard about it, and it was suggested to Isser Harel that the agent be brought back to Israel.

"Why?" asked Isser, "he is a grown man, able to look after himself. Surely he's entitled to an affair."

"I agree," said his then deputy, who tells the story, "but his wife might make trouble, which could embarrass us all."

"His wife?" asked Isser, genuinely astonished. "He's married? What does he need another woman for?"

Harel expected from his men great personal integrity. In conventional terms, at least, he himself was the most straightforward of men and would accept no less in others. Yet, certainly, to put it at its mildest, the business in which he operated was not one that naturally calls forth the adjective honest. He trained men to lie, to cheat, sometimes even to kill. He himself, when operating on behalf of his department within the Israeli political establishment, was regarded by his opponents as a kind of bureaucratic Al Capone. Isser Harel was never a man much given to self-questioning, so to him there was no puzzle in this apparent dichotomy, namely, the different standards he laid down as to how his men were expected to behave toward each other, him and the department and how they were expected to operate professionally on the outside.

More subtle minds than his did begin to wonder how Mossad squared these two irreconcilables. One of Isser Harel's deputies, when asked by a new recruit how it was managed, articulated the philosophy best. "Isser," said his lieutenant, "wants honest men to do scoundrels' work. It is as well that he does. If scoundrels were doing our scoundrels' work, then heaven help Israel."

Isser Harel was born in Vitebsk in Imperial Russia in 1912. His father, Nathan Halperin, had been a brilliant scholar at the famous rabbinical college of Volozhin in Poland and came from a family of scholars. His mother, Yocheved Levin, was the youngest daughter of a rich vinegar manufacturer in Dvinsk and came from a family of businessmen.

David Levin, Isser's grandfather, made his new son-in-law manager of the vinegar works in Vitebsk, a job which he carried out with dedication if not enthusiasm. He made few friends in the community; it was not an area in which respect for or real knowledge of the Talmud and the Scriptures were deeply ingrained. Though they would sometimes come to him with their problems, his new neighbors nevertheless regarded Isser's father as prim, humorless and unsociable. What none of them could guess was they

were living at the edge of a vortex from which few if any
would emerge unscathed.

The outbreak of World War I signaled the beginning of
the end of the life they had all known. Isser was only five
years old when his father announced one day, "They've
overthrown the Czar!" The little that Isser remembers of
that time left a powerful impression with him. The family
business was nationalized without compensation. From
one day to the next the family lost everything.

Isser was a Zionist by the time he was sixteen. It was
necessary, he told his family, that he learn to till the land,
and so he left school before his final examinations, and
took his place alongside other like-minded Jewish youngsters for a year's training at a collective farm in Riga. A
year later, in 1929, every one of those youngsters had
decided that the *Aliyah* to *Eretz Israel* * could no longer
be delayed.

That year was a turning point for Zionism. As the Jews
began to enter Palestine in increasing numbers, the Arabs
of the country rose up against the newcomers. There were
then about 600,000 Arabs in Palestine and 150,000
Jews, over half of whom had arrived since the signing of
the Balfour Declaration in 1917. Moslem leaders persuaded the Arab mob that the Jews had designs on the
holy places of Jerusalem and on August 23, 1929, gave
the signal for an attack. A thousand Arabs in three main
groups poured out from the Old City of Jerusalem and

* *Aliyah* literally means ascent, or going up, and came to
mean emigration to Israel. During the long two thousand
years of exile *Eretz Israel* came to have a mystical significance
for Jews all over the world. *Eretz Israel* meant simply "the
Land of Israel." When Jews spoke of "the Land," they spoke
of Israel. From the first Zionist Congress in Basle in 1897,
Zionism had as its declared aim the return of all Jews to
"the Land" and the rebirth there of Jewish national life,
social, cultural, economical and political. Central to the
Zionist doctrine was the concept that when the settlers arrived
in Israel, no matter what their profession or their intellect,
they would work the land and become once again what the
Jews had been before they were forced into exile, a pastoral
rather than an urban people, where souls were deeply rooted
in the soil. Those aspirations gave the *aliyahs,* as the waves
of immigrants were called, a very special character and
imbued the pioneers with a deserved sense of moral rectitude.

attacked any Jew they could find. The call was taken up throughout Palestine. The British administration refused permission to the Jews to set up the armed militia they needed to protect their settlements. As a result, many were destroyed throughout the country, and 133 Jews were killed, including 59 in Hebron, 23 of whom had lived in one house. They had been abominably tortured and their bodies dismembered.

Zionism might very well have died. Instead, rather magnificently, the Jewish youth of Europe responded. Those who had not been Zionists before became Zionists now. Those who had been Zionists decided to delay their *aliyah* no longer.

The qualifying age to obtain an immigration visa was eighteen, and Isser Harel was not yet quite that. So, for the first time in his life, Isser resorted to forged papers and got a counterfeited certificate showing that he had been born a year earlier than he actually had. Finally, on a January day in 1930, he was on his way. At Dvinsk railway station, he bade goodbye to his parents and received from local Zionists what had become the customary gift on such occasions, a revolver and a supply of bullets to go with it—not for personal use but to be handed over on arrival to the Haganah, which was desperately short of arms and ammunition. Eventually, by way of Genoa, Isser Harel arrived at the port of Jaffa and got his first glimpse of the land he had dreamed of for so long. There, a member of the Jewish Immigration Department came aboard. "The British," he said, "will make an inspection for arms. Any of you who have arms, throw them over the side, because if they find one weapon they will refuse entry to you all."

Most followed instructions. Isser Harel did not. He hollowed out a loaf of bread, placed his revolver and bullets inside it, then carefully put the bread under a pile of dirty clothes. Isser Harel's knapsack, the only luggage he had, was searched in a somewhat desultory way by customs. Harel was young, obviously poor, clearly innocent. "Okay," said the Englishman, and the future chief of the Israeli Secret Service entered the Promised Land.

Isser Harel joined a kibbutz near Tel Aviv. He was uninvolved in Haganah activities—he had come to Palestine to work the land and work the land he did. Single-minded, he labored in the orange orchards, wrapping and packing the golden fruit. The only diversion he permitted himself was to court and marry a young Polish girl called Rivka, a match which caused astonishment in the kibbutz. He was solemn and humorless, a workhorse with little time or inclination for socializing. She was gay and amusing, a pretty little girl, always the first to start the dancing and the last to leave. But marry they did, and made a marvelous match.

In 1935 Isser Harel left the kibbutz after the kind of explosive row which was to become so characteristic throughout his career. He and Rivka had worked long hours outside the kibbutz in order to raise the money to pay for their parents' journey to Palestine. Eventually they succeeded, and both sets of parents arrived and settled in Shefayim. As idealistic a community as the kibbutz was, the people who lived in it were after all only human. Even though private property had been abolished and a kind of perfect equality was supposed to have been established, jealousies would inevitably break out.

By chance, Rivka Harel overheard two members of the settlement talking about Rivka's and Isser's parents and complaining that it had been kibbutz funds which brought them to Israel and kibbutz funds which were now supporting them. Both charges were palpably untrue and unfair. When Rivka, deeply upset, told Isser Harel, he flew into a rage. The following morning Isser Harel and his family left the kibbtuz. They had no money and no possessions, but there were plenty of oranges to be picked and packed. The citrus-fruit orchards of Palestine provided the one source of vitally important foreign exchange for the Jewish community. Harel, Rivka and her sisters set to work. Oblivious to politics, Isser Harel was well on his way to becoming one of those entrepreneur businessmen who were beginning to flourish in Palestine. It seemed nothing could stop him from making his first fortune.

It needed the outbreak of World War II to reawaken in Isser Harel the idealism which had brought him to Palestine. Initially, of course, the war made him richer. The British Army needed the produce he was now not only packing but growing. But suddenly making money didn't seem to be quite enough. As impulsively as he had gone into business, Isser Harel now volunteered for duty with the British Army.

The underground organization Haganah, which controlled recruiting in Palestine, would have none of it. Harel was bluntly told that the Haganah determined who would do war service with the British Army and who with the Haganah. For reasons of its own, but probably to establish its supremacy, the Haganah decided that Isser Harel should join its organization, training with special units preparing for what was believed to be an imminent German invasion of the country. After an initial induction period, Harel was asked to observe the rather suspect activities of a German who was living near Herzliya; the Haganah was convinced he was a Nazi spy. Isser Harel took his orders seriously. He broke into the house and found a splendid printing press in the basement, together with an array of inks and stacks of freshly minted banknotes. The Haganah's spy was a simple old-fashioned forger.

A few months later, one unit of the Haganah happened to be a man short: the Sherut Yediot (the underground secret service of the Haganah), or Shai. Shai was then headed by the supremely gifted Israel Amir (originally Zovlotsky). Amir, who would later command the Haganah forces during the siege of Jerusalem in the 1948 war, was a tough, shrewd Zionist of the old guard. He was a squat heavy-set man, with steely grey hair and a grim, forbidding manner. His standards were of the highest. Amir needed a man of relentless stamina who would be prepared to compile files, sift evidence rigorously, and operate out of the limelight. Isser Harel impressed him immediately.

Israel Amir made Harel secretary of Shai's Jewish Division—regarded by many at that point as the least glamorous, least important, and certainly least agreeable division of the underground agency. The Jewish Division's task was no more and no less than to spy on the Jews inside Palestine. It was an unpopular and unpleasant function. Yet it was also essential. The Haganah was fighting not only the Arabs and, from time to time, the British but also its own people, a dangerous minority of Jews inside Palestine (backed by revisionists in the United States and elsewhere) who refused to accept the gradualist doctrine of the Ben-Gurion establishment in Palestine.

The Haganah had two main rivals. Both were extreme right-wing nationalist groups; both believed that the step-by-step approach to independence would inevitably fail.

There was only one way to achieve their goal, these factions believed, and that was by recourse to the bomb and the bullet.

The most senior of these groups, the Irgun Zevai Leumi (IZL), generally known as the Irgun, broke away from the Haganah in the thirties because it opposed the official Zionist policy of restraint toward Arab terrorism. It became virulently anti-British, when in 1938 the British hanged one of its members who had taken part in an abortive attack against an Arab bus near Rosh Pinnah. The Stern Gang, a small breakaway movement from the Irgun, differed only from its elder brother in being even more extreme; both lived by their adopted escutcheon: a rifle thrust aloft by a clenched fist ringed by the motto "Only Thus."

It was the task of the Jewish Division of Shai to seek out and neutralize these dissidents, who in the beginning were not taken too seriously; their number was small, and they could be fairly easily dealt with, often by betraying them directly to the British. When Isser Harel moved into the Jewish Division, the staff consisted merely of himself, his chief and a female secretary. Harel himself was less than an instantaneous success. He lacked the education and polish of most of his colleagues in Shai. Yet in 1944, two years later, when Harel took over as head of the Jewish Division (which had widened its own scope as the Irgun and the Stern Gang attracted more recruits), Harel did so because he had amassed a formidable knowledge on what had become this most sensitive of subjects. For as secretary it had been Harel's job to keep track of the membership of the dissident organizations, to set up files on individual members, to work out the groups' structure, to establish where they met, where they hid their arms, and, if possible, to infiltrate their cells with his own people.

No one had realized that the department dealing with British affairs, once the most important within Shai, would become at independence completely worthless; all the expertise it had developed over the years might just as well have sailed out with the British Navy from Haifa harbor. At the same time the Jewish Division, renamed the Department of Internal Affairs by Ben-Gurion after a visit in 1947, was the only department with any relevance to the new situation; in its files and in its accumulated experience was all the machinery the new State would require for an internal-security service. Only one man had the background and knowledge to head that service: Isser Harel, who by a remarkable combination of accidents, had reached the top of a profession he had never shown any real interest in entering.

Whenever a new state comes into being, internal security becomes a matter of immediate concern. Never was that more so than in the case of Israel.

On the establishment of the State of Israel, Menachem Begin, leader of the Irgun, emerged from hiding in Palestine and declared that his organization would be put at the disposal of the government in the war with the Arabs. On June 1st, Begin announced that the Irgun would integrate its troops into the Israeli Army—except in Jerusalem, where during the whole period of the siege the various resistance groups of both the right and left operated independently. For a time, somewhat surprisingly perhaps, it looked as if the ultra-right-wing nationalists would be content to play their politics straight.

But on June 11, 1948, two events of the utmost importance to Israel coincided. The first was a truce arranged by the United Nations between the Arabs and the Israelis which came into force at 6:00 P.M. on that day. Article 7 of the truce declared that "war matériels shall not be imported into the country or territory of any interested party."

The second event was that at the very moment Israeli negotiators were signing that truce—and in flagrant defiance of Article 7—an old LST bought by the Irgun from the U.S. Marine Corps and reregistered as the *Altalena* (the pen name of Meir Jabotinsky, Polish philosopher and guru of the Irgun movement) set sail from Port-de-Bouc near Marseilles loaded to its gunwales with rifles, machine guns, cartridges and hand grenades, and with more than 800 volunteers from America and Europe ready to fight for the Irgun against the Arabs.

Af first, and somewhat cynically in the light of the truce arrangements, Ben-Gurion did not object. He had reached an agreement with Menachem Begin that the arms should be permitted to land secretly, out of sight of the United Nations truce observers. It was decided that they should be unloaded at Kfar Vitkin, a beach twenty-five miles north of Tel Aviv and well away from prying eyes.

Twenty per cent of the arms, it had been agreed, should go to the Irgun defenders of Jerusalem and the remainder to the regular army.

But while the *Altalena* was still on the high seas, Begin changed his mind about the division of the arms in the face of what he regarded as an imminent sellout by Ben-Gurion and the Israeli provisional government to a peace mission hard at work in Cairo. Armed rebellion, even civil war, with Jew pitted against Jew, was the nightmare the Israeli government now had to face. Irgun soldiers deserted their units in the south of the country, even though those units were facing the Iraqi Army, and came to the beach at Kfar Vitkin to help unload the *Altalena*. But Ben-Gurion was determined to exercise his leadership. The *Altalena* had arrived and was in the process of being unloaded by the Irgun when crack soldiers of the Alexandroni Brigade opened fire. Irgun soldiers on the beach surrendered, but Menachem Begin, who had boarded the *Altalena* earlier, ordered the ship to sail to Tel Aviv, where he beached it opposite the Ritz Hotel in full view of the whole town. It was a direct challenge to Ben-Gurion.

Begin was daring him to use Jewish soldiers against Jewish resistance fighters while the whole country was watching. It was a challenge which Ben-Gurion seized. He ordered the Palmach, whose headquarters were immediately opposite, to storm the rebel ship. A young Palmach officer, Yitzhak Rabin, later Prime Minister of Israel, led the battle on the beach. A cannon was turned on the *Altalena* by the Palmach commander Yigal Allon, later Deputy Prime Minister. Menachem Begin's bluff had been called.

Isser Harel was now entrusted with the responsibility of crushing the Irgun as an armed force. Harel's men scoured the country for Irgun arms dumps and for officers or organization officials who had gone into hiding. Harel's brief from Ben-Gurion was straightforward; all members of the Irgun must swear an oath of loyalty to the Israeli Army and the State. Harel applied himself to this task wholeheartedly and with characteristic relentlessness.

Irgun members were hunted down. But once found, they were, at least at first, treated scrupulously and promised the same rank and position they held in their own organization within the Israeli Defense Forces. Harel himself negotiated with the top Irgun leadership to try to persuade them to take senior positions in the Israeli Army. They turned him down, but only because they had decided to turn the Irgun into a political organization and challenge Ben-Gurion at the voting booth. Democracy had been put to the test and had won through.

There was still the Stern Gang to deal with, however.

The United Nations had named a mediator between the Arabs and the Jews in an attempt to resolve the Arab-Israeli war. His name was Count Folke Bernadotte, a Swedish aristocrat, and he had infuriated all Israelis by proposing a peace plan which would give the Negev Desert to the Arabs.

A few months later on September 17th, 1948, Count Bernadotte, riding in a white United Nations car through the streets of Jerusalem, was cut down and killed by masked men carrying machine pistols who had blocked his car with their jeep. An organization no one had heard of before, calling itself the National Front, claimed responsibility for the assassination.

Within a day, however, Isser Harel was in Ben-Gurion's office with evidence showing that the National Front was no other than the Stern Gang. Harel sought permission to destroy them.

Ben-Gurion was uncertain. Though the Stern Gang was not officially connected to the Irgun, he feared that by moving against it he might push Irgun troops, not yet completely pacified, to come out in force and bring about the civil war which always seemed to simmer beneath the surface of the new State. Harel, who by now possessed the names of almost every member of the old Stern Gang, told Ben-Gurion it would be a quick and clean operation. He had penetrated virtually every cell of the organization and knew just where the quarry was to be found. Ben-Gurion, with some hesitation, agreed.

That night, backed up by army units under a young lieutenant colonel called Moshe Dayan who had been in charge of the sector of Jerusalem in which Bernadotte was killed, Harel's men began their roundup operation. Throughout the country members of the gang went into hiding, but the noose tightened around them. Moving in a series of lightning sweeps, Harel's men succeeded in doing what the British had never been able to achieve, namely, to wipe out the Stern Gang as an effective organization once and for all. In a period of less than two weeks, every arms cache of the Stern Gang, its secret broadcasting station, the names of its double agents in police and security and the directors of its own intelligence service were all safely under lock and key. On September 30, thirteen days after Bernadotte's murder, Friedmann Yellin, the head of the gang, was arrested by Harel personally in Haifa. The Stern Gang ceased to exist.

Yaacov Shapiro, the Attorney General, who after the death of Bernadotte had drafted a law against terrorists making membership in the Stern Gang or similar organizations illegal, now demanded that all members of the gang held in prison be prosecuted. Isser Harel, however, didn't agree. Only those who were thought to be directly involved in the Bernadotte killing should be prosecuted, he believed. The others should be given a chance to integrate themselves into Israeli society. It was compassionate and wise advice which Ben-Gurion immediately accepted.

From now on, Harel would climb unswervingly to the top. But if it was his battle with the right wing in Israel which brought him into prominence, his subsequent battle with the left nearly led to his undoing. He survived the crisis because unlike those rivals who had fallen by the wayside, he had taken care first to ensure the loyalty and support of David Ben-Gurion.

PART II

Early Struggles

Chapter 5

THE PRESS BENCHES were packed as Avraham Bar and Sholman Ahabi shuffled nervously into the dock on January 28, 1953.

It was a most intriguing case, with quite remarkable parallels on the surface at least to Washington's Watergate scandal some twenty years later.

As in Watergate the two men were caught in the offices of a main opposition party to the government in the dead of night and claimed at first to be merely burglars. As in Watergate they were shown to have connections with security services. And, as in Watergate, the office of the Chief Executive denied all knowledge of their activities. And now, just as at the start of the Watergate investigations, the "burglars" themselves were being dealt with by a small district court on the simple indictment of "illegal entry."

The charge was read out. Avraham Bar and Sholman Ahabi pleaded guilty to entering with felonious intent the offices of Mifleget-Hapoalim-Hameuchdet, known throughout Israel and the world as Mapam, a leftist opposition party to the ruling party Mapai, the party of Ben-Gurion, the party of the government, and the party of the establishment.

Ben Ari, the prosecutor and assistant in charge of the Criminal Department of the Tel Aviv area, rose to his feet and demanded that a heavy fine be imposed upon the two men. The judge thought differently. They were fined twenty Israeli pounds each or two weeks' imprisonment. The case was over. Bar and Ahabi were hurried away and disappeared completely from view with virtually every question the case had raised left tantalizingly unanswered.

Most of those questions had been raised (and answered to his own satisfaction) on the morning after the raid on January 28, 1953, by Natan Peled, the head of the Ma-

pam Party. At a hastily called press conference, Peled
made a dramatic statement which made headlines in
every newspaper in the country the following morning:
"For some time we have noticed that our most secret
meetings have been unaccountably leaked to the press,"
Peled declared. "Our men searched the room of Meir
Ya'ari, the secretary general of the party, and found this
apparatus on the underside of the desk." Peled then produced a miniaturized radio transmitter. "When we found
it," Peled went on triumphantly, "we laid a trap, and last
night we caught two men whom we turned over to the police after having questioned them."

"We know who they are," he went on. "They are spies
for Mapai in the pay of David Ben-Gurion." Peled also
announced that when the two men were searched, found
on them were various keys, burglars' tools, and a type-
written sheet giving a training school course outline in the
art of breaking and entering.

The Prime Minister's office denied all knowledge of the
two men. Inquiries to Shin Bet were met with equally
firm denials. But most people could guess where those
course notes came from.

Few events had a greater influence upon the shape and
conduct of Israel's intelligence services than this apparently minor incident.

Isser Harel's job as head of the Jewish Division of Shai
had never been an easy or a particularly pleasant one.
Like small-town life, Israel is a strangely personal society.
Everybody knows everybody else. As Israeli policemen
like to say, if you arrest a man for a crime, the chances
are that he's the cousin twice-removed of the mother-in-
law of your next door neighbor. In political matters, that
problem was still more acute. None of this bothered Isser
Harel. He was singleminded and determined. He worked
by a simple rule of thumb: the enemies of Ben-Gurion
were his enemies, too. In the early days of Israel, those
enemies were on the right; few foresaw that later they
would be on the extreme left. Ben-Gurion's party, Mapai,
was a socialist party. Russia had sponsored the U.N. res-
olution which created the State of Israel. She was a potential ally. Most Jewish leaders spoke Russian fluently.
The kibbutzim from which they came were an expression
of the purest form of Communism.

One of the prime reasons why in the forties the British

Foreign Office was opposed to an independent Israel was because it believed that, through Israel, Russia would get a strategic toehold in the Middle East. On the face of it at least, that did not seem the improbable proposition it might today.

The early settlers, men like David Ben-Gurion, had come to Israel as idealists of the purest kind. Their Zionism was a philosophy of labor: that the Jew, the eternal wandering Jew, would be purified again only by a return to "the Land" and hard physical work. They set up kibbutzim, where all goods were owned in common, where children were brought up by the community and not by their parents, where Marx's basic tenet was actually put into practice—from each according to his means, to each according to his needs.

Ben-Gurion's generation also brought with them from Czarist Russia an authoritarian view of life which brooked no argument. That authoritarianism was expressed through the Jewish Agency and its political arm in Israel, the Israeli Labor Party, or Mapai. By the mid-forties, it was difficult to make much progress in Israel unless you were of Mapai. Party discipline was strict. The party, rather than the party's philosophy, came to matter most.

Coincidental to that, a new paramilitary force was coming into being whose role in the early history of Israel and in the establishment of its intelligence community would turn out to be crucial. To understand the Israeli Army, to understand the Israeli intelligence establishment —and indeed Israeli politcs today—one has to understand the Palmach.

In May 1941, the high command of the Haganah set up an independent underground striking force consisting of nine companies. It was to be the first Jewish standing army since biblical days. Unlike the Haganah, which called up its people if and when they were needed, the Palmach was wholly mobilized at all times, its soldiers enlisted as full-time regulars.

The unit was given the name Palmach, the initials standing for the Hebrew word for "strike force." The Palmach, after vigorous training, immediately went into action and distinguished itself by the dash and élan it showed on the side of the British against the Vichy French in Syria and Lebanon. Palmach troops were used as guides and saboteurs, as members of advance reconnaissance units, and on intelligence assignments behind enemy lines. Both sides benefited from the experience. The British got hard young fighters who spoke and understood Arabic and the Arabs; the Palmach received training in all of the advanced guerrilla and sabotage techniques then available to the British. Many bright "Palmachniks," as they quickly became known, joined the Arab section— those sent into the Arab towns under deep cover. Many claim that the Arab section of the Palmach was in a real sense the forerunner of the Mossad today. Its first commander was Yeruham Cohen, a remarkable man who taught his pupils how to be Arabs (and then how to be soldiers), and in order to do this took them right into the mosques of Jerusalem. Every recruit into the Israeli Secret Service is taught the basic maxim "You can't be a Moslem without knowing how to pray."

Immediately after World War II, operatives from the Arab section of the Palmach moved into the mixed cities of Haifa, Tel Aviv, Jaffa and Jerusalem as well as into the small villages, as the first properly trained and equipped Israeli penetration agents. But at this point, quite by happenstance, the Palmach began to take on a distinctly political character.

During the British Mandate, as a matter of expediency, all Palmach platoons were stationed in kibbutzim throughout the country. It was the best way of hidiing from the security forces and yet remaining together as an operational unit poised for action. The Palmach commander at the time, the young Yigal Allon saw the social dangers inherent in such a situation. If they were not careful, the Palmach would become a financial drain on an already poor and hard-pressed community. Palmach men would be eating the food of workers who were growing just enough to feed themselves. So it was decided that the Palmach had to be self-supporting. Each Palmach soldier undertook to work for two weeks out of every four in the fields of the kibbutz on which he was stationed, spending the second two weeks in training, so that the earnings from the first fortnight paid for his food and lodgings for the month.

This policy, which was soon in successful operation, had a quite unexpected side effect. The Palmach, which was made up of the most dedicated and committed of Israelis and was the elite of its underground military establishment, became highly politicized. Working as agricultural laborers outside of the big cities, the Palmach turned well to the left of the Haganah. Both its noncommissioned officers and commissioned officers refused to wear badges of rank; its soldiers openly questionted the politics of the Jewish leadership. The Palmach, in fact, was quite openly influenced by the Soviet Union: each unit had its own political commissar who taught the Palmach line, members addressed each other as "Comrade," the Palmach songs were Soviet marching songs, and the Palmach heroes were Russian soldiers who had died glorious deaths on behalf of the Soviet motherland.

Although the Palmach operated under Haganah command, fairly quickly relations between the two deteriorated, partly because of politics, partly because, in the nature of an elite, the Palmach began increasingly to regard itself as being an independent force answerable to itself.

If Ben-Gurion was troubled by these developments, he seldom showed it. Basically, he believed that for all its posturings the Palmach could always be relied upon. But by 1948 he was no longer so sure. On June 12, 1948, he exploded in irritation: "The Palmach does a lot of boasting, but does not act in a responsible manner!"

Mapai, Ben-Gurion's Israeli Labor Party and the dominant voice in Israeli politics since the thirties, split in two as it became impossible to encompass the conservatism of the leadership and the radicalism of new recruits within the same party. The new party, Mapam (the United Workers' Party), stood well to the left of Mapai, and, in the view of many, dangerously so. If differences existed between the policies enunciated by certain Mapam leaders and the Russian Communist Party, these were sometimes difficult to discern.

Mapai might still have been the majority party, but support for Mapam was by no means insignficant. At the 1948 general election, the first in the history of the country, Mapam polled 14.77 percent of the votes, became the second-largest party in the country, and took nineteen seats in the Knesset (the governing Labor Party, Mapai, had forty-six). Within only a few months of its founding, Mapam became the leading opposition party in Israel.

What was potentially sinister in the eyes of Ben-Gurion and his party was that Mapam possessed undue influence within the Palmach. Estimates varied at the time, but it seems certain that between 80 percent and 90 percent of the 9,000 rank-and-file members of the Palmach were members of Mapam, and that probably 95 percent voted for Mapam during the 1948 election. Of the Palmach's sixty-four senior commanders, no fewer than sixty were members of Mapam. At the end of 1948, the high command of the Palmach was dissolved. With a permanent standing army within an independent state, there was no longer any military justification for a separate army operating outside the parameters of the regular army. But Mapam and members of the Palmach saw the decision as a political one. Suddenly the left, like the right before it, had a grievance. Israel, they believed, had been taken over by an oligarchy.

Members of the Palmach were already well entrenched inside the Shin Bet. The Palmach's membership had provided a natural and fertile recruiting ground, and Isser Harel had been quick to realize it. In particular, the Palmach filled the ranks of the so-called "Special Department" of Shin Bet, almost certainly the most secret single unit in Israel. It was this Special Department which Isser Harel had used to crack down on the extremist right-wing parties. Given almost limitless powers, the Special Department broke into offices, kidnapped and interrogated suspects, and used eavesdropping or other electronic devices to collect information. When, after the Bernadotte assassination, it was decided to use force against the right-wing extremists, it was the Special Department which led the raids on the Stern Gang installations, recruiting additional men from its own kibbutzim to help.

In early 1949, Ben-Gurion and Isser Harel agreed that the Israeli Communist Party should be put under surveillance. Harel knew well enough that this could cause problems within his own organization, especially within the ideologically left-inclined Special Department, whose job it would be to carry out the surveillance.

Worse, Isser Harel became convinced that the Communists had infiltrated Mapam and were doing so in increasing numbers. He called in a leading member of Mapam, told him about his suspicions that Moscow was seeking to infiltrate the party, and asked him to transmit this warning to Meir Ya'ari, general secretary of Mapam. Ya'ari's answer was brief and to the point: Security (Shin Bet) had no business meddling in the internal affairs of

Mapam, a democratically elected party in a democratic country.

So, in March 1950, Isser Harel, backed by Ben-Gurion, decided on the fateful step of full-scale surveillance of Mapam, the country's principal opposition party. It was left to Isser Harel to sort out the details.

The basic problem he faced was that many senior officers of Shin Bet were ideologically well to the left of Ben-Gurion. The most prominent of these was Major Gideon Lavi (a pseudonym), a brilliant and distinguished soldier who clearly had an outstanding career ahead of him. He had enlisted in the Palmach in 1941, graduated with distinction from a course for platoon commanders and subsequently from the equivalent of today's Israeli Staff College. In 1944, as chief security officer of the Palmach, he was principally concerned with combatting the British, but he was also involved on the peripheries of the battle then being waged against right-wing terrorist groups.

Within the Palmach and the Haganah, Lavi was celebrated for one of the classic intelligence operations run by the Jews before the establishment of the State of Israel: the equipping and running of a printing house on the outskirts of Tel Aviv in 1945 which produced most of the high-quality forgeries so vital to the Jewish underground, desperately in need of the right documentation in Palestine and in Europe. Naturally enough during this period, he had frequent dealings with Isser Harel, and although he left the intelligence community briefly to become chief of staff of the Negev Brigade during the War of Independence, it was no surprise that he was invited back to Tel Aviv by Harel to become the executive director of Shin Bet after Harel became head of the new security organization in 1948.

Lavi made no secret of his politics or of his close connections with the Palmach. But nobody minded about that when the enemy was the Stern Gang. It began to matter a great deal more, however, when the left-wing parties came under suspicion. It was obvious there were difficulties on both sides, which Harel was determined to try to clear up. At a long meeting with Gideon Lavi, Harel set out the case for Shin Bet surveillance of the Communist Party and asked Lavi if either he himself or any of the colleagues whom he had brought with him into Shin Bet would have any ideological problems in carrying through this program. Gideon Lavi thought hard before he told Harel they would be able to cooperate, and he added one important rider. If, Lavi said, these activities exceeded the limits which he and his people regarded as acceptable or tolerable in all conscience, they should be permitted to resign from the service with no recriminations on either side. It was a deal which Isser Harel, now head of Mossad as well as Shin Bet, was glad to accept.

This strange compact lasted for nearly a year and was broken only by Isser Harel's decision to bring the Mapam Party, of which Lavi was a member, under surveillance. Harel, believing that he could not now absolutely count upon Gideon Lavi, took the extraordinary step of going outside Shin Bet and setting up a parallel intelligence service whose sole role would be to effect vigilance over Mapam. Information concerning this organization was restricted to only two or three people within Shin Bet and two or three people within the government. A special fund was established to pay its operatives, and temporary office accommodation was found on the outskirts of Tel Aviv.

Despite the most elaborate precautions, the secret could not be kept for long. Gideon Lavi, a superb professional, found out about it within two months—where it was situated, who worked for it, and how it operated. Coldly furious, he saw the establishment of this secret parallel "Special Department" not merely as a shocking breach of faith, but as a direct attack upon the political integrity of Mapam and proof that Isser Harel was about to hand over Shin Bet lock, stock and barrel to David Ben-Gurion to be used by him in order to crush all opposition to his policies.

With the same weapons Isser Harel was using against Mapam, Gideon Lavi struck back. (Members of his office, all like him ex-members of the Palmach, members of Mapam, and members of a Mapam kibbutz, began to scrutinize the work of Isser Harel's Special Department, reporting their findings back to Mapam.) It must be said that while it took Lavi only two months to discover the existence of the parallel Special Department, it took the Special Department six months to discover that it had been penetrated. When it did, the explosion was only

barely muffled by the thick padding of secrecy which surrounded Shin Bet.

Gideon Lavi, of course, had to resign. It could have
been worse for him. According to Isser Harel, Lavi's special unit was not satisfied merely with conducting surveillance over the special squad, but also spied upon members
of the Western diplomatic community and stole classified
material belonging to Shin Bet. Most seriously of all,
they were doing all this on behalf of an organization
known as the Security Committee of Mapam. If these
charges had been proved (if it could have been shown
that Gideon Lavi and his men, all members of the staff
of Shin Bet, were actually agents responsive to the orders
of an outside organization, albeit an Israeli one), then
they would have been guilty of a criminal breach of the
Israeli security laws.

Nothing, however, could be proved. Gideon Lavi himself when faced with the evidence wrote in a scornful
memorandum: "I have never taken part in any spying
activities on behalf of Mapam. The organization I set up
within Shin Bet was internal to Shin Bet. I did report to
leaders of the Mapam that they were under surveillance.
This I had the right to do. However, I did not turn over
any information about Shin Bet and I did not receive
any orders from anyone else."

Each of the Mapam men inside the executive office was
closely questioned about his activities. Most confessed to
spying upon their non-Mapam colleagues and also upon
Western diplomats, but they described this as a "free-
lance" action which had nothing to do with their work at
Shin Bet.

Most were fired immediately. Some were given a second
chance within the department. Before Gideon Lavi himself left, he made sure that another Mapam man had his
key job. The blood flowed liberally—so liberally that
there were fears that the press and public would hear
about it.

That they didn't, that no charges were brought against
any of the Shin Bet people, was in fact due to the realization by Isser Harel that any leak would cause enormous
damage to Shin Bet and to Ben-Gurion. Quietly, with as
little fuss as possible, a remarkable episode in the history
of Shin Bet was buried. The corpse, however, refused to
lie down.

Major Gideon Lavi packed up his possessions and returned to the kibbutz he had come from, but within two months he was back again in Tel Aviv, this time on the invitation of the Mapam leadership. He was asked, and he agreed, to set up within the party a secret bureau portentously called the Department of Self Defense. There was no doubt, of course, against whom the Mapam Party believed it needed defending: Shin Bet and its director Isser Harel.

Lavi was a superb choice for the job. He knew Shin Bet and its agents. He himself had selected and trained many of them. He knew the way they operated. He understood the equipment they used. He knew, too, the *modus operandi* of Isser Harel, whom he still met from time to time in a Tel Aviv coffeehouse, and he understood Harel's obsessions.

But initially the pickings were lean. After the fiasco of his "special squad," Harel was keeping a low profile. From time to time Lavi unearthed Shin Bet informers within the Mapam Party, mainly small-time clerks in the offices, who were being paid five Israeli pounds for each item of information; he discovered that Mapam's telephones were being tapped and that on one occasion the office had been broken into, almost certainly by Shin Bet. It was harassment, but nothing which couldn't be handled.

It wasn't until toward the end of 1952, nearly two years after Lavi had left Shin Bet, that the war between Mapam and Shin Bet reached fever pitch, for it was then that Isser Harel made the fateful decision to use the very latest CIA equipment made available to him and actually bug the headquarters of the Mapam Party.

A small group of his top specialists broke into the offices of Party General Secretary Meir Ya'ari. In fact, it was not an easy room in which to plant a radio transmitter. It was simply furnished, contained only a small yellow desk and a few plain chairs. But it was enough for Harel's men. They converted the desk into a miniature broadcasting station. Because the bug was very small it could, with the aid of a little carpentry, be inserted in the space left between the end of the drawer as it slid into the desk and the desk itself. The aerial, easily disguised, simply coiled the length of the desk beneath the paneling. A listening device was placed in an office specially rented for the job just 200 meters away, and from then on every

word uttered in Ya'ari's office went simultaneously onto
the tape recorders of Shin Bet.

Unfortunately for Harel, Ben-Gurion made use of the
tapes a little too crudely. Every day the Mapai press carried
detailed stories of the fierce debates within the inner counsels of Mapam, often reporting verbatim accounts of the
discussions. Meir Ya'ari suspected a leak from a member
of the general counsel and asked Gideon Lavi to investigate. Lavi was experienced enough to know that it was
highly unlikely anyone would be able to leak detailed reports with such complete accuracy. The answer had to be
that Meir Ya'ari's office was bugged.

On January 25, 1953, after most of the workers had
left the building, Gideon Lavi entered Ya'ari's office and
began his search. He turned it inside out, but found nothing. He was about to leave empty-handed when suddenly
he remembered that the central drawer of the desk hadn't
closed properly when he'd tried to push it in. He went
back and looked at it more closely and found the bug resting in a small plastic box at the back of the drawer. The
time was 6:45 P.M.

With the bug still in position, Lavi rushed to a small
perfume shop and bought a plastic soap box of about the
same size as the box which contained the eavesdropping
instrument. Within an hour he had rounded up leading
members of the Mapam Party and told them of his discovery. He had an immediate plan of campaign. They
would start a discussion in the general secretary's office on
Mapam policy and then after a few minutes he would rip
out the bug, and replace it with the empty soap box. Shin
Bet, he told his colleagues, would be bound to send in a
team to repair it or replace what they would assume to be
a faulty piece of equipment.

A group was set up to watch the office under Shimon
Avidan, a commander of the Palmach, a general in the
military reserve, and later controller of the Ministry of
Defense. Nothing happened that night, or on the night of
January 26th. January 27th looked as if it would pass
peacefully as well when, a few minutes after midnight, a
small car drew up on the pavement opposite the building.
There were four men inside. One of them remained in
the car. The second took up an observation point outside
the building. The two others, armed with false identity
cards together with keys and a little screwdriver, entered

the building. Without putting on any lights, they went up to the second floor and approached the door which connected the four rooms of the offices. Silently they opened the external door, then picked the lock of the door immediately on their right. Slowly they pushed the door open and immediately were fallen upon by the men who had lain in ambush for them.

The Mapam men knew that they had only a few moments to get the truth out of the interlopers. Shin Bet, Lavi had warned, would follow orthodox procedure. The Police Department would have been warned in advance by Shin Bet that they would be raiding the offices of Mapam that evening. If anything went wrong, the police would rush to the spot to protect the men who had conducted the break-in and secure their release. As soon as the man in the car realized that his colleagues were not returning, he would go to the nearest police station for help. Shimon Avidan asked the two men why they were there. They had come to steal, they said. That earned them a few punches and kicks. They then told another version. They had recently arrived from Russia, they said, but their family had been forced to stay behind. Their plan was to wreck the Mapam offices in an act of revenge for the party's defense of the Communist countries. Time was now running out. Shimon Avidan grabbed one of the men, pushed him to the door, and placed his fingers in the jamb. "Now," Avidan said, "you opened this door illegally. I propose to shut it very slowly. Your fingers, however, will remain in position unless you tell me the truth."

That was enough for the Shin Bet burglar. He admitted he belonged to Isser Harel's organization, and that he had joined only months previous.

Minutes after the confession, the police arrived and "arrested" the two men. The following day, Mapam held a press conference in which they produced the bug and the course notes. In those days it was forbidden to make public reference to Shin Bet and so the burglars could only be described as "messengers of Mapai." But no one, not even Isser Harel, knew until many years later the true story of how his men had been discovered. No one in Israel knew of the bitter fratricidal quarrel which had rent the entire Israeli Shin Bet. Finally it was a standoff. Mapam refused to pass on to the police the bug, knowing full well that if they did so it would disappear, never to re-emerge. The police claimed that if they didn't have it, they could not pursue the burglars with the full rigors of the law. The men were fined by the courts, an attempt to get a parliamentary debate was quashed, and that was that.

Whether the bugging of Mapam was justified or not, it must be said that on January 26, 1953, the day before the bug was found, the ultra-left faction inside the Mapam Party walked out and made common cause with Israel's Communist Party. Moshe Sneh and his principal lieutenant, Avraham Berman, fascinatingly enough brother of Jakub Berman, Stalin's principal hatchet man in Poland and Minister of the Interior of the Polish government, had lost their struggle to turn Mapam into just another shadow of the Communist Party. Most of the extreme left membership of Mapam went with him, but those who decided to stay were rooted out and expelled by Mapam itself in the months that followed.

Though he added to his list of enemies, Isser Harel, protected by Ben-Gurion, emerged after the Mapam affair relatively unscathed. Whether the bugging of Mapam headquarters was justified or not is still very much an open question. Harel's supporters say that the Sneh group, which had close relations with the Soviet Embassy in Tel Aviv, did represent in its attempt to take over a major political party a real danger to the democratic institutions of the State. Mapam people say that as events proved, the party was well able to look after itself and did in fact expel its Communist or near Communist members. Harel's interests, they believe, were the political interests of Ben-Gurion, not the interests of the State as a whole.

Though Isser Harel would today indignantly deny this charge, the whole affair did have an immense influence upon Harel personally and upon Israeli intelligence institutions as a whole. Never again would Shin Bet or any other Israeli intelligence organization dabble in internal politics. Only in exceptional circumstances would Shin Bet recruit men like Gideon Lavi with such strong and definable political connections. It does not expect its people to be political eunuchs; it does expect them to be dispassionate enough not to wear their politics on their sleeves.

As Harel was later to tell David Ben-Gurion, Shin Bet

would never get the full-hearted support of the Israeli population if it seemed to be playing a political game in Israel. Shin Bet had to be above politics—above suspicion. It is to its credit that it has learned that lesson well.

Chapter 6

ON DECEMBER 7, 1953, a shock wave hit Israel with titanic force. David Ben-Gurion, Prime Minister and Minister of Defense since the creation of Israel, announced his resignation from the government, effective immediately. True, he had attempted to give his countrymen warning when, three months earlier, he had gone on extended leave. But no one really believed that he would go through with his frequently declared intention of retiring. Like Winston Churchill, he was not a man who was universally loved, but also like Winston Churchill, he was not merely a politician but an institution. It was difficult to imagine life without him. Most Israelis sensed that the men he left behind had lived for so long under his shadow that their capacity for independent thought and action had been significantly eroded. Nowhere did this matter more than at the Ministry of Defense.

Ben-Gurion regarded the Israeli Armed Forces as being his personal creation. He supervised training and promotion. He pushed young men up through the ranks of high command faster than was possible in any other army in the world. He used their spirit and their sense of adventure to the advantage of the country, while all the time carefully and patiently balancing these qualities of youth with the enormous weight of his own experience. But when David Ben-Gurion departed, worn out by years of struggle going back as far as the twenties and thirties, the very foundation stone of the edifice he had so carefully built up was pulled away.

Moshe Sharett, the new Prime Minister, was a very different man from Ben-Gurion. His credentials were, of course, impeccable. He was highly intelligent, a superb linguist, and a born diplomat. Ben-Gurion was an activist or, as Golda Meir has put it, "a man who believed in doing rather than explaining and who was convinced that what really mattered in the end—and what would always really matter—was what the Israelis did and how they did it, not what the world outside Israel thought or said about them." But "Sharett," as Mrs. Meir put it, "was immensely concerned with the way in which policymakers elsewhere reacted to Israel and what was likely to make the Jewish State 'look good' in the eyes of other foreign ministers or the United Nations. Israel's image and the verdict of his own contemporaries—rather than history or future historians—were the criteria he tended to use most often."

The new Minister of Defense, Pinhas Lavon, was a legacy of Ben-Gurion's, presumably because Ben-Gurion regarded Lavon as being rather in his own mold. Senior colleagues in and out of the government, people like Golda Meir and Shaul Avigur, had strenuously opposed his appointment, but Ben-Gurion had refused to listen.

Pinhas Lavon was without question the single most remarkable man in the government. Intellectually, he stood far above most other members of the government. His sharp tongue was a feared weapon which he used to good effect. He was learned and a magnificent orator. But he lacked ministerial experience, and his ability to get on with people was always seriously in question.

He was an oddly attractive man, though angular and stooped, with very little hair and a magnificent pair of black bushy eyebrows. Most of his difficulties arose from the contempt in which he held most of his colleagues in his party—a contempt he didn't bother to conceal.

Pinhas Lavon's relations with Moshe Sharett, the new Prime Minister, were appalling from the start. While they were both still working in an "acting" capacity, Sharett wrote to Lavon:

Between the Prime Minister and Minister of Defense [Ben-Gurion] and myself, there was a practise of providing advance notice of every serious act of retaliation against any of the neighbouring countries, or any forceful step against the Arab population of the State. This procedure was not followed with regard to the curfew and the search in Tira or the operations carried out on the night of the 12th of this month. Therefore, I must request you henceforth to give me sufficient advance notice of any serious operation of the types I mentioned, which you have ordered or which have your approval.

On August 19, Sharett wrote to Lavon:

Your refusal to participate in collegial consultations is very surprising and creates a very serious problem. If the intention is to bring about my resignation as acting Prime Minister, there could be nothing simpler. Is that what you desire?

And on May 24, 1954, when Sharett was full rather than Acting Premier and Lavon full Minister of Defense, Sharett wrote to him rather pathetically:

Security measures are not being reported to me as they should be. Things occur that are not being brought to my attention. I hear announcements on the radio and later read about them in the papers without knowing the true background. The proper arrangement would be for me to know the facts if at all possible, before the official version is released. I should know the facts, and it is up to you to take the initiative.

Lavon's relations with the Army—or at least an important section of the Army—were bad, too. He regarded most soldiers as being bureaucrats in uniform. He quarreled immediately with his Chief of Staff General Mordechai Maklef who realized quickly that Lavon was a dangerous choice as Minister of Defense. Though he communicated these fears to Ben-Gurion, Maklef was ignored, and he resigned. On the morning of his own final resignation as Prime Minister and Minister of Defense, Ben-Gurion accepted Maklef's resignation and appointed his own political and military godchild in Maklef's place: Lieutenant General Moshe Dayan.

A potentially explosive situation now existed within the Defense Ministry. For the first time, it had its own minister (previously the role had always been combined with the Prime Minister's office), and he was a man whom many regarded as being psychologically unfitted for the role. He not only didn't get on with his Prime Minister, but despised him, and his Prime Minister lacked the political muscle to remove him. As for the Army, it had a new Chief of Staff, General Moshe Dayan, clearly a brilliant and charismatic leader, but one who lacked experience at the higher levels of administration and leadership and was already, to the dismay of half the cabinet, not merely a soldier but an active politician.

The director general of the Defense Ministry, Shimon Peres, was young and unquestionably able, but he was a callow man who was already showing signs of a weakness which has worked to his disadvantage ever since, that arrogance shown by men who, believing they have great minds, possess merely good ones. Both Dayan and Peres were ambitious—in the view of some, unhealthily so.

The chief of Military Intelligence, Benjamin Gibli, was not a man particularly suited to the job he held, either. Though it was true he had a wide intelligence background, having been chief of the Jerusalem District for Shai during the siege of the city in 1948, and had been with Military Intelligence ever since, he was primarily a front-line soldier—a man who possessed more than his fair share of flair. What he lacked was the kind of deep analytical mind so vital in the chief of an intelligence organization.

Dayan, Peres and Gibli all welcomed Lavon to the Ministry of Defense and backed him to the hilt. They realized immediately that they had in him a strong minister capable of holding his own against anyone in the Israeli Cabinet, including the Prime Minister. He was a man who had been converted to the concept of action, a man who responded with fervor to the brashness of youth. They knew that he was Ben-Gurion's choice and that the establishment disapproved of him. Those, as far as they were concerned, were qualifications enough.

Benjamin Gibli, with whom Labon got on particularly well, asked the minister to have one matter put right straightaway. In respect to "special operations," Military Intelligence had not been master of its own house for some time. In order to avoid rival Israeli agencies falling over each other in the field, a system had been established which gave Military Intelligence the right and duty to plan all special operations and also the right to nominate the target. But Military Intelligence was not permitted to put its plan into operation without the final authorization of Mossad. It was Mossad's finger, in fact, upon the trigger.

Mossad's right to vet the work of Military Intelligence turned Military Intelligence into the junior service of the two. This situation became apparently codified a few months after the original instruction when Ben-Gurion set up a joint intelligence committee with the head of Mossad as ex-officio chairman. He became known as the *Memuneh*, or "father figure" of the intelligence community, a title given to every head of Mossad since. Another effect upon the status of Military Intelligence had to do with the rise of Isser Harel. As head of Mossad, Harel was answerable directly to the Prime Minister; the chief of Military Intelligence was answerable to the Chief of Staff. Isser Harel used his direct access to the top to establish a very special relationship with Ben-Gurion. Conversely to Harel's right of access, Ben-Gurion had an inflexible rule that affected Military Intelligence: no army officer in uniform could attend the Cabinet or the Foreign and Defense Committee of the Knesset. Though Mossad was already suffering from a lack of research facilities permitting it properly to evaluate the intelligence material it collected, this seemed more than made up for by its director's unchallengeable right of entry into the Prime Minister's office.

Gibli, backed all the way by Dayan and Peres and almost certainly encouraged by Ben-Gurion himself (who turned Sde Boker into a kind of Prime Minister's office in exile to which all his young lions would go for advice and encouragement), saw in Ben-Gurion's departure an opportunity to restore to Military Intelligence its former independence. For Ben-Gurion and his immediate entourage, this was a crucial switch of policy, developing out of the fact that none of them believed Sharett had the stomach to approve *any* special operation. While Sharett was Prime Minister, decisions of this nature would have to be made outside his office—and thus outside the office of Isser Harel, too.

Pinhas Lavon undertook to push the change through a reluctant Cabinet. Isser Harel presented a carefully argued paper showing the inherent dangers of permitting the organization which conducts special operations a totally free hand to carry them through. The Prime Minister himself pointed out rather acidly that even the current rules had not stopped the military from conducting border operations without first seeking the approval of ministers.

To the shame of the Cabinet then, Lavon was able to ride roughshod over all objections and get his way. It was a decision which was ultimately to destroy him both as a politician and as a man. It was a decision which would bring about the break up of the government's party and send Ben-Gurion himself into embittered political exile. It was a decision which would befoul the Israeli political scene for years to come and one from which Israeli Military Intelligence would take years to recover.

One operation—Operation Suzanna—played by the new Lavon rules, would in time to come eat its young.

It had been a mess from the very beginning, long before Lavon himself arrived at the Ministry of Defense. In mid-1951, John Darling, apparently a British businessman working as an export salesman for a British electrical apparatus firm, arrived at Cairo airport from London. John Darling's real name was Avraham Dar. He was an ex-officer in the Palmach, a man with a ready grin and a firm handshake for every occasion, and an agent of Israeli Military Intelligence. Somewhat Arabic in appearance, he had more critics than admirers. To many he was too much the second-hand-car salesman, clever but lacking the kind of analytical mind a first-class agent operating on his own in hostile territory requires.

Colonel Gibli of Military Intelligence took the view that in any future war, Israel should possess a fifth column inside Egypt to blow up Egyptian civil and military installations and generally disrupt Egypt's ability to wage war successfully. It was Avraham Dar's—or John Darling's—job to find Gibli a team, a group of sleeper agents inside Egypt, ready to be activated at the touch of a button.

Once John Darling had established his cover with the authorities, he immediately called upon Dr. Victor Sa'adi, the head of an undercover Zionist organization called "Together" whose aim was to assist the emigration of Egyptian Jews to Israel. Sa'adi, young and idealistic, put his organization at Darling's disposal, and Darling began to recruit local Jews at full spate. He divided his organization into two cells, a Cairo section and an Alexandria section. He put Dr. Moshe Marzouk of the Jewish Hospital in Cairo in charge of the Cairo cell and Shmuel "Jacques" Azar, a handsome twenty-four-year-old schoolmaster, in charge of the Alexandria cell. Both sections were to continue to recruit on their own, and of course did so from the circle of people with whom they had been brought up. Though only in their teens or early twenties, they considered themselves a rather cosmopolitan group, living as they did in two of the most ancient and sophisticated cities in the world, where everybody of any account spoke four languages and had absorbed the cultures and traditions of them all.

One of the girls was Victorine "Marcelle" Ninio, recruited by Sa'adi and Darling. She was beautiful, well known in Cairo, with a wide circle of friends, and was a girl of enormous vitality and vivacity. There was Robert Dassa, a clerk, short, always cheerful, looking more Egyptian than the Egyptians, at home anywhere, proud of his Jewishness, yet a stout defender of Arab culture and traditions. There was Victor Levy, who was to become the leader of the group, a student engineer, very much the man about town until he was "captured" by a girl as attractive as he was goodlooking, Marie-Francis, a teacher of English.

In 1952 Gibli decided that the team should be brought to Israel for training. In direct charge of the operation was Lieutenant Colonel Mordechai "Motke" Ben-Tsur, a huge bear of a man, an ex-field intelligence officer in the Palmach, a basketball player of championship potential, and now the officer commanding Unit 131, the single most secret unit in the Israeli Army. Unit 131 ran all of Military Intelligence's special operations from its small, cramped and untidy officers down a nondescript street in the old Arab town of Jaffa.

As C.O. of the unit, Motke Ben-Tsur, along with Gibli himself and Isser Harel, sat at the very apex of the Israeli intelligence community. Ben-Tsur organized the transportation of the team from Egypt to Israel with professionalism and skill. Marcelle Ninio, on instructions from John Darling, set up a travel agency called Grunberg Travel of which she was in charge of ticketing. So it was that all six members of the team could buy tickets to Europe without arousing the suspicions of any curious travel-agency clerk or inquisitive official who might get in the way of their "holiday" in Europe which would be interrupted by a secret trip to Israel.

But on arrival in Israel, when they were taken to the

Army Intelligence School outside Jaffa, the few outsiders who were allowed near them realized immediately that a terrible tragedy was in the making. An ex-Palmach officer then on the staff of Mossad was detailed as one of their weapons-training officers. He was appalled to discover the kind of people with whom he was dealing. These were no natural-born saboteurs. These were gentle, idealistic, sensitive city dwellers, who would always be more impressed with the romantic concept of what they were doing than involved with the work itself. What was even more alarming was the fact that they all knew each other, were friends from years back, had gone to the same schools, and, as far as he could gather, the entire network left behind in Cairo (which was being kept informed by Marcelle with postcards on which messages were written between the lines in invisible ink) was also made up of old friends from school or college days. This was amateurishness in the extreme. If Egyptian security penetrated one section of the organization, they would have the whole lot in the bag. To know Marzouk's organization, all you had to know was his friends. There were no cut-outs, no dead-letter boxes. If the group wanted to discuss something, they simply met in a Cairo or an Alexandria coffeehouse. If what needed saying was really important, really secret, then they met in one or another's apartment. Ben-Tsur seemed sublimely unaware of quite how outrageous these arrangements were.

It was unforgivable. The expertise of how to organize an espionage network in a hostile country had existed in Israel for years. Security (Shin Bet) had mastered the techniques as a defensive measure in order to combat Russian and Arab penetration attempts in Israel. Those techniques were available to Mossad through Isser Harel, who was now head of both organizations, but Military Intelligence, determined to keep its distance, had never sought to plug itself into this invaluable and vital body of knowledge.

There was a further serious blunder in the selection of these young people, a serious breach of regulations for which the authors of the plan would not be forgiven. During the Iraqi crisis in 1951, when Jewish emigration was being threatened by the activities of Israeli agents in Baghdad, Shaul Avigur sought from David Ben-Gurion an important statement of principle: Never in future should any Israeli intelligence organization make use of local Jews or local Jewish organizations. Avigur's point was succinctly made: the creation of the State of Israel must not bring suffering but hope to local Jewish communities around the world. If, he said, the Egyptian authorities find a spy ring run by Israelis in Egypt, then the Israelis will suffer. If they find that local Jews are involved, then the whole Jewish population will suffer. That has been the golden rule for the Israeli intelligence services ever since.* Darling's team of saboteurs were not only *local* Jews, but they belonged to definable organizations, all of which would suffer greatly if the team was caught. While it existed, the team posed a threat not only to the Jewish population of Egypt, but, if the saboteurs were found with weapons and explosives, to the entire Jewish population of the Arab world.

That aside, the training program under the unrelenting discipline of Ben-Tsur didn't go ahead uneventfully either. The weapons-training instructor found himself not only teaching small-arms drill but reinforcing the team's basic Zionism, which was being bullied out of them by Ben-Tsur's attitude.

Eventually trained—and well-trained too—in the use of weapons, explosives, radio communications and the like, each member of the group made his own way back on his Grunberg Travel ticket to Egypt, there to await orders. The scene was now set for an authentic tragedy. The Cairo these young people returned to was a different city than the one they had left. The venal King Farouk had been deposed. A revolutionary junta had seized control of the country. A man called Gamal Abdul Nasser was emerging from the shadows as the real leader of the free-officers movement.

* I suggested to a senior Israeli intelligence man that, while I accepted that this rule may exist in theory, in practice it was difficult to see the Israelis not making use of the Jewish contacts they possess around the world. "If the rule didn't exist in theory, then it would have to exist pragmatically," he said. "If you are looking for Israeli agents, where better to look than the synagogue, the local Jewish organizations, houses of the ghetto, or among Jewish business leaders. Obviously that's where any rival security agency is going to look, and equally obviously because of that we have to stay, even if we didn't want to, well away."

The Egyptian *coup d'état* was warmly welcomed by the Israelis at first. There was a feeling in the air that with a completely new political situation in Cairo, the opportunity existed for a fresh start between the two belligerent countries. Gamal Nasser, himself a self-proclaimed socialist, seemed to many Israelis, themselves socialists, to represent the urban, educated modern man with whom they could do business.

But despite the private feelers that went out immediately to the new Egyptian government, it soon became clear to the Israelis that Nasser's concept of Arab nationalism, so closely equivalent to their own concept of Jewish nationalism, probably made an arrangement between the two sides rather more difficult than less.

The main planks of Nasser's foreign policy also made the Israeli government uneasy. The Suez Canal was Nasser's first target. The canal itself, though it ran through Egypt, was owned by the British and French governments, and Britain was entitled by international treaty to maintain troops in what was known as the Canal Zone in order to protect it. Both arrangements had caused offense within Egypt, and Nasser was determined to bring them to an end as affronts to Egyptian pride and sovereignty.

By and large, the international community sympathized. Farouk had been so universally despised and his government so cynical and corrupt that the young architects of the revolution began with a huge fund of good will from the whole of the Western world. As far as Israel was concerned though, the leopard may have changed its spots, but that didn't make the animal any less dangerous. But Israel could only watch while its allies paid court to the Egyptian government and wonder whether the world was truly beginning to slip away. All the signs seemed to be pointing in that direction.

British and Egyptian negotiators were sitting down in Cairo working out plans for the orderly evacuation of the Canal Zone by the British Army; if this agreement was reached, it would create substantial change in the strategic balance of the area. At one stroke, a Western army would be removed from the scene, an army which up till then could have been expected to interpose itself between the warring parties in any new conflagration. Israel stood suddenly very naked.

Equally worrying, the attitude of the United States of

America under President Dwight Eisenhower towards
Israel was changing visibly and disturbingly. The Americans were negotiating an agreement to supply arms to
Iraq—the only Arab belligerent of the 1948 war which
had not yet signed an armistice agreement.

On the political front, U.S. Assistant Secretary of State
Henry A. Byroads told Israel in a carefully prepared
speech that peace in the area depended upon her "de-
Zionizing" her policies: "To the Israelis, I say that you
should come to truly look upon yourselves as a Middle
Eastern state and see your own future in that context
rather than as a headquarters or nucleus, so to speak, of
world-wide groupings of peoples of a particular religious
faith who must have special rights within the obligations
to the Israeli State."

All of this, of course, created a deep sense of gloom inside Israel. Though Colonel Nasser had done nothing
overtly to harm Israel, he and the Egyptian press made it
plain enough who the real enemy was. Israeli diplomats
in London and Washington made little headway warning
the Western powers of the nature of the new regime with
which they were dealing. This was not, the Israelis tried
to hammer home day after day, a popular revolution;
moderates in Egypt were put into prison, and the country
was becoming a police state; Nasser had ambitions far beyond the geographical boundaries of his country.

As the world refused to listen, Sharett's basic political
philosophy, that everything could eventually be gained by
negotiation rather than by war, was beginning to look
rather threadbare.

Nowhere was he more criticized than at the Ministry of
Defense. Pinhas Lavon's profound contempt for his Prime
Minister was the unreported scandal of this administra-
tion. Lavon either ignored Sharett or humiliated him in
Cabinet, knowing full well that Sharett lacked the muscle
to fire a man appointed by Ben-Gurion.

Lavon, however, was considerably more isolated than
Sharett knew. Lavon had quarreled with both Moshe
Dayan and Shimon Peres. They, however, had little time
for Sharett either, and instead of reporting their problems
to him, they told David Ben-Gurion. Lavon had quarreled with Isser Harel, too. He bypassed Harel even more
easily than he bypassed Dayan and Peres. It was a
wretched, unhappy, and dangerous situation.

That, then, was the international and internal political background to Operation Suzanna. To this day nobody quite knows whose idea it was, nor does it much matter. Intelligence agencies the world over are a bit like film companies. They "buy" hundreds of scripts—some too fantastic to believe—very few of which actually go into production. Nor does anyone know for certain who it was who pressed the button. In the muckraking dispute which followed, Lavon was to blame Gibli, and Gibli was to blame Lavon. All that is known is the precise incident which persuaded one or the other to set the ball rolling.

It was, in fact, a Mossad intelligence report out of London which tipped the balance. Mossad had gotten hard information out of the Cabinet office to the effect that an agreement ending a British military presence in the Canal Zone had been drafted between Britain and Egypt. Any day Britain would be announcing the evacuation from Egypt and the Canal Zone of all its forces.

The philosophy behind Operation Suzanna was simple —childishly so. Israel's political, military and strategic position in the Middle East was being irretrievably weakened by the failure of Western policymakers to discern the truth of the nature of the Egyptian revolution. They had been manipulated by clever Egyptian public relations; the true face of Nasser was being concealed by a skillfully contrived mask.

Israel's task was to rip that mask away; it had failed to do so by diplomacy, now direct action was called for. The public and the governments of Britain and America must be shown the latent hostility to the West and Western influences which existed within the Egyptian revolution. Operation Suzanna was to achieve that end. According to the plan, British and American property in Egypt— embassies, information and cultural centers and commercial buildings—was to be attacked and burned. Communists and the ultra-right-wing force, the Moslem Brotherhood, would be blamed. The Egyptian security forces would be forced to crack down on them, and they would respond in kind. The country would be racked with civil unrest, and at last the Egyptian junta would be seen in the West for what it was. So, at the eleventh hour, the West would change its policies and British forces would be obliged to stay.

Naive and almost insane, the plan rolled inexorably

forward. Israeli agents in Cairo and Alexandria—the Darling ring—would be activated; their task: to burn down American and British installations and then stand back while the Egyptians took the blame.

Months earlier the network had lost its chief, Avraham Dar, who had been recalled to Israel. In his place, Tel Aviv sent a twenty-seven-year-old under the alias of Paul Frank. With his blond hair, blue eyes and good looks, he looked every inch the German his passport showed him to be. His cover was that he was the representative of a large German electrical equipment company. The kind of man always conscious of his image, he had included in his cover the fact that he had been an SS officer during World War II, and he carried the papers and the pictures to prove it. With the natural flair of an actor, he settled easily into Cairo society.

Coincidentally, another Israeli, Max Bennett, also a German Jew, whose macabre cover was that he was a representative for a firm specializing in artificial limbs for wounded soldiers, arrived in Cairo. He was there on other Military Intelligence business unconnected with the Darling ring. Max Bennett hadn't been in Cairo long before Tel Aviv lost contact with him entirely. The back-up network through which he could channel his messages had broken down. He was in Cairo with no way of communicating with his spymasters in Tel Aviv.

Every agent of every major espionage agency in the world knows what to do in these circumstances. He simply moves to a neighboring territory and picks up the threads of a network established for him there—a network which might be no more than a dead-letter box, making it unnecessary for him to make direct contact with anyone. Probably that is what Bennett would have done, but Tel Aviv was impatient. Marcelle Ninio, the young female member of the Darling ring acting as communications officer, was contacted and asked to get in touch with Bennett so that he could use her radio equipment to keep in contact with base.

Bennett—whether he knew the mortal danger to which he had been exposed or not we will never know—was now inextricably involved in the Darling ring. Two unconnected networks had been brought together because of the bungling ineptitude of their employers. They could never be unbound.

In June 1954, Paul Frank received a message from Tel Aviv which put him on the first flight to Paris to meet Ben-Tsur, the controller of the Darling ring, in order to receive his instructions. That meeting was to be one of the most fateful in the whole history of Israeli intelligence.

Chapter 7

THE TWO MEN sitting at the Chez Maitena Café on the Boulevard St. Germain one June day in 1954 could not have been more different in looks, temperament or experience. Motke Ben-Tsur was a career officer who most colleagues predicted would go far in Israel's military hierarchy. By contrast, Paul Frank, according to one perceptive friend, had about him that air of almost manic desperation worn by men who know they are losers but hope to hide that fact from the world.

The son of a distinguished Viennese socialist politician who before the war was imprisoned by the Austrian government, released after the Anschluss and immediately rearrested by the Nazis because he was a Jew and sent to Dachau and Buchenwald, Paul Frank's real name was Avraham Seidenwerg. He had served in the British Army, trained as a paratrooper, and distinguished himself with the Palmach during the siege of Jerusalem. Initially, he had commanded troops protecting the road linking Jerusalem with the outside world, and then became company commander of the Harel Brigade in the city itself, ending up at the age of twenty-two with the rank of major.

Stupidly, weakly, he spoiled it all for himself by appropriating what he later called an "abandoned" refrigerator and installing it in his home. The refrigerator was military property, the theft was discovered, and after an incredibly long two years of investigation, Avri was court-martialed, sentenced to eighteen months' imprisonment, and stripped of his rank. On appeal, the charge of theft was withdrawn but he was found guilty of conduct unbefitting an officer, and though his prison sentence was withdrawn, he was reduced to the rank of private in the reserve and left the Army.

He was spotted by Avraham Dar and recruited by Motke Ben-Tsur when he was at the lowest point of his fortunes. His wife was divorcing him, and he was out of work. He was perfect material for a dangerous mission into hostile territory. He had military training and experience. He had nothing to lose and everything to gain. He needed work, but in Israel work of anything but the most menial kind was difficult to find for a man who had been court-martialed. He believed he belonged in the Army and was grateful to be given a second chance. Like all agents, he was assigned a *nom de guerre* by which he would be known in the department—El-Ad Saatchi, or "Ever Luminous"—and then a field cover name with which he would enter Egypt: Paul Frank. His real name, Avraham Seidenwerg, would continue to exist only for his family and friends.* For Avri's field cover, Military Intelligence borrowed the name of a man of about his own age called Paul Frank who was living on a kibbutz in the heart of Israel. He had been born in Willmars, Germany, and emigrated to Palestine in 1937. Avri went to interview him to dig out all he could about his background before going to Germany and using the real Paul Frank's birth certificate to get a genuine German passport, then

* The whole question of cover names is seldom understood by writers of spy fiction. Most agents have three. The first is the *nom de guerre*. This is the name which is used in the intelligence agency. In any organization, a large number of people are involved in handling a staff member. Salaries and expenses have to be paid, secretaries transcribe reports, so that in time a dangerous amount of paper about a man who may be in an exposed position is circulating throughout the bureaucracy. It is vital, therefore, that an agent have a cover from his own people. In the field, he will have a code name, perhaps the name of a flower or a fruit, again to guard against too many people knowing the cover name he is using as he goes about the everyday work on his mission. The third name, the official cover, under which he openly operates, is the most difficult of all to establish. In the case of Avri Seidenwerg, it had to be assumed that at one time or another Egyptian security would check him out. Everything about the name had to hang together.

embellishing that past by reconstructing the background of a Paul Frank who had served in the German Army.

It took Avri nine months, from March 1953 to December 1953, to establish a history for himself and develop business contacts that would permit him to go to Cairo as a genuine businessman seeking outlets for German electrical equipment in Egypt. Finally he was activated, with orders to proceed to Cairo.

Paul Frank fitted easily into the then rapidly growing German colony of Egypt. Though he was specifically instructed not to go in for conventional espionage, he did manage to acquire details of rockets the Egyptians were developing with German help (which went in to the El-Ad Saatchi "volumes"* at Military Intelligence headquarters) and the plans for a vast underground oil pipeline. Then, at the end of May 1954, he received a message written in invisible ink ordering him to Paris.

It was as the result of that message that he was now sitting under the canopy of a Parisian sidewalk café on a warm day in June, listening to the head of Unit 131 outline Operation Suzanna. He, Paul Frank, would be case officer for the operation. Avraham Dar, who had set up the sleeper network which Frank was now ordered to activate, had disqualified himself by being a "bit of a braggart"; another agent, who had been establishing his cover as an Arab returning home from South America, had at the last moment lost his nerve. Max Bennett, already in Cairo, was unsuitable for this kind of operation. It would be Paul Frank's job to awaken Avraham Dar's "sleepers" and use them to launch acts of sabotage and terrorism in Alexandria and Cairo against Egyptian, American and British targets—to light the flame which it was hoped would soon engulf all of Egypt.

The Alexandrian cell was to be activated first, leaving the Cairo cell for later. The operation would begin in a small way, fire bombs in public places and American and British installations. After that, key members of the governments and military advisers from outside were to be assassinated. Frank would receive his instructions from coded messages on the Voice of Israel, in radio programs

---

* Agents' original reports are kept in files under their *noms de guerre*, and in British, American and Israel intelligence their individual files are known as the "volumes."

beamed to the outside world, or by secret radio messages (he was assured the sleeper team possessed up-to-date receivers and transmitters) or by invisible ink. But the public radio broadcasts would be the most important means of communication. Targets would be designated by a code system. Frank would be in complete charge.

Paul Frank returned to Egypt on June 29th and quickly went to Alexandria to make his first contact with a member of the group, Philip "Henri" Nathanson. He knocked at the door and a middle-aged woman answered. Speaking English, hoping to conceal from the group his Israeli identity, he asked for Philip. "Ah," said the woman, "you must be Robert," a remark which was not likely to put him at ease. The whole family apparently was eagerly awaiting the appearance of "Robert the spy," the cover name the team had been given for its new director. Philip Nathanson, then only nineteen, was equally casual and promised that next day he would arrange a meeting with Victor Levy in front of a bookstore. Patiently, Frank exhorted him to use code names only. Whatever merits his team possessed, Paul Frank realized, a sense of the need for security was not one of them.

Victor "Pierre" Levy quickly destroyed any illusions Paul Frank might have had that the team possessed a full operational network only awaiting orders to spring into action. He and Nathanson, he said, were eager to act. But another friend and member of the team, Robert Dassa, needed convincing. Samuel "Jacques" Azar, a fourth, was uncertain, too, while the man trained as wireless operator for the group, Elie "Alex" Cohen, who many years later would write his own magnificent chapter in the history of the Israeli Secret Service, was not available. The biggest problem, however, was that Meir "M.," who had been given 500 Egyptian pounds (approximately $1,500 at the rate of exchange at that time) by headquarters in order to set up a bomb factory, had not only not done so but was refusing to return the money. Their inventory of explosives and the like was pathetic. Nevertheless, with this tiny group as his nucleus, Frank decided to go ahead, and he asked Levy to stand in as a radio operator and send the first message to base. It read: "Contact established. Phase two to be executed without delay."

But a delay was inevitable; the group simply wasn't

ready for action. Levy was having difficulties with both the radio and his team. Dassa and Azar were still not sure whether or not they would help. So Frank again traveled from Cairo to Alexandria to Apartment 107, Rue Hôpital 18, which when it wasn't being used as the studio for Azar's painting classes, was a shambles of radio equipment —earphones, crystals, transmitter, a Morse key, and the like.

Gently, Paul Frank tried to show them the basics of security despite the sinking feeling in the pit of his stomach that if they hadn't learned them already, it was probably too late to teach them now. His very presence in the room was a breach of all the regulations. As case officer, he should have been known only to the leader of the group, Victor Levy, and then only as Robert. But he had already met Philip Nathanson, and here he was with two others, Azar and Dassa. He quickly won them over and began checking the radio gear. This was another blow. Military Intelligence's spare SAMIR trasmitter and the Zenith portable radio needed to power it were with the Cairo cell. They had to be collected, but that would mean yet another unauthorized approach by Paul Frank; someone else would know of his presence in Egypt.

Nevertheless, despite all these difficulties, on July 2nd, at 11:00 A.M., Paul Frank's eager but pathetically amateurish team was ready to act. The target was the central post office in Alexandria. Levy and Nathanson simply walked in with their small packages of explosives, slid them into the mail-chute slot, and walked out again. Within minutes the explosion went off with a dull thud, and fire racked a corner of the building.

But if the raid had been successful, the planned political fall-out was quite decidedly not. The strictly censored Egyptian press didn't mention the bombing at all, and the information was kept away from foreign correspondents.

The start of a campaign which Israel hoped would produce headlines like TERROR CAMPAIGN HITS EGYPT began without even a whimper. The sabotage team itself was not particularly happy either, and there were problems of morale. But even more serious were their difficulties with Meir "M." When Levy demanded back the 500 Egyptian pounds which the team badly needed to purchase materials to make more explosives, Meir made it plain that if he was pressed again they would have "reason to fear" him. It was a chilling reminder of the danger all of them were in. Frank knew he had to sort him out one way or the other, but fortunately perhaps for Meir M., events moved too quickly for Frank ever to confront him.

On July 10th, new orders came from Tel Aviv. ". . . and here," said the announcer on Radio Israel, "is the answer for Mrs. Saatchi. To improve the coffee party, add English cake or something similar." To Paul Frank, alias El-Ad Saatchi, listening on his car radio, the meaning was clear: Attack a British installation "or something similar." So an American building would do.

Frank timed the next explosion for July 14th and nominated U.S. Information Services libraries in both Alexandria and Cairo as the targets; he also wanted to hit a streetcar terminal in Alexandria, but the team told him they only had enough acid to make two incendiaries. What he had been led to believe before he left for Cairo was simply wrong: not only was the "sleeper" team physically unequipped to handle the operation—regarded as vital to the very existence of Israel—but it was riven with ideological problems and lacking the most basic psychological tools for the job it was supposed to do.

Equally, Motke Ben-Tsur had been hopelessly ill informed about the possibility of purchasing any extra explosives on the spot. He had believed these could be obtained either from pharmacies or directly from manufacturers of chemicals. In fact, as Frank was to discover, the Egyptian authorities had instituted a system whereby each purchaser had to sign a special ledger which was checked as a matter of routine by the security police.

However, Samuel Azar had finally won the battle with his conscience and agreed to commit himself totally to the team. Frank now had four saboteurs—making a simultaneous attack on the two libraries possible.

The attack on the 14th went off without a hitch. Frank had bought some eyeglass cases, carried by everyone in a country where sun-glasses were the norm, and he stuffed these with the incendiary devices. The small eyeglass-case bombs were placed near the film libraries and caused immense damage. This time the Egyptian authorities were unable to keep the story under wraps, and on July 15th the Middle East News Agency carried the first accounts of a new wave of terrorist attacks in both Cairo and Alexandria. The story was picked up and reprinted immediately in Israeli newspapers but was virtually ignored elsewhere. The fuse was taking a long time to burn!

The sabotage team was now without any acid with which to ignite their explosives. To make matters even worse, communications with headquarters had broken down altogether. Neither the team's own transmitter nor its receiver was functioning properly, so they had no idea whether their messages to base at scheduled transmission times were getting through. Radio Israel also gave no new instructions, but neither did it call off the action.

At this point Samuel Azar took a small bottle of sulphuric acid from the laboratory of the technical school where he worked part-time, enough for another five fire bombs. Frank timed new attacks for July 22nd—the anniversary of the Egyptian revolution and a major public holiday throughout the country. Cairo and Alexandria would be *en fête,* and any acts of terrorism then would cause major dislocations. They would also be bound to enrage the junta, who would regard them as an insult to the revolution and could be expected to respond with ferocious attempts at revenge on their political opponents of both the right and left.

There were three targets: the Rivoli Movie Theatre in Cairo, which would be hit by Dassa and Azar; the checkroom of Cairo's main railway station; and the Rio Movie Theatre in Alexandria, where Nathanson and Levy would plant their eyeglass-case bombs.

In Cairo none of the bombs ignited properly. They merely fizzled and were extinguished before any real damage was caused. But, tragically, in Alexandria, the bomb went off ahead of time, while it was still in the pocket of nineteen-year-old Philip Nathanson as he stood patiently waiting in the queue of the Rio Movie Theatre. Suddenly, to the horror of the crowd, his pocket all but exploded as the bomb material ignited.

Captain Hassan el Manadi of the Alexandria Special Branch, who was on duty outside the cinema, tore off the garment, stamped out the flames, and calmed Nathanson, who was lying stunned on the pavement. But when the captain picked out of the smoldering pocket the remains of an eyeglass case still studded with explosive material, he knew immediately that he had discovered one of the bombers for whom the entire Egyptian security apparatus had been looking. Operation Suzanna had come to its inglorious conclusion.

It didn't take the Egyptian police long to pick up the rest of the team along with others on its periphery. One contact led in a straight line to another. All over Cairo and Alexandria Jews were rounded up for questioning. Very little of what was euphemistically described as "hard screening" was necessary to establish the connection from Nathanson to Levy, to Azar, to Dassa, and then deep into the Cairo network, to Dr. Marzouk, Marcelle Ninio, and on to Max Bennett, the Israeli agent who had accidentally become entangled early on. Somehow Paul Frank, who quickly realized what had happened, managed to remain free. He cabled to an emergency address in Europe:

PIERRE AND COMPANY WENT BANKRUPT. I REMAIN HERE TO SAVE WHATEVER CAN BE SALVAGED OF OUR INVESTMENT. PLEASE ADVISE. RELI [a nickname for his son].

It was Tel Aviv's first hint of the disaster. It was only on July 26th, four days after the arrest of Nathanson, that Egyptian security had the case wrapped up and were able to announce that they held ten men and one woman on charges of sabotage, arson and espionage.

The Egyptian press dressed the story in purple. "A bloody Zionist gang has been arrested and charged with the recent wave of arson attacks on public places in Egyptian cities," one paper whooped. It seemed so incredible a charge that initially even sophisticated Egyptians didn't believe it. Outside Egypt, no one did. To Israeli Premier Moshe Sharett, these were "despicable slanders designed to harass the Jews in Egypt."

It was only after that statement was issued to the international press that Sharett heard the truth from Lavon, that a security operation had gone sadly wrong.

Only Paul Frank emerged from the cauldron safe and sound. He flew out on August 6th, a full two weeks after Nathanson's arrest, having first sold his car and arranged his business affairs. His cool demeanor was remarkable; apparently, he had kept his nerve until the very end. He was back in Israel when everyone had long given him up.

Paul Frank's debriefing report, "The Pierre Affair," should have been enough on its own to cause a tremendous shake-up within the entire Military Intelligence establishment, revealing as it did the professional incompetence of the whole operation. But the Cabinet was concerned with the philosophy behind Operation Suzanna, not with the bungling of its execution. It wanted to know who had authorized what Sharett privately described as this "criminally insane melodrama." There were only four men who could have launched the operation. The first was the Minister of Defense, Pinhas Lavon. He told the Prime Minister that the operation had been discussed in his presence, but that he never gave the final authorization for it to proceed. The second was General Gibli, the chief of Military Intelligence. He said that a verbal order was twice delivered to him from Pinhas Lavon to go ahead with the attacks. The third was Moshe Dayan as Chief of Staff, but he had been in Washington during the attacks on the American libraries and so could be ruled out. The fourth was Paul Frank, who could have initiated the action on his own with no orders from anyone.

But Paul Frank was able to show that he received his orders from Motke Ben-Tsur, who received them from Gibli, who claimed he received them from Lavon. So either Lavon or Gibli was lying. It was an appalling situation, kept under deep wraps within Israel not only because the implications were almost too horrendous to contemplate—namely, that either the Minister of Defense or the head of Military Intelligence was a liar—but also because nothing must be said, nothing must be permitted to leak out which could in any way be seized upon by the Egyptian prosecutor as evidence that Israel accepted the guilt for the extraordinary charge he was about to make.

In Cairo matters had indeed taken a fearful turn. A full show trial was laid on for the accused. The Egyptians had been handed a real-life Zionist spy ring of the kind which their more lurid newspapers loved to speculate about, and they were determined to exploit it to the full.

One by one, in January 1955, the defendants climbed into the dock to give their evidence. But Max Bennett, a major in Israeli intelligence, twenty-seven years old, the only real professional of them all, the only one who by talking could do lasting damage to the State of Israel, decided where his duty lay. Methodically, he removed a rusty nail from his prison cell door and with cool deliberation hacked open his veins and died a few hours later.

All but one of the defendants pleaded guilty. Dr. Moshe Marzouk, not in the sabotage ring, declared: "I am guilty but not the way the first charge puts it," which was entered as a not-guilty plea. He stated in his testimony: "John Darling [Avraham Dar] deceived us. I refused to cooperate with him as soon as I found out he had other motives in mind."

Victor Levy declared: "I have confessed everything I have done, but I want the court to know I took the whole affair as fun. I am an Egyptian before being a Jew, and at no time did I think I was causing harm to Egypt, my country. I will never live or die an enemy of Egypt."

Samuel Azar, the quiet intellectual, declared: "I never meant to betray Egypt. I dumped an incendiary device in the sea rather than hurt innocent people and my country."

Marcelle Ninio doesn't talk now about how she was treated in prison by the Egyptians. But she was young and attractive, and one can imagine what happened. Twice she threw herself out of the window of police headquarters in an attempt to kill herself, and twice she failed. At the trial she courageously faced the court, and when asked to repeat the confession she had made to interrogators, she declared simply: "I don't remember what I said. They mistreated me."

On January 29th, the verdicts were handed down. In the face of what had actually happened, they were, to say the least, somewhat illogical.

Moshe Marzouk, the young doctor head of the Cairo cell, not involved in Operation Suzanna, who had been nervous and fretful about his role, sentenced to death. Samuel Azar, who had agreed to come in only at the last minute, constantly concerned about his dual allegiance to both Egypt and Israel, sentenced to death. Victor Levy, the head of the sabotage squad, strong and willing, sentenced to life at hard labor. Philip Nathanson, who had needed no persuading either, sentenced to life imprisonment. Robert Dassa, also a willing accomplice, got only fifteen years. And Victorine Ninio, not involved in the actual bombings, also got fifteen years. Mayer Zarran and Meir Meyouchas, both on the edges of the Cairo ring, got seven and five years respectively; two others were acquitted. Another Egyptian Jew called Carmona, about whom little is known, like the gallant Bennett committed suicide before the trial opened.

Ironically, if the acts of sabotage which led to this vast show trial did nothing to sway public opinion in the West about the nature of the Egyptian regime, the death sentences for Marzouk and Azar did. Not only did no one really believe the charges, but the sentences themselves were regarded as barbarous. Pressure for clemency was put on Nasser by virtually every political figure of note in the West. Perhaps because a few weeks earlier Nasser had hanged ringleaders of the Moslem Brotherhood, there was no political formula by which he could now commute sentences on two Jews.

In the cold early dawn of January 31, 1955, Dr. Marzouk and Samuel Azar were led into the courtyard of Cairo's Central Prison and then up on the platform of the scaffold. In minutes it was over. The first agents in the history of Israeli intelligence to be executed by the enemy had their lives thrown away needlessly on an ill-considered operation.

Two days after the Cairo executions, on February 2, 1955, Pinhas Lavon resigned in an extraordinary letter to the Prime Minister:

> During the two hearings that went on for weeks, I was kept at arm's length. Neither you nor any other member [of the Cabinet] tried to speak to me (except Eshkol, with whom I did not wish to speak for reasons which some worthy people may perhaps not understand), as if I were afflicted with a loathsome disease. I was anathema. I could not know what you thought, claimed or accused. I was an object of pity or for settling accounts. Your conduct and that of the members excluded me from the group and from collective responsibility. But you are not the only ones who are free: I am also free, and this is to inform you that I am no longer prepared to be the friend of people who have liquidated their friendship with me. I hereby tender my resignation as Minister of Defense and from the government.

This extraordinary letter, speaking volumes about the state of mind of Pinhas Lavon during this crucial period, was not, of course, published at the time. Indeed, the very news of his resignation was kept secret until the one man in Israel who could maintain morale in the Army during a period of such crisis would agree to come back and serve once more as Minister of Defense. His name, of course, was David Ben-Gurion.

Mrs. Golda Meir was deputed to see him and ask him to return to the government and take over the Defense portfolio. With a superb sense of theater, Ben-Gurion turned up at the Knesset on February 21st, still wearing the khaki shorts he wore on his kibbutz, to hear Prime Minister Sharett announce that Lavon had resigned when "his proposals for organizational changes in the direction of defense affairs had not proved acceptable to the Prime Minister," and that David Ben-Gurion had agreed to serve in his place.

Those members of the Cabinet who knew the truth were amused by Sharett's explanations as to why Lavon had resigned. There was nothing in what Sharett said which was not literally the truth. For Lavon had indeed proposed two organizational changes which had not been accepted by the government: the instant dismissal of General Dayan and Shimon Peres.

Certainly if Lavon was to be believed—that he himself had not given the operational orders for Suzanna—then Dayan and Peres were part of a dangerous conspiracy. But members of the government, insofar as they themselves knew the story, preferred to believe Dayan and Peres rather than Lavon.

Even before the Cairo sentences were delivered, Prime Minister Sharett had set up a secret "Committee of Investigation" on January 2nd which, he hoped, would settle the matter once and for all. For there were two completely distinct versions as to what had occurred.

The first version was given by those on trial in Cairo. They had confessed to acts of sabotage on July 2nd, 14th and 22nd. However, Colonel Gibli was now telling another story: that he got the order from Lavon to activate the plan only on July 16th, so that Military Intelligence was responsible only for the abortive attacks on two cinemas on July 22nd; the previous acts of sabotage had been carried out by others, perhaps the Communists or the Moslem Brotherhood. As for the "confessions" of those on trial, they had been wrung out of the accused by torture.*

* The team that took part in Operation Suzanna is now back in Israel. Though they have no way of knowing who gave the

Lieutenant General Yaacov Dori, a former Chief of Staff, and Judge Yitzhak Olshan, the president of the Supreme Court, began interrogating witnesses in a small flat in Tel Aviv in order to preserve secrecy. The issue which faced them had by now reached alarming proportions. If Gibli and the Army officers within his own department and the Ministry of Defense were to be believed, then the Minister of Defense had certainly launched an inept operation inside Egypt, but one of no great consequence, and was now seeking to pin responsibility on his staff.

If, however, Lavon, and therefore almost certainly the accused in Cairo were to be believed, then it appeared as if a group of Army officers had taken it upon themselves to launch terrorist attacks for political motives against Western property in Cairo and Alexandria without first seeking any political authorization to do so and were now prepared to perjure themselves in order to destroy an unpopular Minister of Defense.

Gibli was able to show the committee that twice, once on July 15th after a general staff meeting and once on July 16th when he visited Lavon at his apartment, he had had private conversations with Lavon. He had received the order, he said, on the 15th, and had gone to Lavon to discuss it further on the 16th. Dayan, who had left for America on July 7th, a week before the attacks on the libraries, though five days after the attack on the general post office in Alexandria, told the committee that he knew nothing of the operation itself, though presumably he would have done so if the order had been given prior to the attack on the Alexandrian post office. Lavon, he said, had made a habit of approving of military operations before they occurred and then disavowing them if they went wrong. Lavon, he went on, had always insisted on maintaining direct contacts with the Army at several levels—bypassing Dayan's office; he was suspicious and mistrustful of the general staff and took to interviewing junior officers in his office, behind Dayan's back, about operations,

---

original order, they are able to confirm that they were responsible for the attacks on July 2nd and 14th as well as the one on the 22nd. In this respect at least, Gibli's evidence to the committee does not appear to square with the facts, as they are known now. Equally, of course, Dayan was still in the country on the 2nd, when the first attack is now known to have taken place.

apparently in the hope of proving that Dayan was submitting false reports.

The most damning testimony against Lavon, however, came from the man from Cairo who, back in Israel, had temporarily dropped his cover name of Paul Frank and become Avri Seidenwerg once again. His evidence bore out Gibli's in every particular. He had used the sabotage team, he said, on only one occasion, and that was on July 22nd. His team had not initiated the attack on July 2nd or the attacks on the American libraries on July 14th. Motke Ben-Tsur, as head of Unit 131, confirmed Avri Seidenwerg's testimony.

In the light of such overwhelming professional testimony provided by the Chief of Staff, the chief of Military Intelligence, the chief of Operations and the case officer, it is surprising that the Olshan-Dori committee came up with the verdict that it did. Said the two-man committee in summing up:

> In the final analysis, we regret that we have been unable to answer the questions put to us by the Prime Minister. We can only say that we were not convinced beyond any reasonable doubt that the senior officer did not receive orders from the Minister of Defense. We are equally uncertain that the Minister of Defense did, in fact, give the orders attributed to him.

If this had been a stock-exchange inquiry into possible corrupt practices by a listed company, then the fact that honors were even might have been a satisfactory solution. But this inquiry concerned the veracity of the secret intelligence arm of the State itself and whether its officers, aided and abetted by officers and staff within the Ministry of Defense, had taken part in a conspiracy both to launch an offensive strike in another country and then to cover up the truth once that strike had failed.

Boiled down to its essentials, Judge Olshan's and General Dori's verdict left open the possibility that such a conspiracy did, in fact, exist. It was the most appalling blow the Army had ever received, and even raised a question mark over the nature of democracy in Israel.

In the light of the Olshan-Dori findings, changes had to be made. Gibli left his post, but certainly not in disgrace. He went back to the regular Army, where he performed with great distinction during the Suez war a few months later. Pinhas Lavon went back as general secretary of the Israeli Trade Union Movement, a job which still kept him very much in the public eye and preserved his political base. Motke Ben-Tsur lost out altogether. He was offered another posting in the Army but at the same rank. He knew he could never again exert the influence he had had at Military Intelligence, so he resigned and went into the reserves. Avri Seidenwerg—Paul Frank—was sent back to Germany, where Military Intelligence felt he could still be of use.

Operation Suzanna had apparently run its course—and claimed its victims. But not everyone in Israel was satisfied. There were still too many unanswered questions; too many obvious lies had been told.

It was Isser Harel, deep in the shadows, who would continue probing for the truth of this bizarre affair, impelled by the steadfast conviction that unless the truth was established, Israeli intelligence would be haunted by it for years to come.

PART III

The Big Leagues

Chapter 8

WHEN BENJAMIN GIBLI RESIGNED in the aftermath of the Lavon affair a natural successor was at hand. Yehoshaphat Harkabi had been brought in as deputy chief of Military Intelligence when Gibli had first been appointed, but he fell out with his chief and during the whole period of the planning and execution of Operation Suzanna was in Paris on study leave. Thus, fortunately for the service as well as the State, Israel had an experienced officer available untouched by any breath of scandal from the Lavon affair.

"Fatti"—his diminutive—Harkabi is the kind of man whom, save for rare circumstances, armies are only able to recruit in time of war. Only thirty-five years old when he took over from Gibli as head of Military Intelligence, he was to have a profound and lasting influence upon a profession which he entered almost by accident. An intellectual first and foremost, he was one of the most brilliant academic Arabists in Israel, a man who on the face of it would look more at home in a university senior common room than in an officer's mess. Harkabi and his parents before him were born in Israel.

Scarcely out of his teens, after having taken his degree in philosophy at Jerusalem University, with Arab affairs as his second subject, he was picked as a high flier by the Jewish Agency. After intense competition he attended, together with twenty-four others, a special course designed to prepare the most brilliant of the young Israelis for top diplomatic posts in the new State which they were sure would soon come into being.

A cheerful man, inclined to corpulence, he quickly established that not only did he have a brain, but he had great physical and moral courage. Caught in the siege of Jerusalem, he showed himself to be a brave and popular officer. Like many other company commanders, he was deeply critical of the way the austere commander of the Jewish forces in the city, David Shaltiel, was conducting the fighting.

Other Haganah officers grumbled. Harkabi marched into Shaltiel's office, stood stiffly to attention in front of his desk, and told Shaltiel that Harkabi and his battalion no longer had any confidence in his command. Emboldened by Harkabi, other company commanders followed suit. But it did little good. Shaltiel coldly dismissed these representations and, to the disgust of many, removed Harkabi from his post and ordered him out of Jerusalem. Believing his military career had been brought to an abrupt end, Harkabi made the long dangerous journey to Tel Aviv through enemy lines on foot and presented himself to the Ministry of Foreign Affairs, which then had a staff of five.

He was welcomed with open arms by Walter Eytan, the first director general, and made head of a department of which he was the only member and asked to compile a list of all the heads of state of the varying countries around the world, as well as the names of the Foreign Ministers, all of whom Israel proposed to approach to plead for recognition.

Harkabi did it the easy way—absorbing his first real lesson in intelligence: if information can be collected from overt channels, it is wasteful to get it by covert means. He left Eytan's office, walked around the corner to a bookstore, and purchased the up-to-date copy of the Statesman's Yearbook. It was Harkabi's first contribution to Israeli intelligence.

Harkabi remained in the Foreign Ministry with an obviously brilliant career ahead of him as a diplomat until 1950, when the Army, forgiving him for what had occurred in Jerusalem, decided that it needed him more. He was sent to a school for battalion commanders and was called for at the end of the course by General Yadin, the then Chief of Staff, who asked him to accept the appointment of deputy head of Military Intelligence. Yadin bluntly told him that they intended to appoint Gibli as chief of Military Intelligence, but because there were doubts concerning his judgment it was vital to back him up with someone else, a man whose academic career was as distinguished as his military service. Harkabi was the only possible candidate, Yadin said. If he turned down the job, then Gibli would not be the next director. Harkabi went to meet Gibli and asked him to explain the workings of Military Intelligence. Gibli took out a piece of paper, drew an organizational chart, and pushed it across for Harkabi to see. Amused, yet warming to Gibli immediately, Harkabi accepted.

It was a decision he was seldom to regret. He found that Military Intelligence was one of the few areas where he could combine his love of research and analysis with his yearning for action. He set up a research department which is today his real monument—probably the finest center of Arab studies in the world. Analysis and evaluation, he would tell his people time and time again, are everything. Israeli agents who were risking their lives sending back material which was more easily available in the pages of *Al Ahram* were gently discouraged. The natural inclination of any intelligence chief to set more store by intelligence obtained from clandestine sources was constantly being evaluated. The word *Intelligence* with a capital *I* is undeservedly glamorous, Harkabi would say. There is a better word, and that is *knowledge*. He set great store by what he described as human intelligence rather than mathematical intelligence; he taught his men how to enter the minds of the opposition. Like Boris Guriel before him, he was less interested in the number of tanks the opposition possessed than what they intended to do with them. But Harkabi was also a man of action, not afraid to wage war on those he saw as the enemies of Israel.

On April 12, 1955, the Palestinian resistance movement grew up from being a loose collection of disorganized, frequently warring factions to a tightly knit, professional guerrilla organization. It was on that day that Palestinian leaders were summoned from Gaza to Cairo. When they had come previously seeking aid from the Egyptians, they'd had to make do with third-class hotels and patronizing officials. This time it was different. Large government saloon cars ferried them around town; they were put up at the elegant Shepheard's Hotel; they were fêted by ministers and generals. Finally, Gamal Nasser himself received them and embraced each member of the delegation. The battle for the homeland had now begun. The Palestinians themselves were to be in the vanguard. The Egyptian government would train their soldiers and, until the Palestinians were ready to take over, command operations. They would be given arms, money, and whatever else they needed. If the Palestinians seek a genuine date in history when the Palestinian revolution caught fire, then it was on that warm spring day in Cairo in 1955 when Nasser made the Palestinian cause his own.

The Palestinians got down to serious training immediately. With Egyptian officers and NCO's in charge, an initial force of 700 men was prepared to launch major retaliatory strikes into Israel. The days of hit-and-run were over. A new name was found for the guerrillas to give their fight a spiritual legitimacy. They were to be called the Fedayeen, an ancient and honorable Moslem title, given to those among the faithful who were willing to sacrifice everything, including their lives, for the cause.

It didn't take long for Harkabi to hear about the Fedayeen. It wasn't long, either, before they struck. The Fedayeen were ordered into action for the first time on August 25, 1955, and they continued nightly raids right through to August 30th, attacking vehicles and buildings, blowing up a Radio Israel transmitter, laying ambushes and mines, and killing five Israeli soldiers, seventeen civilians and wounding some twenty others. The raids produced an uproar in Israel. Suddenly everyone began to take the Palestinians very seriously indeed.

Ben-Gurion demanded reprisal raids of the utmost ferocity "to teach them a lesson," but Harkabi preferred a more sophisticated approach. The Fedayeen, young men fighting for what they regarded as their homeland, had more in common with the spirit of the Israelis themselves than most of the population was prepared to acknowledge. It was the "fat cats" who sat back in comparative comfort, after sending another raiding party on its way, who were to be condemned and punished. Harkabi lost no time in establishing who was the fattest cat of them all —Lieutenant Colonel Mustapha Hafez, the chief of Egyptian intelligence in the Gaza Strip and the man personally charged by President Nasser with training the Fedayeen and launching them on targets inside Israel. No less dangerous was Lieutenant Colonel Salah Mustapha, the Egyptian military attaché in Amman, the officer inside the Egyptian intelligence community who was similarly preparing the Palestinians in Jordan for action against the Israelis.

If Israelis had been murdered, these were the men who had directed the assassins' arms. Kill Fedayeen and more would spring up to replace them; kill their Egyptian commanders and the Fedayeen would become like a branch without a tree. In October 1955, Harkabi went to the unusual length of issuing a public warning to Hafez, by naming him in the press as the true commander and organizer of the Palestinians. Nine months later, Mustapha Hafez was dead.

On July 13, 1956, a short announcement in the Egyptian official daily, *Al Ahram,* read: "Colonel Mustapha Hafez, who was stationed in the Gaza Strip, was killed when his vehicle ran across a mine. His body was transferred to El Hafish, and from there flown to Cairo." The article concluded with these words: "The dead man was among the Palestine war heroes and those who fought for Palestine's freedom. History will mark his acts of valor to his credit. His name spread fear in Israel." A few days later, French Street in Alexandria was changed to Hafez Street.

The Israeli press also reported his death, but they had a different version. Distinguished commentators on Arab affairs wrote that Hafez had been stripped of his position as chief of intelligence by Nasser because of the anger Hafez's activities had caused among the Palestinians. He had left the area and returned only a few days before his death to clear up his effects and had been killed by the Fedayeen to avenge the death of their colleagues, whom Hafez had cold-bloodedly sent to their slaughter in Israel.

While the world's press was trying to make sense out of these two wildly varying reports, the news came that Colonel Salah Mustapha, the Egyptian military attaché in Jordan, had died on the operating table in the Italian Hospital in Amman after a mysterious explosion. Officially, it was stated that an unknown assailant had thrown a hand grenade at Mustapha's car. Before he died, Mustapha himself explicitly blamed Israel. Five days later, President Nasser announced that he would nationalize the Suez Canel. Hafez and Salah Mustapha were forgotten, as the world now concentrated upon a crisis which could—and did—lead to war. Yehoshaphat "Fatti" Harkabi had got away with it. For the first time in its history, the Israeli intelligence community had set about the assassination of its enemies. Not only did it succeed, it did so in an operation which left behind no undesirable political fallout; the finger which pulled the trigger had been superbly camouflaged.

The principal target, Colonel Mustapha Hafez, was no easy hit. He was a man who left little to chance. He knew he might well be on an Israel "death list" and took the appropriate precautions. Thirty-six years old in an army where it was difficult at that time to become a colonel until one's mid-forties, his brilliance was unquestioned. In the 1948 war, he had been captured by the Israelis and was one of the few Egyptian officers successfully to break out of a POW camp and, in a genuinely heroic trek, make his way back to the Egyptian lines. He was an outstanding soldier—brave, resourceful, and above all a man of high intelligence.

Harkabi had pored over his dossier looking for the weak point in Hafez's armor. The weak point, Harkabi decided, was the colonel's ambition—not ambition of an unworthy sort, but a professional determination to establish a network of his agents inside Israel at almost any cost. Shin Bet had already picked up some of these men, and were astonished at their low calibre. Harkabi realized that the explanation for that was Hafez's belief that any agent was better than no agent at all.

One such man was an Arab Palestinian called Mehmoud Salamin El Talwouka. He had worked for the Egyptians and the Israelis too, for many years in and out of Gaza, a double agent, in the business simply for the money, which was handed him by both sides. The Israelis never had any doubts from the very beginning that El Talwouka was controlled by the Egyptians. But he was permitted to believe otherwise, given a long rein in the hope that one day he might lead the Israelis to other Egyptian agents of some significance.

Hafez, however, in his desperation to infiltrate Israel had no reservations about El Talwouka's capacities, or, if he had, he pushed them to the back of his mind. El Talwouka, a man who knew Israel and the Israelis, was prepared for the most important journey of his life.

His instructions were simple: once he had crossed the frontier, he should present himself to border guards and demand to see intelligence officers. He should then offer his services on a full-time basis to the Israelis.

It worked like a dream. Within hours of arriving in Israel, he was pouring out his heart to three Israelis whom he knew only as Sardak, Ebenezer and Absolum, who listened sympathetically to his story of his resentment at the way the Egyptians were using the Palestinians of Gaza to do their dirty work for them. In turn, they reassured him as to how much his work in the past had been valued by them, and now that he proposed to concentrate entirely upon working for Israel in an undercover role, he would have many important missions to fulfil.

The report of the conversation was on Fatti Harkabi's desk within an hour. An idea which had already half formed in his mind was slowly beginning to take final shape. It was at the end of May 1956, four months after El Talwouka had been activated by Colonel Hafez, that Fatti Harkabi decided conditions were right to spring his trap.

Sardak, Ebenezer and Absolum met El Talwouka for the last time. This time, they told him, they had a mission for him of supreme importance. Only he could be trusted to carry it out. Sardak gave him a book which El Talwouka had time to flip through while it lay in his hands. It was an instruction manual for a radio transmitter and coding instructions of the kind a secret agent in a hostile country might require.

The book, he was told, had to be delivered urgently to a very important man in the Gaza Strip, the local commandant of police, Commander Ludvi El Ahabi. Sardak gave El Talwouka an Egyptian 25 grushen note and, to El Talwouka's astonishment, a green business card belonging to Commander El Ahabi with the right-hand corner neatly snipped off. El Talwouka was told that he should take the package to El Ahabi's house, together with the banknote and the business card. First, he should hand over the small denomination bill. El Ahabi, said Sardak, would ask where he got it; El Talwouka would reply by handing him the business card and then finally the book.

El Talwouka crossed the border without incident, hurried to the first Egyptian position he could find and demanded to see the officer in charge. He told 22-year-old Lieutenant Bagi Ismaru to put him in direct telephone touch with Egyptian intelligence headquarters in Gaza, and he also asked him, because El Talwouka was now thinking about his own skin, to order his soldiers to fire forty or fifty shots into the air. He explained that he wanted the Israelis to believe that he had either been killed or captured.

In an army where personal initiative is not at a premium, the lieutenant refused the request until he received orders from higher authority. He tried to telephone intelligence headquarters, but couldn't get through, so a Captain Ismail drove El Talwouka into town and delivered him to the interrogation block. El Talwouka, now in a high state of nervous excitement, gave the code word and demanded to see his own superior officer, Captain Asaf. Asaf was eventually contacted on the telephone; he told the guard to inform Colonel Hafez.

The time was now 7:20 P.M. Colonel Hafez was enjoying a drink on the bench in his garden overlooking the Mediterranean. With him were his two principal assistants, Major Petri Mahmoud and the man who was to be his eventual successor, Major Americ El Haribi.

So when the guard came into the garden with Asaf's message, Colonel Hafez immediately rose, beckoning Major El Haribi to accompany him. The arrival of El Talwouka would unquestionably be an interesting diversion. By the time Hafez reached the cell, El Talwouka was gibbering with frustration. But, at last, seeing Hafez, he handed over the package which had been dangling inside his trousers. Hafez listened patiently as El Talwouka told him how he had been asked to hand over the package to the local police commander, El Ahabi, and then, with an apparent sense of mounting excitement, sent for Major Mahmoud, still in the garden, to come and listen as well.

Mahmoud entered the interrogation room but left again immediately to get an extra chair. On his way back, he was waylaid by a telephone call—it was to save his life.

There was no stopping El Talwouka now. He showed Hafez the 25 grushen note and El Ahabi's green calling card, cut at the corner. The package had been so wrapped that it was comparatively easy to open to inspect the contents and reseal it so that no one would ever know that it had been opened. Slowly, Hafez pried it open. Something fell from the wrapping, and he bent down to pick it up. Precisely at that moment, a huge explosion rent the building. Major Mahmoud broke in through the wreckage and found the three men apparently mortally wounded. They were rushed to the hospital at Tel Asahir in the suburbs of Gaza, where at 5:00 A.M. Hafez died, whispering a blessing to his sons and the workers at the office before he did so. Harabi and El Talwouka recovered, though they were to remain invalids for the rest of their lives.

The general prosecutor for the Gaza Strip took statements from the injured men at the hospital and ordered an immediate search of El Ahabi's office and home. El Ahabi denied all knowledge of El Talwouka or that he had any contact with the Israelis. The calling card was easily explained: it was one of many which he sent to friends and relatives when he was on holiday, and must somehow have fallen into the hands of the Israelis. The upper corner had been cut off because it was there he had always inscribed a simple message. El Ahabi was completely cleared—it was obvious that he was but one element in a multifaceted Israeli plot in which all the parts of deception and intrigue fit together at the moment of the explosion.

The assassination, of course, put Colonel Salah Mustapha, who as Egyptian military attaché in Amman was in charge of the Fedayeen in Jordan, very much on his guard. He died because he made the classic mistake of ignoring the obvious. He should, and in most circumstances probably would, have suspected the package addressed to him which his chauffeur brought from the central post office. But the wrapping could not have been more artfully chosen, franked with the seal of the United Nations headquarters in Jerusalem where Colonel Mustapha had many friends. He tore open the parcel and found inside the recently published memoirs of Field Marshal Gerd von Rundstedt, *The Commander and the Man.* When he opened the book, the cunningly concealed and triggered bomb blew his car in half. Colonel Mustapha died shortly after.

The Fedayeen, ill prepared and disorganized, were three months later pitched by Nasser into the Suez war and were virtually destroyed by the Israelis. It took the Fedayeen years to recover from that catastrophe and from the death of Colonel Hafez. There were not again a power to be reckoned with until after the Six-Day War in 1967, when once again they became, in the words of one Israeli intelligence chief, not merely deadly but dangerous, too!

Today, intelligence experts inside Israel regard the
Hafez operation as being, if anything, too sophisticated.
Harkabi and the men who planned it were banking upon
too many imponderables. They assumed that El Talwouka
would be taken straight to Hafez; they assumed that
Hafez would open the package. Too many things could
have gone wrong. El Talwouka's case officer, Captain
Asaf, for example, might well have met El Talwouka and
opened the package himself.

Yet nothing did go wrong. Harkabi had played it exactly right in an operation which bore all of his trade-
marks. He had so successfully entered the minds of the
opposition, so exactly predicted how they would behave
in a given set of circumstances, that it is almost as if they
had been programed by him. It *had* to be Hafez who
would have opened the package because no one else
would have dared do so.

Two men were assassinated—for the first time the classic espionage phrase "Terminated with Extreme Preju-
dice" was stamped on the file before it was consigned to
the vaults. There had been no international recriminations, no political fallout. The operation gave meaning to
a phrase in one of the manuals which all recruits at the
training school for both Mossad and Military Intelligence
are required to study. "The mind is the most powerful
weapon we possess." Harkabi had shown how the intellect can be polished to become an instrument of murder.

Chapter 9

HOWEVER SUCCESSFUL the Hafez operation had been,
Harkabi was unable to resist the encroachment of Isser
Harel upon Military Intelligence for very much longer.
Harel had long since thought that the occasional duplica-
tion of functions between the two agencies was wasteful
and competitive. The fiasco of Operation Suzanna permitted him once again to assume overall control of Mil-

itary Intelligence's special operations, and he now possessed the personal authority to ensure that this control was rigidly applied.

Unable to launch operations of its own without the approval of Harel, who now was able to insist that every detail had to be approved by his own people, Military Intelligence lost much of its zest for deep-penetration special operations. Harkabi himself took this philosophically. He had always regarded the importance of special operations as overstated. Too often they were used simply to impress ministers. Many operations run not only by Israel but by every major secret-service agency in the world, he believed, could not be strictly justified on purely professional grounds. Yet though this was undoubtedly true, it was a difficult line to sell either to his own colleagues in the military or through them to the Prime Minister, to whom Harkabi, unlike Isser Harel, had no direct access. With activists like Gibli and Ben-Tsur out of the picture, Harkabi set about making Military Intelligence a haven for intellectuals, where research and analysis, previously very much poor relations, were given parity with unit 131.

In a sense Harkabi ducked out of a fight with Harel over special operations, not because he was afraid of the battle but because he believed it was not worth fighting. This view had been very much reinforced as a result of the Suez war. Determined to get back to the Suez Canal, Britain and France and Israel had connived together to attack Egypt. The idea of the operation was for Israel to attack in the Sinai Desert and for Britain and France, as the old guaranteeing powers of the Suez Canal before it had been nationalized by Nasser, to send in their troops under the guise of intervening between Israel and Egypt to save the canal from war damage. The Israeli Army and Air Force performed brilliantly and achieved all the objectives set, yet politically the war did Israel's reputation in the world, especially in America, very little good. The territory it won, including the Gaza Strip, had to be restored, and though United Nations troops moved in to separate the antagonists and most important of all to "guarantee" Israel's right of shipping through the Gulf of Aqaba, this arrangement was at best a volatile one.

The whole Suez-Sinai campaign was a monument to inept political intelligence, not only Israel's, but Britain's and France's as well. For a month before the invasion, a tripartite intelligence team of Israeli, British and French intelligence officers set up headquarters in Cyprus in order to pool information in readiness for the attack, but the quality of logistic information which came from that quarter proved to be extremely poor. The British, who had the strongest intelligence apparatus in the whole of the Middle East, came up with very little. Probably this was so because their tradition of absolute secrecy was so deeply ingrained that the British representatives could not bring themselves to share information they had with two allies whom they certainly would have regarded with the deepest suspicion. The French were more forthcoming, but much of their information, while sound enough, was not of sufficient depth to assist field commanders in anything but the most marginal way. As for Israel, her intelligence community produced a great deal which was useful, including superb maps of the Sinai Desert of a quality never previously available and probably better than the Egyptians possessed themselves, but Israeli intelligence had gone wrong in seriously overestimating the capability of the Egyptian Army to resist, which had the effect of placing Israeli armored divisions very frequently at the wrong place at the wrong time.

To Israeli military commanders, this mattered a great deal. More than any other arm in the world, the Israelis could not afford the luxury of moving men and equipment into an area where they would lie even momentarily idle, because by so doing they would denude another front where such equipment might prove essential. Israeli military leaders knew as they withdrew that the Suez war, peremptorily brought to an end by the Americans, would one day have to be fought all over again. It was up to Harkabi to prepare Military Intelligence for the future war by refining intelligence-collection techniques and by setting up the wherewithal to analyze that intelligence correctly.

So Military Intelligence withdrew somewhat into the background, partially because of pressure from Harel, partially because of Harkabi's personality, and partially because for the first time since Chaim Herzog had laid down a template for its organization, Military Intelligence began to perceive its real function, namely, to set forth an order of battle, to know and evaluate every unit of the enemy, to assess their weaponry and their power to use it, and to put the information down alongside offensive and defensive operational plans constantly being prepared by the general staff and come to day-to-day conclusions concerning the correctness of Israeli's military posture right down to platoon level.

This left Isser Harel with a clear field in the area in which he reveled—special operations. Though he despised the glamorization of his trade in books about James Bond (he once went to see a James Bond film to see what all the fuss was about and left appalled), in truth, it was not the work that Bond did which he found unappealing, it was the image of the urbane sophisticate which was so much at odds with the kind of men Harel was recruiting. His was a serious business which deserved to be treated seriously. He did not regard the choosing of fine wines a necessary part of his training program.*

Already, by the time of Suez, Isser Harel's international reputation among the intelligence agencies' chiefs had been secured. One great coup put him into the big league. At a secret session of the Soviet Communist Party Congress on February 25th, 1956, Nikita Khrushchev had launched an extraordinary attack upon Joseph Stalin, whom he accused of using his position as party leader to make himself supreme, of permitting the execution on false charges of loyal Communists who had opposed him, of mistakes in agricultural policies, of failure to pre-

---

* Ironically, in the late forties, two or three Israeli agents in Europe were reported to local police as being "suspicious" characters (suspected of being Russian spies) because of their quite remarkable lack of knowledge of normal procedure when checking into a hotel and how to behave once they had arrived. Having lived all of their lives on kibbutzim, never having entered, let alone stayed in, a smart international hotel, they were completely at a loss. At the same time, a resident Israeli agent in Paris was so appalled at the table manners of an agent passing through who had also come direct from a kibbutz, where such niceties were treated with some contempt, that he wrote a report home calling for classes in basic decorum as standard procedure during the training course. Harel, most reluctantly, was forced to keep "good manners" in the training program and eventually was even prevailed upon to include an education in wines as part of the curriculum. Israelis drink very little as a rule, and so Israeli agents working in Europe need to be taught, if they are to blend into the landscape, how to read a wine list and menu.

pare for the German invasion, of strategic blunders during the war, and of responsibility for the break with Yugoslavia in 1948. The speech was, of course, political dynamite, confirming everything about Stalin's rule both in Russia and the satellites that the West had been saying for years. It came as a terrible shock to Western Communist parties, but more particularly to pro-Stalinist leaders still in power in Eastern Europe. However, only summaries of the speech were made available to the public, and the CIA's Allen Dulles was determined to get hold of and publish the complete text. The race was on to score a major propaganda victory over the Soviet Union.

Isser Harel had only a tiny network in Russia, consisting of just one Mossad-trained case officer. No Mossad operative was less active than he. He had been inserted as a precautionary measure, to be used only *in extremis,* perhaps in the illegal emigration of prominent Russian Jews if the Russian Jewish community were ever again to come under pressure.

The Mossad man had been given strict instructions not to engage in any illegal activities or do anything to expose his hand. The Israelis knew only too well what the discovery of a genuine Israeli spy ring could do to the three million Jews trapped in the Soviet Union. Equally, Isser Harel knew that it was unlikely that his man would ever be able to find anything in Russia which was not available to the CIA and which the CIA would not, if it involved Israel, pass on. Nevertheless, the Khrushchev speech was as important to the Israelis as it was to anyone else, and Isser wanted a copy of the speech badly enough to instruct his man to move sufficiently out of the shadows to try to get it. It would be left entirely to his discretion as to the degree of danger he would expose himself to, but if at any stage he felt that his own security could be compromised, he should withdraw.

With instructions as soft as these, it is even more remarkable that the agent succeeded against the most intense international competition. The CIA was turning Russia and Eastern Europe inside out in a frenzied attempt to buy the speech at almost any price. The British had entered the bidding as well; their own SIS having taken a heavy battering, their image badly dented by major security lapses, they hoped that getting the Khrushchev speech would restore something of their lost prestige. Precisely how the Mossad man did it is still a closely guarded secret, as indeed it is a closely guarded secret that the Israeli Secret Service succeeded where the others failed.

The story of the full operation will probably never be told—certainly not while those who could be hurt by the information are still alive. There is, however, some evidence to suggest that the Mossad case officer had recruited into his network a junior diplomat at one of the East European embassies whom he needed to make out passports should he ever need to move a Jew out of Russia in a hurry. This diplomat was able to make an unauthorized copy of the speech and dispatch it to his own foreign office by diplomatic pouch. There, he had a friend waiting who took delivery—a friend who was told that the diplomat was smuggling stuff out of Moscow, a fairly common occurrence at that time. He was told to take the package to a restaurant where in return for a sum of money believed to be $5,000, he should hand the package over.

Within hours, the speech was in Western Europe and handed to another Mossad representative, who took it to Israel.

Once Mossad evaluators were convinced the document was genuine, Isser Harel had to make the decision as to what to do with this, the greatest triumph of his professional life. The temptation to release the text in Israel was almost overwhelming. It would have enhanced the public prestige of Israel as well as Mossad itself. Every secret-service chief knows that the greater the fame of his service, the more effective it can be. Israel at that time had not yet established the image of an omnipotent secret service which strikes so much terror into the enemy. Censorship was such that Israeli newspapers never even mentioned that the Secret Service existed at all; no one outside of a very small circle had ever heard of Mossad. (The Prime Minister had a year earlier mentioned Shin Bet, the security agency, in Parliament, thus releasing the press from its obligation never to refer to it in print. But that confused the foreign press, who right up to the mid-sixties were still referring to Shin Bet as if it were Israel's principal secret-service agency.) Here was an opportunity to put Mossad on the map . . . to pitch it into the world's headlines and keep it there. Against that was the awareness that if Israel were shown to have been the country which got the document, then Russia would no doubt find some means of exacting vengeance upon its Jewish citizens. That, in the end, proved to be the decisive consideration. There was only one capital from which the document could be safely released—Washington. Isser Harel himself flew to America to negotiate the transfer.

There he met James Angleton, one of the most remarkable men ever employed by the CIA. No one in the world knew more about the machinations of the KGB and the secret world of the Communist colossus. Angleton had established a loose connection with the Israeli Secret Service principally because of personally making contacts with Israeli agents pre-independence—in Italy, where he was fighting the secret war then being waged to prevent a Communist takeover of the country. He had maintained those friendships and become a spokesman for Israeli interests within the CIA at a time when the agency was veering sharply over to the Arab side. It was natural, then, that Isser Harel should go directly to Angleton, both because of the value of his expertise in helping to authenticate the document and the knowledge that in any subsequent "trade" negotiations, Angleton could be expected to deal fairly with Israeli interests.

The price Harel demanded was a high one: no money, but a formalized swap agreement by which each side would automatically exchange information on the Arab world, excluding only that material which fell into the highest possible security classification. Allen Dulles accepted the deal without demur and as a mark of his good faith confirmed Angleton as head of the Israel desk while still keeping him in charge of counterespionage. It was an odd arrangement, but with the Israeli account in Angleton's hands, Isser Harel could be sure that the CIA would not renege.

The Khrushchev speech was handed over to Ray Cline of the intelligence-analysis department of the CIA, who confirmed its authenticity. The decision was to publish and the document was handed by the State Department to the New York *Times*. On June 4, the *Times* ran the report in full, probably the longest report it has ever published, and the world knew for the first time the full horrors of Stalinism.

The effects were dramatic. Radio Free Europe made

sure that the whole of Eastern Europe knew what Khrushchev had actually said. It wasn't long before the workers of Warsaw and Budapest rose in defiance of their masters. All over the world young men and women deserted the Communist Party in droves. It was part of the deal with the Americans that the CIA should be permitted to take the full credit for what was perhaps the most successful espionage coup since the end of the Second World War. But those few people within the profession who knew the truth suddenly realized that they had a newcomer in the big league of international espionage.

There was a more direct and infinitely more important payoff as well. James Angleton stuck steadfastly to the provisions of the swap arrangements, which had the effect of ensuring that virtually every CIA man in the Middle East was also working at second hand for the Israelis. The young lions who had been running the Arab accounts suddenly discovered that they had been totally outflanked, as the CIA's policy changed almost overnight, in an extraordinary *volte-face,* from being largely pro-Arab to becoming almost totally pro-Israeli.

The Angleton view was that the interests of the United States lay in propping up the Jewish State militarily and economically. Very quickly, that view became the received wisdom of the CIA, then of the State Department, and ultimately of the presidency. It is an oversimplification to say that *that* was the prize Isser Harel won for the Khrushchev speech, but the speech provided the spur and put the CIA and its powerful chief Allen Dulles deeply into the debt of the Israelis.

Inside Israel, Isser Harel's great coup and the extraordinary diplomatic benefits for Israel which he extracted from it made him now quite unchallengeable—more powerful than most ministers. He had already established his mastery over Military Intelligence; now he was able to crack the whip.

But there was still one piece of important business left undone. The appalling fiasco of Military Intelligence's Operation Suzanna had left a nasty smell which Harel was determined to eradicate. He had been convinced all along that the whole truth of this episode had not come out, and that the entire Military Intelligence hierarchy had lied to the Olshan-Dori committee in order to cover up their culpability in the planning and the execution of the operation. To a man like Isser Harel, whose own deeply defined set of moral principles made him at times a difficult man to work with, this was a shocking betrayal of the very basis of his calling.

Democratic control over any secret-service agency is always difficult. Spymasters operate out of the public gaze; the operations they conduct on behalf of the state are not open to normal debate because of the very secrecy in which they take place. When spymasters conceal the truth from the few men who are entitled to know it, then indeed these agencies become Frankenstein monsters, out of control and dangerous to the very fabric of the state they are pledged to serve. Isser Harel, whose own personal politics are extremely right-wing and authoritarian and who was often suspected by his enemies of not perceiving this vital principle, did, in fact, throughout his entire career, cling to it with a fanatical determination, even when all power lay in his hands. If one were to look for one single thing to mark out Isser Harel's greatness, then it would be that at the pinnacle of his power, he not only willingly accepted that he was an official answerable in every way to the Prime Minister, but insisted upon it.

With an almost biblical sense of righteousness, he set out to clean the Augean stables. Men of his choosing were put into senior jobs in Military Intelligence, the most significant appointment, the head of Unit 131, going to one of the great heroes of Israeli folklore, Jossi Harel (no relation). Jossi Harel had been captain of the *Exodus*, the famous immigrant ship which had tried to make it through the British blockade after the war, but otherwise he had no experience at all in what was a highly specialized field. Others were cleared out, to the anger of the Army, but even Moshe Dayan was not powerful enough to stop Harel from what some regarded as the neutering of the whole operation.

But Isser Harel was after one man in particular—Avri Seidenwerg, alias Paul Frank. Harel was convinced that Paul Frank was at the heart of the Suzanna conspiracy. He was certain, too, with nothing better than a hunch to go on, that Paul Frank had only managed to escape from Egypt because he had sold out to the Egyptians. Harel had been stunned when he discovered that Military Intelligence had sent Frank back into the field to Germany, where he was operating an import-export firm using the same name, Paul Frank, he had used in Egypt and, indeed, calling his firm Paul Frank Import-Export, with himself as sole owner. To Isser Harel and all his associates this was a special kind of madness. Not only had Paul Frank been named in the Cairo trial, he had been sentenced to death *in absentia*. How on earth could he operate on behalf of Israeli interests when his cover had been so well and truly blown? Even if Frank were as pure as the driven snow, there were overwhelming reasons of national security why he should not have been permitted to live at large in Europe. He knew too much about the Israeli security apparatus. It would not be beyond the capability of the Egyptians to kidnap him, take him to Cairo, and extract from him everything he knew. He was, in short, a security risk. But, to Isser Harel's astonishment, Fatti Harkabi held firm, and refused to bring Frank home. This excited Harel's suspicions still further. If Military Intelligence refused to accept the very good reasons as to why Frank's presence in Germany could be a potential risk for the whole service, then they must want him out of Israel for a special reason. By the summer of 1955, Paul Frank's movements were dogged by Isser Harel's men.

By January 1956, Fatti Harkabi could no longer resist Harel's insistent demands that Paul Frank be brought back to Israel, but he refused to accept any suggestions that Frank was actively betraying his country. Harkabi knew all too well the burden that Frank was carrying through his knowledge of the cover-up operation, a burden which Harkabi shared. A year earlier Gibli's secretary, a woman called Dalia, had admitted to Harkabi that she had been asked to alter a vital letter of July 19, 1954, from Gibli to Dayan, changing the words ". . . following the conversation we had, the boys were activated" to read: "Upon Lavon's instructions, we have activated Suzanna's boys."

Harkabi knew, too, that alterations had been made on other documents relating to the operation, and that documents, including a copy of the vital radio transmission which instructed Frank to go for British or American installations, had been removed from the files. Harkabi, however, decided not to do anything about it. His motives were mixed. First, he owed a loyalty to the Army and to its Chief of Staff, Moshe Dayan, who would, he believed,

inevitably be involved if the criminal acts which had
taken place were ever to be properly investigated. Second,
he did not believe that any possible good could come
from an investigation. Those responsible had been removed. It had been a miserable affair which was best
forgotten.

But Paul Frank remained a problem. Harkabi tried
unavailingly to persuade him to leave Military Intelligence altogether and, indeed, promised to seek to have
his rank and seniority restored provided he joined the
Tank Corps. There, Harkabi reasoned, he would be safe
from Harel's constant vigilance. But Frank, by now ob-
sessed with his own role in the drama, refused pointblank.
Instead, in April of 1956, with his father dying of leuke-
mia in Vienna, he obtained permission—after some delay
caused by Harel's obstinate refusal to permit Frank to
leave the country—to return to Europe to see his father.
He remained in Europe for the rest of the year, but this
time he was in Vienna not as Paul Frank but as Avri
Seidenwerg, traveling on his own Israeli passport. It was
at this point that he began making mistakes. Apparently
hooked by his life as a spy, he could not leave well
enough alone and drove to Salzburg, where he informed
the authorities that he had lost his passport and got a new
one issued in the name of Paul Frank. It was, of course,
a gross breach of regulations, compounded by the fact
that he then used that passport to travel within Europe.
By now, Frank's behavior could no longer be ignored
even by Harkabi. He refused to return to Israel with a
rank of major in the Tank Corps and made it plain to
everyone that he intended to remain in Europe. To Harel,
this was additional evidence of his guilt.

Then, suddenly, perhaps because of his father, whose
illness was reaching its final stages, or perhaps because of
the sense of injustice he felt at being hounded by Harel's
men, Frank decided in January 1958 to return to Israel
and tell all he knew about the Suzanna cover-up. It was
to Motke Ben-Tsur, his old chief at Unit 131, that Frank
wrote, informing him of his intentions. Motke's reply was
incautiously cautious, and would do more to destroy his
reputation than anything he had done up till then. "Let
me tell you a story I read recently in the newspaper," he
wrote back. "Then draw your own conclusions."

The President of the Spanish Olympic Committee was invited to the Soviet Union to participate in an Olympic festivity in Moscow. The President politely rejected the offer. When questioned by friends as to why he had done so (for rarely was such an honor bestowed upon citizens of Franco's Spain), the President replied: "Everything you say is true. They have promised me the best hotel in the city; they have promised me free movement wherever I want to go; they indicated all the cultural events were open to me; they even sent me a first class ticket on Aeroflot . . ."

His friends chimed in: "So why did you reject the invitation?"

The President replied caustically: "Because the ticket was for one way only."

Motke Ben-Tsur's meaning was plain. Nevertheless, when his father died, Paul Frank flew to Tel Aviv, where he went straight to Gibli's house and told him that he was going to blow the lid off the scandal. Whether Paul Frank was bargaining for his own immunity from prosecution is not clear; whatever the case, matters had gone too far now for anyone to help him.

A few days later, he was picked up for questioning and after nine months of interrogation was finally, in October 1958, arraigned before a district court in Jerusalem and charged with the photographing and possession of top-secret Military Intelligence material and with making unauthorized approaches to Egyptian military officers in Europe.

In truth, despite all the surveillance which had been carried out on him, the prosecution actually had very little evidence. Certainly, he had met Egyptians, but there was no proof at all that he had used these contacts to pass on secret information. He had in his possession when arrested (though they were actually found later) photographs of documents he should not have had, including extracts from the top-secret "Violet File," one of the most sensitive files in the whole of Military Intelligence, as well as film (again from the vaults of Military Intelligence) of secret Egyptian rocket installations which he had photographed himself while in Egypt. There has not to this day been an entirely satisfactory account of how this classified material came to be in Frank's possession. His claim that they were planted on him by Isser Harel's men in order to use him to open up the Pandora's box of the Suzanna affair simply doesn't pass muster. Isser Harel's loyalty to Ben-Gurion was absolute; the interrogation of Frank had revealed that if there was a cover-up, it would touch Ben-Gurion himself. Framing Paul Frank was not in Harel's interests at all; nor, of course, was it something that Harel could ever tolerate doing.

The prosecution's position that this material had been stolen in order to be passed on to the Egyptians never quite fitted, either. Frank was able to show that the documents had never left Israel, though there was no reason, if he proposed to pass them on, he couldn't have done so when he was given permission to visit his sick father. Also, he had left the case of documents in the safekeeping of a colleague in Military Intelligence—hardly the action of a man who believes he has something to hide. The documents were to be one more mystery in what was about to become a *cause célèbre*, which would within eighteen months force the final resignation of David Ben-Gurion.

In the meantime, however, Harkabi was forced to resign. He did so in April 1959, together with the Chief of Operations, in the aftermath of incredible confusion when they both authorized a trial mobilization without receiving Cabinet approval. To the astonishment of the Prime Minister, the whole country left their offices and factories in response to code calls on the radio to join their reserve units. It cost millions of dollars in lost production, as well as being a great muddle—nothing more serious. Nevertheless, as a gesture, Harkabi and the Chief of Operations were asked to resign. Harkabi was told by Ben-Gurion that he could return after a month, but he decided he'd had enough and went abroad on study leave, eventually to take his place as a professor of international relations and Arabic studies at Jerusalem University.

So, as a result of a silly misunderstanding, the least well-known but perhaps one of the most effective chiefs of Israeli Military Intelligence retired. His term of office had been constantly marred by echoes of Suzanna. He was to hear more of it yet.

In July of 1959, the Frank trial opened in secret session in Jerusalem. Frank's innocence or guilt was to be established by three judges. The trial lasted until September, as Paul Frank and his counsel slowly and gradually forced the court to accept as admissible evidence his story of the cover-up. Motke Ben-Tsur lied repeatedly to the court, but was ultimately forced to admit that the letter in which he referred to the invitation of the Spanish Olympic President to visit Moscow was a warning to Frank not to come home. Colonel Ariel Amiad, chairman of the independent Army investigation into the affair (begun as a result of Frank's allegations while in custody), took the witness stand to say that Ben-Tsur had admitted to him in private that documents had been falsified, but had said that he would deny this if ever put into a witness box. The testimony of Major Shlomo Millet, who had been Frank's supervising case officer for much of the operation, was even more damaging. He described how he had opened the file and in accordance with normal procedure organized an index. Eventually, Motke Ben-Tsur had taken the file over. Millet testified that he could see that the file had now been changed—it had even been placed into a new binding—the index was missing, and documents which he knew had once existed in it had been removed.

In particular, he told the court, he had personally taken to the Israeli radio station the taped order to commence the second sabotage action in Egypt. This, too, had disappeared and was no longer in the file.

Nevertheless, the court found Frank guilty in August 1959 of all charges and then postponed sentences. Their verdict ran to eighty pages. Paul Frank was, of course, most interested in that part which concerned him; others were more interested in the recommendation of the court that allegations made by Frank against General Gibli and Colonel Motke Ben-Tsur should be brought to the attention of the Chief of Staff.

But the cat was already out of the bag. In February, 1959, Jossi Harel, the hero of the *Exodus* who for a short while had been head of Unit 131, had called upon Pinhas Lavon and told him of the discoveries about the cover-up he had made while working at Military Intelligence. Lavon had waited a long time to clear his name, gradually becoming more and more bitter as the years went by. Now he informed David Ben-Gurion about this new evidence and insisted upon a full inquiry. Ben-Gurion asked his military secretary, Colonel Chaim Ben-David, to conduct a preliminary investigation, and on July 15th he reported to Ben-Gurion that there could be no doubt that documents had been forged. In September, having received the report from the Frank court-martial, Chief of Staff Chaim Lascov set up an official board of inquiry under the chairmanship of Justice Chaim Cohen, specifically to investigate

> Whether any measures were taken by the "Senior Officer,"* his assistant or any other officer in the bureau in question to induce witnesses in general and the third man in particular to perjure themselves to the Olshan-Dori Committee that investigated the "security mishap" or the Minister of Defense and Chief of Staff and whether false evidence was actually given.
>
> Whether any alterations were made in the documents of Operation Suzanna or other documents connected with the investigation carried out by the above-mentioned committee and, if so, by whom.

The Cohen report turned out to be little more than a whitewash. Forgery, they said, had not been proved, "nor have the suspicions . . . been substantiated." As for the famous letter of July 19, 1954, sent by Gibli to Dayan, police experts testified that no changes had been made in the letter they were asked to examine.

The whole affair had now taken on enormous political importance. The opposition parties saw it as a stick with which to beat the Government, and were doing so successfully every day. David Ben-Gurion saw the attacks as personal, aimed at senior officers in the Army like Dayan, and, through them, straight at him. The Cohen report gave him and his friends the opportunity of going on the offensive. If all those who had claimed forgeries were believed, there seemed little in the way of clearing Gibli completely from the charge at the heart of the matter,

---

* From the moment that Pinhas Lavon heard from Colonel Jossi Harel, the whole affair for the first time came out into the open, and occupied the front pages of Israeli newspapers for months to come. However, the dictates of censorship made the story hard to follow for the ordinary reader. Gibli was referred to throughout as the "Senior Officer," Ben-Tsur as the "Reserve Officer," Paul Frank as the "Third Man," and Operation Suzanna as a "security mishap."

namely, that he had ordered the operation without the knowledge of the Minister of Defense, Pinhas Lavon. So General Gibli asked for a full-scale judicial inquiry into the whole affair from beginning to end. But the majority of the government, heartily sick of the whole business, and perhaps realizing that the Cohen committee report was not so clear-cut as Ben Gurion seemed to believe (it said that forgery had not been proved, not that it had not occurred), vowed to end the matter and over the violent opposition of Ben-Gurion set up its own Ministerial Committee of Seven with a brief as wide or as narrow as it wished, that is, "To review the material and to tell the government what in our opinion should be done in the future."

Attorney General Gideon Hausner flew to Paris and spoke to Fatti Harkabi about his claim that Gibli's secretary, on the instructions of Mordechai Ben-Tsur, had told him that she had changed the letter of July 19. Hausner then confronted Dalia, a friend and admirer of Gibli's, who at first denied this. But finally, tearfully, she admitted the truth. Hausner together with Dalia returned to Tel Aviv, where she was held for police interrogation. Once again, somewhat oddly, she changed her testimony. She was no longer so sure, she said, that the letter she had changed was the letter referred to. On December 21st, the Committee of Seven made its findings public.

> Lavon did not give the direct order for the 1954 action.
> This committee sees no need for further inquiry.
> No one but Gibli and Motke Ben-Tsur bears any responsibility for the mishap.

Bitter and angry, Ben-Gurion took six weeks' leave of absence and then threatened his colleagues with his resignation, because "this country cannot live by whitewashing lies, misrepresenting facts and perverting justice." The members of Mapai, Ben-Gurion's party, were by now bewildered and frightened. It was Lavon, they decided, who had begun this campaign of denigration against the Army and Ben-Gurion, and it was Lavon who should suffer for it. He was stripped of his position as general secretary of the Histadrut and retired a lonely and bitter man. He had partially won the fight to clear his name, but had lost the political battle in the process. He died in January 1976.

Ben-Gurion was never to permit the affair to rest, believing, perhaps rightly, that if his side of the case was not accepted by the historians, then his role in the history of Israel would have Lavon's shadow cast over it. He finally resigned as Prime Minister in 1963 and worked almost full-time to get a full-scale judicial inquiry opened in the case, but his successor, Levi Eshkol, and his Cabinet would have none of it. At last, in 1964, failing to convince the government of the necessity of such an inquiry, Ben-Gurion removed himself from Mapai, the Labor Party, taking with him his two protégés, Moshe Dayan and Shimon Peres, to form the breakaway Rafi Party. He would never forgive his ex-colleagues, who he believed had deserted him.

So, fitfully and tragically, what was always erroneously described as the Lavon affair came to an end, the loose strings still hanging in the wind. To the Israelis at the time it had come as a disturbing revelation of how close Israel could come to an elected dictatorship, with the Army and not government ministers in charge of events. The Israelis were, of course, overreacting. Every country has had its Lavon affairs—times when the bureaucracy gets out of hand and then covers up its guilt. In Israel, the cover-up was forced out into the open and ultimately destroyed the government. Democracy is no guarantee that men will do no wrong; it merely provides the means by which they can be brought to account.

With the affair itself dissolving into the history books, only the puppets were left, still to be accounted for. The original men and one woman of the "sleeper" team, sentenced to long periods of imprisonment, were serving their time in the infamous Tura Prison near Helwan on the Nile. They had reason to feel bitter. Mustapha Amin, the Egyptian editor and journalist, and friend and confidant of Nasser, told one of them that after the Suez war in 1956, he had been sent to Washington by the Egyptian President to negotiate at second-hand with the Israelis through the Americans. He was given carte blanche by Nasser, told to accept virtually everything the Israelis demanded, and, indeed, was specifically told to accept any exchange proposals made for the young Jews in their Egyptian prison. To his and Nasser's astonishment, no request of any kind was made by the Israeli authorities.

At the time Victor Levy and his friends, not knowing of the tremendous row in Israel, could have no idea why this chance to gain their release was not grabbed by the Israeli government. Now they suspect that their presence back home would have added further embarrassing complications into an already hideous situation. As it was, they had to wait until the Six-Day War, when they were exchanged for what seemed to be virtually the entire Egyptian army.

Today they lead quiet and successful lives in Israel. As Victor Levy says: "We all lived happily ever after."

That was not to be the case for Paul Frank. To the astonishment of his attorney, he was sentenced to twelve years' imprisonment—a barbarous sentence in the light of the evidence produced against him at his trial. The suspicion must linger that the court was prompted not by what they heard in court, but by outside suggestions made to them by Isser Harel and others that Paul Frank had betrayed the original Suzanna team. He served out his time and now lives in the United States.

Chapter 10

THE DATE WAS May 23, 1960. Jerusalem was abuzz with rumors that the Prime Minister would be making an important announcement in the Knesset, the Israeli Parliament, that afternoon. So when David Ben-Gurion walked in just before 4:00 P.M., the chamber was packed to the roof. There were not many people, however, who noticed a remarkable and unique occurrence.

A few minutes before David Ben-Gurion was due to stand to make his statement, none other than Isser Harel, then forty-eight years old, slipped into a seat reserved for senior officials behind the table where Cabinet ministers sat. Never before had Isser Harel put in what amounted to a public appearance. He was one of those men who positively gloried in remaining anonymous—a man whose picture had never appeared in any newspaper, whose name was censored out of correspondents' copy, a man who permitted acquaintances to believe he was simply a grey-faced bureaucrat, permanently buried beneath a pile of paper in some dark and dusty government office. Now he had come out into the open in order to taste, as far as it was possible for him to do, public recognition for his greatest triumph.

There was a hush when Ben-Gurion climbed to his feet. His statement was brief and matter of fact, devoid of emotion in content though the emotion broke through in his voice.

"I have to announce to the Knesset," he said, "that a short time ago, one of the greatest Nazi criminals was found by the Israeli Security Services, Adolf Eichmann, who was responsible together with the Nazi leaders for what they called the 'Final Solution of the Jewish Problem'—that is, the extermination of six million Jews of Europe. Adolf Eichmann is already under arrest in Israel, and he will shortly be brought to trial in Israel under the Nazis and Nazi Collaborators (Punishment) Law of 1950."

There was a single sob from one Knesset member and then wild cheering and clapping as the news sank in. Adolf Eichmann, who represented what was subsequently so exactly and so brilliantly described by Hannah Arendt as the "banality of evil," was now in the hands of a people he had quite deliberately and apparently with no moral scruples sought to exterminate.

There are brief moments in time when a single incident can unite a whole people. There seemed an almost divine sense of justice in his capture. That feeling did not last long, but for that day and the days which immediately followed, there was a mixture of tears and joy throughout every Jewish community in the world—tears for the deeds this man had done, joy for the fact that the Jewish people had risen sufficiently strong from the funeral pyre upon which he had sought to cast them to sit now in judgment upon him.

For Isser Harel, the occasion meant much as well. He himself had led the task force which had gone into the Argentine to kidnap Eichmann and bring him to Israel in an operation which was as daring in conception as it was brilliant in execution. Eichmann's capture had become an obsession for Harel, and would remain a constant theme in his conversations for years to come.

The capture of Eichmann had another effect, too. The moment of Ben-Gurion's announcement was the moment that Israeli intelligence was thrust upon the consciousness of the world. Suddenly, Israeli intelligence was on the map, and Israel's enemies became a little more fearful of the tiny State on their doorsteps. Israelis abroad found it that much easier to recruit agents, who needed no more convincing that they were dealing with professionals, while agents playing a double game for the Arabs felt that much less sure of themselves and on at least two occasions within a month of Eichmann's capture threw in the towel because the strain had become unbearable.

The kidnaping of Adolf Eichmann was in truth one of the classic covert-intelligence plays of all time—with agents operating thousands of miles from home, traveling on forged documentation, relying on their own resources and moving to eliminate or (in this case) capture a single target. It is a fascinating case study of sheer technique of the kind employed not merely by the Israelis but by the intelligence agencies of the super powers, from whom the Israelis learned most of their lessons in the first place. There was the usual quotient of mistakes or misfortune which hits any such undercover operation, any one of which might have exposed Harel and his task force of eleven to the authorities. There were also the compensating pieces of luck that saved hours and sometimes even days of tedious surveillance.

There has never been an intelligence operation which has gone completely according to plan, and that is the secret of why so many otherwise sane men maintain a lifelong fascination for the art. Yet no intelligence operation has worked at all where there has not been the most painstaking planning, the most relentless dedication to detail.

Contrary to what was claimed after Eichmann's capture, Mossad had never seriously gone into the business of finding and apprehending Nazi war criminals. This was not out of a lack of interest but rather a lack of resources, and many a "Nazi hunter" coming to Tel Aviv seeking financial and moral support was turned away. Nevertheless, Eichmann, the man who organized and ran the Final Solution, was different.

It took Mossad nearly two years, from the first tentative sighting of Eichmann to his final capture, to establish that he was, without question, the man they were after and then to plan and execute his kidnaping. Once all doubt had been removed that the man calling himself Rikardo Klement who was living in a suburb of Buenos Aires was Eichmann, Isser Harel dropped everything else to concentrate upon his capture.

There was no doubt in anyone's mind about the difficulties this would entail. The Israeli team would be operating thousands of miles away from Israel, in breach of all international law. If things went wrong, the repercussions —political, diplomatic and professional—would be serious. Communications with Israel would be difficult, and task-force leaders on the spot might be faced with the necessity of crucial decisions without any possibility of advice from headquarters.

So Isser Harel persuaded Prime Minister Ben-Gurion that, in these most special of circumstances, Harel himself should be on the spot in Buenos Aires in order to take personal responsibility for the operation. For the head of Mossad to take over what were, in effect, the duties of a case officer was without precedent either in Israeli intelligence or indeed any other intelligence service in the world. But Harel regarded the capture of Eichmann as being the single most important mission ever entrusted to him. Normal considerations no longer applied; everything was justified, including blowing his own cover, as Harel has made clear in his published account of the operation.

At one point, when the Israelis had Eichmann in their hands in Argentina and were awaiting the chance to move him out of the country, a decision had to be made as to what action they should take if the police found their hideaway. Harel's instructions were explicit. Gabi Eldad, the commander of the task force, would handcuff Eichmann to himself and dispose of the key. While the rest of the team attempted to escape, Gabi would await the arrival of the police, inform them that the man manacled to him was Adolf Eichmann, the war criminal, and demand to see the most senior Agentinian official in the vicinity. As Harel later wrote:

I also thought . . . that I had no right to subject Gabi to the ordeal of interrogation and trial all alone so

I said to him, "When you're caught with Eichmann and brought before a senior police officer or a high-ranking civilian government official, you will disclose that you are an Israeli and explain that you were acting under the instructions of another Israeli, the leader of a group of volunteers you belong to. . . . This group, you will tell them, received information that a resident of Argentina known as Rikardo Klement was actually Adolf Eichmann, the man in charge of the extermination of the Jews in Europe during the Second World War. The group came to Buenos Aires to check the truth of the information. If they found that the man was really Eichmann, they intended capturing him and handing him over then to the Argentine authorities to be judged for his crimes against humanity and the Jewish people. . . . You will tell them that the name of the leader of the volunteer group is Isser Harel. You will give them the address of the hotel I am staying at and the name under which I am registered there. . . . When you've given them my name and the address of my hotel, you will tell them the following: Isser Harel ordered me to give his name and address to the Argentine authorities. He will explain to you himself the motives for the actions of the group he heads, and he will take upon himself full responsibility for their activities, in accordance with the laws of the State and the principles of justice and morality."

For the head of a secret service, whose very name was a state secret in his own country, to agree to give himself up in this way was extraordinary. Very often the biggest secret an agent who is caught possesses is the identity of his case officer. But in the Eichmann kidnaping, the team were all experienced Mossad, Military Intelligence, or Shin Bet veterans with a good deal more to impart than that. Yet here was Isser Harel, ordering his men to hand him over to the authorities. Gabi protested, but Harel according to his own testimony told him: "This operation . . . has nothing in common with anything we have ever done before. As far as I am concerned, it is a humane and national mission that transcends all others, and its success is more important in my eyes than any other consideration.

I am acting in this matter according to the dictates of my conscience."

Harel was, of course, never called upon to make the sacrifice. On May 11, 1960, at 8:05 P.M., in Garibaldi Street on the outskirts of Buenos Aires, Rikardo Klement, whose real name was Adolf Eichmann, ex-chief of Subsection VI of the Reichssicherheitshauptamt (RSHA), the main security department of the Nazi regime, commissioned by Heinrich Himmler to bring about "the Final Solution of the Jewish Problem," was walking home after having gotten off the bus from work. Israeli commandos snatched him from the street and sped away to the sanctuary of a "safe house." Within minutes of his capture, Eichmann confessed to his true identity. On May 20, he was flown out of the Argentine to Israel, was put on trial almost a year later, on April 11, 1961, was found guilty of crimes against humanity, and on May 31, 1962, became the only man apart from the unfortunate Captain Toubianski to suffer the death penalty in the history of the State of Israel. He was hanged at Ramle on May 31, 1962.

The blow-by-blow account of the capture of Adolf Eichmann has been told and retold elsewhere, notably by Isser Harel himself in his book *The House on Garibaldi Street* (Andre Deutsch, 1975), so I will not go over the same ground here. But some mention of techniques employed in the capture of Adolf Eichmann may be useful in indicating how meticulously the Israeli Secret Service plans its operations. Only Mossad's treasurer could put a price on what this operation cost, but a figure of $250,000 would not be far off.

Long before the operation itself, three Israeli investigators flew to the Argentine to make a preliminary reconnaissance. As a result of their investigations, a special office was established within Mossad, headed by a senior agency executive, to do nothing but collect material on Eichmann and other German war criminals believed to be still on the run. Within a few months, a subsection of that office was set up to deal with the complex problems of getting an Israeli team into Argentina and also of getting them out again. By the time the senior executive was finished, he had a thousand-page manual covering every possible eventuality.

It was one individual's job to do nothing but make the travel arrangements—a kind of one-man "travel agency."

It was decided that at least twelve people, including Harel, would be needed in the Argentine for the snatch, all of whom had to travel on different flights, come from different parts of the world, with forged passports and a variety of visas. No one traveler could have any connection with another. In some cases in order to maintain absolute security, the documentation with which they entered the country would have to be different from the documentation with which they left. They obviously couldn't be seen traveling from Israel, yet some of the Argentinian consulates in Europe and elsewhere asked for character references from the local police of their area of residence before they were prepared to grant visas. One way round this problem was to book a tour of Latin America making Buenos Aires merely a staging post, but obviously the whole party couldn't use the same method. Health regulations posed other stumbling blocks. The travel officer and other people Harel recruited in Paris to help him (without telling them the purpose) were forced to undergo a long series of innoculations and medical examinations in a variety of names so that the necessary documentation could eventually be placed into the right passport.

The main difficulty, which was to turn out to be a blessing, was that Argentina was celebrating the hundred and fiftieth anniversary of its independence. The Argentinian authorities, expecting political leaders and heads of state from all over the world, were extremely jumpy about security. So not only did the Israeli documents have to be of the highest standard, but the team itself had to observe the most rigorous conspiratorial techniques to keep clear of the Argentinian authorities as well as to avoid alerting Eichmann.

One passport and one set of papers are seldom enough for an agent operating abroad. If the authorities get on to him, they will do so initially in the name under which he is traveling. So if he is to have any chance to make a getaway, he must be able to change identities in midstream. Sometimes he can hope to secrete an extra set of papers in the false bottom of a suitcase, but that is risky and potentially disastrous. It needed only one customs officer to sense there was something not quite right about any one of the Israelis, order a thorough search, find a false passport, and the whole mission could have been compromised. Because that could not be allowed to happen, a documentation expert who would be prepared to make up new documents on the spot was brought in as a member of the team. Given the name Shalom Dani by Isser Harel in his book on the Eichmann affair, he was one of Mossad's most talented forgers, a genius in his field. Dani entered Argentina with all the tools of his trade—the various cards and delicate paper, the extraordinary range of inks, the array of pens and brushes and so forth—all quite unremarkable to the customs officials because Dani was an "artist" according to his passport. He even carried with him an example of his "oeuvre," which was made up of so many architectural details, so many tiny scrolls, detailed letterings and facets that no one could reasonably doubt his need for such specialized paraphernalia.

Eli Yuval was another member of the team chosen because of a special talent. He is one of Mossad's top make-up artists as well as someone with the mechanical and technical ability to put his hand to anything. When a man is being watched, as Eichmann was for many days before his capture, one problem for any team limited in number is that sooner or later someone will begin to notice the same agents in the same cars in the same area. Cars are easy enough to change. The Israelis simply hire the vehicles they need, then turn them in for different ones after a short time. Eli Yuval's job was to "change" the people, too.

Dina Ron was the only female member of the team, a full-time Mossad operative. Her role was to be the "girl friend" of the operative who had rented the safe house in which Eichmann was to be kept after his capture until he could be moved. It was a passive role but a vital one in order to maintain "normality" in case of police inquiry.

The safe-house situation itself seems extraordinary. The Israelis actually rented seven houses or apartments for this one operation. The first was an apartment in the city given the code name Maoz, or Stronghold, which was to be the headquarters of the whole operation; here Shalom Dani would do his work, and here Isser Harel could meet his team and direct operations, particularly at the early stages. Another safe house was code named Tira, or Palace, and was designed as a possible prison for Eichmann after his capture. Others were rented and kept as reserve houses in case a widespread search was mounted for Eichmann and he had to be moved to other hiding places or in the event that any members of the team needed new places to lie low.

What with the numbers of cars which the team needed to rent and the seven houses, the amount of documentation Shalom Dani had to prepare from his workroom in Moaz was quite enormous. Nobody is going to rent a house to a casual stranger who is not armed with references, bank accounts, and a great deal of "paper." And it was obviously important that the houses were not rented in the names used by the team as they entered the country or the names which they were likely to use when they left. There could be no trace left of any of them. There is no greater problem for any secret-service operation than this vexing and even nightmarish question of identities and the documentation required to back them up. When Ehud Revivi, second in command of the assault team, checked into his hotel in Buenos Aires on first arrival and presented his passport, he was unlucky enough to draw a reception clerk who came from the same home town as Revivi gave on his passport, a town Revivi had never been to in his life. The clerk chatted away happily about local people and sights, and when Revivi reached for the visitor's form to complete it, the clerk just told him to sign and he would fill in the rest himself. But Revivi, by now in a complete panic, had totally forgotten his cover name and had quickly to seek an excuse to get his passport back to take a look.

Isser Harel himself, despite having Maoz as an operational headquarters, used an extremely effective technique in order to keep in touch with the whole team during the initial surveillance and during the operation itself. Every member of the team was given an itinerary of cafés in Buenos Aires which Harel would use as a kind of mobile headquarters. Harel would spend the first half of every hour in one café and use the second half to walk to the next. Only if meetings lasted more than an hour would he take a taxi. It was an exhausting schedule for him, but it did mean that very few meetings would ever be held in the same café more than once. If he were noticed at all in any single café, it would only be as someone who stopped in for an occasional coffee and who on rare occasions was joined by another. Nothing could be apparently more innocent or less conspiratorial than that. On the actual day of the operation and immediately after it, Harel stepped up the pace and cut the time sequences by a half so that he was virtually at all times in touch with or at least available to the members of the team. Not for the first time in an intelligence operation, the national airline, El Al, was pressed into service. Harel persuaded the directors to make a Britannia available, officially to fly in the Israeli delegation led by Abba Eban, who was then the Israeli Permanent Delegate to the United Nations, but in actuality in order to have transport available to fly Eichmann out after his capture.*

The plan worked perfectly. The special plane flew into Buenos Aires and unloaded its V.I.P. delegation to attend the independence ceremonies. While it was on its way, Rafael Arnon, a young Israeli who happened to be in Buenos Aires, was prevailed upon to feign sickness and have himself admitted into hospital suffering from vertigo as a result of a motorcar accident. He was provided with symptoms by an Israeli doctor and was carefully instructed so that he would be released on the day the special flight was leaving with a certificate from the hospital showing that he required further medical attention. Eichmann was going to be taken aboard drugged and dressed as an El Al crew member, but if the crew car was stopped by customs, then Arnon's papers, including the genuine medical certificate, could be shown. As it happened, this proved unnecessary. For two or three weeks, a senior El

* Abba Eban was not told the real purpose behind the special flight, and, when he discovered it, angrily denounced those responsible for compromising his own diplomatic status by making it appear that he was an active participant in a breach of international law thus reducing his moral stature at the United Nations. His mood was not helped when an Isser Harel remark drifted back to him to the effect that the only man in Israeli official life who would not for a moment wonder why an El Al Britannia was being made available for him—and, indeed, would regard it simply as showing proper deference to his position—was Abba Eban. Eban, many believe, got his own back when Harel left the service. Harel was anxious to publish his account of the Eichmann capture, but because of Eban's resistance in Cabinet had to wait fifteen years before his book got into print. Amusingly perhaps, though the names of other V.I.P. passengers on the special flight figure in the book, Abba Eban's name appears nowhere. Harel has always had a long memory.

Al staff man had lived almost day and night at the airport making arrangements for the special flight and ingratiating himself with customs and airport workers. He sat in the front seat of the El Al car as it approached the barrier leading to the tarmac and was cheerily waved on his way. At exactly five minutes past midnight on May 21, 1960, the Britannia lifted off the tarmac of Buenos Aires airport, and Adolf Eichmann, the mindless petty bureaucrat who had so efficiently organized the slaughter of six million Jews, was on his way to the gallows.

Chapter 11

ISSER HAREL'S PRESTIGE and authority were now at their height; yet within a few months of his return to Israel in triumph with Adolf Eichmann, the seeds of Harel's destruction were sown. As we have seen, Harel owed his position and his unique status not merely to his remarkable abilities, but to the absolute loyalty he had shown David Ben-Gurion, and the Prime Minister had reciprocated in full. Their relationship meant that few dared criticize Harel's actions or call into question his view of the function of a modern intelligence agency.

This relationship began to come apart over what is known in Israel as the Israel Ber case. Ber, one of the most influential men in the country, was military adviser to Ben-Gurion and a penetrating military theorist with an international reputation, as well as being the official historian of the Israeli Army. He had a colorful biography, had fought with the International Brigade in Spain, had enjoyed a distinguished career in the Haganah, and now, in the early sixties, was much sought after at home and abroad as a lecturer and writer on military affairs.

Dr. Ber was not a pleasant man either in looks or manner. He was contemptuous of those he regarded as beneath him, condescending and arrogant. Up to 1953, he had been far to the left in Israeli politics, then almost overnight he switched allegiance and became one of Ben-Gurion's most loyal supporters. Many people—including Moshe Dayan—mistrusted him from the beginning, but none more than Isser Harel, who regarded Ber with the deepest suspicion and loathing. For years Harel had hugged to himself the thought that Israel Ber was a Soviet agent. Several times Harel had had reason to warn him about taking classified documents out of the Ministry of Defense to his home, and several times Ber had complained to Ben-Gurion about Harel's attitude toward him. Ben-Gurion had taken Ber's side, and when Harel proposed that Ber be kept under surveillance for a limited period, Ben-Gurion had expressly and frostily forbidden Harel to do anything of the sort. Then, according to the official report on March 31, 1961, Isser Harel was preparing to go to the theater when the telephone rang at his home. The chief of counterespionage of Shin Bet was on the other end, demanding a meeting immediately.

His agents, he said, had been tailing a Soviet diplomat who was suspected of engaging in espionage in Israel. They had watched the Soviet agent give a black briefcase to a man he met in the street. That man was Israel Ber. Without informing Ben-Gurion or anyone else, Isser Harel arrested Israel Ber that night; shortly after, Ber confessed to having been a Soviet spy since the Suez war. The stories he had told about his life before he came to Israel proved to be all fiction. Instead of fighting in Spain, he had been a small-time clerk in a Zionist organization in Vienna. Yet he was a kind of genius, a man with a brilliant mind, who sold his country's secrets to the Soviet Union not simply because he needed the money, but because he believed that Israel had not granted him the honors he felt were his due.*

Ben-Gurion's reaction to Israel Ber's arrest was a mixture of horror that his military adviser was a Soviet agent and fury at the way Isser Harel had handled it. Ben-Gurion found it difficult to believe that Harel's agents had

---

* Some Israeli writers persist in describing Ber as Israel's Philby. This is something of an exaggeration. Ber, of course, did have access to sensitive material, much of it no doubt of great value to the Soviet Union. But he never reached a position whereby he was privy to the really major secrets of the country. Even as Ben-Gurion's military adviser, he did not have the security clearance for that.

happened upon the meeting between Ber and his Soviet case officer by chance. What was more likely was that, contrary to Ben-Gurion's direct instructions, Harel had ordered that Ber be put under Shin Bet surveillance. The fact that Ben-Gurion was out of town when the arrest took place only added to his suspicion that Isser Harel had flouted Ben-Gurion's authority, and had done so in such a manner as to cause the Prime Minister maximum embarrassment.

Human nature being what it is, the fact that Isser Harel had turned out to be right and the Prime Minister wrong did not much help matters. David Ben-Gurion set an exaggerated premium upon whether or not he could trust his closest associates. Those whom he trusted were permitted remarkable liberties, those who were not were kept at arm's length—and heaven help those who had once been in the former category and in Ben-Gurion's eyes had betrayed him!

David Ben-Gurion could be grossly unjust, and so he now was to Harel. Hurt and bewildered, Harel reacted badly, too, and began making common cause with those in and out of government who were seeking Ben-Gurion's removal from public life. Harel believed his own position was unassailable: the man who had caught Eichmann and exposed Israel Ber could not be disposed of lightly. Nevertheless, Harel's great sheet anchor was gone. Criticisms that had been muted began to be expressed more openly, and Harel's next big case brought those criticisms very much to a head. To Israelis, this extraordinary story became known as the Schumacher case.

Yosselle Schumacher was an eight-year-old boy who, in 1960, with the help of the boy's grandfather, had been kidnaped by a fanatically religious Jewish sect from his parents, whom the grandfather had reason to believe were not prepared to bring him up as an Orthodox Jew.

Religion has been a divisive factor in the State of Israel from the very beginning. The Labor Party, Mapai, never had an overall majority, and in order to carry out its program had to rely upon the votes of members returned to the Knesset by Orthodox Jewish parties. In return for their support on other matters, these religious parties imposed upon the government many of the strict laws of Orthodoxy, which only a very small proportion of the population actually subscribed to in their daily lives.

What may not be generally known is that within Israel is also an ultra-Orthodox community who are deeply and passionately opposed to the State of Israel itself; they believe the State of Israel is an abomination in the sight of God, a heresy equal in its awfulness to when the people of Israel worshiped a golden calf while Moses spoke to the Lord on Mount Sinai. For the Bible, which foretold the dispersal of the people of Israel, also foretold that they would come together again only at the Last Judgment.

These ultra-Orthodox Jews regularly petition the United Nations about the illegality of the State of Israel —an illegality not, as the Palestinians would have it, in the sight of man but in the sight of God. Their enemy is not the Arabs but the government of Israel and those Jews who have dared to defy the ordinance of the Almighty, who have dared to restore Israel, to gather in the wandering Jew, before God has given His signal.

Ida and Alter Schumacher, a tailor by profession, had come from Poland to Israel in 1957 with their two children, Zina and Joseph, whom the family called Yosselle. Ida's father, Nahman Shtarkes, was a tough Orthodox Jew of the old school who had faced everything that life could throw at him and still come out on the other side with his zeal undiminished. Three things kept him going: his religion—he was a member of an ultra-Orthodox sect known as the Hassidim of Breslau—his family, and his hatred of Communist Russia. He had good reason to hate. During the Second World War he had been sent to the Gulag Archipelago, lost one eye, and saw his youngest son murdered by a bunch of Jew-baiting Russians. He had preceded his daughter and his son-in-law to Israel, and welcomed them ecstatically, though Alter Schumacher, his son-in-law, was not sufficiently Orthodox to be the man he would have chosen for his daughter himself.

The Schumachers found life in Israel difficult. After a long period of unemployment Alter finally found a job as a textile worker; his wife worked as a photographer's assistant. They decided to buy a small apartment in a suburb of Tel Aviv, but in order to do so they were forced to make many financial sacrifices, even to the extent of sending their children away from home for what they hoped would be a brief period. Zina was sent to a religious institution to live and Yosselle to his adoring grandfather.

In one of Ida Schumacher's letters to an old friend in Russia, she had complained about life in Israel, questioning the wisdom of ever having left Russia in the first place and hinting that they might want to return. Somehow this letter got into the hands of old Nahman, and he took these lamentations of a woman in great distress literally. Not only would his daughter be taking his grandson back to the land Nahman hated above all others, but also, he assumed, the child would be converted to Christianity there. His one duty now in the face of God was to save Yosselle's soul.

In late December 1959, with the fortunes of the Schumachers slowly improving, the parents called at old Nahman Shtarkes' house to bring their son home again. But Yosselle wasn't there. Slowly it dawned on them that Grandfather Nahman was not going to let them have their child back.

The Schumachers called in the police. On January 15th the Court of Appeal in Israel ordered the old man to return Yosselle to his parents; he refused to do so. Two months later the police reported to the court that it was unlikely that any one could find the child.

As Nahman was carted off to prison for contempt of court, a national storm broke over his head. He himself refused to say anything. He had done his sacred duty. The police were convinced that, in any case, others had helped to spirit the boy away and that he was in the hands of the ultra-Orthodox. The country was divided right down the middle. The Chief Rabbi of Jerusalem, Rabbi Frank, endorsed old Nahman's position and called upon the faithful to come to his aid. The Supreme Court called the kidnaping "the most despicable crime ever to have been committed in the whole history of Israel." Orthodox ranged against non-Orthodox. Israel was on the verge of a kind of holy war.

In March 1962, with the boy already gone for over two years, Isser Harel told his astonished senior executives that he had undertaken to Ben-Gurion to find Yosselle; as in the Eichmann case he would require virtually the full resources of the agency to help him. This time, however, even his own people questioned his judgment. Joel Morab, the chief of Shin Bet, argued furiously that this was a matter for the police, a social and religious question that had nothing to do with Israel's secret intelligence agencies. But Harel was adamant. The boy, he said, must be brought home to his parents. Israel's Secret Service had social as well as political duties to perform. The opposition to Mossad involvement from all sides only seemed to make Isser Harel more determined. Yosselle would be found, and Harel would do it. So it was that Operation Tiger was born.

One thing was certain: Yosselle had been spirited out of Israel long ago. So Harel, once again personally in charge of the operation, moved his headquarters to the Mossad office in Paris in order to be better able to direct his forces, and his agents began the long job of scouring the world. There were ultra-Orthodox communities in Italy, Austria and France, they existed in Switzerland, Great Britain, Belgium and South Africa, and most particularly of all they were to be found in America. But, ironically, the Israeli Secret Service, which had so little trouble infiltrating Arab countries, had considerable difficulty making any significant inroads into these Jewish Orthodox communities. Trained to act as Moslems if necessary, none of the agents really knew how to behave like ultra-Orthodox Jews. As one agent complained to Isser Harel, every gesture gave him away. Centuries of persecution had equipped the Orthodox—much more so than their non-Orthodox brothers—with an almost extrasensory, built-in alarm system which warned them of the approach of strangers and allowed them to pick up threats to the community as soon as they arose. Isser Harel's much-vaunted operatives were reduced to impotence in the face of these extraordinary people, their co-religionists.

But just as these communities had a feel for danger, Isser Harel had a feel for the truth. Since his earliest days in intelligence, he had been reading files, learning how to draw conclusions from a series of apparently unrelated incidents. Most of the reports his agents brought back, along with the film they had shot secretly inside the Orthodox communities, had produced nothing. Yet Harel knew that somewhere, in one or another of these communities, Yosselle Schumacher was being kept hidden. It was a flash of the purest inspiration that opened the case up— the kind of second sight only the great detectives possess. Isser Harel had managed to recruit one Orthodox Jew called Meir to help in the search. One day in casual conversation in Paris with Harel and some of his lieutenants, Meir told a story he had heard from a group of ultra-Orthodox Jews living in France who were all followers of a remarkable local rabbi, a great scholar and teacher, regarded as something of a holy man, an Old Testament prophet reincarnated.

According to Meir, during the war a beautiful blue-eyed young French girl had fallen under the influence of this rabbi and had been converted to Judaism. Thanks almost entirely to her, the community had survived the Nazi occupation. Able to move at will among both the Jewish and the French communities, with a natural aptitude for clandestine activities, she had been the perfect link between the community and the French Resistance and had persuaded the Resistance to protect this small band of Jews from the Nazis.

To everyone else listening this was merely a good story. To Isser Harel, it was the break he had been waiting for. With nothing to go on save Meir's account, without even the woman's name or present whereabouts, Isser Harel to the amazement of his colleagues turned his entire investigation to a massive effort to find the girl. If Yosselle had been smuggled out of Israel, Harel argued, then someone completely trusted by the Orthodox community, yet able to pass as non-Orthodox, would have to be involved. There would be few such people in the world; this Frenchwoman was one of them.

Her name was Madeleine Féraille; she had fought with the French Resistance during the war and as a result had come into contact with the Orthodox community. After the war she did some business with the community in imports and exports, and, in 1951, divorced her Catholic husband Henri because she had fallen in love with a young rabbi. She converted to Judaism and followed her new husband to Israel, changing the name of Claude, her son by her first marriage, to Ariel. When her husband left her she sought consolation in extreme Orthodoxy. She dressed in the prescribed manner, obeyed the laws of Judaism precisely, and lived in the Orthodox community in Jerusalem.

Having taken the Jewish name of Ruth Ben-David, she remained for a time in Israel before returning to Europe. A check with Immigration in Tel Aviv established that she had visited Israel twice during the period that Yosselle could have been abducted. It was enough to change what had been till then in Isser Harel's mind only a hunch into hard conviction. She was quickly tracked down by Mossad agents outside Epernay near Rheims in France.

Mossad men piled into the town to find out all they could about her. They quickly established that she had frequent contacts with a London jewel merchant called Joseph Domb. His file, too, was Telexed from Tel Aviv, and it showed precisely what Harel expected. He belonged to the fanatical Satmar sect, a sect that was bitterly anti-Zionist and anti-Israel. Domb was a member of a branch of the Satmar in north London, and what was more, Shalom Shtarkes, the son of old Nahman Shtarkes, was living in London, too.

The problem facing Isser Harel was that though he believed Madeleine had been responsible for spiriting the child out of Israel, it was quite possible that in the interests of security she would not now know where the child was, even though there were apparent references to him in the letters to her son in Israel Harel had arranged to have intercepted. And there was no more chance, Harel knew, of getting Joseph Domb to talk than there had been of persauding Shtarkes to do so. Merely to take in Madeleine would be to gain little information worth having and at the same time would warn the Satmar that Mossad was hard on their tracks.

Isser Harel had already in fact decided that one man was worth watching. His name was Rabbi Shai Freyer, a mohel, that is, a rabbi who specializes in circumcising newborn boys. Rabbi Freyer's name had come up frequently during the investigation. He was a man who liked to travel, deeply anti-Zionist, greatly religious, and yet, as was apparent from the way he operated, was not averse to ensuring that his arcane profession produced the maximum possible income. Operation Tiger, from being a straightforward search, now turned into an espionage operation of remarkable sophistication, the purpose of which was to get both Madeleine and Rabbi Freyer into Israeli safe houses in the same city at the same time so that they could be simultaneously subjected to questioning.

Isser Harel and his team set about working out the details of what is known in the trade as a "gambit." There could be no question of simply kidnaping one or other of them; neither were nationals of Israel, the Israeli team was operating outside its national boundaries, and the international uproar if anything went wrong could be imagined. The means Isser Harel chose were as elegant as anyone could expect to find in a spy novel—and illustrate perfectly the lengths to which an espionage service must sometimes go in order to achieve its ends. By then Yosselle's safe return to Israel had become as important to Harel as any operation he had conducted. It had become an obsession.

Rabbi Shai Freyer was the first fish the Israeli team sought to land. In June 1962 a man called upon another mohel in Paris. The man, swearing the rabbi to secrecy before he spoke, told a remarkable story. He was, he said, in perfect French, the son of an important official in Morocco. He had fallen in love, he said, with a beautiful Moroccan Jewess and in time had abducted her and forced her to marry him. In order to gain her love he had converted to Judaism, and had married her, secretly, in a Jewish ceremony. In public, he appeared the devout Moslem, but in private with his wife, he followed the laws of Judaism. His wife, said the young man, had now given birth to a son in London, and he needed a mohel who could carry out the circumcision rite, yet keep his secret. If his father or any of his relatives discovered the truth, the young couple and their child might lose their lives.

The rabbi suggested that he bring the child to Paris so that he could perform the ceremony himself, but the prince rejected that immediately. Paris, he said, was too dangerous; there were many too many North Africans living in the city. He would invite the mohel to London, he said, but it was a dangerous undertaking and the prince advised against it. The rabbi had no desire, whatever the fee, to expose himself to trouble, and at the young prince's urging, wrote a letter of introduction couched in the vaguest of terms to Dr. Homa, the president of the association of Orthodox mohels in London. A few days later, the prince, accompanied by a friend and confidant, called upon Dr. Homa. This time the prince had a slightly different story to tell. His wife, he said, was in Morocco, recovering from childbirth, but was prepared to travel to the Continent for the circumcision ceremony. All expenses for a mohel's trip would, of course, be paid, and the fee would be a handsome one. However, the mohel would have to be a man used to travel, at home in the world at large.

The "gambit" had been perfectly played. Dr. Homa immediately suggested Rabbi Freyer as the only possible candidate for such a job and wrote a letter of introduction to him for the Israelis. It is worth pausing for a moment to ask why Mohel Freyer was not approached from the very beginning, instead of going through this rather complex charade. In an operation of this kind nothing can be left to chance. If a first approach had been made to Freyer and he had rejected it, perhaps feeling that things were not quite right, well, that would have been the end of that. As it was, he was psychologically ready to believe what he had been told because the visitors who now came to see him in London had been recommended to him by a man of great repute, utterly trustworthy. If Homa hadn't recommended Freyer but someone else, difficulties would have been put in the way of the other candidate until, inevitably, Freyer's name would come up, suggested not by the prince but by a member of the Orthodox community. In fact, the gambit was so well played that the Israelis got to their man after only two moves.

Freyer was delighted to receive the commission. He would, he said, travel anywhere, even Morocco if necessary. The prince, swearing him to secrecy once again, told him that he would go to Morocco, collect his wife and son, and then rent an apartment in Geneva on June 20th so that the ceremony could be conducted there. The rabbi was given first-class air tickets and money to cover his other expenses, and he promised to be present.

In the meantime, a gambit was being worked out for Madeleine. This was a bit more difficult. A proposal that her son in Israel be held as a kind of ransom was rejected on the grounds that she might well seek the support of the Orthodox community, who would report the story to the international press, causing grave embarrassment to Israel. Nevertheless, for all its flaws, that seemed the most promising plan of the many considered and rejected until chance played into Isser Harel's hands. Chance, of course, needs to be helped along, and for months Mossad had been intercepting Madeleine Féraille's mail. One letter turned out to be a reply to an advertisement she had apparently placed in a newspaper offering her country house for sale. It was the perfect means of approach. Immediately, one of Harel's men wrote to the box number offering more money than she was asking, explaining that he represented an international company looking for a country house in France to be used as a vacation home for its executives. Madeleine accepted the bait and a few days later was showing a representative of the company around the house. It was, he said, exactly what they were looking for and told her he would recommend purchase. The company wanted to move fast, he said, and explaining to her that his principals would be in Geneva on June 21st, he asked her to meet him and his superiors at the Hotel Beau Rivage so that they could sign the papers and hand over a check. She agreed immediately to be there.

Shai Freyer arrived on schedule and was met at the airport by his Moroccan prince and driven straight to the apartment in Geneva. It was while he was actually laying out his instruments that to his astonishment several other men walked into the room, sat down, and began asking him about Yosselle. With an awful feeling of finality, Freyer immediately understood what had happened. He was in the hands of Mossad. He had fallen into a trap. There was a shock in store for Isser Harel as well, several hours later, anxiously waiting in another apartment for news. Not only had Freyer denied all knowledge of the boy, Harel was told, but his interrogators were convinced he was telling the truth. Harel's instructions were firm: Freyer was to be told that he would not be released until the boy was found on the grounds that to do so would breach security of Operation Tiger. Freyer had become prisoner of the Israeli Secret Service in the heart of Switzerland.

The following morning Madeleine arrived, looking extremely elegant. (As Ruth Ben-David, in the company of Orthodox Jews, she wore the clothes of a devout Jewess. When dealing with the outside world, she was very much the Frenchwoman, Madeleine Féraille.) Speaking in English, she opened negotiations about her house in the lobby of the Beau Rivage. After an hour or so, a message came from the lawyer they were expecting saying that he had been held up on another deal; since all the relevant papers were at his house, he suggested that they meet there for the sake of speed and convenience. Madeleine agreed immediately. Shortly they arrived at a small but elegant house on the outskirts of the city. As Madeleine walked through the door, another agent telephoned Isser Harel, who had set up a communications network with Tel Aviv in his Geneva apartment; a message was flashed to headquarters, who, in turn, and within seconds, communicated with a certain radio car in Beer Yaacov. Two Shin Bet agents got out of the car, went up to Ariel Ben-David, Madeleine's son, and told him that he was under arrest. A brilliantly conceived operation had come to fruition. Everything now depended upon whether either of these two prisoners knew where Yosselle was and whether they could be persuaded to cooperate.

Madeleine, when she realized what had happened to her, contemptuously refused to do anything of the sort. In any case, Isser Harel, quite aware that an ex-member of the French Resistance was not likely to respond to ill-treatment, ensured that she had every comfort. Unlike Rabbi Freyer, she did not say, "I do not know anything"; instead she said, "I will _tell_ you nothing." But in the meantime, in Tel Aviv, Ariel Ben-David was being a little more cooperative. He admitted that his mother had helped in the kidnaping, and this admission was used against Madeleine, along with threats that Ariel would get a stiff prison sentence for aiding and abetting if she did not now help the authorities.

After forty-eight hours, it was clear that no one was getting anywhere, so Isser Harel himself moved out of the shadows, arrived at the house and confronted Madeleine across a table. Slowly and carefully, watching every word, he spelled out the moral wrong which had been done the boy's parents. No one, he said, was fighting religion; they were fighting for the right of parents to bring up their child as they wished. They were also fighting to unite Israel, not divide it as this issue had done.

Everyone in the room knew that this was the point of no return. She would either crack now or she would retreat even further behind the wall she had erected around herself. As if playing for time, she asked Isser Harel to prove that he was who he said he was, an authorized representative of the government of Israel. Without a moment's hesitation—and to the utmost astonishment of his men—he pulled out his diplomatic passport, made out in his own rightful name, and pushed it across the table to her. Both the spider and the fly now lay exposed to each other—and for several minutes each said nothing.

Suddenly it came out in a rush. The boy, now called Yankele, was with the Gertner family, 126 Penn Street, Brooklyn, New York. And then she burst into tears.

Mossad immediately sent a message to Ambassador Avraham Harman in Washington, telling him to inform the FBI. Harman suggested there might be difficulties. The Satmar sect controlled a huge chunk of votes in New York, and America was in the middle of congressional elections. Exasperated, Isser Harel got on the telephone himself to Harman and, despite or perhaps because of Harman's hints that the FBI might be monitoring the call, told him to approach Attorney General Robert Kennedy immediately and demand instant action. That was enough. Within hours, accompanied by a resident Mossad agent in Washington, the FBI had Yosselle in their hands, and on July 4th he landed at Tel Aviv airport to be reunited with his deliriously happy parents.

As for Madeleine, when Isser Harel found out how capably she had managed getting Yosselle out of Israel on a passport she herself had doctored, dressing him as a girl, taking him to America and putting him in the safekeeping of the Gertner family, he knew that she was a natural agent, and he immediately offered her a job. But, suffused with guilt, she turned him down and eventually married the seventy-two-year-old head of Neturey-Karta, one of the most fanatical of all of the sects in Mea Shearim, the Orthodox quarter of Jerusalem.

So "the Yosselle affair," as the Israeli public knew it, or Operation Tiger, as it was known within Mossad, was triumphantly concluded. The whole operation was a good illustration of Isser Harel and his methods, and showed the magnificent Harel intuition at its sharpest. Here was a man who was prepared to play his hunches to the limit—and to operate outside the law in a foreign country confident that the ends would justify whatever action he took.

All these were the very great strengths of a very great intelligence chief. They were also, at one and the same time, his weaknesses and would, not long after Yosselle came home, prove to be Harel's undoing.

PART IV

End of an Era

Chapter 12

IN 1958, after Fatti Harkabi had been forced to resign as chief of Military Intelligence, the Army had turned once more in desperation to Colonel Chaim Herzog, the man who had first formed the unit under Isser Be'eri and had already once served as director after Be'eri was disgraced. Herzog was brought out of retirement, given his general's stars and asked to resume command. It was a wise and profitable move.

Mossad's Isser Harel was then at the zenith of his career and influence. There was simply no point in having at the head of Military Intelligence a man who would be bound to clash with the powerful head of Mossad.

Chaim Herzog is a man of great ability and a fine speaker, a man constitutionally incapable of joining internecine intrigues. Yet he has always been sufficiently a personality in his own right to ensure that whatever else happened, the flag of Military Intelligence would be kept flying. A natural diplomat, with enough of the politician in him to keep his head in the upper strata of Israeli politics, extraordinarily articulate and persuasive, a brilliant organizer, Herzog managed to keep Military Intelligence as a credible organization during a period when Mossad was very much king of the castle.

It is an extraordinary fact that when Herzog finally retired in 1962, he was the first Israeli chief of Military Intelligence to do so in the ordinary course of events. Each of the other chiefs of Military Intelligence—Be'eri, Gibli and Harkabi—had been forced out, their careers clouded by scandal. Herzog's greatest achievement was to restore to Military Intelligence its self-respect, and in so doing to make possible the appointment of General Meir Amit—which would in time lead to an historic shakeup of the entire Israeli intelligence community.

Meir Amit was a soldier's soldier, one of the first of the

Israeli commanders who would regard it as not only right but natural to lead from the front lines. He was a flamboyant personality who while serving as Moshe Dayan's second in command during the Suez campaign had learned the importance of being a general who is seen and known by the troops—not necessarily liked but always respected.

He had risen from the most traditional of Israeli backgrounds. His mother had been an early pioneer, and he was born in Tiberias, then moved near Tel Aviv. For most of his life before entering the Army, he lived and worked on a kibbutz, and he developed much of the personality of a typical kibbutznik—independent, somewhat arrogant, a bit contemptuous of those who lived in towns. He served as a company commander in the War of Independence, and first came to Dayan's attention in 1951, when Dayan was in charge of the Southern Command and Meir Amit was one of his brigade commanders. In May of that year, Amit led an attack on a Syrian position on the Israeli side of the Jordan River's entrance to Lake Kinneret. In the face of withering Syrian fire, Amit pressed ahead with the attack until the Syrians were driven back, but twenty-seven Israeli soldiers were killed in the action and many others wounded. Amit came under harsh criticism from GHQ for persisting in the attack when his losses were so high, but Dayan, who visited the area twice after the troops returned and closely cross-examined the young Colonel Amit, rejected these criticisms out of hand. The action, he said, far from being a failure as GHQ maintained, was a success. The objective had been achieved, and the officers and men of the attack force had shown the kind of spirit Israel needed—courage and perseverance under the most adverse conditions.

When Dayan became Chief of Staff, he appointed Meir Amit as his chief of Operations and thus the second ranking officer in the Army. During the Suez war, Dayan spent most of his time on the battlefield flitting between command posts, leaving Amit as chief of Operations to run the war. It was an extraordinary opportunity for a man everyone believed would inevitably become Chief of Staff of the Israeli Army. But, in 1958, two years after Suez, his career was abruptly terminated. Strongly believing in the concept of a "fighting general," Amit took a refresher course at a paratroop training establishment and went up for a practice run; when he jumped, his chute only partially opened. For days, it was a question whether he would live or die, but he pulled through. His army career, however, seemed at an end.

After he spent eighteen months in the hospital, the Israeli government under its retraining program for retired senior officers sent him to Columbia University to take a master's degree in business administration. He chose to write as his thesis a paper which compared the military —one extreme of society where everyone has rank and knows his place, where orders are given and received, where everything is on paper, where there's a "book" to go by—with another Israeli societal grouping, the kibbutz. He came to the conclusion that the unwritten laws of the kibbutz could have an even more powerful effect upon its members than did the written laws of the Army on its soldiers. It seemed to him that this was relevant to the Army—that if soldiers understood what they were doing and why they were doing it, then they would do it on their own volition, not because they had been ordered to. It was a concept he was never to forget.

It was his old friend Moshe Dayan who first proposed that Meir Amit would be an outstanding chief of Military Intelligence to take over from Herzog. It was a daring suggestion and one which Isser Harel fought from the beginning. Amit, he argued, had never had any experience whatsoever in intelligence; he was a man of action rather than an administrator, and would, Harel hinted, create precisely the sort of problems which Gibli, a soldier out of a similar mold, had.

But Army Chief of Staff Zvi Zur was prevailed upon to make the strongest representations to David Ben-Gurion, still doubling as Prime Minister and Minister of Defense, that the Army must be allowed to appoint its own senior men without outside interference, and Meir Amit was gazetted as chief of Military Intelligence.

Virtually overnight the relationship between Mossad and Military Intelligence changed dramatically. Meir Amit was not the kind of man easily able to play second fiddle to anyone; neither, having worked for Dayan all those years, was he prepared to mince words when he believed that things were not going quite right. He had one enormous advantage over Isser Harel—and indeed over everyone else in the whole of the intelligence establishment in Israel: he had been a battlefield commander, and he knew the importance of good intelligence to the fighting soldier. He constantly enunciated the principle that the bulk of the Israeli intelligence effort should be concentrated upon the "confrontation states," those Arab countries which adjoin Israel, in order to get the intelligence needed by Israel in time of war. The quality of battlefield intelligence was not good enough, he said, because its importance was insufficiently understood by Harel.

Meir Amit became more than chief of Military Intelligence, he became the focal point for those in government and the Army who had been steadily growing more and more critical of Isser Harel's supreme power and the way he was using it.

While Israelis in the know still nudged each other in the street when Isser Harel went by and said, "That's the man who caught Eichmann," Amit loudly expressed the views of those senior army officers who believed that Harel's job was not to chase aging Nazis throughout Latin America but to use the resources he commanded to gather information about the strengths and weaknesses of the Jordanian, Syrian and Egyptian armies.

If the nation and its political leaders regarded these other operations as essential, then it was Harel's duty to ensure that they were not allowed to interfere with Mossad's primary function of giving advance warning of any assault of whatever kind upon the integrity of the State. As Amit saw it, Harel had not discharged that duty.

To attack Isser Harel was to attack a living legend, and there weren't many in Israel who gave Meir Amit much chance of surviving the bruising confrontation they knew would inevitably follow. But Meir Amit was doing more than involving himself in a mere power battle—the by now traditional struggle for ascendancy between Mossad and Military Intelligence. He was proclaiming an alternative philosophy, criticizing the very fundamentals in the way Isser Harel conceived of his job. For the first time Harel was on the defensive. Suddenly and without precedent, he was being forced to justify himself. Up till then ministers who had had run-ins with Isser Harel were told by the Prime Minister when they complained that Isser had a job to do and it couldn't be helped if a few knuckles were bruised in the process. The arrival of Meir Amit changed all that. His message was that if Isser Harel had a job to do, he wasn't doing it very well. He was out-of-date. He was living from day to day, from operation to operation, a kind of super sleuth performing on the world stage instead of as effective head of a modern secret service.

It didn't take long before Meir Amit's argument was bolstered by the march of events. On July 6, 1961, to jubiliation in Israel, the nation had launched its first rocket (calling it "Shavit 2," a bit of misinformation bound to make the Arabs wonder about the secrets of "Shavit 1").

Officially, the Israelis let it be known that the rocket, operating on solid fuel, had been designed for meteorological research purposes. But there wasn't a government in the world which doubted its military applications.

Almost exactly a year later on July 21, 1962, it was Egypt's turn for jubilation: her scientists successfully launched four rockets—two of the Al Zafir (Victory) type, with ranges of 175 miles, and two of the Al Kahir (Conqueror) type, with ranges of 350 miles. President Nasser didn't bother to conceal the purpose of his new weapons. Their names made that plain enough, and Nasser's proud boast that they were capable of destroying any target "south of Beirut" rubbed the point home.

The alarm in Israel was considerable, but it would have been greater still if the general public had realized what a shocked government only now discovered: that Israeli intelligence had virtually nothing on these rockets whatsoever. The Mossad files were empty.

Every warning that Meir Amit and his friends had ever issued abut the danger to Israel of the then-current intelligence strategy—or lack of it—was illustrated as cheering crowds of Egyptians watched the rockets being trundled through Cairo in a military procession marking the anniversary of the revolution. "What are we spending our intelligence budget on," asked Amit rhetorically, "if we get our information from a public speech of Gamal Nasser? All we need for that is a portable radio!"

Brutally stung by these charges, Isser Harel promised Ben-Gurion that he would have all the facts about the rockets on his desk within three months. In actuality, Harel managed to hand the definitive report on Nasser's rocket program to the Prime Minister on August 16, 1962, less than a month after the Egyptian President's announcement.

It had all started during the immediate postwar period, when ex-German-army officers with nowhere to go but into Allied internment camps found that there was a place for them in the sun training the Egyptian Army. Ex-officers of the Afrika Korps who had failed to reach Cairo with Rommel now did so under their own steam. The first batch were men with very good reasons indeed to disappear—people like Leopold Gleim, who had headed the Gestapo in Warsaw, and SS General Oscar Dirlewanger and Willi Brenner, who had helped organize the Mauthausen concentration camp. In 1951 their number was swollen by people with something rather more concrete to offer when General Wilhelm Fahrmbacher, a distinguished artillery officer, arrived with forty ex-Wehrmacht officers, mercenaries prepared to sell their very considerable expertise to the Egyptian Army. Their success can be judged by the fact that after the revolution they were asked to stay on, and indeed Nasser increased their strength considerably. An officer who had been on the staff of General Heinz Guderian became chief adviser to the Egyptian armored brigade. World War II frogmen, demolition experts and paratroopers were drafted into the Egyptian military training schools, and, perhaps most significantly of all, fifteen German test pilots and technicians replaced British experts at the De Havilland aircraft assembly factories which had been set up in Egypt by the British during the days of King Farouk.

The biggest catch of all, however, was a certain Dr. Wilhelm Voss, who had managed the Skoda works during the German occupation of Czechoslovakia and had been a senior figure in the German munitions industry throughout the entire war. He brought in with him a leading German scientist, one of the fathers of German rocketry, Rolf Engel, then working for the French at the National Office of Aeronautical Research, and put him at the head of an Egyptian company called Cerva, charged by the Egyptian government with the design and manufacture of tactical rockets. Just as he had been recruited by Voss, Engel persuaded Paul Goerke, a German electronics engineer who had been at Peenemünde (the top-secret wartime

German research station working on guided missiles), to join him in Cairo.

The first group of scientists and technicians who went to Egypt had not, in fact, been very well treated. Salaries were not high, and money for research was limited. By the time that General Fahrmbacher decided in 1958 that he had had enough and left, the scientists had mostly already gone and Cerva disbanded.

In 1959, President Nasser decided to try again and put General Mahmoud Khalil, a former head of Egyptian intelligence, in charge of a top-secret project called the Bureau of Special Military Programs to provide Egypt with all of the latest weaponry of war, particularly locally manufactured jet planes and rockets, so that Egypt would not have to depend upon the outside world for weapons essential for its continuing struggle against Israel.

Though the Second World War was long since over, Germany was still a fertile recruiting ground for the talent Khalil needed. Under the four-power occupation agreement, Germany was forbidden to manufacture its own rockets and jet planes; any German aeronautical engineer was forced to find work outside Germany if he wished to pursue his chosen profession.

It was because of this very special set of circumstances that the advertisement which Khalil put into several West German newspapers under the help-wanted section "Aeronautical industry in North Africa requires specialists . . ." attracted more replies from distinguished scientists than would appear inherently probable. At the same time, Khalil signed a contract, completely open and above board, with Willy Messerschmidt for him to build an aircraft plant. He also found the ideal man to run it: Ferdinand Brandner, a remarkable Austrian engineer who had been captured by the Russians at the end of the war and offered a deal. If he and his team designed a Russian jet engine for heavy aircraft in five years he would be permitted to go home to Germany. Both sides stuck to the bargain.

Ferdinand Brandner developed a 12,000-horse-power turboprop which was used for the vast Tupolev 114, one of the biggest transport planes in the world. When he had finished his work, Brandner went home, but he found the aeronautics industry in the West rather choosy about the people it employed. Brandner had held the rank of an

SS colonel, and this proved to be a serious disqualification for the kind of work he wanted to do.

By 1960, the Egyptian aircraft industry was ready to start work. Messerschmidt's factory, where the airframes would be built, was close to completion near Cairo with the code name "136," and near by was Brandner's engine plant, code named "135." But Khalil, who was nothing if not ambitious, was also planning to build rockets, which he believed would lead to the eventual destruction of Israel, and the most secret factory of all—code name "333"—was under construction near Heliopolis. Almost certainly without realizing it, the Egyptians had established a perfect screen for their activities at Factory 333. Factories 136 and 135 claimed all Mossad's attention, while 333, employing over a hundred German technicians, escaped detection even after the man put in charge of it had been completely "blown" by the Israeli Secret Service in November 1962. Khalil had found his rocket scientists at the German government-sponsored and financed Stuttgart Institute, a scientific establishment working on weather satellites and the like. Most of the scientists there were deeply frustrated men, very much in the backwater of international rocket technology, men who had not been considered important enough by either the Americans or the Russians to grab after the war for the enormous missile race into which the postwar world had been plunged.

The head of the institute was a Dr. Eugen Sänger, who at the end of the war had been working on a wonder rocket plane, one of the most secret projects then being developed by Hitler's scientists. That was unquestionably the high point in a career which had gone downhill ever since. He had worked for a while for the French, but returned to Germany hoping that the Stuttgart Institute would provide a better setting for a man with his ideas. But the work at Stuttgart was low grade and uninteresting, and Sänger was anxious for a fresh challenge; the Egyptian project, as outlined to him by Khalil, provided just that. The Egyptians were prepared to offer him anything —including the chance to launch his own earth satellite— and naïvely Sänger accepted, despite the fact that the institute was expressly forbidden by the Bonn government to do any work for foreign countries. Sänger recruited virtually the entire institute to work with him. Professor Paul Goerke, the expert in electronics and guidance systems who had worked in Egypt in the fifties, was delighted at the chance of going back. Wolfgang Pilz, who, like Sänger, had once worked for the French on their Véronique rocket, was head of the Stuttgart engine department, and he eagerly agreed to join the team.

There were others, too—men like Dr. Hans Kleinwachter, an electronics expert, and Dr. Ermin Dadieu, head of Stuttgart's chemistry department. The technicians and engineers at the institute didn't need much persuading either, and fresh from their technical schools they went to Egypt in droves. There they were known by the German colony as *Sänger Knaben*—a play on words meaning either Sänger's boys or choir boys. The choir boys were very quickly spotted by Mossad, but it was assumed that they must be working for the aircraft factory.

The flimsy cover story for factories 136 and 135 was that the Germans were building a flight trainer. Mossad knew differently. The Egyptians were attempting to build their own high-performance fighter, and the Israelis even had got hold of some of the blueprints to prove it. This didn't worry Israel unduly.

All the advice that Isser Harel received was that designing a plane of this kind and building it were two very different things. Industrialized countries like Britain and France had found it difficult enough, and however many German technicians the Egyptians imported, it was believed that an underdeveloped country like Egypt simply would not be able to provide even the minimum industrial backup such a project would require.

In 1961, Isser Harel had sufficient information about the activities of the Stuttgart Institute and Dr. Sänger to permit the Israeli government to lodge a formal protest with the Bonn government. Sänger was forced to end his contract with the Egyptian government, but many of his colleagues resigned their positions at the Stuttgart Institute and went and worked for the Egyptians full-time. Extraordinarily enough, a great deal came out at that time about the Egyptian rocket program—that, for example, the Egyptians had promised members of the institute a total of 2,000,000 marks if they produced a rocket, and that more than a quarter of this amount would go to Sänger, who had already received a large advance. Harel's men had also established the identities of Egyptian dummy companies operating in Switzerland and the nature of the scientific equipments and parts that they were shipping to Cairo.

Yet, despite all of this, it hadn't actually occurred to anyone at Mossad to take any of this very seriously—and certainly no one knew that by the time Sänger had been exposed, the Egyptians were already testing engines for liquid-fuel rockets weighing from four to twenty tons, a cross between the old wartime V-2 and the more modern French Véronique.

With the benefit of hindsight, it is almost impossible to understand why no one in Tel Aviv was able to put together the information they possessed and come up with the assumption, based upon pure logic, that there had to be a factory somewhere in Egypt designing and manufacturing rockets. But the fact is that no one did. And, as we have seen, it was only after that huge military procession in July 1962, when an exultant Nasser stood at attention as twenty rockets draped with the Egyptian flag were paraded before him and another four test-launched to prove to the world that these were not mere mock-ups, that Mossad began to assemble the jigsaw of their material.

It has been said that none of the atomic spies did nearly as much damage to the security of the atom bomb as the decision to drop the bomb on Hiroshima. Nothing did as much harm to the security of Egypt's greatest secret than Nasser's proclamation of it to his people. It took Mossad literally three days to discover the whereabouts of Factory 333—and only another three weeks to gather material for Isser Harel to produce his comprehensive report to David Ben-Gurion.

The prime document in Mossad's possession was a letter from Professor Pilz, who had taken over from Sänger as head of the scientific team, to Kamil Azzab, the Egyptian director of the factory, dated March 24, 1962. Pilz asked Azzab for 3.7 million Swiss francs to buy components for 500 Type 2 and 400 Type 5 rockets.

The significance of that letter could not be overstated. Egypt was not merely building rockets for prestige purposes, it was preparing a veritable arsenal to let loose on Israeli cities in time of war.

Isser Harel was now thoroughly alarmed. He had apocalyptic visions of an imminent attack on Israeli centers of population with rockets raining from the skies killing thousands at a single strike.

Conversely, Meir Amit played down the significance of what the Egyptians were doing. Because of the magnificent Military Intelligence research department Amit had inherited from Harkabi and Herzog and the ability of Amit's academically trained research staff to discriminate between hard fact and sheer fantasy, he reported to Shimon Peres, the Deputy Defense Minister, that the Egyptians had a long way to go before they posed any real danger to Israel. All the reports Amit had showed that the Germans and Egyptians were having immense problems in perfecting the proper guidance system and were nowhere near solving them.

As for Isser Harel's dire predictions that the Egyptians were building some kind of doomsday device, Amit dismissed this out of hand. Even if they were planning to stuff their warheads with some fearful explosive, it was highly unlikely that either the Russians or the Americans would ever permit a situation whereby these could be used. It was the considered view of Military Intelligence that Nasser's rockets posed a potential threat to Israel, but were not an immediate danger.

Isser Harel disputed this angrily, but for the first time in many years his advice was not accepted by the Prime Minister. Harel wanted Ben-Gurion to take a strong public position and to inform West German Chancellor Konrad Adenauer that unless every West German citizen working on the rockets was withdrawn, the most serious implications concerning relations between Israel and West Germany would inevitably follow.

It was bad advice—an emotional rather than a practical response to the situation. Such a letter from Ben-Gurion to Adenauer could not have achieved anything. The West German Chancellor would merely have been pushed into a corner from which he would be unable to extricate himself, and relations between the two countries would have to be broken off altogether.

Working to Meir Amit's altogether more balanced conclusions, Shimon Peres suggested a much lower-key approach, a more-in-sorrow-than-in-anger note from him to German Defense Minister Franz Joseph Strauss, advising him of what had occurred and expressing the conviction that the German government must be embarrassed by the knowledge that Germany was assisting the Russians and the Egyptians to destroy Israel. He asked Strauss to say whether he believed that German citizens had the right to manufacture weapons of war in the troubled Middle East, pointed out that the German scientists were working against the West German government's efforts to normalize its relations with the Jewish people, and expressed confidence that the German government would put pressure on the scientists to give up their work.

Isser Harel was far from satisfied by what he regarded as the lily-livered response of the Israeli government to a terrible danger, and he was bitterly angry that his advice had been rejected in favor of what he regarded as the complacent attitude of Military Intelligence. This was not, however, a simple question of two intelligence chiefs falling out. Politics was also very much at the heart of the debate. Amit sided with Ben-Gurion's young lions like Peres and Dayan, who wanted Israel to get closer to Europe—particularly France and Germany, especially as they were prepared to support a nuclear program. Isser Harel supported the Mapai veterans, led by Foreign Minister Golda Meir, who advocated closer relations with the United States and a conventional, non-nuclear arms program.

By now, all of Mossad was working on the Egyptian rockets, and certainly some of the material they produced was alarming. Professor Wilhelm Gross, one of the fathers of the atomic centrifuge, the uranium skimmer, appeared to be in contact with the Egyptians, and it was thought that he could be negotiating the sale of a centrifuge which would permit Nasser to produce fissionable material. The presence in Cairo of a young German woman chemist called Mathilde Rosenfleder was believed to be connected to a chemical-warfare program. Dr. Hans Eisele, who had been a concentration-camp doctor and had fled Germany in 1958 just before he was due to go on trial for crimes against humanity, was also in Egypt. Mossad agents established that he was the medical officer of Factory 135, but the thought that he might be working on bacteriological weapons could not be discounted.

What Isser Harel needed, however, was direct evidence, not mere supposition, to convince the skeptics inside Military Intelligence and their friends in the government

that they were almost criminally playing down the frightening implications of the rocket program. In September
1962, he believed that was what he'd got.

It was brought to him by an ex-officer in the Wehr-
macht, an Austrian scientist called Otto Frank Joklik, who
contacted the Israelis at one of their European embassies. Joklik's story was a remarkable one.

He had just come from Cairo, Joklik said, where he had
been involved in the missile program. The Egyptians, he
said, were working on a "poor man's atomic bomb" containing strontium 90 and cobalt 60. It needed just one to
be dropped on Israel for the soil and the atmosphere to be
poisoned for generations. It was Joklik's job to procure
the materials for the bomb in Europe and get them to the
Egyptians. More investigation by Isser Harel appeared to
confirm the essential validity of the Joklik story, whatever
his motives in coming across. The Egyptians *did* have,
according to him, two top-secret programs, one code
named Cleopatra, for the manufacture of Hiroshima-
type bombs, and the other Ibis, a radioactive weapon
capable of destroying all living things.

Though both the CIA (by now very much involved)
and Meir Amit's Military Intelligence remained obsti-
nately unconvinced throughout all of this, it was difficult
for anyone to escape the general mood of hysteria now
sweeping over the whole of Israel, a mood largely created
by Mossad-inspired scare stories which appeared daily in
the press. With Joklik's testimony bearing out everything
Harel had said, the Harel bandwagon was now unstoppa-
ble.

Harel's solution was a drastic one. As the official approach to the German government had failed to achieve
anything, direct action was called for. If the German
scientists were not prepared to leave Egypt willingly, then
they must be persuaded. Not since the killings of Colonel
Hafez and Colonel Mustapha in 1956 had the Israeli Secret Service employed assassination as a legitimate
weapon in their battle with the Arabs. Isser Harel himself
regarded such measures as morally repugnant and seldom
efficient. It is rare for there to be one man who is so
precious to the other side, so irreplaceable, that his death
would seriously affect the outcome of any struggle save
for in the very short term. But the German scientists in
Egypt fell precisely into that category. Scientists don't

grow on trees. Dispose of or frighten off those working in Egypt then, and it was hard to see where Nasser would find their replacements. "We must make it plain to these gentlemen," said one of Harel's deputies darkly, "that a trip to Cairo is a visit to the front line."

So Operation Damocles (the sword hanging over the head of every German working for the Egyptians) was conceived and planned. The Israeli Secret Service had declared war.

Chapter 13

ISSER HAREL'S INFORMATION about the Egyptian rocket program was coming largely from one of the most remarkable agents that Mossad has ever had in the field. His name was Wolfgang Lotz, one of the truly great characters employed as a spy since the end of the World War II.

The Israeli investment in Lotz had been enormous. His cover was that of a wealthy ex-Wehrmacht officer and horse breeder. To maintain that fiction, not only did he need a stud farm, which he quickly established when he arrived in Cairo at the end of 1960, but the life style to match it. Lotz had always been one of those men born with a positive talent for living well, but without the wherewithal to do it. Now with the part scripted for him in Tel Aviv, he actually became, to all intents and purposes, the gentleman of wealth and background whose role he was required to play.

His new skin fitted him so perfectly that it seemed realer than the real Lotz, who had been a comparatively junior officer in the Israeli Army. Lotz had been born in Mannheim, Germany, in 1921. His father Hans was not Jewish, and was a theater director in Berlin, later appointed director of the Hamburg State Theatre. His Jewish mother Helene was an actress who, after divorcing Hans, emigrated to Palestine with the young Lotz in 1933;

there she sent him to an agricultural school in Ben-Shemen, where he became an expert horseman. At the outbreak of World War II, speaking Hebrew, Arabic, German and English, he joined the British army and spent the whole of the war years in Egypt and North Africa, finishing up with the rank of quartermaster sergeant and the nickname "Rusty" because of the rust-red handlebar moustache he affected. After service with the Haganah, he joined the regular Israeli Army and fought in the Suez war, attaining the rank of major.

It was Military Intelligence, at that time under Harkabi, that first spotted his potential. He had a great deal going for him along with his Teutonic good looks and his flawless German. Because he had a German father, he was entitled to a German passport under his real name and could thus travel to Egypt with perfectly genuine papers. Because his father was not Jewish, it was not hard, either, to construct a German biography for him from 1933 on, when, of course, he had actually left Germany. At that time, he had been a student at the Mommsen Gymnasium in Berlin. His new life simply prolonged his stay at Mommsen until graduation, then put him into the 115th Division of Rommel's Afrika Korps in which he supposedly served throughout the war. During World War II, the British Army had used him as an interrogator of POW's from that very corps, so that he knew the names of units, officers, as well as many details of their exploits. After the war, according to his fictional biography, he had gone to Australia to breed race horses, but returned to Germany out of homesickness only to find the new postwar Germany very little to his liking. Now he was looking for a more congenial part of the world in which to settle down.

In late December 1960, working for Military Intelligence, he had arrived in Egypt and quickly got himself an introduction to the fashionable Cavalry Club in Gezirah. The honorary president of the club was General Youssef Ali Ghorab, officer in charge of the entire Egyptian police force and as such a man of immense influence and prestige. Enormously impressed by this good-looking German, a spectacular horseman who appeared to have a great deal of money to splash around, it was the general who first proposed that Lotz should set up a stud farm in Egypt and settle there permanently breeding Arabian thoroughbreds. Six months later, Lotz, known by his Tel Aviv handlers as "Horse," returned to Europe to report to his masters. He had done more than brilliantly. He had established himself at the highest level of Egyptian society, was a welcome guest at the home of prominent Germans, and had close and warm relations with important senior Egyptian army officers. What was more, he was enjoying life immensely. That sense of introspective loneliness which can hit an agent working in a hostile territory had left him only a few days after arrival. There were problems, however; by becoming the high-living hard-drinking ex-German officer of his cover, Lotz had taken on as well the streak of reckless irresponsibility such a man would almost certainly possess.

The old Lotz would have played it by the rules; the new Lotz, created by Israeli intelligence, found that impossible. He was constantly in trouble about money. Great sums were passed to him to set up his stud farm in Egypt and to maintain the fiction that he was a rich man in his own right. But shortly after he had arrived in Egypt, all special operations were transferred, to Mossad, and so Mossad rather than Military Intelligence became his employers.

Isser Harel's paymasters—echoing Harel's own puritanical approach to money—were not satisfied with Lotz's simple accounting methods: two sheets of paper, one a round figure for income and the other a round figure for expenditure. As far as Isser Harel was concerned, Lotz's stud farm in Cairo was an asset belonging to the Israeli government, and he required a full accounting of how it was run, as well as the number, cost and present value of its horses. On one occasion, Lotz was hauled over the coals when in the books he presented one horse was unaccounted for.

He was told to hand in more detailed explanations as to how he spent such enormous sums of money, and was asked for receipts to justify some of it. Lotz acidly inquired if there was a special Israeli government form he could ask Egyptian generals to whom he had "lent" money to sign. As for the missing horse, he promised to ask the permission of the Egyptian government to receive an auditor from Mossad to go over his establishment in order properly to assess its value. Though he had been moved over to Mossad, his case officer, a colonel in Military Intelligence, stayed the same. He managed to persuade Isser Harel that Lotz's usefulness depended very much upon his buccaneering quality—which made him a good spy though a bad administrator.

But even Lotz's colonel would be astonished—and angered—when he was to discover a year too late an extraordinary breach of discipline, breathtaking even by the standards of "Horse." Naturally enough for this larger-than-life agent, it all began on the Orient Express. He boarded the train on June 3, 1961, from Paris and, being very much a lady's man, chose a compartment occupied by what he described as "a tall, extremely pretty, blue-eyed blonde with the kind of curvacious figure I always had a weakness for." They began talking, and when she got off at Stuttgart, Lotz was determined to see her again. In response to his ardent requests over the telephone, she came to Munich, and within two weeks they decided to get married. Lotz thought of asking the permission of his chief, but rejected it on the very good grounds that it would almost certainly be denied. The problem, of course, was that he couldn't marry Waltraud, who was from Heilbroun in south Germany and a graduate of a Swiss hotel school, without revealing to her that he was a secret agent. Practical reasons—apart from any emotional considerations—made that essential. After all, his main transmitter was hidden in the scales of his bathroom in Cairo! Before they were married, Lotz told Waltraud merely that he was involved in espionage; subsequently, he revealed that he was an Israeli. Waltraud absorbed it all and indeed gloried in the knowledge. Married life was to be exciting indeed.*

* This whole episode is so extraordinary that some experts doubt if it is as simple as it seems. In his excellent book *Gehlen—Spy of the Century* (Random House, 1971), the British journalist and historian E. H. Cookridge, who specializes in espionage affairs, says that the Gehlen organization made a secret agreement with the Israeli Secret Service under which Gehlen agreed to train an Israeli to be infiltrated into Egypt. That Israeli, according to Cookridge, was Wolfgang Lotz. Cookridge states also "it has never been established whether the lady [Waltraud] whom he had brought with him from Germany was also in the game and perhaps attached to

If at first Isser Harel was a bit suspicious of Lotz and his accounting methods, this was soon swept away by the sheer power of his personality, as well as by the nature of his achievement in infiltrating the target area so successfully. Behavior which would have merited the sternest retribution if indulged in by a lesser man, in Lotz was overlooked with amused chuckles. The more outrageous he was, the more Tel Aviv seemed to like him. Spymasters—and Harel was no exception—tend unconsciously to behave a bit like a woman choosing cosmetics, the more expensive the product the better it has to be. Lotz was certainly expensive, and so it was to Lotz that Isser Harel chiefly turned for information on the rockets program.

That decision proved to be a mistake. Lotz had many attributes, but a sharp, analytical mind was not one of them.

Not the kind of man ever to accept that he might be out of his depths, Lotz's transmissions to Tel Aviv, based upon boastful but purely illusory claims of the Egyptian and German sporting and society fraternity with which Lotz mixed, fueled Isser Harel's belief that the Egyptians really were close to perfecting the ultimate weapon in their continuing war against the Israelis.

Operation Damocles, designed to drive German technicians out of Egypt and so bring the whole program to a grinding halt, initially employed Lotz. As an activist, not a thinker, he performed brilliantly.

The first step was to warn the German scientists individually about the personal danger they faced if they continued with their work. Using Lotz as the postman, Isser Harel addressed letters to various scientists, all, of course, bearing Egyptian postmarks to bring home to them that nemesis was at hand.

A typical letter read:

---

him by courtesy of his Pullach [Gehlen's headquarters] instructors."

Cookridge, in fact, is quite wrong to suggest that the German secret service had anything at all to do with Lotz. And Lotz's marriage is one of those bizarre incidents which occur from time to time in "the game" for which it is tempting to seek complex explanations when none exist.

Dear Doctor,

The work you are doing on behalf of the Egyptian government may have a significance in this part of the world which you may not even suspect. While science has no boundaries, similar research being carried out by your colleagues in America, Europe, and even Russia is being done on behalf of governments who at least claim that they have no intention of using the terrible weapons they are manufacturing unless they themselves are attacked first. Of course, if the world is to survive at all, all of us must rely not simply upon the good faith of these governments but that enlightened self-interest will in the end triumph over ideology. It is impossible to believe, however, that the government which you are currently serving so brilliantly can ever be prompted by similar considerations. There can be little doubt that once the weapons systems you are helping to build have been perfected, they will be used in order to wipe Israel from the map. The government of Israel does not believe that it will ever successfully be able to appeal to Egyptian self-interest. It is dealing with a leader and with a government hell-bent on war —irrationally holding to the belief that it will emerge unscathed from the resultant conflagration. I believe, however, that I may be able to appeal to your own sense of self-interest in the hope that I can persuade you to resign your work here and return to Europe. Israel will never permit the Egyptians to manufacture weapons which could destroy Israeli cities and wipe out great centers of population. It must therefore act decisively now to make sure that work on these weapons is never completed. During Wold War II the Allies sought to destroy Peenemünde, its installations and the men who worked there, from the air because of the danger this work posed to their cause. Without actually going to war, which Israel does not want, such a solution is not available to us. That means that individual Israelis worried for the security of their country must seek out and, if necessary, destroy individuals of other nationalities whose work could reduce the dream of 2,000 years to ashes.

I beg of you as a fellow scientist to heed what I say most seriously.

This letter, my dear colleague, must, I regret, go un-signed.

About fifty of these letters, none of which were exactly the same, went out to scientists on all levels. Nobody knows precisely what their effect was. Though some of the more junior staff did leave Egypt, this could well have been because they had finished the work they had been contracted to perform. The letter campaign did, however, have an immediate indirect value. Suddenly, the plush-lined life these scientists had settled into didn't seem so comfortable after all. The leading scientists carried guns with them wherever they went; extra security staff were brought in to protect them and their families. Most of them believed that the Israelis had struck once already, in the same month—July 1962—that Nasser unveiled his rockets.

Hassan Khamil, an Egyptian industrialist who was overseeing from Switzerland the program to procure equipment for the designers of these rockets, chartered a plane to take him from the island of Sylt in Denmark to Düsseldorf. At the last moment, he canceled his plans, but his German wife did take the flight. The plane crashed in Westphalia, killing the pilot and Madame Khamil. Though this was a pure accident, to the by now thor-oughly paranois German scientists, it was at best an omen and at worst an Israeli assassination attempt.

It wasn't until September 1962 that Isser Harel got ap-proval for the final stages of Operation Damocles. Meir Amit did not object, though he made it plain that he still believed the dangers posed by the German scientists were being grossly exaggerated and that Operation Damocles was an exaggerated response. Nevertheless, Amit was forced to accept that the diplomatic efforts to dislodge the German scientists had failed, and that even though their activities in Egypt may not have been so dangerous as Mossad was insisting, it was an unarguable proposition that Israel would be better off if they were not doing this work at all.

In any case, what is known is that at 10:30 A.M. on September 11, 1962, a dark-skinned man, possibly an Egyptian (as witnesses reported later), went into the of-fices of Intra, the main purchasing agency for the rocket program in Schillerstrasse, Munich, and left a little later with the manager, Dr. Heinz Krug, an ex-officer in the German Army. When he had been gone for twenty-four hours, his wife telephoned the police reporting her husband missing. Two days later, Krug's car was found. Apart from an anonymous telephone call to the police informing them that Dr. Krug was dead, there were no more clues. Neither Dr. Krug nor his body has yet been found. Over two months later, on the morning of November 27th, Miss Hannelore Wende, secretary to Dr. Pilz, director of Factory 333, where the missiles were actually being manufactured, opened a large parcel addressed to Dr. Pilz which, according to its return label, had been sent by a prominent lawyer in Hamburg. As she opened it, the parcel exploded. She was badly injured.

A day later, on November 28th, another parcel arrived at the same factory, addressed to the general office. It had come by sea from Hamburg and was marked "specialized literature." An Egyptian employee, despite what had happened to Hannelore Wende, thoughtlessly tore open the package. Five people were killed in the explosion. The investigation showed that the Stuttgart bookshop on the parcel label did not exist. On November 29th, two more parcels arrived from Stuttgart with similar designations. But this time the Egyptian security authorities were alerted, and the parcels were found to be laced with explosives.

On February 23, 1963, Dr. Hans Kleinwachter, the expert in electronics who was working on the vital guidance system for the rockets, turned into the quiet cul-de-sac in Lorrach where he had his house when another car suddenly overtook him out of nowhere and screeched to a stop in front of him, blocking his way. There were three men in the car, one at the wheel, one in the passenger seat, and one in the back.

According to Kleinwachter's subsequent testimony to the police, the man sitting next to the driver got out, asked for the house of "Dr. Shenker," and then suddenly, without warning, pulled out a pistol equipped with a silencer and fired straight through the windshield. Miraculously, Kleinwachter emerged relatively unscathed. The windshield somehow deflected the force of the bullet, which lodged in the thick woolen scarf he was wearing. Kleinwachter, who was armed, tried to get at his own gun in the glove compartment, but he was too slow. The man who had attacked him ran to the car and the three made good their getaway before abandoning the car. There was only one clue which the police busily checked; nestling in the map pocket of the abandoned car was an Egyptian passport made out to one Ali Samir. It was a nice touch. Ali Samir was one of the top men in Egyptian counter-intelligence. His alibi checked out completely. At the time of the attack, he was having his picture taken in Cairo. The message of that passport was not, however, lost on anyone. The Israeli Secret Service was not only able to get one of the German scientists, but was able to involve the very man who was supposed to be protecting him. How could anyone regard himself as safe?

But ironically, it was the "soft" approach rather than these events which proved to be the undoing of Operation Damocles. Isser Harel was still setting much store by Otto Joklik, the Austrian who had first alerted him to the Ibis and Cleopatra projects. Now he asked Joklik to help Israel persuade German scientists to stop the work they were doing. Professor Paul Goerke, the presiding genius of Factory 333, had a daughter Heidi, a lawyer living in Freiburg, an attractive little town on the Swiss border. One day, on her way home from the office, Otto Joklik suddenly emerged from a doorway and began walking along beside her. Quietly, he told her that he knew where her father was and what he was doing. The Israelis, he said, *no matter the cost,* were determining to stop Goerke from working on these weapons of mass destruction. As her panic mounted, he told her that provided her father left Egypt, no one would have anything to worry about. The moment he stopped working for Nasser, Goerke could be assured of not being molested. But if Goerke remained where he was, then that would be another story. A few days later, Joklik telephoned Heidi at her home and said, "If you love your father, come on Saturday, March 2nd, to the Three Kings Hotel in Basle at 4:00 P.M., and I will introduce you to my friends."

Extremely frightened, Heidi immediately got in touch with a former German Army officer who was working for the Egyptians and whose telephone number she had been given by her father in case she observed any suspicious activity around the house. The officer, in turn, had the sense to notify the police.

The security authorities in Germany and Switzerland

had a fortnight to prepare their trap. Joklik had made no secret of the fact that he had come from the Israelis or that Israelis would be present at the meeting. His own trail was quickly picked up in Zurich, while border police were ordered to keep a look out for any suspicious-looking Israeli entering the country. On March 1, 1963, a fair-haired young man with a trim moustache, carrying a passport identifying him as an official of the Israeli Ministry of Education, Joseph Ben-Gal, arrived at the Italian frontier. He was somewhat vague about the purpose of his visit, was followed and seen to check into the Three Kings. Heidi turned up at the appointed hour the next day with her younger brother and a man she introduced as a friend. The Swiss police had bugged the table so that every word spoken was overheard. Detectives sat at neighboring tables, and police cars surrounded the hotel. Apparently suspecting nothing, Ben-Gal and Joklik talked to Heidi for over an hour. Ben-Gal told her that the Israelis had nothing against her father, for he had never been a Nazi, and only objected to the work he was now doing.

Dr. Pilz, on the other hand, Ben-Gal told her, *was* a Nazi and could expect to receive no mercy. Neither Ben-Gal nor Joklik made any specific threats, but they offered her a plane ticket to Cairo in order to try to persuade her father to come back to Germany. Eventually, receiving no firm promise from Heidi, the two men left. They were not picked up straightaway, but were followed. They went to the station and caught a train to Zurich, where they entered the lakeside Kongress Haus; there a masked artists' ball was in progress. They had a drink at the bar, shook hands and parted. Joklik was picked up at the railway station and Ben-Gal near the Israeli consulate. Both were arrested, but no formal announcement was made for a fortnight. The Germans were told and immediately put in a request for their extradition on the grounds that the threat to Heidi Goerke had been made in Germany, and also because the two men were wanted on suspicion of the attempted murder of Hans Kleinwachter.

Mossad and its director, Isser Harel, faced a crisis of monumental proportions. One of its agents stood accused of attempted murder in a European country; the implications of that for the whole of the service as well as for Israeli's foreign relations could hardly be more grave. Harel acted with increasing—and sometimes irrational

—anger under the pressure of these events. He had pursued the German scientists with such relentless zeal partly because they were German; their activities, he believed, could not be isolated, related simply to themselves, but were part of a larger, historic, specifically *German* conspiracy against the Jewish people. If Germany was now demanding the extradition of Joklik and Ben-Gal, then this was surely concrete evidence of official German ill will toward Israel.

Several members of the government, led by Israeli Foreign Secretary Mrs. Golda Meir, agreed with this analysis. Like Isser Harel, Mrs. Meir saw the world in black and white, made up of heroes and villains with few shadings in between. Urged on by Isser Harel, she proposed to colleagues that Israel send a special envoy to see Chancellor Adenauer demanding that Germany withdraw the extradition request over Ben-Gal and Joklik and insisting that he take immediate and concrete steps to stop the activities of his scientists in Egypt.

David Ben-Gurion was on holiday in Tiberias, and Isser Harel was sent to see him to secure his agreement to this proposal. But Ben-Gurion refused. Unlike Golda Meir and Isser Harel, he knew perfectly well that though Bonn probably was embarrassed by the activities of its scientists, there was nothing the German government could reasonably do. If a German scientist wanted to work abroad, then that was a privilege he possessed as the citizen of a democratic country. Equally, with regard to the extradition request, the German Chancellor could not interfere with the due process of law. If the prosecuting authorities believed that they had sufficient evidence to seek the extradition of the two men, then there was little or nothing Adenauer could do. Any approach to Adenauer, in the view of Ben-Gurion, would be counterproductive; it would merely embarrass him, sour relations between the two countries even further, without producing any benefit for Israel.

Ben-Gurion was motivated by other considerations as well. He was seeking to create in Israel the concept of a "New Germany," to show his fellow countrymen that Germany was not merely trying its best to expiate its past sins, but could become an important ally, which might be crucial to Israel in the years ahead. Israel simply could not afford to stand aside and permit the past to become a stumbling block, inhibiting Israel's ability to withstand the future. Germany not only had been pouring millions in reparation payments into the Israeli treasury, but was also secretly supplying Israel with ultramodern weapons at only ten percent of their value as well as with other vital military equipment free of charge.

The argument between Ben-Gurion and Harel was at very much the same point as it had been seven months earlier when the Egyptian rockets were first unveiled, with the additional complication that Isser Harel had badly stumbled in his response to the threat he perceived.

Meir Amit, too, had hardened his position. Despite Wolfgang Lotz's reports, Amit, always skeptical about the degree of danger to Israel, was now positively contemptuous. The Egyptians, he believed, were nowhere near building an atomic bomb, and all their work had produced only crude and unimportant results.

Ben-Gurion, to Isser Harel's disgust, accepted Amit's evaluation. Harel took the view that the Prime Minister was sacrificing the security of the State at the price of his German alliance. It was a bitter charge to lay against a man who for so many years had been Harel's greatest champion, and it placed into grave doubt the ability of each to go on working with the other.

In the meantime, however, something had to be done about Joseph Ben-Gal. Ben-Gurion authorized Harel to call in Israel's top editors to try to mobilize domestic and international opinion in order to secure his release, but asked him to play down the significance of the Egyptian rocket program. Isser Harel appeared to ignore Ben-Gurion's instructions when he met Israeli newspaper editors next day. He told them about Joklik's testimony, about the kind of work he had been doing in Egypt, and helped three papers to send their top investigative reporters to Europe to look into the activities of the firms—the names of which he supplied—that the Egyptians had set up as purchasing conduits for fissionable and radioactive material.

If the press had been alarmist before, now it became positively hysterical. Suddenly the newspapers were full of the most remarkable stories—products sometimes of the fertile imagination of their authors and sometimes of their friends in Mossad. An alarmed and frightened public was informed that the most brilliant scientists Nazi Germany had ever produced were now manufacturing weapons capable of waging biological, chemical, nuclear and radioactive warfare against Israel. Right out of the comic strips came death rays and fatal microbes and other amazing devices against which the country would be defenseless. "Perhaps we're being too complacent, after all," said Meir Amit dryly when he read these accounts. "Egypt doesn't only want to destroy Israel—it's about to take over the world." The campaign, both in the press and in the Knesset, soon took on a distinctly anti-Ben-Gurion character.

The Prime Minister still continued his vacation, believing that if he were to hurry back to Tel Aviv, he would only heighten the sense of crisis. There was no one available to restore some sense of proportion to the debate. On March 23rd, Ben-Gurion's own Foreign Secretary, Golda Meir, rose to her feet in the Knesset and declared: "The activity of the German scientists and experts in producing weapons for Egypt that she intends to use for the destruction of Israel and her people constitutes a serious threat to our survival. If that criminal activity continues, the German people must accept responsibility for it. The German government has a duty to cause the wicked pursuits of its citizens to cease and to terminate their services to the Egyptian government."

Enough was enough. On March 24, 1963, nine days after the announcement of the arrest of Ben-Gal, with Ben-Gurion's own party split, the opposition and the press howling for his blood, and his security services apparently out of control, David Ben-Gurion returned to his home in Tel Aviv in order to take control of a desperately deteriorating political and diplomatic situation. His first act was to order Isser Harel to come to see him, and like two angry bulls, they faced each other across Ben-Gurion's living room.

Chapter 14

DAVID BEN-GURION FELT BETRAYED. Gravely weakened by the Lavon affair, which was still exuding its poison, he now faced a new crisis involving his security services. The battle had become a political one, and the Prime Minister believed that Isser Harel was primarily responsible for that. Certainly, Ben-Gurion's German policy seemed in ruins. The opposition parties at last had an issue around which most Israelis, unaware of the sober evaluations of Military Intelligence, could unite, namely, a bitter detestation of Germany—always just beneath the surface—and a conviction that a people which had massacred six million Jews were now stoking up the furnaces to finish off those Jews who were left.

Ben-Gurion's main complaint—when he faced Harel —was against the press. It had distorted his position and had grossly exaggerated the possible danger that the German scientists posed for Israel. It could not be overlooked, either, that there was enough of a common denominator in the reports to indicate that the journalists were getting their information from a central governmental source. Harel did not even try to disguise the fact that for those stories for which there was a source (not the more outrageous ones), he was it, and he admitted that it was on his instructions that three journalists had been guided in the direction of the Egyptian purchasing missions in Europe that produced some of the most alarming stories of all.

Isser Harel went on the offensive and launched a withering attack upon all those, particularly inside Amit's Military Intelligence, who were in his view so complacently and dangerous disparaging the Egyptian capability, especially in Factory 333 in Heliopolis. Ben-Gurion heatedly replied that the precipitate response Mossad had made in Switzerland and elsewhere to the problem posed by the scientists had had the effect of turning international public opinion against Israel at a time when, especially if Harel's evaluations were correct, Israel more than ever before needed world sympathy and support.

Ben-Gurion went on to defend his German policy and its importance for Israel. West Germany, he said, politically (in the European context) and economically had once again become a world power. She would not be ignored, would thrive with or without Israeli support. Matters were now, said the Prime Minister, very finely balanced. During his recent visit to Israel, Dr. Gerstenmayer, President of the Bundestag, had promised to do what he could to establish proper diplomatic relations between the two countries and to help prepare the way in Germany. This, said Ben-Gurion, was an important, and to Israel, vital pledge. But Isser Harel dismissed it. The Prime Minister, he implied, had permitted himself to be tricked. Harel's information was that Gerstenmayer was absolutely opposed to the normalization of relations between the two countries and would campaign against it. "If that is what you believe," Ben-Gurion told Harel, "then I must tell you that I have no faith either in the source of your information or the information itself."*

Ben-Gurion brought the meeting to a close, but before he did so he told the chief of Mossad that he would ask the Parliamentary Committee of Defense and Foreign Affairs to be convened in order that Ben-Gurion could appear before it and use that opportunity to tell the Knesset and the country the truth about the German scientists—how the issue had been manipulated by some people for political purposes.

There was only one course open to Isser Harel, and he took it. He returned to his office and wrote a letter of resignation.

Ben-Gurion knew only too well that once the news got out that Isser Harel had resigned over the issue of the German scientists, the government itself might find it difficult to survive. So he replied, in his own handwriting, that he could not accept the resignation.

Isser Harel seemed to accept this situation and on the

---

* Subsequent events were to prove that Ben-Gurion had been right in his judgment.

following day, March 25, 1963, turned up at his office as usual. But there was another letter there waiting from the Prime Minister. It asked Harel to put in writing: (a) what information he had concerning the manufacture of non-conventional weapons by the Egyptians, (b) what information he possessed concerning German industrial firms supplying this weapons program, and (c) to name the sources for the above information.

Though this was a perfectly proper letter for the Prime Minister to write, preparing, as he was, to face a vital Knesset committee, it wounded Isser Harel to the depths of his being. Hitherto his information had been regarded as sacrosanct—no one questioned its reliability or demanded to know from where it came. Bruised by what had already gone before, sensitive now to any slight, he regarded this letter as a mortal insult.

Outraged, he picked up the telephone, called Haim Israeli, director of the Defense Minister's office (Ben-Gurion was, of course, Minister of Defense as well as Prime Minister), and demanded that someone come over and pick up his keys. He was leaving—and leaving for good.

By 11:00 A.M. he had cleared his desk and left the building. At the age of fifty, his long and distinguished career had all but come to an end. Desperately, his colleagues in Mossad tried to get him to change his mind, but he was adamant.

Isser Harel subsequently rationalized his resignation to the Israeli journalist Michel Bar-Zohar, as reported in *Spies in the Promised Land*, as follows: "Ben-Gurion wanted to convene the parliamentary Committee of Defense and Foreign Affairs and tell it that the Egyptian rockets were no threat to Israel. If he had done so, I would have been the first to testify before the committee, and I would have been obliged to contradict Ben-Gurion, for, to the best of my knowledge, the rockets were very much a threat indeed. Ben-Gurion would have lost face; his colleagues in the coalition government would have rebelled against his authority; he would have been forced to resign. I myself resigned in order to prevent his calling the committee."

This was, of course, nonsense. Ben-Gurion did call the committee, did present to it Meir Amit's estimates, and did successfully convince them. Isser Harel left for no better reason than his pride. For Israel, it was very much the end of an era.

There can be little doubt that during his career Isser Harel had developed into one of the great secret-service chiefs of the world. With his small select staff, he had turned Israel's intelligence operation into a formidable and hugely successful effort.

Internally, where he controlled Shin Bet, he had been almost wholly successful. During the late fifties, when the Russians, with some initial if limited gains to their credit, were seeking to penetrate Israeli society, Isser Harel took on the KGB and its operation on Israeli terrain and defeated it. Israelis caught in the Russian web—and there were many ex-Russians among them with extreme left-wing sympathies—were quickly flushed out. It was all done quietly, efficiently, and with a minimum of fuss. Arab attempts to set up espionage operations on Israeli soil practically all came to nothing. During the Six-Day War, when Israel had the opportunity to interrogate thousands of Egyptian and Syrian officers, many of field rank, the interrogation teams never once came across an instance where the enemy possessed significant intelligence about Israel obtained by clandestine methods.

Internationally, Harel's achievements had been even more spectacular. Mossad was recognized within the trade as one of the most daring, ambitious, and professional services in the world. The Israeli intelligence services had become feared and respected. That this was so was almost wholly due to Isser Harel, one of the truly great spymasters of all time.

But like so many great men, his strengths proved also to be his weaknesses. He was an obsessive personality— a magnificent gift most of the time for a man with his job, but dangerous when the obsession was about a matter of minor importance and led him to neglect a major concern. He was, above all, intensely loyal to the people who worked for him, but expected that loyalty to be repaid with an unquestioning allegiance to his judgments. Most gave that allegiance gladly, for he was adored by his staff, but it led to an unhealthy lack of criticism of virtually everything said or done by Isser Harel within the intelligence community.

It was because Military Intelligence, alone within the intelligence community, constantly sought independence of thought and action that Isser Harel was constantly at war with it. He regarded Military Intelligence as a rival, not as a partner. He made little use of its massive research facilities and was deeply suspicious of its intelligence evaluations. He was a man who liked to go out on his own operations and gravely mistrusted what he regarded as armchair spies, intellectuals sitting in little offices in Tel Aviv reading Arab newspapers, and then attempting to tell him what was *really* going on in Cairo.

During all the years that Isser Harel ran the service no one can remember seeing the head of research of the Foreign Ministry at any meeting of any importance. What was at the very beginning conceived as an independent reference point had pretty well ceased to exist. Harel could never stand potential rivals—and clearly a strong head of research might have been one. Harel had ignored the department so completely and over such a long period that it had become virtually moribund.

All this left Isser Harel hopelessly exposed during the affair of the Egyptian-German rockets. Military Intelligence, whose chief was at least as tough as Isser Harel, a man certainly not prepared to be swept aside by the civilians of Mossad, had to be listened to. It soon became very clear indeed that the quality of Amit's material, its breadth and its scope, its scientific and political sophistication compared to the sketchy, seat-of-the-pants evaluations which came, as someone said at the time, not from Isser's files but from Isser's soul, simply could not be ignored.

It needed only a glance at the evaluations the two men submitted to realize that while Isser Harel had far from proved his case, Meir Amit, even if he was not necessarily right, had put forward a thesis impossible to disprove. Isser Harel didn't see the argument in that light at all. To him, it wasn't a question of whether or not Amit might be correct, what mattered was that Mossad should stand preeminent and that, whatever the circumstances, its view should prevail. Isser Harel would, of course, deny that this untenable position was the fulcrum of all of his actions during these critical days. Yet those who know him well—and admire him—accept that Isser Harel's battle against the German scientists was really a battle for power inside Israel itself. That battle he finally lost.

There was no obvious successor to Isser Harel in sight. In any case, few believed that his resignation would stand for very long. David Ben-Gurion first tried to reach Joel Morab, the head of Shin Bet, to take over the agency temporarily, but when he couldn't be immediately found, Meir Amit, the head of Military Intelligence, was asked to assume command until a new director could be appointed.

The following day, Meir Amit strode into Mossad headquarters knowing he faced one of the sternest challenges of his career. Already the warning signals had been sounded. The previous evening, one of the most senior and respected departmental controllers of Mossad had called Amit at home and informed him peremptorily that the senior Mossad man had no intention of working for him. That morning, as Amit moved into Isser Harel's office, the hostility of virtually every Mossad employee from top to bottom was not only obvious in the sullen and angry faces he saw all around him, but was put to him directly by senior executives. Amit's position, in fact, could not have been more difficult. He had taken over Mossad at a moment's notice while still retaining control of Military Intelligence.

Though most in Mossad thought that Harel would be back within a few weeks, his differences with Ben-Gurion forgotten and forgiven, they were extremely disturbed to find that Meir Amit, head of Military Intelligence, was taking his place. This was the man who in the eyes of almost everyone was responsible for Isser Harel's temporary eclipse, the man who had led the increasingly vocal attacks within the defense establishment against the agency and its director—and he was now *inside* Mossad headquarters. If Isser Harel was coming back, then the devil was keeping his seat warm for him.

Meir Amit didn't make it any easier for Harel's supporters. Now that he was inside Mossad, his criticisms became more vocal, not less so. What astonished him most was the complete absence of any real chain of command other than in the most surface sense. In Harel's Mossad, there had been one boss, Harel; below him was everyone else. With Harel gone, Mossad was running around like a chicken without a head. Amit had been brought up in a completely different tradition, a tradition which demanded that in any battlefield situation, the commanding

The great Isser Harel who, more than any other man, was responsible for establishing the international reputation of Mossad. *(Photo courtesy Israel Press and Photo Agency)*

Defense Minister Pinhas Lavon, the man at the heart of the Lavon Affair. *(Photo courtesy Camera Press)*

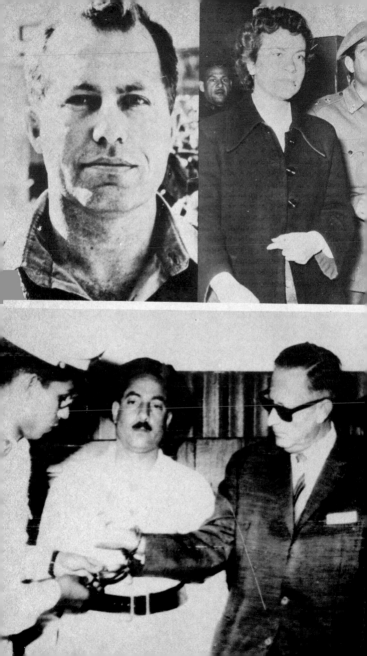

Top row, left to right: Avraham
Seidenwerg, alias Paul Frank, alias
El-Ad Saatchi, photographed in
Ramona Prison, Israel. *(Photo from
a private collection)*

Marcelle Ninio on trial for her life
in Cairo. *(Photo courtesy Keystone
Press)*

Meir Amit, the only man to head
both Military Intelligence and
Mossad. *(Photo courtesy Camera
Press)*

Benjamin Gibli, chief of Military
Intelligence throughout the
disastrous Lavon Affair.
(Photo courtesy Jewish Chronicle)

Left: Handcuffs for Wolfgang and
Waltraud Lotz just before their Cairo
trial in 1955. *(Photo courtesy UPI)*

Above, left: Zwicka Zamir, the unassuming chief of Mossad who took on the Palestinians. *(Photo courtesy Erica)*

Above, right: General Yehoshaphat Harkabi, the intellectual who became chief of Military Intelligence. *(Photo courtesy Jewish Chronicle)*

Left: Alfred Frauenknecht, the man who stole the blueprints of the Mirage for the Israelis. *(Photo courtesy AP)*

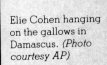

Elie Cohen hanging on the gallows in Damascus. *(Photo courtesy AP)*

Admiral Mordechai Limon,
the man behind the daring
escape of the missile boats
from Cherbourg.
(Photo courtesy AP)

Ehud Avriel: long before
independence and right
through to the sixties, he
was never far from the
center of the Israeli intelligence community. (Photo
courtesy Camera Press)

General Aharon Yariv, the genius who ran Military Intelligence for and during the Six-Day War. *(Photo courtesy AP)*

General Eli Zeira, chief of Military Intelligence before and during the Yom Kippur War. *(Photo courtesy UPI)*

General Shlomo Gazit,
head of Israeli Military
Intelligence after the
disaster of Yom Kippur.
(Photo courtesy AP)

General Yitzhak Hofi,
current head of Mossad.
(Photo courtesy Starphot)

officer knows that, if he goes, his deputy can take his place, and so on, right down the line of command, with the unit not faltering for a moment. Mossad was not merely faltering, it had virtually ceased to function. Every senior Mossad man worth his salt was temperamentally and emotionally tied to Isser Harel. So inspired a leader had he been and so all-encompassing was their loyalty to him that, for the moment at least, he was more important in their eyes than the organization itself. Isser Harel was Mossad and Mossad was Isser Harel; it was inconceivable that one could be divorced from the other.

There was much, however, that was wrong with the organization. In many respects, Mossad was antiquated and in no position—with or without Harel—to keep pace with its extraordinary reputation. Harel had been persuaded to install a computer, but Harel mistrusted gadgets of all kinds. When younger members of the organization timidly suggested that it might be put to greater use, Isser Harel would quickly trot out the latest story he had read in a newspaper of some computer overcharging a customer by a million dollars or a bank crediting a customer with all the gold in Fort Knox. The point was, of course, that Harel prided himself primarily upon having created an organization where sheer human intelligence was employed to combat the enemy—an organization in which the resources of the human mind would be always greater than anything that modern technology would produce.

That concept was a flattering one to the people who worked for Harel. To Amit, however, it implied a special kind of arrogance. Nobody in Mossad, as far as he could discern, had thought out properly what the real function of Mossad should be. While its "special operations" capacity, as it had shown time and again, was at a high pitch of excellence, the whole organization was geared to operating on a day-to-day basis, with no long-term objectives and no overall operating philosophy, which meant that it was not effectively using the strictly limited resources of money and manpower it had available to it. What this meant in practice was that while Mossad had proved supremely capable in, for example, getting assistance to beleaguered Jews during the Algerian civil war, it had been less successful in predicting the outcome of that war or assessing the significance of the outcome to Israel.

Meir Amit lost no time in making these views known in the most trenchant terms, and senior Mossad executives replied in the only way left to them, namely, to resign. Within forty-eight hours of Amit's arrival, Isser Harel's deputy and three of the agency's most experienced executives walked out the door. Persuaded by his colleagues in the Army to try to mend his fences, Amit brought the Mossad station chief in Paris back to Tel Aviv as his deputy in the hope that this would persuade Mossad rank-and-file that Amit's appointment did not mean an Army takeover, but he then undid any good this posting might have achieved by consistently ignoring his deputy's advice and keeping him out of his inner counsels.

For several weeks, various delegations called upon Isser Harel and David Ben-Gurion in an attempt to persuade them to bury the hatchet. Almost certainly this effort would have been eventually successful—even given the fact that both were hard and obstinate men—but suddenly, on June 16th, at the end of a routine Cabinet meeting, David Ben-Gurion, tired and embittered, principally by the Lavon affair, announced his resignation—and this time he went into the political wilderness never to return.

Meir Amit was still only the acting head of Mossad, doubling as chief of Military Intelligence. As long as Ben-Gurion was Prime Minister the chances of Amit's being confirmed in Harel's place were slim. But now, with a new Prime Minister, the 67-year-old Levi Eshkol, the situation had changed.

Sorting out this problem clearly had to be one of the new government's first priorities. Eshkol himself was not the most decisive of men. A joke about him was making the rounds of Tel Aviv to the effect that when before a Cabinet meeting the waitress asked him if he wanted tea or coffee, he replied "Half and half." The Cabinet itself was deeply divided as to what to do. On the one hand, his Deputy Prime Minister Abba Eban and his influential Minister of Agriculture Moshe Dayan pressed confirmation of the appointment of Meir Amit. Golda Meir, the Foreign Secretary, and Moshe Shapira, Minister of the Interior, supported Isser Harel.

The pro-Harel campaign was fought ruthlessly. Files were missing from Mossad to make life difficult for Amit;

information was withheld from him within the department on the remarkable grounds that as he hadn't been confirmed, he lacked the security clearance to see the director's most secret papers; and executives, almost working to rule, refused to do anything but the most routine work. The press was fed with pro-Harel material in an enormous and effective PR operation.

Within the Cabinet, the principal objection to Amit was that he was a soldier. This argument had then—as it has today—a great deal of force. With a general in charge of Mossad, how would the Cabinet know if the intelligence they were receiving had not first passed through a military screen, "marked" by the chiefs of staff in order to ensure that it fitted into their own preconceptions. Ben-Gurion himself had always insisted upon civilian control of the armed forces. Never during his premiership did a military chief of intelligence attend a meeting of the Cabinet or Foreign Affairs Committee of the Knesset. Seldom was the Chief of Staff permitted to do so.

Yet soured by the nature of Israeli politics, Ben-Gurion more and more tended to regard the Army as the salvation of Israel. In his old age he imbued the Army with an almost mystical quality. It represented to him all that was best in Israel. He saw the Lavon affairs as an attempt by easy-living and corrupt politicians to drag the Army down—a betrayal of all that he and his contemporaries had stood for. That was a view which many military men shared, and some Israelis were even beginning to talk about the imminent dangers of a military coup (talk which reached its height just before the Six-Day War).

Meir Amit was shrewd enough not to try to dispute that there could be dangers if a military man in charge of Mossad owed his primary allegiance to the Army. But, as he told his friends, just because Moshe Dayan was Minister of Agriculture, did not mean that Israeli farmers were being marched to work or made subordinate to the Chief of Staff. His loyalty was first and foremost to the State and to any institution, be it civilian or military, which the State asked him to serve.

Amit's supporters, meanwhile, began to dismantle the Harel legend. Harel, they charged, had neglected the prime area of his responsibility—namely, the so-called "confrontation states," those Arab countries which have common borders with Israel—for the sake of more glamorous "adventures" in Europe and elsewhere. No one doubted Harel's genius or his great contribution to Israeli intelligence. But he had outlived his usefulness. Not only had he failed to provide sufficient high-grade information for Israeli commanders on the battlefield, but by his constant interference in the affairs of Military Intelligence he had made it difficult for that body to perform *its* duties.

At the beginning of September 1963, Levi Eshkol could put off his decision no longer. He arrived at a typical Eshkol compromise, unsatisfactory to all parties and unworkable. Meir Amit was confirmed as chief of Mossad: his brilliant deputy at Military Intelligence, Colonel Aharon Yariv, was made chief of Military Intelligence; and Isser Harel was brought back as an intelligence overlord, operating out of the Prime Minister's office with the responsibility of briefing the Prime Minister on all matters relating either to military or political intelligence. It was an unhappy period for everyone. Meir Amit, to the amused contempt of Mossad staff, moved into his new headquarters, tore down Harel's simple office, and set himself up in some style with paneled walls, expensive office furniture, and an outer office containing his secretaries, all completely at odds with what had been, up till then, Mossad's spartan tradition. But though Amit established a proper chain of command, laid down firm operational procedures, and introduced the latest technological aids, he was unable at first to break through the resentment of his appointment and so put Mossad to work once again.

The great problem was, of course, Isser Harel in a job which demanded of him the least of his many talents. Harel was an operational commander, at his very best in the field. He was not good at evaluating material or exercising cool judgment in the face of conflicting advice from opposing quarters. Amit and Yariv were both hostile and uncooperative, and though Harel returned that small favor by ensuring that he received information from Mossad which had bypassed Amit, frequently having access to it before Amit had himself, this only exacerbated relations between the two without in itself being effective enough to permit Harel to maintain a grip on the organization.

Amit responded by isolating the rabidly pro-Harel men in the department, and he brought in new people, often from Military Intelligence, and set up an inner circle excluding Harel's men. Neither man emerged from this battle of wills with much credit, though slowly the sympathies of the younger men at Mossad began to swing towards Amit. There was no questioning that he was intent on modernizing what had become a somewhat creaky structure. And he himself was an attractive man, dynamic and forceful.

Mossad had seriously underestimated Meir Amit from the very beginning. They had apparently overlooked the fact that he was not just another superannuated general looking for a comfortable niche, but a man who had all the qualities to be a Chief of Staff of the Israeli Army. It took some time to sink in, but ultimately Mossad realized that though he was a very different man from Isser Harel, Meir Amit was a worthy successor. To their surprise, old Mossad hands found themselves liking the general and excited and stimulated by his concepts. They particularly appreciated the fact that Amit brought with him one priceless gift—Unit 131, the unit which ran special operations. He was able to do so, to cut through all the argument, during the period when he ran both Military Intelligence and Mossad. Because of those unique circumstances he returned to Mossad an operational facility which, without him, it would almost certainly have lost forever.

On the other hand, it must be said that with the departure of Isser Harel, an indefinable quality left Mossad that has never really been successfully replaced. Under Isser Harel, Mossad was both human and humane, though few of Isser Harel's enemies—who are legion in Israel—would believe that he possesses either attribute. In a fight, he would give no quarter. His personal politics are far to the right. He pursues his enemies to the grave and beyond. Yet he possessed a shining integrity and a deep sense of personal honesty which gave a very special character to the Israeli service. He recognized that his was a dirty business, yet still passionately believed that his people should have the standards he insisted upon in their personal and professional life.

He didn't like employing women, because he believed that sooner or later they would be drawn into situations where they would be obliged to use their sex in order to achieve their objective. He was simply not prepared to put anyone into that position. At various times, "assasinations" were put up for his consideration, and until he was unnerved by the situation with the German scientists, he had always rejected such a course with so much passion ("We're not paid killers!") that younger members of the staff, hungry for real action, became afraid even to suggest it. On one occasion, when during an early planning session on the capture of Adolf Eichmann, a staff member proposed a contingency plan to kill Eichmann should things go badly wrong, Harel snapped angrily that the mission was designed to bring Eichmann out of the Argentine to face trial in Israel. If that proved impossible, then the mission had failed, and Eichmann would have to be let go.

Something of that quality was lost when Meir Amit arrived, and it has been steadily eroded ever since—though to this day compared to most secret-intelligence services Mossad's standards are still of the highest. But Amit was a soldier with a soldier's directness. If someone's in your way, he would tell his men, you use the greatest fire power you can muster to blow him away. It would be wrong to say that Amit and his successors were not men of principle. They were simply more flexible, more attuned to the modern world, less dependent upon instinct and upon human reaction, demanding only that the job be done and not too concerned about the methods employed, save that they did not embarrass the service or the State of Israel.

Perhaps the greatest advantage the new team brought with it was that for the first time in the history of the country, Mossad and Military Intelligence operated, without rancor, in harness one with the other. Aharon Yariv, who became a general when he took over from Amit, was an immediate success at Military Intelligence.

Yariv had always been one of the Army's high fliers. In 1950, at the age of twenty-nine—and looking about twenty-one—he was a full colonel, studying at the prestigious French War College in Paris. The commandant of the school took one look at him and ordered him to attend classes in civilian clothes. "You really look too young for your rank, and it might upset the other students," he said.

After Amit made Yariv his deputy at Military Intelligence, the two men were a formidable combination. Yariv by then had shed his youthful appearance and seemed very much the university professor rather than the soldier—a small man, with alert, very sharp eyes and grey hair, a man who liked to communicate and to explain, but who weighed the questions carefully, an analyst and an intellectual who surrounded himself with the brightest young men he could find and then encouraged them to dissent from orthodox opinion, to argue and to disagree.

While others in the Israeli intelligence community basked in Allen Dulles' remark that the Israeli service was one of the finest in the world, Yariv found such exaggerations ludicrous. The CIA and the KGB were, he told his people, the two greatest intelligence agencies in the world because of the size and the scope of their activities. It was arrant nonsense to pretend that Israel was in the same league. As for comparisons with countries like Britain or France, Israel temporarily had a slight edge in one area only: operational intelligence. In the Middle East, war was an ever-present threat; in Europe it was a distant nightmare. Israel had to know exactly the precise deployment of the forces of its surrounding enemies; its political situation demanded it. That fact alone made Israeli intelligence different—gave it its sense of urgency, impelled some of the brightest people in the country to enter its service.

Yariv was clear-headed, too, about making use of intelligence once it had been collected. There is a natural tendency among intelligence agencies around the world to keep the secrets they have gathered—often so painfully—very much to themselves and a few senior commanders. An agent's report is transcribed, read by the chief of intelligence, and then stamped TOP SECRET and hidden away from view. Intelligence becomes an end in itself—the art of collecting information for information's sake. The TOP SECRET stamp, Yariv decreed, could be "our greatest enemy."

Yariv insisted that intelligence should continually be evaluated to see what units in the Army (as far down as platoon level) could make use of it. After Yariv became involved, company and battalion commanders suddenly began receiving constantly updated maps of the regions in which they were operating, as well as a flow of information on the nature of the opposition they faced in their immediate sector. But Yariv insisted that this shouldn't be a one-way flow. Intelligence officers within each unit were instructed to send back to headquarters every scrap of information; all of it went into the intelligence pot to re-emerge in the form of another updated intelligence map or the like.

Isser Harel had been a great intelligence chief. But Amit and Yariv over the next few years were to prove an extraordinary combination whose achievements surpassed anything Israeli intelligence services had performed in the past.

PART V

Day of the Generals

Chapter 15

MEIR AMIT LOST NO TIME in introducing reforms and a major restructuring of the service. The most important change, of course, followed naturally from his appointment and the relationship he had established over the years with General Yariv. It was to bring Mossad, for the first time, into a partnership with Military Intelligence and end for the time being at least the constant internecine warfare between these two branches of the Israeli intelligence community. Within Mossad itself, Amit formalized—and in view of some of the old-timers—bureaucratized the loose organization which had existed under Harel. In so doing, he lost for good the agency's ability to operate as a single unit. What he gained, however, was probably more important, even if the results appeared to be less spectacular.

With day-to-day access to the researchers at Military Intelligence and operating within narrow perimeters set down by Meir Amit, each Mossad departmental head stuck closely to his specialization, be it operational or geographical, which paradoxically had the effect of widening rather than narrowing their horizons. Where previously, problems were dealt with on an ad hoc basis when they arose, now everyone employed by Mossad was expected to regard intelligence in philosophic terms. Even Amit's insistence that the most valuable intelligence was that which had a direct application to the battlefield did not prove as restrictive as many had imagined it would; nor did it mean that Mossad's operational capacity (which actually expanded) had to be subordinated entirely to the needs of the military.

Again, perhaps paradoxically, systematic analysis, with the help of computers, of data from all over the world showed that events apparently unrelated to the Middle East in faraway countries could have significant implications for Israel, even if this was not immediately obvious. Thus when a Mossad operative in an African country reported that a minister had angrily complained to him that a recent Russian arms shipment had included a great deal of old and unserviceable equipment, contrary to promises they had received when the agreement was signed, and this matched fragmentary reports of similar incidents occurring elsewhere in the world, it seemed probable that the Russians had withdrawn equipment intended for these countries and had included it in a massive shipment to an area which the Russians regarded as politically more important. When, therefore, a few days later, agents in Cairo reported that Egyptian ordinance and supply officers were making a tour of inspection of the Soviet Union, it took very little imagination to see where that shipment was destined. As a result, long before anything had been signed or even agreed between the Russians and the Arabs, the Israelis were able to tell the Americans what was almost certainly about to take place and ensure that America would be ready, at a moment's notice, to match anything the Russians introduced into the area.

While Amit had a great deal of faith in the new technology of the craft, he knew as well as anyone that all the technical devices in the world would never replace or even reduce the role of the secret agent. Neither, as Amit was quickly to learn, would all the psychological tests and exhaustive deep-vetting really establish anything but a rough and ready guide as to how the agent will ultimately perform.

One of the first men infiltrated by Amit into hostile territory was a young Israeli sent into Beirut, which, through an Arab city, was nevertheless a comparatively soft option compared with, say, Cairo, Damascus or Baghdad. Everyone had great hopes for him as a man who would one day rise high in the service. He was keen and ambitious; he had proved himself brave in combat and resourceful while serving with the Israeli Army. Like every Israeli agent, he had undergone the most complete psychological screening and had emerged with flying colors. He arrived in Beirut by plane and went straight to the hotel room which had been booked for him in advance, and then, despite all entreaties, simply refused to emerge. The mere act of passing through customs at

Beirut airport on a forged passport had taken so much out of him psychologically that he suffered a nervous breakdown there and then.

The matter became more serious when it became plain that he could not even emerge from his hotel room to leave the country. Mossad was faced with a bizarre situation in which it looked like one of its men might be spending the rest of his life in a smart Beirut hotel, a total recluse stranded forever far behind enemy lines. In any event, a very embarrassed Mossad was forced to seek the assistance of the CIA to bring him out. He was drugged and taken home on a stretcher; there he not only immediately recovered, but begged for a second chance. Needless to say, he didn't get one.

Soon, however, real catastrophe was to strike Mossad. Two of the greatest spies ever to work for Israel, Elie Cohen in Damascus and Wolfgang Lotz in Cairo, were both arrested. Not since the unfortunate Max Bennett, who was so carelessly entangled with the Lavon team in 1954 and picked up in Cairo (and later committed suicide in his prison cell before being called to testify at his trial), had an Israeli member of the Israeli intelligence services been caught in an Arab country.

Both Elie Cohen and Wolfgang Lotz were remarkable men in a remarkable trade—deep-penetration agents operating inside enemy territory and knowing full well that one mistake could mean their lives. Though Wolfgang Lotz's information to Isser Harel during the affair of the German scientists had proved less than reliable, his value to the Israelis was nevertheless enormous and should not be underrated. Although he was never really qualified to deal with the highly technical information he had been asked to obtain and assess, his great strength, of course, was that he constantly floated around in the upper reaches of Egyptian society, mixing freely with generals and security chiefs. Meir Amit, if initially, like Harel, a little skeptical about Lotz, soon appreciated his importance and pumped him dry. Amit wanted everything from Lotz—gossip, rumor, information of any kind on any subject—and Lotz always had more on hand than he could reasonably send on his bathroom transmitter. In the end, the pressure on him from Tel Aviv to unload his material almost every night (material which was vital to the remarkably accurate picture which the computers of Military Intelligence and Mossad were building up on Egypt's political, military and economic strengths and weaknesses) proved to be his undoing.

On February 22, 1965, Wolfgang Lotz and his wife Waltraud returned to their splendid Cairo home after a trip to Mersa Matrouh. As they walked in the front door, they were met by members of the Egyptian security services, who were lying in wait for them. Nobody except the other side is ever absolutely sure what it is that finally gives an agent away. But Lotz himself was told—and there is no reason to disbelieve this—that his radio transmissions had been finally tracked down. Certainly he had been using his radio a great deal, staying on the air every night longer than was consistent with security. Interestingly, only a month earlier, on January 21, 1965, Elie Cohen, almost certainly the greatest spy Israel has ever had, was also given away by his radio transmissions.

Mossad took the view that there had to be a link between these two events. It wasn't long before, from independent sources, Mossad established—to its satisfaction at least—what this link was. Concerned that its Arab allies were proving very leaky vessels indeed, GRU (Russian Military Intelligence) had insisted upon a major overhaul of local security in both Cairo and Damascus. Suspecting that the Israelis had agents in both capitals transmitting information by radio, the GRU brought in their very latest radio detection vans together with Russian crews to operate them. Within a few weeks, they tracked down both Lotz and Cohen—an extraordinary achievement in counterintelligence terms.

Astonishingly, Lotz's German cover stood up throughout his interrogation and trial. Regarded with some distaste merely as a German mercenary who was working for the Israelis for money, he was put on trial on July 27, 1965, and was sentenced to life imprisonment. Waltraud Lotz was sentenced to three years' imprisonment with hard labor. Both, together with the Lavon team (whom they met in prison), were exchanged for 500 Egyptian POWs, including nine generals, at the end of the Six-Day War.

Elie Cohen was less fortunate. He was executed in the main square of Damascus, called Martyr's Square, at 3:30 A.M. on Tuesday May 19, 1965. He was allowed one last message to his family and wrote:

* * *

My wife Nadia and dear family,

I am writing you these last words to entreat you to stay together. I beg you, Nadia, to forgive me and to look after yourself and the children. Make sure they get a good education. Take care of yourself and them; see they want for nothing. Always stay on good terms with my family.

Also, I would like you to marry again so that the children may have a father. You are entirely free to do this. Don't, I beg you, spend your time crying over what is no more. Always think of the future.

I send you all my last kisses; you, Sophie, Iris, Shaul, and all my family. Don't forget a single one of them. Tell them that my last loving thoughts were of them.

Don't forget, any of you, to pray for the salvation of my father and the deliverance of my soul.

My last kisses .... Shalom

Elie Cohen

Elie Cohen was born in Alexandria in 1924 and lived there until he was thirty-two years old when he finally emigrated to Israel. He was brought up as a devout Jewish boy and had thoughts of becoming a rabbi in the local Jewish quarter; his parents were proud Oriental Jews who owned a small tie shop in the city.

Like most of the young Jews in Egypt during that period, he soon became immersed in Zionist politics, but went further than most by joining the illegal Jewish underground led by Samuel Azar, who was subsequently to be executed by the Egyptians after the failure of Operation Suzanna. Elie (often known as Alex) Cohen's first trip to Israel was as part of that underground in order to train as a wireless operator. The intention was to use him on Operation Suzanna, but he was not available at the time, and though he was picked up by Egyptian security for interrogation, he was able to convince them that despite having known Azar, he had had nothing to do with the operation. Thereafter, though he did some work for the largely locally run, secret Jewish-emigration organization, he could not be used for espionage purposes in Egypt, not only because the Egyptians were bound to regard him with some suspicion, but because the rule that local Jews must never be recruited to spy in their own countries had been rigorously reapplied.

In 1957, he arrived in Israel. Originally he worked as a translator of Arab newspapers in the Ministry of Defense, but the work bored him and within a year he left to work as an accountant with the Central Marketing Agency of Industrial Concerns, run by the Israeli trade-union movement.

All this time, without his knowing it, Mossad had been keeping an eye on him. He already had rudimentary training, and some experience of clandestine activities. He had lived all his life in an Arab country, had spent some time underground. His potential was obviously enormous. While he could never be sent into Egypt— there would be too great a chance of recognition—Syria, one of the most difficult of the Arab countries to penetrate, was another matter. His family had originally come from Aleppo in Syria, and he could remember as a child the family speaking the Syrian dialect of Arabic at home. The fact was that while there was no doubting his patriotism, Elie Cohen felt more at ease in an Oriental environment than he did in an Israeli one. The Arab culture was something he had discovered was dear to him, and he missed it.

Although he was married, Cohen needed no permission to become an Israeli deep-penetration agent, and for an arduous two years he trained for the role.

The problem was that unlike Lotz, who could travel to Egypt as a German and gain quick acceptance, the only way Elie Cohen could make similar progress in Damascus was to become a Syrian. Syria, unlike Egypt, is a country that has always been suspicious of foreigners, even non-Syrian Arabs, and its people have long been taught to keep outsiders at arm's length.

To turn a man into a resident national of a country not his own is an ambitious undertaking if his cover is to pass muster for more than a moment. Elie Cohen, though of Syrian-Jewish background and with a great natural advantage, had to be carefully and patiently taught not only to lose his Jewish identity but also his Egyptian background. To a certain extent, his carefully prepared biography would help cover any cracks, but very little, if anything, could be left to chance.

By the end of 1960, Elie Cohen was ready. His Mossad

controllers had worked out a neatly packaged identity tailored to match his own background as closely as possible. His name was Kamal Amin Taabes, of Syrian parentage but born in Beirut in 1930. His family had emigrated to Alexandria in 1933 and then in 1947 had gone to Buenos Aires. There, as an adult, he had started an import-export business which had made him a reasonably wealthy man. It was the kind of biography that would fit thousands of Arab families, uprooted so many times by poverty and the turmoil of war and revolution in this century.

There were more than half a million Arabs living in Buenos Aires alone, with a large Syrian contingent, and he could fit into that group easily enough. If his Syrian accent ever let him down, this could easily be explained by the fact that he had spent all of his formative years in Egypt and Latin America. If he seemed to know more about Egypt than Syria, then that would be because it was Egypt where he had lived. The only problem was that he spoke very little Spanish, but a crash course at a language laboratory in Jerusalem soon took care of that.

Elie Cohen, traveling for the first time as Kamal Amin Taabes, arrived in Buenos Aires at the beginning of 1961 in order to establish the Latin American connection and, as Mossad hoped, make the contacts in the Syrian community that would give him the credibility he would need when he was ready to move to Damascus. He did better than anyone had dared to imagine. Liberally assisted by large sums of Mossad money, the import-export business he established quickly began to thrive, giving him sufficient cachet to be able to move comfortably in the upper reaches of the Syrian community.

Within nine months of his arrival in Buenos Aires, he was prepared for the biggest step of all—the journey to Damascus. By now a well-established personality both in the Syrian community and with the Arab population in Buenos Aires, Cohen let it be known that he intended to fulfill a lifetime's ambition to visit, for the first time ever, his homeland, Syria. Armed with letters of introduction, on January 1, 1962, he sailed on the liner *Astoria* from Genoa for Beirut. He was traveling first class, with an upper-deck cabin, and quickly fitted in with the other wealthy Arabs aboard. Nine days later, helped by an influential Syrian he had met on the ship who had driven him across the Lebanese-Syrian border, he at last arrived in Damascus, the target area.

Within a few days, he announced to his new friends with some emotion that after years of wandering, he had at last come home, and he had no intention of leaving ever again. Syria was his native land, and this was where he intended to spend the rest of his days. Quickly, he rented an elegant flat in the center of town, opposite the headquarters of the Syrian general staff, well aware that many of his neighbors would be bound to be Syrian army officers. Once established, he set up his radio transmitter, cunningly concealed in an apparently ordinary electric food mixer; his antennae, which he now fixed to the roof, had been brought in as an extra long flex to his electric shaver. He was ready for action.

From then on, for three years almost to the day—save for holidays he took in Israel with his family—Elie Cohen operated out of the Syrian capital on behalf of Mossad. He communicated either through his radio or through a method which had proved effective for other Israeli agents. A firm run by Mossad was set up in Switzerland to deal with *objets d'art* Cohen purchased in Syria to export to Europe: this served both as his cover and as a method of smuggling out material hidden in hollowed-out pieces of furniture.

It would be hard to exaggerate Elie Cohen's importance or the quite extraordinary ability he showed as an agent. Very different in manner to Lotz, quiet, unassuming, and modest, these very qualities helped him to infiltrate the highest councils of the Syrian Ba'ath Party and of the nation. Singlehanded, he sketched almost the entire Syrian fortifications along the Golan Heights and on the Plain of Damascus, established every detail of how the Syrians were proposing to divert the waters of the Jordan in order to pump Israel dry, charted the first Syrian official involvement with the PLO, told Israel of the precise nature and caliber of Soviet weapons made available to the Syrians, discovered the number of Syrian pilots capable of flying Russian MiGs, detailed the precise Syrian order of battle, and, of course, accurately plotted the political upheavals that were so characteristic of Syria during the period that Cohen was in residence.

Elie Cohen's reports were a model of their kind. He was always careful to name his sources, to understate rather than overstate his information, and he had an almost uncanny ability to analyze correctly and put into perspective every shred of conversation he picked up.

On several occasions, he was taken on a tour of inspection of the Syrian fortifications around Kuneitra and once actually stood on the Golan Heights looking down at Galilee spread like a multicolored counterpane before him. Simply looking at the topography convinced him that the Syrians were probably right to believe that their positions were unassailable but also made him more determined than ever to map out with as much precision as possible the quite remarkable Maginot-type defensive lines which the Syrians were building. He was actually transmitting when Colonel Ahmed Sweidani, head of the Syrian intelligence and counterespionage service, and his men burst into the apartment. They kept Cohen in the flat for three days insisting that he continue making transmissions to Tel Aviv. He did so, but subtly altered the speed of his Morse key—a signal agreed upon before he left Tel Aviv—making plain that he was in enemy hands.

So Meir Amit already knew the worst when Cohen was forced to send his last message. It read: "For Prime Minister Levi Eshkol and Secret Service Chief Tel Aviv from Syrian Counter-intelligence Service. Kamal and his friends now our guests in Damascus. Assume you will send all his colleagues. Will give you news of his fate shortly."

Some 500 Syrians (a mark of the extraordinary range of his contacts) were arrested in the days following Cohen's capture, and three Syrians who had become close friends of his were put on trial with him, though there was no evidence at all that they were anything but innocently involved. The Syrians, of course, could never be sure whether Elie Cohen was alone, whether he was a member of a network, or whether he had managed to suborn Syrian citizens to work for him. He was terribly and cruelly tortured during his interrogation to find out, but he had nothing to tell. The man from Israel had been a man alone.

Elie Cohen's trial was a farce. He was refused a defense counsel, and the press were excluded from all but the opening stages. The trial ended on March 19th, and the death sentence was pronounced on May 1st. Sentence was confirmed by President el-Hafez, a man who personally knew Elie Cohen and who had once accepted a mink coat as a present to his wife. Despite an international campaign in which world leaders, including the Pope, appealed to President el-Hafez for clemency, the televised execution was carried out and the body, left hanging for six hours, draped with a white sheet proclaiming his crime as thousands of Syrians trooped past.

It is always difficult to place the achievements of a spy in perspective. In the case of Elie Cohen, that problem is magnified a hundred times. Because the Syrian Ba'ath Party at the time was in an ideological dispute with the rest of the Arab world, Lebanese newspapers in particular took the opportunity to print the most extraordinary stories of Cohen's exploits, stories designed to embarrass the Syrian government, which was posturing as the only true enemy of the Zionists and the "imperialists."

These newspaper reports were picked up and amplified by the Israeli press after Cohen's death, making it difficult now for anyone—even Mossad itself—to pick out fact from fantasy. Evidence given at the trial can no more be regarded as reliable than could evidence at a Russian show trial in the thirties. Witnesses were playing a part written for them by the prosecutors; defendants had been tortured into submitting to this charade.

But some things are certain. It is indisputable that during the three years Cohen worked in Syria he kept up an extraordinary work rate, broadcasting home material of immense importance which was not available to the Israelis from other sources. In Israel, the Elie Cohen volumes burst at the seams with the information he supplied, most of which was made available within hours to combat units serving on the Syrian border. To the people of Israel, he became a national hero. To Meir Amit and Aharon Yariv he was quite simply the ultimate professional. When, on Day 5 of the Six-Day War, the Israeli Army swung round and stormed the Golan Heights, taking what had been regarded by most military men as an unconquerable fortress in a few hours, glasses were raised within the offices of Military Intelligence in Israel to the memory of Elie Cohen, who, more than any other single individual, had made that assault possible.

Chapter 16

IN THE WEEK that Meir Amit officially became head of Mossad, on March 25, 1963, he took the trouble to visit senior military men as well as top civil servants in virtually every government ministry in the country. It was first and foremost a public relations exercise, forced upon him, he believed, by the very strong feelings which his appointment had created in certain ministries. However unpopular Harel had been in some quarters, he was universally regarded as being irreplaceable. Meir Amit did, however, have another purpose in making these courtesy calls. He wanted to explain what he believed the objectives of Mossad ought to be and get in return an idea of what kind of services the ministries expected the agency to supply. Only General Mordechai Hod, chief of the Israeli Air Force, could come up with a specific request. If, he told Amit, Mossad really wanted to earn its keep, then it should bring him a MiG-21.

The MiG-21, if Russian claims were to be believed, was the most advanced strike aircraft in the world. In 1961, the Russians, under conditions of maximum secrecy, began introducing this aircraft into the region, and by the time Meir Amit took over Mossad, the MiG-21 was in service with the Egyptian, Iraqi and Syrian air forces. It was an aircraft about which no one in the West had anything but the vaguest details

Its speeds, armaments, its performance capabilities, its instrumentation, its defensive equipment, all vital information if the Israeli Air Force was to be given a chance to counter it, were all unknown quantities. General Hod had made his request before, and preliminary inquiries by agents in all three countries where the plane was stationed had indicated that the Russians had made it a condition of supplying the aircraft that they should be responsible for security, crew training and maintenance.

Elie Cohen had managed to get a picture of one of the aircraft at its special secret airbase in Syria; this was as close as anyone had got.

The fact was that the Russians were well aware that by stationing squadrons of the MiG-21s outside the Soviet Union, they were risking its secrets passing to the West. Security was therefore extremely tight. Men chosen for MiG training were hand-picked—the cream of their respective air forces. Appointment to a MiG-21 squadron was the highest honor that could be granted to a pilot. These were not the kind of men who could be bribed or would talk loosely in public. As a result, neither Mossad nor Military Intelligence had made any progress at all. Just before Christmas in 1964, a man called at the Israeli embassy in Paris and asked to speak to the military attaché. He said that he didn't have an appointment but that what he had to say was of such major importance he felt sure the attaché would wish to see him. The military attaché was not in the building at the time, and so a young second secretary was deputed to see the stranger in one of the small conference rooms of the embassy. The man got straight to the point. He explained that he would not return to the embassy; nor would the Israelis ever hear from him again. He had come to the embassy only to deliver an important communication from a friend in Iraq. The message was that if the Israelis wanted a MiG-21, they should telephone a certain number in Baghdad and ask to speak to Joseph. Joseph would arrange it. Astonished—and also amused —the Israeli diplomat asked for more information. The man said that he didn't have any, shook the diplomat by the hand, and walked out into the streets of Paris leaving neither a name nor any clue as to where he had come from. All the Israelis had was the name Joseph and a telephone number.

The young diplomat wrote out a brief report and sent it down the corridor to the Mossad office within the embassy. No one took it too seriously. Espionage freaks are to be found everywhere and cause almost as many problems to secret-service agencies as do opposition agents. The more paranoic they are, the more convincing their stories; often they come up with elaborate and convincing dossiers, all of which have to be checked out at great expense, wasting precious man-hours chasing after a chimera.

But Amit, when he learned of the incident, took a different view. However unlikely the Paris approach might seem, it simply had to be followed up. That number in Baghdad had to be telephoned, and he wanted within twenty-four hours a written proposal as to how this should be done.

Michael Sharon (a pseudonym), the head of operations, a tough ex-Palmach officer who had worked his way up through Mossad from its inception and who had been one of those in the agency most deeply opposed to Meir Amit when he first arrived but had grown to respect and then like him, called together a team of three to provide an operational plan.

The biggest danger as far as Mossad was concerned was not that the mysterious caller was an espionage freak, but that he was an opposition agent rather clumsily luring the Israelis into a trap. It was, therefore, out of the question for anyone in any existing Israeli network in Iraq to make the telephone call. It would be equally dangerous for an Isreali agent in Baghdad even to attempt to check the number with the local telephone exchange. Presumably the Iraqis would have that well covered.

Michael Sharon's plan assumed—as it had to—that this was indeed a trap. Therefore, someone had to be inserted into the country with sufficient experience and intelligence to make an accurate on-the-spot assessment of the contact (should he exist) and his proposal; at the same time the agent could not know too much about Israeli intelligence, which he might betray under torture, and could not be given the use of any existing Israeli facilities or call upon any Mossad network in Baghdad for help. Whoever was chosen for the mission, said Sharon, had to know in advance that he would almost certainly be going to his death.

Meir Amit himself came up with a possible candidate. He had come across and had been most impressed by a young field intelligence officer in Military Intelligence. He had trained as a paratrooper, had a good degree in Arabic studies from Jerusalem University, and spoke fluent English and Arabic. His family had been in Israel since the turn of the century. Even his grandfather was a

sabra. His name was Yossef Mansor. Still a lieutenant,
he had already been marked out for early promotion,
though as yet he had not dealt with any security matter
of great sensitivity. He was ideal in every way. Mansor
was located, and arrangements were made for him to
meet Amit and Sharon. He knew who Amit was, of
course, but Sharon introduced himself only as Michael.
He left nothing to the imagination in his description of
the dangers inherent in the mission. For what it was
worth, Sharon said, his staff believed that the man who
called at the embassy in Paris was almost certainly a
fantasist and arguably a dangerous one. Mossad had
come across such people before. He would be at the other
end of the line and as soon as the call was made would
inform the Iraqi authorities, whom no doubt he had
been plaguing with his reports of Israeli spy rings for
years. This time, however, he would have a real Israeli
spy to hand over.

Meir Amit concurred with everything that Sharon had
said but added this rider. The MiG was important to
Israel. Nobody would be asked to volunteer for what was
on the face of it a crazy mission if the product they were
after was not really so important. Michael Sharon put it
more brutally. At this moment, he told Yossef Mansor,
the MiG is more important than you are. Mansor was
asked to think it over, but he refused to do so and agreed
to go to Iraq then and there.

Overriding the objections of Sharon and others, Meir
Amit decided that in order to help Mansor, Mossad
should risk exposing one of its most successful operations.
Years earlier a firm engaged in the manufacture of sophisticated electrical and medical equipment had been
set up in Europe to do genuine business with the Arab
world in particular but the rest of Europe and Africa as
well. The firm, which had become one of the leaders in
its field (and made a handsome profit every year), was a
cover operation for Mossad and had been used on frequent occasions to send Israeli agents into the Arab world
with the credentials of export salesmen for the company.
So well established had it become that there was never
any difficulty about getting visas for its people or even in
setting up branch offices in many Arab capitals.

Amit well understood that if Mansor was walking into
a trap, then this sophisticated operation could well come

under intense suspicion and might even be forced to suspend operations altogether. There was, however, only one man (working in Cairo) then in the field on behalf of the firm, and he was ordered to return to Europe. If Mansor was caught, then only the firm, not individuals, would be compromised. It was, nevertheless, a tremendous risk to take.

Four weeks later, armed with false papers that showed him to be an Englishman specializing in X-ray equipment (a subject in which he had been given a crash course), Yossef Mansor flew into Baghdad and checked into the splendid old Baghdad Hotel on Sa'adon Street. For a week, he made the rounds of hospitals and Health Ministry officials, pushing his equipment (he turned out to be a natural salesman), all the time mentally preparing himself for the one telephone call he had come to Iraq to make.

Finally, he knew he could put it off no longer. To serve as a slim kind of cover, he took two senior officials of the Ministry of Health to dinner in one of Baghdad's best restaurants, and then halfway through the meal excused himself in order, he said, to make a business call. As he dialed the number, his legs were trembling. Someone answered at the other end, and he asked for Joseph. He had mentally expected "Joseph" to answer and was unprepared for the question "Who's speaking?" Falteringly, he described himself as "a friend from out of town," thinking, as he spoke, that that was probably a mistake. He gripped the receiver for over a minute in his damp hands before Joseph came to the telephone. Mansor knew that Mossad had been angry with the second secretary in Paris for at the very least not having arranged a simple code, but it had been agreed between him and Sharon that he would say: "It was nice to meet your friend, perhaps we can get together to discuss the matter." Now he completely forgot all of this and asked, feeling rather foolish as he did so: "You are *the* Joseph?" It was Joseph, who seemed to be as calm as Mansor was agitated, who saved the situation. "Are you the gentleman who met my friend?" he asked. Mansor mumbled that he was and found himself agreeing to a meeting in a Baghdad coffee house at noon the following day. He had to go to the toilet to calm himself after the call, knowing that he had broken every single instruction given him in

Tel Aviv. *He* should have nominated the meeting place, not Joseph; *he* should have suggested a time, not Joseph. He wondered whether he should phone back and change the arrangement but realized that would be even more ridiculous. He returned to the table, but, as he later told Mossad, he couldn't remember anything about the conversation for the rest of that evening or even recall how he got back to his hotel.

The next day, as he sat out under the awning of a café in the middle of Baghdad, he knew, without anyone's having to tell him, that his panic had caused him to break one of the most important instructions of all. Not only had Joseph told Mansor where to meet him, but he had asked Mansor to describe how he would be dressed so that Joseph would be able to recognize him. This was an appalling blunder. Instead of being the ferret, he had become the rabbit. He should have been told what Joseph looked like and not the other way round. If he had, he would now be sitting waiting for his mark in the café across the street, ready to move out fast if anything didn't look quite right. Instead, he sat there, imagining everyone's eyes on him and expecting any moment to feel the heavy hand of Iraqi security on his shoulder. He nearly fell out of his seat when, dead on the strike of noon, the chair opposite him was taken and a man smilingly introduced himself as Joseph. Joseph was sixty, if he was a day. His face was dark and deeply etched, setting off magnificently his snowy white hair. He was dressed in a suit which looked as if it might have been handed on to him. They each ordered a black Turkish coffee, and Joseph took a sickly piece of Arab pastry, all the while observing Mansor closely.

Mansor will remember to the rest of his days Joseph's opening words: "It was nice of you to come," just as if Mansor had dropped in for tea and not flown into a hostile country on a forged passport, putting his very life on the line. It was, he thought, all a rather sick joke. This old man had managed to turn Mossad inside out because of some wild fancy, which probably wasn't even worth an explanation. One thing was for sure, however, he had nothing to do with Iraqi security—he was evidently too gentle for that. For the first time since he'd arrived in Iraq seven days before, Mansor felt the luxury of calm.

"We are," said Mansor, realizing that he had to go on

with the pretense for at least this one meeting, "most interested in the merchandise of which your friend spoke." "You mean," said the old man, "the MiG." Mansor swallowed hard and nodded. "It will cost a lot of money," the old man went on, "and much time. But I think it can be arranged."

Almost despite himself, Mansor felt a tingle of excitement. There was something so majestically serene about Joseph, so certain, that he found it difficult to dismiss what he was saying out of hand. He tried another tack: "My friends don't understand how you will be able to achieve this where others, to be frank, have tried and failed." Joseph smiled and proposed another meeting, where, he said, they could talk more fully. It was set up for the following day—on a park bench this time, away from the crowds.

It was there that Joseph told Mansor his story. He had come from a poor Jewish Iraqi family, and at the age of ten had been indentured as a servant in the house of a rich Maronite Christian family. He had never attended school, could hardly read or write, and yet, as the years went by, he established for himself a very special position in the household in which he worked. He was still in theory a servant, but more and more the whole family had come to rely upon him for advice and guidance, in personal as well as in business matters. His influence within the household was remarkable. He had known and looked after the head of the house since he was a baby. He had approved his marriage and had looked after his children with the same love and care he had lavished on their father. No secret was kept from him, no family conference was ever convened without his presence or without his having the last word. He had become more than part of the family, he had grown to be a kind of spiritual father to them all. Two years previously, an event had occurred which had changed his life. He and the head of the house had had a violent disagreement in the course of which the Maronite Christian, losing his temper, threw Joseph's illiteracy in his face and accused him of being nothing without the family. A few hours later, the father had deeply apologized to him, and, in Arab fashion, the two had embraced to show that no ill-feelings existed between them.

Joseph, however, knew that though what had been

said had been spoken in anger, there was, nevertheless, justice in the words. He existed only in relation to the family. There and then, at the age of sixty, he decided that that was not quite good enough. The only other identity he possessed was his Jewishness—something he had never given a moment's pause for thought during any part of his life. He didn't know any other Jews, and to the degree that he thought of Israel, he did so with the animosity of a true citizen of Iraq. Now he set about in search of his heritage. The Jewish population of Iraq had been decimated in the early fifties; nevertheless some Jews still did live on in Baghdad. Among them Joseph found a teacher, a local rabbi who instructed him in the Bible and the Jewish faith. He joined a small discussion group which met once a week to discuss Judaism and Israel. All of those who attended, Joseph observed curiously, while not wishing to go to live in Israel, nevertheless felt profound ties with the country and its people. They were Zionists as long as no one ever suggested they should go to live in Zion. It was a feeling Joseph grew to share. His loyalty to his family was absolute—but so, too, was his newfound loyalty to Israel. Six months later, Joseph discovered the means by which he believed he could serve both. The Iraqi government was putting pressure on the Christian Maronite minority. At a family conference, the father revealed how it was becoming increasingly difficult to manage his business due to government interference, how they were being financially squeezed, and also how his friends had been imprisoned on trumped-up charges. He felt he could be next. If only, he said, we had a means of getting out.

His eldest son, Munir Redfa, however, felt none of these pressures. Brought up and educated in Arab schools, more Iraqi than the Iraqis, he was a deputy squadron leader and a brilliant pilot who had been chosen to fly the new MiG-21 supplied by the Russians, one of the fastest and best fighter planes in the world.

It was his talk of this Russian wonder plane, and of the millions the Israelis would pay to have a look at it, that gave Joseph his idea. His influence on the boy was such that he believed he could persuade him to fly to Israel. In return, he would get from the Israelis a guarantee to bring the entire family out to safety and sufficient funds to permit them to live in the style to which they had been accustomed in Baghdad.

Joseph was the kind of man who only saw simple solutions to complex problems. He persuaded a friend from the study group going to Europe on business to leave his message with the Israeli embassy. Then he sat back and waited, confident that the Israelis would call. Mansor asked him how much money the family would need. He had thought about that, too—half a million pounds sterling. For himself, he wanted nothing, not even a safe passage.

A week later, Yossef Mansor was back in Tel Aviv reporting to Meir Amit. As far as the story could be checked without drawing attention to himself, Mansor had done so. He had confirmed that Joseph's family existed and that there was a son in the Iraqi Air Force. The rest, including the fact that he was flying MiG-21s, had to be taken on trust.

Mansor himself had been completely won over by the simple directness of Joseph, but he had more difficulty in transmitting that feeling to senior personnel inside Mossad. Only Meir Amit needed no persuading. But so determined was he to get a MiG that, as his deputy said rather caustically at the time, he would have believed that Joseph was a setup only if the President of Iraq told him so himself. The professionals were considerably more skeptical. At worst, one said, Joseph was working for the Iraqis, luring an Israeli espionage team deep into the mire. At best, he was a shakedown artist who no doubt would soon be demanding money on account.

It came as something of a shock to the pro-Joseph group within Mossad when Joseph did just that two months later, when Mansor was sent back to seek more precise details from Joseph as to how he believed the operation could be carried out. The family, said Joseph, would need convincing very early on after he had put his plan to them that their interests would be properly looked after. Therefore, he would propose to them that a trusted uncle who needed medical treatment would request permission of the authorities for an exit permit allowing him to go to Switzerland. It would be up to the Israelis to see to it that a sizable advance would be waiting for him so that he could cable the family that the Israelis could be trusted.

When pinned down to the exact sum the uncle would regard as sufficient, Joseph proposed a figure of a quarter of a million pounds sterling.

Even Mansor was shocked by the amount and for the first time began to entertain doubts. But Joseph, as Joseph was always able to do, convinced him that he was not being unreasonable. He had thought it all out most carefully. The pilot would only go if the family had been properly provided for. The family would only go if they knew that they had a real opportunity of re-establishing their family fortune outside Iraq. The fact was that whatever political difficulties they faced, they enjoyed a standard of living far higher than most Westerners ever dreamed of. Rather than leave Iraq in penury, they would take their chances and stay. When the time came for him to sell his plan to the family, he would need to be able to talk about very large sums of money indeed. He would also need to be able to propose a plan which would convince them that the Israelis could be trusted.

Needless to say, this explanation did not go down too well in Tel Aviv. Mansor was dismissed as a naive young man who had been taken in by a professional con man, and Amit was strongly urged to drop the matter altogether.

But Meir Amit thought otherwise. His position was simple: Israel stood to lose half a million pounds and stood to gain a MiG-21. If it was a gamble, it was one Israel could not afford not to take. Cabinet approval for the operation came quickly once Amit had briefed the Chief of Staff Yitzhak Rabin, who became as enthusiastically committed as he was. To the military, this operation was the most important that the intelligence service had ever mounted. If successful, the impact—particularly upon the air force but also upon the other services—could not possibly be overstated.

Whatever view the professionals took about the likelihood of success, once the decision had been taken, both intelligence agencies threw themselves into the operation with total commitment. Because the stakes were so high and the "Joseph" factor so puzzling, very little could be left to chance. Though Meir Amit had criticized the way Isser Harel had used virtually the whole of Mossad on a single operation, he now did precisely the same, justifying himself on the grounds that the sum of all current Israeli intelligence activity did not measure up to the vital importance of this one operation. Meir Amit was, of course, gambling with more than money, he was gambling with his career. It is doubtful whether he could have survived the ridicule if Joseph had turned out to be what some believed he was right to the end, a clever trickster. For eighteen agonizing months, nobody could be sure.

Michael Sharon continued in charge of the operational planning. He was a good choice. He still had grave doubts about the whole mission, and so would not make that classic error of believing Joseph because he wanted to believe him. Healthy skepticism, provided it did not become obstructive, was essential if lives were not to be thrown away needlessly.

He now took a remarkable step. He removed from Iraq almost the entire Israeli network which had been built up over the years. He couldn't risk accidents, he couldn't risk chance encounters which could destroy everything. Then he set up five operational teams. Team No. 1 consisted of Yossef Mansor, assisted by a radio operator. Mansor's job was to remain in Baghdad and set up a business front with his radio operator officially employed as his assistant. Once in position it would be his job to maintain contact with Joseph and also, if possible, the family. Team No. 2, consisting of four men, would also be in Baghdad covering Mansor without his knowing it. Mansor was given a dead-letter box communication in Baghdad with this team and they with him, but who they were, how many, or what their function was he had no idea. Their basic function was to help Mansor and his radio operator out of the country if anything went wrong, or to take over from Mansor if it looked as if he was losing control of what was clearly going to be a delicate as well as hazardous mission. Team No. 3, consisting of three men, was put into Baghdad for two or three months in order to keep the family under observation through electronic means. (As it turned out, this team was never able to establish anything of any value, and they were withdrawn early for fear that this kind of physical surveillance might betray the whole operation.)

Team No. 4 came from Military Intelligence and consisted of six men, who were put into Kurdistan. Their function would be to keep contact with the Kurds, who, it was hoped, would be persuaded to assist in transporting the family out of the country.

Team No. 5 was stationed in Ahwaz in Persia. They would help in the evacuation of the family. A diplomatic team was also sent to Washington and Turkey in order to seek landing and refueling rights should this become necessary. The direct flight from Iraq to Israel is over hostile territory all the way. Even if this did not matter too much —it was thought unlikely that the Jordanians could get anything into the air to intercept the MiG—the Israelis knew that the Russians were aware of the dangers of pilots on training missions flying their aircraft to the West and therefore kept fuel tanks only half full, probably making the journey from Iraq to Israel impossible without refueling if the Russians maintained this policy in Iraq.

Joseph in the meantime was biding his time. But he did have one real shock for the Israelis which he wanted to have clear before he made his first approach to the head of the household, namely, the sheer size of the family to be transported out of the country. He was not talking, as had previously been assumed, merely about a wife and children but two parents, grandparents, aunts and uncles, nephews and nieces, as well as two old family retainers. Michael Sharon absorbed this extraordinary demand as he had so many others without flickering an eyelid. Nevertheless, it obviously created huge problems, not merely how to get them away physically, but how to ensure that one or other didn't at least hint to friends that they were leaving the country and for good. A student of human nature, as all successful spymasters have to be, Sharon took the view that it would be inevitable for one or other of this large group of people, if they were in on the secret, to find the temptation to talk—however elliptically—irresistible. Iraqi security men were everywhere; one word out of place and the operation—along with all those participating in it—could well die there and then.

Joseph, as always, had the simple answer to an apparently complex problem. The flight of the family would have to be arranged in such a way that the majority would not know where they were going until they were away. As every last one of them prayed every day for the chance to leave Baghdad for good, they would not be too upset if the decision as to how this was to be done was taken from their hands.

With everyone in position, it was now up to Joseph to use the influence he said he had to talk the family round. It took him close to four months. First, he worked on the father, convinced him of the feasibility of what he was suggesting, and then the son, Squadron Leader Munir Redfa, who was at first shocked and then slowly came to see how only in this way could he and his family be certain of a long-term future. But he was still indecisive, struggling between his sense of patriotism and his filial duty, when Meir Amit, daily in contact by radio, had a brain wave. The CIA and the Pentagon wanted the MiG as much as anyone. So, over a weekend, he flew to Washington himself to inform the CIA director that Mossad had a MiG-21 on the line and only needed a little CIA help to reel it in. The Americans leaped at the opportunity.

So it was that a senior diplomat at the American Embassy in Baghdad met Joseph and Squadron Leader Redfa at a prearranged spot one night to explain how vital it was for the whole Western alliance, in its fight against Communism, to get hold of this aircraft. The following day, the diplomat flew home, never to return, in case the pilot went to the authorities. But he didn't. Now satisfied that he wasn't being asked to work merely for the Israelis, whom he had been conditioned to regard as the enemy, but against the Russians, and at the same time that he could help himself and his family, he informed Joseph he was prepared to go.

At this point, Munir Redfa was invited to Israel. Together with a Mossad operative—an attractive woman, posing as a rich American—he flew to Paris on holiday. There, false papers were provided him, and he was brought to Israel, where he met the commander of the Israeli Air Force, General Mordechai ("Motti") Hod, who was able to reassure him about his escape route and about arrangements for his family. This extraordinary journey was strictly unneccessary, but it committed the pilot to the Israeli cause as well as helping to give him confidence in the ability of the Israelis to bring out his family.

Back in Iraq, Michael Sharon now began slowly and carefully to knit all the pieces together. There was no problem about the uncle's getting his exit permit to take a cure in Switzerland. There he was paid the money and watched over day and night by another Israeli team just to make sure that he stayed put. He sent a postcard to Joseph in a prearranged code that the Israelis had fulfilled their part of the bargain.

A friendly doctor was found to provide a medical certificate stating that Munir Redfa's son needed urgent treatment in London. Nothing was more natural than that he, accompanied by his mother, should leave the country immediately.

Now D-day was approaching fast. The pilot was visibly suffering from cold feet. His main concern was that he might fly the aircraft out to Turkey only to discover that his father and mother and other relatives had been abandoned. At one point, he was refusing to move at all unless he had confirmation that they had all reached safety. Clearly this was impossible.

The Israeli plan for the family was comparatively simple. In the hot Iraqi summer, it is normal for wealthy families to move to the foothills of the mountains of Kurdistan. The Kurdish rebellion had made this more difficult, but nevertheless there were still spas well out of the troubled areas where people could take houses away from the heat and dust of Baghdad.

The Israelis, who were supporting the Kurds militarily, made arrangements with Sheik Banzhani, leader of the Kurdish tribes, to smuggle the family from their cottage through the Iraqi lines into the mountains, where they would be picked up by helicopter and flown to nearby Ahwaz in Persia. All of this would take twenty-four hours —twenty-four hours in which their absence might be discovered.

To wait, as the pilot wanted, for them to get to safety before he made his move could easily mean disaster. Eventually, it was agreed that two events—the arrival of the helicopter in Kurdistan and his flight—should be simultaneous. The date fixed for the operation was August 15, 1966, when his duty roster showed that the pilot would be on an early-morning training flight from his base near Mosul in northern Iraq. On the actual day, nothing went wrong. Once in the air, the pilot suddenly banked his plane, put on his afterburners, and was over the Turkish border before the Russians knew what had happened. With U.S.A.F. Phantoms flying escort, he put down at a secret CIA base, refueled, and with more fighter escort planes made his way out over Turkey and the Mediterranean, where Israeli fighters waited to escort him to Israel.

At the same time, Michael Sharon's fourth team had performed their part of the operation with little trouble. They had met the whole family at a pre-arranged spot, where the family had ostensibly gone for a picnic. Two fast cars, previously rented in Baghdad, took them just south of the Iraqi lines, where they waited for nightfall. A platoon of Kurdish guerrillas who had used this spot as one of their main infiltration points into Iraq picked them up and, traveling by mules through the night, took them to the helicopter pickup point. The chopper arrived exactly on time, and in thirty-five minutes the whole family had been ferried to safety. Within days, a new identity had been found for them all, and they were permitted to disappear to live the rest of their lives in peace and security.

On May 2, 1968, on the twentieth anniversary of the founding of Israel, the Israeli government, in defiance of the United Nations, organized a vast military parade through the streets of Jerusalem. It was, of course, a double celebration. Only eleven months previously, the Israelis had won in what came to be known as the Six-Day War one of the most famous victories in modern military history.

At 10:00 A.M., watched by half a million people, the parade began. A plane painted bright red swooped over the city to the cheers of the population. There were not many in the crowd who realized that they were cheering not an Israeli Mirage, which had made victory possible, but a Russian MiG-21.

General Amit and his men from Mossad and Military Intelligence could not, of course, take part in the parade. So the MiG-21, the capture of which had been one of Israeli intelligence's greatest triumphs, had to do the job for them. The Army high command's way of acknowledging the supreme role which intelligence had played in that victory was to permit Mossad's MiG-21 to lead the parade.

Chapter 17

THE SIX-DAY WAR was to prove to be the ultimate test of the Amit-Yariv axis at the head of the Israeli intelligence community. There are some pro-Arab modern historians who still insist upon maintaining that because Israel launched the first strike, it was Israel that started an aggressive war of conquest against her weaker Arab neighbors. Alternatively, it is claimed that somehow the Israelis manipulated President Nasser, or, as Ambassador Charles W. Yost of the American U.N. delegation put it, contrived the crisis, because "it is difficult to see how any Israeli leader could have failed to foresee that such repeated massive reprisals must eventually place the leader of the Arab coalition in a position where he would have to respond."

There is no question that two events—a raid on the Jordanian village of al-Samu in which 18 Jordanians were killed and 134 wounded on November 15, 1966, and an air battle between Syrian MiGs and Israeli Mirages over the Plain of Damascus in which six MiGs were shot down on April 7, 1967—had the effect of uniting the normally suspicious Arab nations.

But even prior to these events, Meir Amit was reporting to the Cabinet that the Egyptians at least, bolstered by Russian arms, were confidentially preparing staff position papers which were being circulated to corps commanders on battlefield tactics within the boundaries of Israel itself. It has subsequently been claimed that, within his heart of hearts, President Nasser knew that he could not win a war against Israel, but if this is the case, he did nothing to transmit his views to the generals, his closest advisers or his allies.

The war really began on May 16th, when President Nasser ordered the U.N. Emergency Force (which had held the two parties apart since the Suez campaign of

1956) out of Egypt. U Thant, the U.N. Secretary-General, complied with almost indecent haste, and the vacuum was quickly filled by Nasser, who poured 100,000 Egyptian soldiers and 900 tanks into the Sinai Desert to add to the six Syrian brigades backed by nearly 300 tanks which had already massed on the Golan.

Six days later, on May 22nd, President Nasser imposed a blockade on the Straits of Tiran, Israel's outlet to the Red Sea. The whole world knew that Israel regarded freedom of navigation through this international waterway—a right specifically guaranteed her by the world's maritime powers, including the United States, Britain, Canada and France in 1956—as being so fundamental that any attempt to deny so Israeli ships passage would be an automatic *casus belli*. But to the disgust of the majority of Israeli generals, Eskhol wavered. War, he believed, was the ultimate obscenity. He had every reason to attack immediately, but he risked seeking diplomatic solutions first.

There was more than an edge of hysteria in Israel during those dangerous days. Apart from the 1948 War of Independence, Israel had not fought a full-scale war against the Arabs alone. There were even some in the Army who doubted Israel's capability to do so, especially if Eshkol, by keeping the diplomatic pot on the boil for too long, lost Israel the ability to launch the first strike. Criticism of the government became wilder and wilder in the press and in private, until Eshkol was forced to bring in General (Reserve) Moshe Dayan, then a civilian and a member of Parliament, as Minister of Defense to reassure both a nervous population and an edgy Army.

Only one man in the whole military hierarchy kept his head during these days of intense turmoil: The chief of Military Intelligence Aharon Yariv, known to his friends as Ahrele, had laid the Egyptian and Syrian order of battle against Israeli strategic operational plans so many times that the thought that Israel could lose the war he knew would inevitably come that year did not occur to him for a moment. It was Yariv who was pressing for war because he knew that war could be won. So finely tuned was his intelligence apparatus that he was able to predict an outcome which was to astonish the world when it was all over. Despite all the experience every Israeli senior officer had had of the decisive effect accurate intelligence could and did have on their military actions, particularly against terrorist encampments in Jordan and Syria, it needed, for all their staff training, a huge effort of imagination to understand how this same careful and detailed application to particulars could and should be brought into play in the vast arena of a full-scale war. As far as the public was concerned, all of this passed them by entirely. Ahrele Yariv had until then always shunned publicity (though subsequently he was to go rather the other way), and he was virtually unknown outside the Army, a long way removed from the glamorous generals Israelis were beginning to treat the way other countries treated their film stars.

Yariv was born in Moscow in 1921, the second son of a pediatrician, Dr. Haim Rabinowitz. In 1925, Dr. Rabinowitz moved his family to Lithuania, where he was a leading Zionist. His elder brother, Gutman, was also involved in Zionist affairs, but Ahrele himself took little interest in politics until one day a Lithuanian staff officer came to talk to his class. The officer preached about patriotism and service, and how the future of the nation resided in the army. He then noted that there were only two kinds of "incurable dodgers," the gypsies and the Jews.

From that moment on, Ahrele became not only a Zionist but a boy determined to stand and fight in a Jewish army. The whole family emigrated to Palestine in 1935 and, not finding an army to join, Yariv went to an agricultural school and joined the Haganah. Though small, thin, and apparently rather undernourished when he arrived, his natural qualities of leadership soon asserted themselves and within a short time he became head of the pupils' committee. A keen soccer player (he was a first rate goal keeper) and outstanding at his lessons, Ahrele, according to those who were at school with him, had about him that indefinable aura which marks out some boys at an early age.

When war broke out, he joined the British Army immediately, and, as a young officer, became A.D.C. to Major Ephraim Ben Artzi, the only Palestinian Jew to become a battalion commander during the war. He left the British Army with the rank of captain and, like Fatti Harkabi, applied and was accepted for the Jewish Agency's "Institute of Advanced Studies," which was in reality a training course for the diplomats the new State of Israel would require immediately upon independence. But, like Harkabi, he was pulled out by the Army. Their need was greater. He became, in turn, adjutant to the Haganah Chief of Staff Yaacov Dori, then to Yigal Yadin, who was to become Chief of Staff in 1949 and was then head of operations, and the guide and personal assistant to David ("Miki") Marcus, the brilliant American soldier who was killed by accident by one of his own men during the Battle of Jerusalem.

After the fighting, Yariv became first a pupil and then an instructor at the Israeli Army's senior war college for battalion commanders, then being run by Yitzhak Rabin. He was the only non-Palmach instructor on the course, but soon proved that he had no need to apologize for his background. It was after he returned from France, where he attended the French Military College (one of his classmates was General Gamal Faisal, who was for a period Chief of Staff of the Syrian Army), that he had first the opportunity to put his own mark on the Israeli Army.

He headed a team whose brief was to establish Israel's first Staff College, and when, in 1956, it was ready to open its doors, he became its first commander. Though the curriculum has changed many times since he ran it for a period of two years, the Staff College is still today regarded in the Army as very much Ahrele Yariv's. He put enormous emphasis not merely upon arcane military arts but upon establishing what he described as a "college of thinking," a university for mature students, where logic and philosophy figured almost as prominently in the curriculum as weaponry and tactics. He went straight from that post to becoming Israeli military attaché in Washington, where he astonished the Pentagon not merely by asking to go on night maneuvers with the American marines but, instead of watching the action from headquarters, by insisting on spending the time with lower ranks at platoon level. Back in Israel, in March 1960 he was given what he had always wanted, the command of a brigade. Held by now in considerable esteem, he commanded the Golani Brigade. But it wasn't to last long. The man whose only real ambition was to be a fighting general was simply too finely attuned to staff work, where his talents were badly needed, and so in the summer of 1961, when Meir Amit became chief of Military Intelligence, Yariv was appointed his deputy.

Brought up on the spit and polish tradition of the British army, Yariv has always been very different from most senior Israeli officers. He speaks quietly and apparently shyly; he was known as a disciplinarian, yet most who have ever served closely with him have remained firm and admiring friends. Unlike most Israeli generals, he dislikes personal publicity and told one reporter who wanted to write a profile about him for his newspaper that he disapproved of turning the I.D.F. (the Israeli Defense Forces) and its officers into "a kind of *son-et-lumière*." The morale of the Army, he said, should not revolve around little stories about its commanders.

It is never quite clear from history whether great events shape great men or great men shape great events. The fact is, however, that Israel, when it entered into the troubled year of 1967, could not have been more fortunate in having a man like Ahrele Yariv at the head of its Military Intelligence Service. Here was an officer whose intellect could not be faulted, who had personally taught most of the operational commanders, and who himself had distinguished battlefield experience. Most of the top commanders had been his students at the Staff College. There may have been some who didn't much like him, but there could have been none who didn't admire and respect him. In a trade where intellectuals are natural targets of suspicion, Yariv had a brain which was both widely recognized as being outstanding and at the same time one which, as a staff officer put it, indubitably wore I.D.F. uniform.

But even Yariv would have to admit that if it hadn't been for his immediate predecessors, Military Intelligence would not have been the finely honed weapon it was when he came to take over. Harkabi had given him one of the best research and analysis departments in the whole of the Middle East. Herzog had shaped the whole into a superbly organized machine, and Amit had refined it so that Military Intelligence was totally battle oriented.

Perhaps most important of all, work done by one of the most remarkable men ever employed by this intelligence service or any other had reached the point where it could be put to daily use. The man was Yuval Ne'eman, a highly distinguished Israeli scientist, now professor of physics at Tel Aviv University, who served for over ten years as a colonel in Military Intelligence under Gibli,

Harkabi and Amit and was now leader of a new right-wing political party.

Ne'eman was not the first intelligence man to understand the uses of the science of computerology and high technology in the world of espionage. But he was the first within any service in the world, save perhaps the Russians', to have the mind and the background to design equipment or himself have equipment designed specifically to meet the needs of this somewhat arcane profession.

Yuval Ne'eman was born in Tel Aviv in 1925 and educated at the Imperial College, London, where he took his doctorate. To the astonishment of his friends, to whom he appeared the archetype scientist—brilliant (they called him "the Brain") but unworldly—he not only fought in the War of Independence, but proved to be an outstanding success as a soldier.

After the 1948 war, the Army encouraged him to stay on and, like so many others destined for high rank, he was sent to the War College in Paris; he returned home after graduation to become one of the senior deputies in Military Intelligence.

Ne'eman's "message" suffered the duel disadvantage of being both revolutionary and expensive. Future wars, he predicted, would be won by electronics. The greatest intelligence officer in the world, he said, would be a mere child against an inferior enemy armed with a computer. In warfare a Chief of Staff required instant intelligence. Without computers, he would either not get it or what was supplied to him would not be exact. Between wars, a government required constant surveillance of the potential enemy. The traditional spy still had his uses, but electronic watch stations, which would keep the borders under constant observation and detect the smallest movement for analysis, were bound to take over part of his function, leaving him free for other work, perhaps in the political field, no electronic gadget yet devised could do.

To cost-conscious Israeli ministers and bureaucrats who had somehow imagined that Ne'eman was brought in to invent things like exploding suitcases or fountain-pen guns, this came as something of a shock. For he proposed an investment of many millions of dollars in hardware which he freely admitted would be outdated every five years as ever-newer technology came along to replace it.

To many army men, the concept of spending billions on equipment which doesn't, as one of Ne'eman's friends remarked contemptuously, "go bang" was sacrilegious. The Ne'eman thesis today hardly appears very startling, but in the early fifties it was revolutionary.

In any case Ne'eman was given the money and the resources. Within a few short years, perhaps only the Americans could match Israel's impressive computer-linked electronic warning systems. Much of Ne'eman's work was completely original. It was he who invented the system of the computerized tracking of submarines. NATO's northern and southern boundaries are protected by his electronic watch stations, first erected in the Sinai by Israeli forward patrols who went into the desert to bury sophisticated equipment to serve as an early-warning alarm system for any unexpected Egyptian movements.

The Ne'eman revolution did not take place without occasional traumas. In 1960, Israel partly mobilized because the alarm went off in the Sinai and the computers predicted an imminent invasion. What was a comparatively low-level Egyptian military exercise would have almost overnight escalated into full-scale war if the human genius for genuine understanding as distinct from mere computing had not intervened to override the electronics. The system was modified and refined until it was as sophisticated and advanced as similar systems anywhere in the world, and certainly far outstripped anything possessed by medium-sized powers like Great Britain and France.

There comes a point in the life of an organization when, because of a variety of circumstances, it reaches as near a state of perfection as is inherent within the concept which framed it. With Ahrele Yariv heading Israeli Military Intelligence at the start of the Six-Day War, that state had been reached. It could not have come at a more fortuitous moment.

At 7:30 A.M. on June 5, 1967, the first wave of Mystère and Mirage supersonic fighter-bombers took off from their secret airbases inside Israel, swept out over the Mediterranean and back in again from the west, completely putting out of commission sixteen Egyptian airfields and the planes on them. Within two hours—by 9:30 A.M.—the Israelis destroyed nearly 400 Arab aircraft and wrecked by similar attacks in Jordan and Syria the entire Arab air force. The war was virtually settled there and then. Brigadier General Mordechai Hod, the Israeli Air Force commander, described this as a victory "beyond my wildest dreams," to which one of Yariv's intelligence officers remarked that the general must have been sleeping during all of their briefings. The first-strike strategy—to hit the Arab MiGs before they got off the ground—had long been part of Israeli doctrine, but it was Yariv who refined it to the point where chance was ruled out of this most spectacular of military operations.

"Know your enemy" was not, Yariv told his heads of department, merely a figure of speech; it had to be taken literally. It was not enough to know Arab strategy on the grand scale; Yariv wanted to know everything about every Arab unit down to the menus served in the sergeants' mess.*

First priority was given to the Arab air forces. High-flying aircraft as well as more normal intelligence channels had established the whereabouts of every airfield in the Arab world. But Yariv insisted that each one should be personally inspected by Israeli agents. Over a period of eighteen months not a single airfield was omitted, and many of the more important ones were visited more than once. Sometimes it was easy, sometimes, in rear stations deep in the heartland of Egypt, it was difficult, but Yariv's long arm stretched to them all. Most of the stories of how this was done still remain classified, but one or two are beginning to emerge. At one strategic secret fighter station where MiG-21s were kept on permanent alert near El Faiyum, 150 miles from Cairo, an ex-Israeli army officer got a job as a mess waiter in the senior officers' mess. So impressively did he perform his duties that he came to the notice of the local commanding air officer of the region, who used him as a batman whenever he went on tours of inspection of airfields within his command.

At another airfield, run by the Russians, a chief technician who believed he was working for Egyptian security authorities was told that the Russians were making false reports about the serviceability of their planes. He was asked to provide a weekly log indicating the state of pre-

* As a neat piece of propaganda, the Israelis made sure that the 3,000 Egyptian POWs taken during the war were rather better fed while in Israeli hands than they were at their own bases.

paredness of every aircraft in the station, as well as details about every pilot and fellow technician on the base. He was never to know that in fact he was working for the Israelis. Agents everywhere were encouraged to submit even the smallest scrap about life on the various bases they had been assigned to. Yariv wanted names of pilots, their marital status and information on their families. He wanted, he said, to know everything there was to know about base commanders—whether they were liked by their men, whether they were disciplinarians, whether they'd achieved their rank through ability or influence. For over eighteen months, this material literally poured into Tel Aviv, where Israeli air force officers, seconded by Military Intelligence, built up almost as detailed a picture of the Egyptian Air Force as the Egyptians themselves possessed.

It was that dossier which decided the exact moment of attack for the Israeli Air Force. For it showed conclusively that between 7:30 A.M. and 7:45 A.M. the Egyptian airbases and radar stations were at their most vulnerable.

As far as the latter were concerned, the night shift ended at 8:00 A.M. The men on the screens and their controllers would be tired, their concentration at a low ebb as they mentally prepared to hand over responsibility to a new crew, who would be arriving shortly.

As far as the airmen were concerned, the timing was more subtle. Reveille for pilots at virtually every base in Egypt was at 6:30 A.M. Breakfast was served at the officers' mess between 7:00 A.M. and 7:30 A.M., after which the pilots would be walking between the mess halls and their rooms, often in bungalows around the airfield, to pick up their flying gear. Ground crew would be busy during this period, too. It was normally at that time that those aircraft which had been in hangars overnight for servicing purposes would be rolled out to their stands, naked and vulnerable.

Meanwhile, in Cairo, senior officers of the army, air force and navy would have left their homes and embroiled themselves in those extraordinary Cairo traffic jams for which the city is famous in order to be at their desks at 8:00 A.M. They, too, during these crucial moments when decisions would need to be made on the run would be out of touch, a vital consideration in a country where subordinates do not easily make decisions in the absence of their superiors.

It was Yariv who chose the time and place of the first engagement—and he chose well.

The enemy air force was caught on the ground. Radar didn't pick up the incoming Israeli planes over Egypt because they came from such an unexpected direction and flew so fast and low at a time of day when the operators were, in any case, predisposed to ignore the unusual by their desire to end their shift. Of course, some Arab planes did get off the ground, but the runway charts the Israeli bombers possessed were so accurate that every first-strike forward airfield in Egypt was out of commission and most of its aircraft destroyed within minutes of the start of the war.

On the ground, Israel intelligence proved to be just as effective, hamstrung, ironically, only by the speed of the Israeli advance. Yariv had patiently collected details of every unit in the Egyptian, Syrian and Jordanian armies, including the fire power of each as well as an assessment of its general competency. Intelligence officers stationed with every Israeli unit received from HQ a complete breakdown of the formation they faced on an hour-by-hour basis, but so quickly did the Israeli Army move that even Military Intelligence's computers found it difficult at times to keep up.

The Arab communications network and their battle codes had been broken long ago, largely thanks to Ne'eman. Not an order was relayed by radio on any of the fronts that the Israelis didn't have as soon as those for whom it was intended.

On one occasion, a large Egyptian tank formation in the Sinai got lost and Tel Aviv realized what Cairo didn't, that its commander was temporarily out of contact with his headquarters. So an Israel commander took over. With a dossier of the tank formation before him, an Israeli controller told the commander to change radio frequencies and put the tanks under his wings. For the whole of the war, like robots these tanks moved backward and forward in the Sinai under Israeli control, always well away from the fighting and from any Israelis. After the ceasefire, the Israeli controller was ordered to direct his unit to the nearest POW camp, but for a moment he demurred. He had begun to feel the stirrings of affection for his little army, and argued that—not having done any harm to Israel—they should be permitted to go home. He was overruled on the grounds that Israel wanted the tanks and that the men themselves would be unlikely to remain in Israeli custody for long!

Meanwhile, on the Jordanian front and in the Sinai, too, the quite exceptional quality of Israeli Military Intelligence was also making itself felt. The Jordanians in particular had relied heavily for their defense upon tank traps and mine fields, which required elaborate keys to disentangle. To the astonishment of King Hussein's commanders, Israeli ground forces swept through them as if they did not exist. Every mine field had been marked by the Israelis, who possessed the ability to decipher the secrets of virtually all of them.

On the Golan, Elie Cohen and agents like him had carefully mapped every Syrian fixed position. The Syrians had apparently assumed that if anyone attempted to storm what they regarded as an impregnable fortress it would be on the widest flank, and so their defenses were established in depths and breadths along the whole of the heights, backed by several divisions at the summit to hold any attack which did manage to break through along a single sector.

The Syrians believed they were safe and, indeed, some American senior officers who visited Israel in 1966 and saw the heights concluded that any attempt to capture them would result in such enormous loss of Israeli life that no Israeli Government could ever afford even to try.

Yariv had a model built of the area which was constantly updated as new information came in. This model was the center of months of study by staff officers until the weakness of the Syrian defensive positions became clear. Like the French, who depended upon a Maginot Line which the Germans could bypass, so the Syrians dug deep into their mountain, safe from air attack, their guns in fixed positions dominating the slopes before them. For a long time, the Israeli Army considered the possibility of a mass paratroop drop on the summit until Elie Cohen was able to tell Yariv that this was what the Syrians expected and would be prepared for. Another approach was needed.

When the time came for the Israeli assault, Moshe Dayan himself was not convinced of success, but every other officer on the general staff was sure that by taking what amounted to a single road, dealing only with Syrian defenses along a needle-narrow corridor, and using their air superiority to clear defenses at the summit, the Israeli forces could pour in enough armor and men to hold a position, which could then be reinforced by a second wave who would come back down the mountain again.

It is a matter of history that the plan worked magnificently and that, in rather less than a day's fighting, the Golan Heights were secured. It would be wrong to suggest that Yariv planned the assault, but equally wrong to deny the extraordinary influence which the Israeli intelligence community under Yariv had upon the plan. For it was out of the volume of intelligence Yariv gathered that it became clear there were only two real options in Syria open to Israeli commanders: either to attack along a line of advance apparent to any strategist with the help of Yariv's model or not to attack at all. The victory of the Golan Heights had as its midwife Aharon Yariv. When asked if he was surprised at the speed of the victory, he replied simply that he was paid *not* to be surprised.

One incident above all others in the Six-Day War showed with what ruthlessness Israel was prepared to both fight a war using the modern tools of intelligence and deception and to protect itself against even friendly intruders. When the war began, King Hussein of Jordan was uncertain whether to intervene. As far as the Israelis were concerned, once engaged with the Egyptians, they very much wanted to do battle with him. The conflict was seen by Israeli military men as the chance once and for all to "clean up" the borders, to establish new buffer zones, and to defeat not merely the Egyptians but the armies of all the confrontation states so decisively that Israel would be secure for another generation.

So, throughout the first day of the war, radio messages from Cairo to Amman were first blocked and new information inserted, then quickly rerouted on their way. While the original signals made it clear that the Egyptian Army was in retreat along the whole length of the front, the message Amman received via Tel Aviv was the opposite—that large formations of Egyptian tanks were breaking through in the Sinai and inflicting devastating losses on Israeli formations. Hussein was invited by apparently jubilant Egyptians to join in and enjoy the fruits of victory. As this was also the message being pumped out, for internal propaganda reasons, by Cairo radio the Jordanian King ordered his army and air force into action.*

On June 7, after the Old City of Jerusalem had already been taken, the Israeli Ambassador to Washington was called to the State Department. He was told that the Americans would back an Egyptian request for a cease-fire, and when the Israelis objected, it was made plain to him that the Americans knew that Jordan had been lured into the fighting by signals deception.

This was a major breach of Israeli security—a breach which could have immense diplomatic repercussions after the war was over. After Suez, Israel had been forced under pressure from the United Nations to hand back all of the territory it had won. Israel was determined that this time things would be different, but in order to be sure, it needed to be able to sustain the argument that Israel had been the victim of aggression. Even though Jordan had indubitably attacked Israel, the knowledge that she had done so with some Israeli connivance was not something Israel wished the world to know about. But the Israelis also knew that if the Americans had "read" these signals, they were also "reading" Israeli battle intelligence as it flowed in by radio on all three fronts. This was serious. A war was still being fought and a great deal of mopping up was still needed before the country's new frontiers could be secure. If the Americans were listening in to war communications, the risk that these could leak via anti-Israeli elements in the State Department and the Pentagon was too great to be ignored.

Once they realized that their signals were being intercepted, it didn't take the Israelis long to discover that the USS *Liberty,* a CIA spy ship packed with the latest electronic equipment, was stationed in the eastern Mediterranean some fifteen miles north of the Sinai Peninsula and was receiving the entire signal output of the Israeli Army and Air Force and broadcasting much of it back to

---

* At the end of the war, Nasser telephoned King Hussein, and they both agreed they'd tell the world that the Israelis won the war because American Air Force pilots had flown attack missions. The Israelis taped the whole conversation on a supposedly secure communications network and played it to a press conference.

Washington. Almost simultaneously, once they knew this, on the direct orders of Dayan, a message was put over the air making it plain to the *Liberty* that it had been spotted and that unless it sailed instantly the Israelis would have to take action. The Chiefs of Staff in Washington had no hesitation in ordering the ship from the area immediately, but the message in somewhat mysterious circumstances was never received by the *Liberty*. In any event the Israelis felt they had no option but to attack. The Americans had been warned and chose to ignore the warning. So on June 8 torpedo boats and jet aircraft with verbal orders to disable the vessel rather than sink it launched three strikes against the ship. Thirty-four U.S. sailors lost their lives in the attack and another seventy-five were wounded, many seriously so. For a few hours in Washington there was talk of a retaliatory air strike against the Israeli base from which the jet fighters had come, but after two or three hours of intensive debate within both the Oval Office and the War Room at the Pentagon, America decided to back down.

President Johnson realized that Israel had called America's bluff. The spy ship had no business in the area in the first place, and only the Russians would gain now from a public squabble between the two countries. So the official Israeli version, though the Americans knew it to be absolutely untrue, was publicly accepted and written into the historical records. The Israeli Air Force, it was said, mistook the *Liberty* for an Egyptian supply ship, the *El Ksair*. Regrets were expressed and eventually Israel paid in full claims totaling more than 1.8 million dollars from members of the crew and their families as well as expenses incurred by the American government for the medical care of those injured. What Israel consistently refused to do was to pay for the damage and repair of the vessel itself. The USS *Liberty,* said Israeli negotiators, had sailed knowingly into a war zone, had spied upon the combatants, and had suffered the consequences. The responsibility for that, said the Israelis, lay fairly and squarely with the Americans.

When it was all over, Yariv's stupendous achievement was obvious to every officer in the Israeli Army who had fought in the war. Every unit had benefited in one way or another—either from his almost miraculously accurate maps or from the detailed knowledge of the enemy and his armaments gathered by Yariv's men. Yariv himself remained typically reticent. One of his men, wearing Egyptian uniform, had been killed by the Israelis during the war, Yariv once told senior officers with some emotion —a sad and ironic end to a master spy about whom we can know nothing. But beyond that, little detail has emerged.

Yariv once said that the job of Military Intelligence is inherently full of contradictions. One has to be an expert in detail and yet be able to see a wide picture. One has to deal in abstractions and yet at the same time have one's feet firmly planted on the ground.

At another point, he was to say "Intelligence is like opium. One can become addicted to it if one loses sight of the aim." Ahrele Yariv's genius lay in his ability never for a moment to lose sight of that aim.

For Israel, Yariv has said, intelligence must make up for the fact that it is a small country surrounded by enemies. Intelligence must give the prior warning that will prevent surprise attack. Intelligence must adopt the motto of the bomb-disposal men in World War II: The first mistake is also the last. Almost exactly six years later, Yom Kippur, 1973, that phrase was to come to haunt the nation.

Chapter 18

AS FAR AS PUBLIC OPINION was concerned, Meir Amit emerged from the Six-Day War sharing the laurels of the outstanding intelligence victory with Ahrele Yariv. News of an extraordinary mission he undertook on his own personal initiative on June 1—when he flew to the United States, called Richard Helms, then head of the CIA from the airport, demanding an immediate audience—spread quickly. The Israeli government had been torn almost to the breaking point by an internecine battle between those in the Cabinet who favored an immediate strike against the Egyptians massing in the Sinai Desert and those who still believed that President Nasser could be persuaded to withdraw through diplomatic pressure. It was Meir Amit who received first from Richard Helms and then from Defense Secretary Robert McNamara if not direct American approval for an Israeli pre-emptive strike then at least acquiescence.

He did so by presenting to them in detail Israeli intelligence evaluations, which cut through the somewhat arid debate inside the Pentagon as to whether Egyptian dispositions were offensive or defensive in character. Whatever Nasser's original intentions, Amit argued, the momentum of his drive into the Sinai could only be halted if Nasser went to war or if Israel did. The Americans accepted this argument, and the last prop of the doves within the Israeli Cabinet was removed.

What the Americans—and most people inside Israel—didn't know was that the same man so ably arguing the case for Israel was himself in the midst of a maelstrom which was close not merely to ending his own career but to bringing down the government and sucking the whole country into a scandal potentially far more damaging even than the Lavon affair. However extraordinary the diplomatic triumph he achieved in Washington, it probably did not begin to outweigh the damage he had already done to Israel's foreign relations. In one sense it had all begun early in 1965, when Isser Harel returned to his profession, this time in the capacity of "Special Advisor to the Prime Minister on Security Affairs," a post created especially for him.

Though Amit had been confirmed as head of Mossad, his enemies believed he would not accept the humiliation of Harel's return for long and would inevitably resign, permitting Harel to step back into the position he so foolishly threw away. They were, however, overestimating their own influence and underestimating Meir Amit's tenacity.

Isser Harel was brought back not really because of anything his friends had managed on his behalf but because of the deteriorating political fortunes of the Israeli Labor Party, Mapai. David Ben-Gurion, one of the party's principal founding fathers, had been in violent disagreement with Prime Minister Eshkol and his Cabinet over its handling of the Lavon affair. Ben-Gurion played rough, and when it became clear that, for all his eminence, the party was not prepared to bow before him, he formed his own party, the Israeli Labor List, or Rafi (from the initials of its Hebrew name), and took Shimon Peres, the Deputy Defense Minister, and Moshe Dayan with him in order to fight the general election due in November.

To the perennially suspicious "old Bolsheviks" of Mapai, anybody who could even remotely be regarded as a Rafi sympathizer had to be treated with the deepest caution. Meir Amit, of course, came at the top of that list. He owed his appointment to Ben-Gurion; he was a personal friend and former aide to Moshe Dayan; and he had always been supported by Shimon Peres. To Eshkol and his friends, who saw political relationships in stark terms, this could only mean that Amit's loyalty could not be counted upon, and that Mossad, with all of its ability to make mischief, would be in the pocket of the enemy.*

Isser Harel was their answer. Once one of Ben-Gurion's staunchest supporters, each man now felt betrayed by the other. Harel's task was to keep an eye on Amit and Mossad and be ready with an alternative scenario for any intelligence proposal the agency put up. In any case, Harel's reinstatement not only made Meir Amit's job more difficult, but soured his relations with the Prime Minister.

On November 2, 1965, the row which had produced such a tempestuous split within the ruling party was brought to a head by a general election that gave Prime Minister Eshkol and the party which had gone into coalition with him a substantial vote, though not a working majority over all of the other parties combined. It was not until January 10, 1966, that Eshkol was able to form a government. In fact, behind the scenes during this entire period, his principal concern was not how to form a coalition but how to keep one of the most damaging and disastrous intelligence scandals Israel had experienced from percolating to the surface.

At the center of what became known around the world as the "Ben Barka affair" was Meir Amit, brilliant and yet impetuous and inexperienced, mixed up against his will in the angry passions of internal politics. At the time, and indeed until publication of this book, the Israeli po-

---

* It was said in Israel at the time only half jokingly that given a choice between Nasser and Ben-Gurion in his Cabinet, Eshkol would choose Nasser.

litical, military and security establishment was kept in total ignorance of what had occurred, while the outside world was permitted only the smallest of glimpses of the true facts behind a major but apparently purely French *cause célèbre*.

What was known was that just after noon on October 29, 1965, Mehdi Ben Barka, a Moroccan opposition leader, then forty-five years old and one of the intellectual gurus of the Third World, was kidnaped outside the Brasserie Lipp in St. Germain des Près, a well-known Parisian haunt for left-wing artists, writers and politicians. He was never seen again. What was not known was that Meir Amit's Mossad was part of an operation which was to lead to the death of this brilliant and talented man, who was shot down in cold blood by Moroccan security men in a villa in Fontenay-le-Vicomte, in the outer suburbs of Paris, a few miles south of Orly airport.

How Mossad came to be involved at all is a remarkable story in its own right, highlighting as it does one of those secret and, on the face of it, unnatural alliances of which there are more around the world than probably anyone can possibly guess.

In the early sixties, King Hassan of Morocco, believing with some justification that his life and his regime were threatened by the new Arab republics, turned to Israel for help. The King had more reason to fear the influence of Gamal Abdel Nasser and the revolutionary spirit which he inspired throughout the Middle East than he had to fear the hated Israelis. He was intelligent enough, too, to learn from the experience of ex-King Farouk of Egypt that the Americans, and certainly the CIA, could always be persuaded that the Arab kingdoms were the reactionary product of the European colonial empires which had dominated the area up to the Second World War, and that it was in the American interest to support the revolutionary anticolonialist ferment which followed. The one country with an interest in an alliance with Morocco was Israel, and so it was to Israel that King Hassan turned.

No one, of course, was to be allowed to know about it, but by 1965 Israel was even providing Moroccan Jews who had emigrated to Israel as the personal bodyguards of the King. Mossad and Shin Bet set up an efficient internal-security and intelligence service training Moroccan personnel in the latest surveillance and espionage techniques. Just as would happen later when Mossad completely restructured the Shah of Persia's secret service, Israel gave King Hassan one of the most modern and up-to-date internal-security services in the region. If one requires a definition of the word *Realpolitik,* then this strange alliance between Israel and an Arab kingdom, formed as it was on the rocky shores of Arab-Israeli hatred, is as good an example as one is likely to find anywhere.*

Israel itself got a good deal out of it in return. Morocco became an important jumping-off point for Israeli agents being infiltrated into the rest of the Arab world, while Rabat was turned into a front-line listening post for Mossad in its eternal quest to record every murmur from the enemy nest. In more concrete terms, when Israel became independent, there was a large Jewish community in Morocco. The King had promised his protection for this Jewish minority in his country, and almost promised to turn a blind eye if any wished to emigrate to Israel. That was good enough for the Israelis, who launched one of the biggest emigration programs of their history under the benevolent eye of the Moroccan Kiing.

All went well until 1965, when General Mohammed Oufkir, Hassan's tough Minister of the Interior, approached Meir Amit about Mehdi Ben Barka, unquestionably the ablest and, in the King's eyes, most dangerous of Moroccan politicians. An ex-tutor of the King, he had been elected president of the National Consultative Assembly in 1956 when Morocco won its independence, but used this position as a forum to expound his left-wing and, by definition, anti-monarchist beliefs and sentiments.

In the late fifties, he was driven into exile, but as so often happens, this increased his influence and prestige rather than diminished it. He became one of the most elo-

---

* It was Isser Harel who, in the late 50s and early 60s, established a series of secret alliances with countries like Morocco, Iran, Ethiopia and Turkey that formed a circle of Third World countries around the Moslem confrontation states. In each of them Harel set up a substantial Mossad presence which, for all intents and purposes, acted as Israel's diplomatic representation, unofficial but no less effective for that. In the late 60s, Mossad had similar arrangements with many African countries; so much so that Mossad's African desk became one of its largest and most important desks.

quent and most widely known and respected advocates of the Third World, and he argued that the industrialized countries had a vested interest in maintaining the poorer countries in a state of abject poverty in order to be able to purchase the raw materials which the Western world so desperately needed at bargain-basement prices. He traveled widely—to the Soviet Union, China and Cuba—and increasingly came to advocate armed revolution, because, he said, power in countries like Morocco was too often in the hands of an oligarchy who ruled at the expense of the people rather than on their behalf. In 1963, the Moroccan authorities claimed that Ben Barka was behind an attempt to assassinate the King, and at a special court hearing he was sentenced to death *in absentia*. When Morocco and Algeria nearly went to war in 1964 over a border dispute, Ben Barka openly supported the Algerians and was for the second time sentenced to death *in absentia* at a trial of Moroccans who had infiltrated from Algiers to fight against the Moroccan Army.

Some time in early 1965, King Hassan let it be known that he would not grieve at the death of his former tutor. The man who listened was General Mohammad Oufkir. Though he possessed an efficient and Israeli-trained internal-security service, General Oufkir could not rely upon the small external-intelligence service which Morocco maintained. Its expertise was geared almost solely to embassy duties. Obviously, it could not run an operation of quite this magnitude.

It was quite natural in these circumstances for Oufkir to approach Meir Amit. As part of the Moroccan-Israeli deal, Israeli agents had for years been observing the activities of Moroccan exiled opposition leaders living either in Europe or in other Arab countries. Almost certainly Ben Barka had been among those on whom the Israelis had been reporting.

But what Oufkir was now suggesting was in a very different league altogether. He wanted Israeli help to eliminate Ben Barka.

Meir Amit agreed to go along, and laid down only one condition. Israeli agents could not be in at the kill. But Mossad would lead a Moroccan team in organizing Ben Barka's kidnaping. What happened to him thereafter would be up to the Moroccans.

As the operation was to be conducted on French soil,

where Ben Barka spent much of this time, Meir Amit and Oufkir sought the cooperation of the French SDECE (*Service de Documentation Extérieure et de Contre-Espionnage*), the French external-intelligence organization which for years had managed its affairs with little political control. Brilliant in many respects, the SDECE had the reputation internationally of being the rogue elephant of the world's intelligence circus. The CIA regarded it as being as "leaky as a sieve," and probably with some justification, for few services had so many departmental heads constantly at loggerheads with one another, all serving different masters, either within France itself or in some cases abroad. The Israelis, however, had always got along with the French service very well. As an ally in the tricky world in which the Mossad was obliged to operate, the SDECE had proved itself extremely useful, principally because its officers did not feel obliged necessarily to receive political authority for its operations. This gave the service a freebooting quality very much like the Israelis themselves but without Israeli discipline and order.

Mossad's contacts within the service tended to be with the ex-OAS elements, those opposed to De Gaulle for what they believed to be his sellout of French interests in the Algerian War of Independence. They had every reason to help Oufkir; Ben Barka was the kind of Arab politician whom they most abhorred.

As always, however, one arm of the SDECE didn't know what the other was doing. As one department was arranging for Ben Barka's assassination, another was organizing a regular monthly paycheck paid him through a French scientific research center, one of the covers for the extensive SDECE operation in Africa.

Be that as it may, Meir Amit himself flew to Paris for talks with Moroccan and French security men early that spring. He kept the purpose of his journey secret except from a very small number of close associates, and whether or not he told the Prime Minister is still a question in dispute. But those who know Amit find it difficult to accept that he would go ahead with an operation of this kind with no authorization whatsoever. What seems most likely is that he told Eshkol, but told him in such a manner that the Prime Minister—who had probably never even heard of Ben Barka—did not take in what it was that was being proposed. What is certain is that no one told Isser Harel, though he was indubitably entitled to know. Relations between the two men were such that on the personal level this was hardly surprising; yet here was an operation whose implications were so far ranging that it is remarkable that personalities should have come into it at all.

The fact was that Meir Amit was determined to run his own shop without outside interference, and so concerned was he about this that anyone whose loyalty to him might be in the slightest way questioned was excluded from his inner councils. Inevitably, this meant that during this crucial period he lost the advice of the healthy skeptics Mossad and every intelligence agency needs.

In fairness, Meir Amit did not create that atmosphere of suspicion and jealousies which had turned his office, temporarily at least, into what was somewhat viciously described at the time by one of his enemies as a "führer bunker"; nor was he responsible for the fact that whether Mossad liked it or not, the organization had become something of a political football, with the loyalty of its senior executives—mirroring the society as a whole—deeply divided. Isolated, unsure of whom he could trust, he acted almost alone, caught up in the excitement of operational details which obscured entirely the extraordinary political and diplomatic risks which such a desperate adventure held for his country.

Teams of French and Israeli agents kept Mehdi Ben Barka under observation for weeks while plans for his elimination were being worked out. Ben Barka lived in Geneva, but it was decided to lure him to France, where the SDECE believed it could more easily cover any tracks which his abduction might leave. That was perhaps the biggest mistake of all.

Ben Barka was told in Geneva by a group of friends that the well-known French film director Georges Franju wished to meet him for lunch to discuss an anticolonialist film he was making. It was an offer Ben Barka accepted eagerly, and he flew to Paris for his rendezvous at the Brasserie Lipp. Just as he was about to go in, three men stepped out from a nearby doorway, flashed their identity cards, and told him he was wanted for questioning.

Two of the men who "arrested" him were members of the French Vice Squad *(Brigade Mondaine)*, Louis Souchon and Roger Voitot, and a third, Antoine Lopez, was an SDECE officer who worked undercover as a customs officer at Orly airport. Ben Barka was driven to a villa at Fontenay-le-Vicomte, the home of George ("Jo") Boucheseiche, a shady underworld figure who had the dubious distinction of owning plush brothels in Paris and Morocco and who obviously had some favors to pay off. There, several of his men—nothing short of gangsters— as well as Moroccan and French security men stood guard. Telephone calls were put through to Morocco to tell Minister Oufkir that Ben Barka was in custody. Code messages were flashed to Tel Aviv to let Meir Amit know that the job had been done, and Mossad men, who had kept well in the background during the actual kidnaping, were withdrawn. Israel's part was over.*

Twenty-four hours later, Oufkir was in Fontenay-le-Vicomte, and in his presence Mehdi Ben Barka was gunned to death. The body was buried in the garden, but was moved a fortnight later, on November 16th, to its final resting spot—the river bank of the Seine this time, northwest of Paris near the Ile de la Grande Jatte.

Unfortunately for those involved, Mehdi Ben Barka

* It will be evident why the author is unable to provide the sources for this chapter, revealing, as it does, one of the most important classified secrets in the history of the State of Israel. The nearest anyone has ever got to the truth so far, despite all the books and films on the subject, was *Time* Magazine which, on December 29, 1975, ran a superb four-page article on the Ben Barka assassination. Within the article, a hint is given of Israeli involvement. It reveals, though not in detail, the Israeli-Moroccan connection, tells how Oufkir approached Amit, but then somewhat oddly goes on to suggest that though Amit put men on to tail Ben Barka, he withdrew them, because there were so many agents on the job already that "they were falling all over each other in the streets of Geneva." Apart from this, the article was astonishingly accurate in every detail of the assassination. I made some inquiries as to how it was that *Time* Magazine seemed to have got hold of the whole story but failed to follow through on the really sensational aspect of it all, the Israeli connection. The answer appears to be that the principal source was an Israeli who was in full possession of the real facts. At the last moment, believing that he could harm the interests of Israel, as well as get himself into deep trouble, he not unnaturally got cold feet and decided to censor the story himself, reducing Israeli involvement to a minimum, before passing the story on to *Time* Magazine.

was to take on a far greater fame dead than he ever had alive. Apart from the fact that the operation itself had been ineptly handled, permitting police quickly to trace his last movements, France, ever since the return of Charles de Gaulle from the wilderness, had become politically the most highly charged nation in Europe, with both the left and the right locked in ideological battle both with each other and with the government. In that atmosphere the disappearance of Ben Barka was like pouring petrol on flames.

The left, suspecting that the government was involved, saw this as an opportunity to create a major scandal (and they were not disappointed), but the scandal, perhaps the biggest in France since the war, though initially stirred up by De Gaulle's opponents, got the head of steam that it did because De Gaulle himself, when he discovered that elements within the SDECE were responsible and that they had acted on their own without ministerial authority, chose to regard the whole affair as a constitutional crisis, an attack upon himself and the integrity of his government. At a special Cabinet meeting called to discuss Ben Barka's disappearance, De Gaulle declared war on all those within the armed forces, the security services and elsewhere who still refused to acknowledge his authority or who sought to undermine his administration from within. "There are some nitwits who take me for a fool," he told his ministers. "The scores will be settled."

This is not the place to describe the quite extraordinary police and SDECE investigation which led to two trials, in one of which Oufkir was sentenced *in absentia* and Ahmed Dlimi, his deputy, who actually flew from Morocco to appear at the trial and who was in actual charge of the day-to-day planning of the operation, was found not guilty. Many witnesses disappeared, some in mysterious circumstances, leading to speculation (some of which was almost certainly well-founded) that they had been murdered to silence them. The SDECE was thoroughly shaken up and reformed, and De Gaulle used the Ben Barka affair to tighten his grip elsewhere, too. Though he was genuinely outraged, De Gaulle was politician enough to see this as an opportunity once and for all to establish his authority and purge those within government departments who had consistently opposed him.

All of this quite remarkable activity in France, the huge

police hunt, the largest in French history, the screaming headlines in the press which continued day after day, and the evident hysteria inside the Elysée Palace, first utterly transfixed Meir Amit's Mossad and then panicked it. Operation Ben Barka had always been regarded as an unsavory but necessary bit of work which the outside world would barely notice but which would tie in Mossad even closer with Morocco, one of its more important allies. Instead, the Ben Barka affair had become an international incident. France, Israel's principal arms supplier and one of her most ardent supporters, was in uproar. Mossad's reputation and, more important, the reputation of Israel was now very much on the line. Meir Amit did what he could to keep the genie in the bottle.

Executives who were in the know were sworn to secrecy, while emissaries traveled to Rabat to remind the Moroccans that if Israeli involvement ever became public, their situation would be made even more embarrassing than it was already. If the king's secret alliance with the Israelis ever became known, his position within the Arab world, already difficult, would become impossible. The French SDECE, who were desperately covering up their own tracks on this seamy operation, and more besides, were warned that if Mossad went down so would they. It wasn't blackmail, it was a sharp reminder that all intelligence services have a vested interest in ensuring that each doesn't wash the other's dirty linen in public.

It is just possible—though probably unlikely—that Meir Amit might have got away with it completely if it had not been for the tense and ugly mood of Israeli politics. The election on November 2nd—three days after Ben Barka was murdered at Fontenay-le-Vicomte—failed to provide a majority for Mapai and the horse-trading was on to patch up a coalition. Ben-Gurion's new party, Rafi, had got ten seats, which put him and his followers as a constantly brooding and hostile presence in the Knesset; though they could be excluded from any coalition, they could not be ignored. Rightly or wrongly—and the truth lay somewhere in the middle—Eshkol and his senior supporters believed almost as holy writ that Rafi's influence was deeply entrenched within the Ministry of Defense and among senior army officers. Almost certainly as part of that struggle, a Mossad executive, hostile to Amit, informed Israel Galilli, one of Israel's most influential M.P.s, about

Mossad's involvement in the Ben Barka murder. Galilli informed Isser Harel, who told Prime Minister Eshkol. The dam had burst.

It was an appalling moment for a man whose party had emerged so horribly mutilated from the Lavon affair and who was at this moment trying to form a government from the shambles that scandal had created. Now, here he was, back again into a security scandal of perhaps even greater significance with the added dimension that, as this was a Mossad operation, he as Prime Minister at that time and officially responsible for Mossad, was intimately involved. A sense of *déjà vu* was highlighted, too, when Isser Harel, who was asked to investigate and did so with relish, reported that, just as in the Lavon affair, the crucial question "Who gave the order?" was probably never going to be satisfactorily resolved. Eshkol himself denied that he ever knew anything about it; Meir Amit insisted that he received prime ministerial authority.

Isser Harel didn't take long to write his report with its bleak recommendations. The principal one was that Meir Amit should resign immediately.

The operation itself had been both immoral and unnecessary, he declared. Assassination was a weapon the Israelis could only afford to use as a very last resort. There were no conceivable circumstances—or if there were, this occasion could not be regarded as one of them —where Israel should perform like a mercenary army such a duty for another state. Israel had no interest in the death of Ben Barka, and should not have got involved. If the story were to come out, the implications for Israel would be horrendous.

As for the question of ministerial authority, if Meir Amit had sought it, he had done so in such an obscure manner that no one had understood the quite extraordinary importance of what he was saying; he had plunged the nation into an appalling crisis, and there was no alternative but that he should go. But Meir Amit was a fighter. He saw the attempt to remove him—spearheaded by his old adversary Isser Harel—as part of a political campaign to shake any possible Rafi supporters out of the higher reaches of government. This was certainly the view taken by Ben-Gurion, Shimon Peres and Moshe Dayan, who, when they got wind of the affair, let it be known to Eshkol that if Meir Amit were sacrificed, then they would see to it that the government would not survive the political conflagration they would ignite. Eshkol was widely regarded in the country as "soft" on security, a man with no power of decision, a "dove" who couldn't be completely trusted on matters of war and peace. It was not difficult to see how Rafi could use the sacking of Meir Amit against him. Eshkol was simply too vulnerable to take the risk.

It is not surprising that in this fevered atmosphere during a period when Israel, in effect, did not have a government that the story leaked out to senior members of the parliamentary party. Determined at all costs to avoid another Lavon affair, they set themselves up as a committee, meeting in absolute secrecy, to review the evidence and make recommendations.

The committee was chaired by Eliezer Shoshani, a veteran of the kibbutz movement and the party's principal eyes on security affairs. Members of the committee included Mordechai Misiyahu, head of the research department of the party, whose wife, in fact, was a senior Mossad executive; Mrs. Santa Yoseftal, who had been general secretary of the kibbutz movement and whose husband was general secretary of the party and Minister of Housing, and who for a period was an active member of Ben-Gurion's "Young Guard"; and David ("Dodic") Golomb, son of Eliyahu Golomb, the legendary commander of the Haganah, who was then regarded as being one of the brightest young M.P.s in the party, with a glittering future before him.

If the party elders hoped that this committee would adopt a low-key approach, they were to be disappointed.

Their report came as a bombshell. Someone, said the committee, ought to resign, and the members were fairly unanimous as to who that should be—Prime Minister Eshkol. Golda Meir, as tough a politician as Israel has ever had, used her very great influence to ensure that the report and its recommendations disappeared without a trace and the members of the committee were punished for their "disloyalty." All were frostily reminded of the terms of Israel's Official Secrets Act, and then frozen out of the party's inner councils. Dodic Golomb, until then the party's fastest-rising star, got the message quickly and within a year was out of Parliament altogether, only returning, older and wiser, to the Knesset in the elections of

1977, but this time out of the labour party as a member of the "Democratic Movement for Change."

Mrs. Meir's tough stance was taken not to protect Eshkol, whose job she coveted, but to protect the party. If Ehskol were forced to go down, the party would go down with him. The uproar in the country and in the Knesset would be such that no Mapai leader in the face of the Ben Barka scandal would be able to hold together, let alone form, the coalition which the results of the election demanded. But if Eshkol was not to resign, neither clearly could Meir Amit. Rafi was there to make sure that he didn't.

So, not for the first time, Israeli party politics intruded into that highly specialized field of secret intelligence and came to be the determining factor in the decision to cover up a scandal. National security was not the consideration. What mattered most to those involved was the continued integrity of their personal public positions.

The one man who would not accept his situation was Isser Harel. Angrily, he insisted that if Meir Amit did not resign, he would. The operation had betrayed both the ethical standards of the service he had founded and the State itself. Vigorous attempts were made in an effort to change his mind. But Isser Harel was adamant, and after only nine months in his new job, he packed his bags and this time left the intelligence community forever.

The cover story to explain his defection was sufficiently believable, too, for there to be little discussion or speculation as to why he went. It was known that he and Meir Amit didn't get on and that Isser was, in any case, unhappy in the role that he had taken—a potentate without a state. So when the Prime Minister's office let it be known that Isser Harel had resigned again, this was put down to a clash of personalities between him and the head of Mossad.

The government was determined to ensure that the Ben Barka affair would not become a public scandal. An indication of how far it was prepared to go came twelve months later, when an Israeli weekly paper, the now defunct *Bull*, a gossip and scandal sheet, printed a story about the Ben Barka assassination, drawn from a French newspaper, which speculated in fairly vague terms about Israeli involvement. The night before *Bull* left the warehouses, police raided the offices, confiscated the whole issue, and arrested two editors under Article 23 of the Israeli Security Laws, only previously used in cases of espionage. Never—either before or since—have such Draconian laws been used in Israel against journalists. Under this article, the two men could have been sentenced for up to fifteen years' imprisonment. For forty-eight hours, the military censored publication anywhere of even the mere fact of their arrest, and then they got a judge to extend the ban. Only in February 1967, two months later, was it lifted. The two editors were sentenced to a year's imprisonment at a secret trial, but thanks to the behind-the-scenes maneuvering of other Israeli editors, appalled at the way the case had been handled (though not really aware of what it was all about) and the threat this posed to their own independence, the two were pardoned and released in April. It was, nevertheless, a severe warning to anyone in Israel as to what would happen to them if they began investigating this story. Obviously, there were people who knew something about it. Justice Minister Yaacov Shapiro's action against *Bull* made certain that they remained silent.

But the nation could not escape from the consequences of the actions of its security services. President de Gaulle was outraged when he discovered the truth, though he had previously every reason to be grateful to the Israeli Secret Service and to Prime Minister Ben-Gurion. During the French-Algerian War, the Israelis had kept in close contact with the French Army in Algiers because of the large Jewish community there constantly under threat of attack. So, when in 1961 the OAS was created, it was a natural development that Israel, as keen on *Algérie-Française* as the OAS themselves, should lock themselves into the organization. But, in March 1961, a prominent Israeli was invited to the home of an OAS colonel in Paris. The colonel had an astonishing proposal. His friends, he said, were planning a coup which would involve the assassination of De Gaulle and requested the help of Israel. If an Israeli Arab could be brought to France to do the job, then blame would be attached to the FLN (*Front de Libération Nationale*). The effect in France would be dramatic, he said. Not only would De Gaulle, who was "selling out" Algeria, be disposed of, but the French people in their anger would reject any compromise solution with the Algerian Arabs. In exchange for Israeli help, said the colonel, when he and his friends came to power, they would ensure that the needs of Israel in the defense field would be furnished by the French, free of charge, for as long as Israel wanted. The Israeli refused to take this talk seriously, advised his hosts that they shouldn't do so either, and left. A few days later, while talking to Walter Eytan, the Israeli ambassador in Paris, he mentioned this bizarre conversation. Eytan knew the OAS and what they were capable of and, unlike his visitor, took the approach very seriously indeed and that day wrote a letter to the Foreign Secretary, Mrs. Golda Meir, to be personally delivered by a senior member of his embassy staff returning home to Tel Aviv. Golda Meir called in her senior advisers. They were agreed that De Gaulle had to be told, even though it was feared that if De Gaulle granted independence to Algeria, this would pave the way to a rapprochement between France and all of the Arab countries. Golda Meir decided that Ben-Gurion had to be informed and that a warning should be sent to Paris in his name. Ben-Gurion reacted with intense fury. Israel, he said, was not a land of assassins. What on earth, he asked, was Walter Eytan doing in not warning De Gaulle straightaway, and that day a telegram went off giving the ambassador precise instructions as to what to do. On March 29, 1961, an Israeli diplomat saw Colonel de Boisseu, the President's son-in-law, at the Elysée Palace to pass on Ben-Gurion's message and the details of the plot as the Israelis had it. De Gaulle himself through unofficial channels sent his personal thanks a few days later.

On April 22nd, the generals struck in a planned *putsch* which had little chance of success while President de Gaulle still lived. If an Israeli "jackal" had been involved, it might have been a different story. As it was, when David Ben-Gurion visited France in 1961, President de Gaulle was able to make this toast: ". . . I raise my glass to Israel, our friend and our ally."

All of that good will was swept away in one stroke by the Ben Barka affair. As far as President de Gaulle was concerned, the implications were that Israel was dealing with the OAS in France, which was still active, still bent on revenge, and indubitably involved through its supporters in the SDECE in the killing of Ben Barka. It meant that Israel was involved in illegal activities on French soil, an affront to French nationalism, and it meant that he himself, whose support for Israel had never been challenged, had been dealt with treacherously.

President de Gaulle was persuaded not to make Israeli involvement public. But he took immediate revenge. Paris had been the headquarters of Mossad in Europe ever since Mossad's formation. It was the most important Mossad installation anywhere outside Tel Aviv, and links between Mossad and the SDECE were intimate. De Gaulle ordered Israeli spies to leave France as soon as practical and shut down their entire operation in Paris. It was a severe blow, perhaps the most severe the Israeli Secret Service has ever suffered.

As for Israel foreign policy, that, too, took a difficult turn following Meir Amit's involvement. The country from which Israel had traditionally bought virtually all of its aircraft and arms turned hostile overnight. The Israeli Foreign Ministry had known nothing of the Ben Barka affair. It was their task to seek to disentangle something from the wreckage. They failed in the face of De Gaulle's intransigence. He was never to forgive Israel, and the price Israel had to pay in the years to come for this incredible lapse proved to be, as those who know the history of French-Israeli relations are aware, a heavy one indeed.

Chapter 19

How FAR President De Gaulle's quite extraordinary hostility toward Israel after the Six-Day War was influenced by his knowledge of what had occurred in the Ben Barka affair will be a matter of dispute until the definitive French official papers of the period are published. What does seem certain is that, barring a deep sense of personal animus, De Gaulle could quite easily have shifted French support to the Arabs without having to go to the extremes he did to cut out the Israelis.

Immediately after the Six-Day War, the French imposed a savage embargo upon the sale of all French military hardware to Tel Aviv, refusing export licenses to equipment ordered, signed for, and sometimes even paid for before the outbreak of hostilities. It was an unexpected and devastating blow to a country which had always regarded France as one of its most important allies and arms suppliers.

When, in the fifties, the Israelis scoured the world for arms for Israel, it was France, both for ideological reasons and because France's arms salesmen have always been among the most aggressive in the world, which stopped and listened. In 1954, a secret agreement was concluded between Israel and France whereby France provided Israel with Ouragan jets. These were quickly followed by the Mystère II and Mystère IVs.

After the Suez War, when the Czechs and the Russians began delivering advanced weapons systems, including MiGs, to the Arabs, the Israelis purchased the Mirage fighter from the French—which once again gave Israel a superiority in the air. This was not because the Mirage was necessarily a better plane than the MiG, but because the Israelis possessed the design and engineering skills to modify the planes (essentially built for a North European theater of war) to the peculiar climatic conditions of the Middle East as well as to the very special tactical and strategic uses to which they would need to be put.

President De Gaulle's first move after the Six-Day War was to order the cancellation of fifty new Mirage IIIs the Israelis had ordered and had indeed already paid for. Virtually the entire Israeli Air Force was "locked in" to the Mirage system. Even if the Americans had been prepared to replace this order quickly with their Phantoms—which they were not—it would not have solved the immediate problem of having developed sophisticated facilities to serve one kind of plane only to find that plane no longer available.

These facilities included, of course, the huge investment in advanced electronics, an industry in its own right, geared to the Mirage system and the Mirage system alone. If Israel was to get new planes from another source (and it was difficult to see immediately what that source would be), then much of this would count for nothing, and the engineers, designers and scientists who had "rebuilt" the

Mirage so that it exactly fitted the specifications laid down by the Air Force would have to start all over again.

If the short-term problem seemed enormous, the long-term prospects, when the Mirages the Israeli Air Force currently possessed were no longer serviceable, were daunting indeed.

Never had Israel felt more isolated. It relied absolutely for its ability to defend itself upon the good will of other nations, who could, as the French had done, change course and deny Israel the arms it needed. Logically, too, this sort of change was most likely to occur at times of extreme tension when suppliers were being asked to choose sides and when Israel would need the weaponry most.

The Israeli Cabinet quickly came to a decision. It would make funds available to the Israeli aircraft industry in order for it to build an Israeli fighter capable of beating the best in the world. A committee set up to consider the problem reported back quickly. Its findings could not have been more pessimistic. It would take perhaps as long as ten years, it reported, to put a purely Israeli jet in the air, and even then, because the Israelis would be starting pretty well from scratch, there was no guarantee at all that the plane which would eventually come off the production line would not prove to be years behind Russian, American, British and French planes being put into service at the same time.

The quickest and safest solution would be to build a copycat version of the Mirage—the aircraft with which Israeli technicians had had so much experience. On the face of it, that should have presented few problems: Why not, asked the ministers, take a Mirage which the Israeli Air Force possessed already, strip it to its component parts, copy and then rebuild it. That proposal was laughed out of court immediately. A modern fighter consists of over a million components, each part of which has been extensively tested and built to minimal tolerances which cannot be reproduced without the blueprints of the engineers who built it. The Swiss, for example, who were manufacturing the Mirage under license, with access not merely to all of the French plans but also to French technical assistance when required, who had no financial problems slowing up their program, still took six years to put their Mirage in the air from the moment they first received the French blueprints. A jet fighter, one engineer told Israeli ministers, is a bit like a human being. The human body has been dissected for years by doctors, but without the original blueprint no one has yet managed to create one!

The world was to discover the Israeli solution just over two years later, when at 4:00 P.M. on Saturday, September 20, 1969, Herr Karl Rotzinger, the owner of a small trucking company in Kaiseraugst, a Swiss town close to the German border, noticed one of his employees, a man called Hans Strecker, appear to load some large cardboard cartons from a storage shed into a Mercedes and drive off through the gates. Rotzinger hurried over to the shed to investigate; there he found three similar cartons, two empty and another full of blueprints. He pulled one of the blueprints out and looked at it closely. Stenciled in large letters on the top right-hand side of the drawing was the word SOLZER—the world-famous Swiss firm engaged in research and manufacture of aircraft engines. Beneath, also stenciled, were the words LICENSE-SENIKAMA, which didn't mean much to Rotzinger at the time, but, as he was later to find out, indicated that the engine parts to which these blueprints referred were being produced under license from the French engine manufacturers Senikama. There could be no doubt, however, as to the meaning of the large stamp in the right-hand corner. It declared TO BE KEPT SECRET FOR MILITARY PURPOSES AS REQUIRED BY MILITARY CRIMINAL LAW.

Herr Rotzinger asked a group of workers near by whether they had noticed when these cartons had arrived and was told that Strecker had, for several months, been moving boxes in and out of the storage shed. Oddly, Rotzinger didn't go immediately to the police. Instead, he waited to confront Strecker when he returned an hour later. Strecker didn't for a moment try to disguise what he was doing. The crates, he said, were being taken over the border so that they could be delivered to the Israeli Embassy in Bonn. Rotzinger asked for some kind of certificate showing this transaction to be legal and told Strecker that unless he could produce one, he would not permit him to remove any of the other cartons. After a few angry words, Strecker left. Still Rotzinger didn't go to the police, but began making his own inquiries. To his ever-deepening disquiet, he found out that Strecker had not only used Rotzinger's Swiss depot to store the mysterious cartons, but had also often kept them temporarily, once he'd driven to Germany, at Rotzinger's small branch depot in Losinger.

At 8:30 that night, Rotzinger finally informed the authorities. The police, hoping that Strecker would return, staked out the warehouses all night, but when he didn't show, they impounded the documents and informed the federal authorities. A week later, Strecker's home was searched to no avail, and on the 29th of the month, an arrest warrant was made out in his name.

Though the Swiss authorities didn't yet realize it, a remarkable coup had finally been blown wide open. The Israeli intelligence services, a combined Mossad and Military Intelligence operation, had quite simply stolen what President De Gaulle had refused to give them, the Mirage fighter, which they believed they had a moral right to own.

It all began in December 1967, a few months after the Six-Day War, when the French organized a conference in Paris for license holders, partial license holders and users of the Mirage supersonic fighter, with its Atar-9 engines, in order to pool experience of the aircraft as it had performed operationally. Present at the meeting were representatives of all the governments and aircraft industries who had an interest in the plane. The Australians and the Swiss manufactured the plane completely in their own plants under license; the Israelis and the Belgians were partial license holders who basically took the aircraft complete, but were responsible for assembly and the manufacture of some parts; and the South Africans, Lebanese and Peruvians purchased complete aircraft.

No aircraft or aircraft engine ever built has quite matched specifications or been sufficiently trouble-free to satisfy all of its customers. The Mirage was no exception, and in order to help sort out these problems, Dassault, which made the air frame, and Senikama, which made the engines, set up a "Users' Committee," which met regularly in order to exchange technical ideas. Brigadier General Dov-Syion of the Israeli Air Force headed the Israeli delegation but took little part in the debate. Partly because the general was seated next to the head of the Lebanese delegation, partly because of Israeli anger with the French, the mass of data available to the Israelis as a result of combat experience in the Six-Day War was not submitted to the conference.

If this was what the other nations had come to hear—and certainly the French were more than curious—they were all to be disappointed. For some reason, the meeting became rather heated. Senikama, the manufacturer of the Atar-9 engine, found itself under considerable pressure, particularly from Herr Frauenknecht, the representative of the Swiss firm of Solzer Brothers, the Swiss license holders. Alfred Frauenknecht was the senior development engineer responsible for the Swiss Mirage program. At forty-three, he was at the top of his profession, an engineer who knew his business, respectable and responsible, who made his criticisms of the Atar engine forcibly and directly, to the embarrassment of the French. Dov-Syion knew, however, that everything Frauenknecht said had been borne out in Israeli combat experience. Outside the meeting proper, Dov-Syion took the trouble to look up Alfred Frauenknecht and take his meals with him. They immediately got on, and Dov-Syion on his own initiative told Frauenknecht some of the Israeli discoveries about the Atar-9 engine, discoveries which he had deliberately kept back from the Users' Committee.

Back home Dov-Syion had some remarkable news for the Israelis. The Swiss government, according to Frauenknecht, had originally ordered 100 Mirage IIIs from the French but because costs had got out of hand they had decided to build only 53. However, the component parts for the full 100—that is, enough to make a further 47 planes—plus the design specifications were all in Swiss hands. If only Israel could get hold of these, it would virtually make up for the 50 which the Israelis had expected from the French. Dov-Syion also said that Alfred Frauenknecht could be helpful. Though not Jewish himself, he appeared to have an emotional attachment to Israel. In conversation with Dov-Syion, he had brought up the question of Swiss guilt during the Second World War, when many Jewish refugees seeking to escape Hitler's extermination camps had been turned back at the border.

The Israelis had suddenly, almost by accident, discovered a small breach in the very heavy French security, and now were determined to widen it. The first step was to gain the loyalty of Frauenknecht. Dov-Syion and others sent him a series of Israeli modifications to the Atar engine which, it was suggested, could be incorporated into the Swiss version. Frauenknecht was delighted, and soon a lively correspondence, both technical and personal, developed between Frauenknecht and his new Israeli friends.

While Amit was responsible for the operation, a standing committee composed of intelligence, Air Force and aircraft-industry people was set up to supervise day-to-day details. It was headed by General Aharon Yariv, chief of Military Intelligence, and Al Schwimmer, the remarkable American Jew who, in 1947, became one of the founding fathers of the Israeli Air Force by purchasing old aircraft in the United States and cannibalizing them to produce serviceable planes for Israel. Since then, Schwimmer had risen to become president and chief executive of Israel Aircraft Industries, which he started from nothing and which now employs 15,000 people.

Initially, the committee decided to try an open approach to the Swiss government via Frauenknecht. A proposal went to him directly from Al Schwimmer's office to the effect that Israel would be prepared to purchase the surplus Mirage components from the Swiss government and in return the Israelis would give up to the Swiss one of the most important secret modifications Israel had made to the aircraft. While the aircraft was being combat-tested in Israel, it had been discovered that the engine had one major drawback: the chances of a fuel-feed failure were unacceptably high. The Israelis had solved the problem by designing an alternate emergency pneumatic system which would cut in automatically when the primary fuel-feed device failed.

The approach was unsuccessful. The Swiss contract with the French stipulated that they could not sell the plane to a third party without the prior approval of the French. Switzerland, the most law-abiding of nations, was not prepared to forgo this obligation even in an under-the-counter deal.

The Mirage committee had foreseen this, and moved to phase two of the operation. It was obvious to them by now that the key to their problems lay in Switzerland—all that was needed was the means with which to turn it.

In early 1968, Frauenknecht received a letter addressed to his office requesting permission for an Israeli officer, a Colonel Shuhan, to inspect the factory in order to help the Israelis plan a similar factory for themselves.

Frauenknecht sought senior management approval for the visit, and when it was granted, he wrote back saying that Shuhan would be warmly welcomed. Almost immediately, the Israeli embassy in Rome was onto Frauenknecht, suggesting an earlier meeting in Berne to pave the way for Shuhan's visit and to map out a proper itinerary for him.

Frauenknecht arrived for this meeting at 10:00 A.M. on April 1, 1968, at the Ambassador Hotel in Zurich. There were two Israelis there to meet him, and they introduced themselves as Colonel Abel of the Israeli Air Force and Mr. Bader, who represented, they said, the European Military Procurement Committee of the Israeli Defense Ministry. The two men were, of course, using aliases. Mr. Bader was none other than Al Schwimmer, and Colonel Abel was Colonel Cain, one of Yariv's senior Intelligence men in Europe, then based at the Israeli Embassy in Rome.*

---

* Since Ehud Revivi, the second in command of the Eichmann operation, forgot his cover name at his hotel in Buenos Aires, there had been another near disaster involving pseudonyms. An Israeli agent spent a night in a French prison after he had checked into a hotel in Paris, deposited his passport with the desk, and then called to collect it later. At that moment he realized that he didn't have any idea of what the cover name was in which the passport had been made out. Desperately, he tried to bluff his way through, but he had aroused the suspicion of the reception staff. The police were called, and he was accused of traveling on a stolen passport. Fortunately for him, it was an Israeli document, and a check by the French police with Tel Aviv alerted them to what had happened. He was released next day with profuse apologies, but he had a good deal to account for to Meir Amit when he got home. These two events persuaded Mossad to change its techniques slightly, especially when dealing with inexperienced people. Instead of names being picked at random, they were chosen (and are to this day) so that they have some connection with the real name.

In the case of Colonel Cain, of course, the pseudonym Abel was a natural. *Schwimmer* means "swimmer" in German. Swimmers swim in pools; pools is *bäder* in German—hence Mr. Bader. It is a simple method but extremely effective. No one, even if they suspect that the man they are dealing with is using a pseudonym, is ever likely to make the right logical progressions from Bader to Schwimmer, but for Mr. Schwimmer the name Bader is not likely to be forgotten.

Amit had decided that the Israeli Embassy in Switzerland should not be compromised in any way because they were still working on the official net. But there was also a sound piece of trade craft involved as well. The Israeli military attaché in Switzerland would be known to the authorities, who might start expressing an interest in his activities if he were known to be having regular meetings with a senior engineer in the Swiss aircraft industry.

In their meeting with Frauenknecht, Bader and Abel came quickly to the point. Israel, they said, desperately needed these fighters. Was there any way, they asked, for the Israelis to deal directly with Solzer and bypass the Swiss government? Frauenknecht suggested that if they purchased the plans for 150 million Swiss francs and then placed an order in addition worth, say, 100 million Swiss francs for turbines and the like which were also made by Solzer, then it was possible there could be a deal. He was urged to make an approach to the company along those lines, but when he did, Solzer rejected the offer. The company was bound, they said, by the previous decision of the Swiss government.

Al Schwimmer, who knew as much about arms dealing as anyone in the world, never had any doubt that this would be the answer. Solzer was far too respectable a firm to engage in any illegal activity. The purpose of his own personal involvement in meeting Frauenknecht was to discover exactly what kind of material the Swiss engineer had access to. The answer was, in the circumstances, little short of dramatic. Every single blueprint of the Mirage and its engine went through his office. Alfred Frauenknecht was in a unique position to provide the Israelis with the information they would need to build their own fighters in five years instead of ten.

The operation to secure the MiG-21 for Israel had been regarded at the time as being of supreme significance. But that seemed almost child's play compared with the importance of Israel's possessing the working drawings of the Mirage III.

The problem, of course, was Alfred Frauenknecht. However friendly he may have been to Israel, it would be hard to imagine a man less likely to betray the secrets of his country or his company. Frauenknecht could not have been, on the surface at least, a more respectable or solid citizen. He lived in a typical Swiss middle-class one-story house near Berne with his wife Elizabeth. They took their holidays in the Swiss Alps rather than abroad and liked nothing better than to sit at home listening to classical music or entertaining friends.

His principal enjoyment seemed to be his work. He had started with Solzer Brothers in 1949 as a junior technician. By 1959, thanks to his dedication and ability, he had become manager of the manufacturing department for jet engines within the company. Though he had climbed far, he continued to live modestly, driving a small Opel and remaining in the same house he had purchased when he first joined the company as a young man. Though a subsequent investigation showed that he was not quite the model Swiss citizen—he had a mistress, whom his wife seemed to know about and, however reluctantly, accept—he was in almost every respect what the Swiss expect their citizens to be: sober, devoted to work, extremely hard-working, conservative in dress and manner, and modest about his undoubted achievements. He was unpromising material as far as the Israelis were concerned, to say the least.

It took three meetings—the last in a bar in the red-light district of Zurich—to persuade him to agree to help. Once in, of course, he could never get out.

What Frauenknecht was not to know was how skillfully he had been psychologically set up by Amit and Yariv. Though both men were certain that official approaches to the Swiss government and to Solzer would come to nothing, they had encouraged Frauenknecht to think that with him as the go-between they would be successful. When the approaches failed, Frauenknecht believed that he had let his new friends down and began to feel a real sense of grievance.

Time and time again, the Israelis (with a psychologist in the background working out the approaches) reinforced Frauenknecht's anger until he had got to the stage where he was personalizing the whole issue, and it had become almost more important to him than to Israel that the Israeli Air Force should have the Mirages. Money, of course, came into it as well. It had been hinted to him in the past that he would be on a commission if the sale went through. Now he learned that he could still earn a considerable sum of money by copying and supplying to the Israelis the blueprints in his care. In fairness to

Frauenknecht, the Israelis always knew that money would not be a prime consideration. He accepted $200,000 (which he probably could have bumped up to a million dollars) as insurance if things went wrong and he lost his job. So Frauenknecht was hooked. The cause, the money, his sense of anger at the way the Israelis (and by extension he himself) were being treated by the Swiss turned this most respectable of men into a spy, a job which he carried out with all the cool efficiency and resourcefulness for which he was known at the company with whom he had been a loyal employee for so many years.

General Yariv, however, still had one great shock in store. Like everyone else, he had seen all those spy movies, where the master spy opens a safe, draws out documents, takes two or three photographs, and escapes into the night with the enemy's master plan. The reality was to prove rather different.

There would be 45,000 blueprints to cover the machine tools alone and 150,000 blueprints for the aircraft. Frauenknecht himself estimated the total weight of all the blueprints at about two tons and thought he would need a year to do the whole job. It seemed a fiendish undertaking—only marginally less difficult, Yariv sometimes thought during planning sessions, than getting the aircraft themselves. But as it evolved, the *modus operandi* was quite brilliant in its simplicity.

The blueprints were occupying one huge room in the Solzer factory, where they were simply taking up valuable space. The Swiss Mirage assembly program had come to a halt, and the prints were no longer required by Solzer. So Frauenknecht went to his superior and suggested that the whole series be microfilmed and the originals destroyed. It was an obvious solution to what had become a storage problem, and he got immediate approval. With two sets of drawings now potentially in existence—the original and the microfilm—an opportunity clearly existed to get one of them away to Israel. The question was how?

Security at the factory itself—by the Swiss military— was strict. If the blueprints were to be microfilmed, then this could only be done under supervision. There would be no chance of making an extra microfilm and no chance of not incinerating the originals. These documents were classified as top secret, and heavy security would apply both during filming and during destruction. But

Frauenknecht had a stroke of genius. Under Swiss law, blueprints of patents have to be retained for fifty years and then are sold as scrap. Frauenknecht recruited a nephew, Joseph Frauenknecht, to help and had him negotiate with the patent office for the bulk purchase of old blueprints.

The rest was plain sailing. Frauenknecht made sure that he was in charge of the microfilm program; once filmed, he had the blueprints packed into cardboard containers, all under the supervision of a security guard. The containers were then loaded into a Volkswagen minibus, which Frauenknecht had purchased in his nephew's name, to be taken to the main incinerator in the town. Frauenknecht, for reasons of security (he told his employers), insisted on going along on the journey to the incinerator. However, he had also rented a small garage en route. There, he had the blueprints he had purchased from the patent office stored, all neatly packed into precisely the same kind of cartons, ordered from the same supplier, as Solzer used to pack the Mirage prints. In a matter of minutes, the Mirage blueprints were swapped for the old patent-office blueprints, and the minibus continued its journey to the incinerator, where an inspector would log the destruction in his furnaces of cartons full of blueprints.

There were, of course, certain blueprints which the factory didn't want microfilmed. These Frauenknecht had to deal with by more direct methods. Fortunately for him (and the Israelis), his mistress worked in the plant archive office, and he simply had to ask her to log them out to him for inspection. By now, the Israelis had a full back-up team in the town servicing their agent. Frauenknecht would simply hand over these documents to members of the team at meetings arranged at hotels, restaurants, parking lots and the like—always a different place, in order to arouse no suspicion—where they would be taken away from him, copied and the original returned.

There was basically no difficulty about getting these particular documents out of the factory and then to Israel because there were relatively so few of them. Yariv's real problem was how to move the great bulk of the rest of the blueprints out of Switzerland. If Frauenknecht tried to move a few crates at a time by air freight, the regular shipments would eventually arouse the interest of Swiss security, which happens to be one of the most efficient and effective in the world.

After weighing the various alternative proposals which were put forth by the committee, Yariv decided that the safest course was to get the blueprints across the border —obviously not to France but to Germany. Four Israeli agents were dispatched to the Rhine bridges to observe the movement of traffic, report on customs activity, and particularly to establish whether there was a likely official who could be bought in order to assist the transfer.

Within a fortnight, Yariv received a list of possibilities, but one man stood out as the most likely candidate. As we have seen, the man was Hans Strecker, a German who had lived most of his life in East Berlin and who was now employed with the Swiss transport firm of Rotzinger & Co. His job was to process through customs all of Rotzinger's trucks, to deal with customs officers on a day-to-day basis and, as Rotzinger was a perfectly respectable firm, to do so on a basis of honesty and trust. He had held the job for a year and was on first-name terms with customs officials on both sides of the border. Strecker was approached in the classic manner used by espionage agents throughout the world. He was befriended by an Israeli agent who was as free with his money as he was with his friendship until the inevitable day when Strecker commented upon the amount of money his friend seemed to have. It was downhill all the way after that. Strecker was told by his friend that he got the money by doing a few simple jobs for friends of his, jobs that involved no danger though they were marginally outside the law. In fact, said the Israeli, there was $100,000 going for anyone who could take across the border over a period of several months a few cartons of papers in the trunk of his car. Strecker accepted the bait and was recruited within hours.

The operational plan was now perfect. Frauenknecht met Strecker only once, in order for Strecker to hand over the keys of a small warehouse which Rotzinger owned. The system worked out by the Israelis was simplicity itself. Frauenknecht would drive a crate of documents every Saturday to Kaiseraugst and deposit the crate in the warehouse. He and his nephew would then go to a local bar, the Hirshen, for a drink. If he had made a safe delivery, he would nod to Strecker. Strecker would then go to the warehouse, load the documents into the trunk of his black Mercedes, drive through customs smiling and chatting with his friends as usual, enter West Germany, and then head northeast through the Black Forest to Stuttgart. There, at a small private airport, a twin-engined Cessna, registered in Italy, would be waiting. The Cessna would fly the plans to Brindisi down at the heel of Italy, where an Israeli aircraft waited to take the plans aboard and fly them directly to Lod and the Israeli aircraft industry.

The first shipment of blueprints was made on October 5, 1968, and at the rate of fifty kilos virtually every week (which was not all that Frauenknecht could manage, but all that the factory could manage to blueprint) was flown out to Israel. For all but a few days of a full year the operation went undetected until the day in September 1969 when Hans Strecker made his mistake, first by permitting himself to be observed loading cartons and then, more seriously, by somehow failing to move one crate of blueprints. No one knows why, because he disappeared completely after being questioned by his director. The explanation is probably no more complicated than the fact that on one of those Saturdays, when Frauenknecht nodded to him across the bar, he simply couldn't be bothered to make the long drive. Thereafter, he was always a crate behind. Human frailty is the great enemy of an espionage service; once again it had intervened to explode a near-perfect operation.

The Israelis, who had been keeping a careful watch on Strecker, quickly realized that the operation was blown, and Frauenknecht was given the code warning by telephone ("the flowers have been spoiled") to give him an opportunity to get out.

But Frauenknecht, perversely perhaps, decided to remain behind to face the music. The day after the federal authorities received the crate of documents they had found at Rotzinger's warehouse, they called in an aircraft-engine specialist to pronounce upon their significance. As it happened, he had an appointment at Solzer's the following morning and telephoned the man who would be chairing the meeting he was due to attend to make his apologies. He couldn't come, he said, because he had been asked by the police to identify certain blueprints which had fallen into unauthorized hands.

That evening, the chairman of the meeting turned up at his house. He was Alfred Frauenknecht. He knew all about the blueprints. They were of the Mirage III and the Atar-9 engine, he said, and he had been responsible for removing them from Solzer's and having them shipped to Israel.

He was kept in prison for a year without trial while the prosecuting authorities tried to work out precisely the scale of his operation. It was a difficult task, but the authorities came to the conclusion that he had passed on something like 2,000 drawings of engine parts, 80,000 to 100,000 drawings of jigs and the like, 35,000 to 40,000 drawings of instruments, 80 to 100 drawings of the plane itself and 15,000 documents relating to other specifications, spare parts and instructions for maintenance—altogether a stupendous haul.

On April 23, 1971, Alfred Frauenknecht was sentenced to four and a half years' imprisonment with hard labor.

Because his time in prison previous to his trial was taken into account and because he was released early for good behavior, Herr Frauenknecht left prison on September 21, 1972. Two and a half years later, on April 29, 1975, together with his wife, he arrived in Israel to watch the maiden flight of the Kfir, Israel's own home-produced fighter-bomber, a Mach-2.2 aircraft based upon the Mirage III, the plans of which this astonishing man had made available to Israel.

Today the Kfir is the workhorse of Israel's supersonic strike force and Israel herself one of the few countries in the world manufacturing its own Mach-2 aircraft. A great many engineers and scientists can take the credit for that, but Alfred Frauenknecht's role in that remarkable achievement can never be underestimated; nor can the roles of Meir Amit and Aharon Yariv, who played him so brilliantly. As Al Schwimmer observed as the Kfir took to the air, President de Gaulle did Israel one hell of a favor.

Chapter 20

THE SABBATH OF SATURDAY, OCTOBER 21, 1967, was drawing to its close. The time was exactly 5:20 P.M. The war of attrition which had followed the Six-Day War was at its height. Brigadier General Alex Argov, captain of the *Eilat*, one of the biggest ships in the Israeli Navy, an old World War II British destroyer, took a turn around his bridge, checking his position, some fourteen miles from the entrance of Port Said. Something in the sky caught his eye and he looked up. Two balls of fire hung momentarily at their zenith high on the horizon before making what appeared to be a slow descent down into the Mediterranean.

He knew immediately what he was looking at, and with a sense of sickening dread pressed the general alarm. One hundred and ninety-nine officers and men of the Israeli Navy moved to action stations and at the captain's orders began firing at will in an attempt to hit the balls of fire now hurtling toward them. It was, of course, useless. Within seconds, two missiles of the Styx type, fired from two Ossa missile boats lying in Port Said, struck the *Eilat* midships. All day, the Egyptian boats, with Russian advisers aboard, had been tracking the *Eilat* on their sophisticated equipment and only when the Russians were convinced that the *Eilat* was in range and their instruments properly calibrated was the Egyptian commander permitted to press the fire button. The two missiles struck the ship's boiler room, splitting the vessel virtually in two. As fires broke out everywhere, desperate attempts were made to keep the *Eilat* seaworthy. But much of the communications equipment inboard and outboard had been destroyed, so that even though an emergency radio was pressed into service, no one at naval headquarters heard the *Eilat*'s distress signal. At 7:20 P.M., the signal was picked up by an Israeli armored column in the Sinai and

267

passed on to Tel Aviv, and rescue ships and helicopters dashed to the scene. The *Eilat* was now on its side in the water. Those who weren't killed or wounded had fought for two hours to save the vessel, but to no avail. At 7:30 P.M., clear now in the night sky, a third missile homed in on its target and hit the ammunition store with a vast explosion.

At last, Brigadier General Argov gave the order to abandon ship, and all who were able jumped into the cold and oily water. A few minutes later, the fourth and last Styx missile smashed into the water, injuring many of the survivors with the force of the underwater shock. Miraculously, of the full ship's company 152 sailors were picked up relatively unscathed, 41 of them had been wounded, and only 47 killed. Yet there could be no denying the scale of the disaster.

Naval history had been made on that day. This was the first time in the history of naval warfare that a ship had been sunk by long-range missile attack. For reasons of internal and external prestige, little was made of this publicly at the time, yet the Israeli general staff now knew what its naval commanders had known for some time, that the whole Israeli Navy was out of date, completely unsuited for the kind of warfare which would be waged from now on in the Mediterranean. Those four Styx missiles not only sank the *Eilat*, in a way they sank the whole Israeli Navy.

During World War II, the *Eilat*, sailing under its commissioned name HMS *Zealous*, had performed valiantly in the North Atlantic. The ship now lying at the bottom of the Mediterranean, sunk by Russian missiles (such is the irony of the shifting alliances of the past fifty years), had accompanied British convoys to Russia bearing vital wartime supplies over one of the most dangerous and treacherous stretches of water in the war to assist Russia to survive the onslaught of their common enemy. Then she had been a force to be reckoned with, capable of 35 knots, carrying four sets of guns, and displacing 1710 tons. In the sixties, in the Mediterranean, she seemed merely slow and cumbersome.

The sinking of the *Eilat* finally closed the argument which had been raging for quite some time between the Chiefs of Staff and the naval command. Ever since the Egyptians got Russian equipment, including missile boats equipped with sea-to-sea missiles, the Navy had been saying that its own ships, mainly World War II castoffs, were completely incapable of meeting this challenge. Somewhat reluctantly, two years previously, the Israeli government had agreed that the Navy should have new boats to meet this potential threat. Nothing was available in the West, which was well behind the Russians in this field, so the Israelis began designing their own boats. These were to be fast and maneuverable, comparatively small, and packed full of on-board instrumentation. Initially, the boats were to be built in Germany, but when in 1965, after massive Arab pressure, the Germans stopped supplying military equipment to the Israelis, the order was transferred to the C.C.M. (Chantiers de Construction Mécanique de Normandie) shipyards in Cherbourg.

It was a godsend for the firm and the port, for this was an area suffering from high unemployment. C.C.M. had no previous experience building vessels of this kind, but with the German know-how already tapped and with the original Israeli designs, backed up by an Israeli technical mission established on the spot, Félix Amiot, the director of the shipyard, was able to guarantee delivery according to specification. Meanwhile, in Israel, military factories were designing and manufacturing the Gabriel missiles and the incredibly complex electronics, which would cost more than the boats themselves, to be fitted to the vessels once they arrived.

The French arms embargo imposed by de Gaulle after the Six-Day War did not initially affect the gunboats— on condition that they were not sent with any military equipment. This was simply a piece of sophistry. The fact was that the unemployment situation in Cherbourg was grave enough to withstand even Gaullist concepts of international morality.

The first five boats sailed for Israel with no difficulty. A permit was in hand for the sixth to make the voyage when, on December 28, 1968, the Israelis attacked Beirut airport and blew up thirteen Lebanese aircraft as a reprisal for a Palestinian attack on an El Al Boeing 707 at the Athens airport on December 26th. The Beirut attack enraged de Gaulle, who declared that the French arms embargo would now be total.

The Israelis moved quickly. Orders were given to sail

the sixth boat immediately, and the seventh stole out of Cherbourg Harbor three days later and made a successful run home. A furious de Gaulle, believing with some justice that he had been tricked, refused to accept the Israeli explanations that there had been a "misunderstanding." Whatever else happened, he told his officials, the remaining five boats must never be allowed to go to Israel.

The Israeli Defense Ministry faced a major dilemma. Very few people—not even the men building the boats—realized the immense importance which Israel attached to these vessels. European eyes, still conditioned by the Second World War, could not take these vessels too seriously. They appeared to be something like the old motor torpedo boats, weapons of war certainly, but not of major significance.

For the Israeli Navy, however, these remaining boats, all near to completion, represented a large proportion of the sharp end of Israel's new Navy; without them Israel could not be an effective fighting force in the Mediterranean, the theatre of war in which it operated. It was vital to the security of the State that they be got to Israel.

Flushed with the success of their military operation in Beirut, one school of thought within the military was that the boats should simply be seized by a party of armed sailors, who would beat off any French resistance and make for the open seas. This was rejected immediately by General Dayan, the Minister of Defense. Such action would be inconsistent with the dignity of Israel and would also create diplomatic whirlpools from which Israel might not be able to extricate itself. If the boats were to be brought home, it would have to be done secretly, using the covert techniques which Israel's intelligence community had learned to employ with such great effect over the years. In August, under the overall supervision of General Yariv, an operational unit was formed with the cover name "Operation Noah's Ark."

The first stage began in the summer of 1969. Admiral Mordechai Limon, head of the Israeli purchasing mission in France, renounced all further Israeli interest in the boats and opened negotiations with regard to compensation. The boats had not yet been completed, and would not be seaworthy until the winter. It was, therefore, vital that the Israeli technical mission in Cherbourg should be permitted to stay on, both to ensure that the vessels were completed to specification but also as a cover for Yariv's operational requirements. It was Limon's job to negotiate this package. The boatyard itself was anxious to continue work on the vessels. It was clear to everyone that if work stopped it would affect the employment situation in the port considerably, so the French government was persuaded that the boats could continue to be built under Israeli supervision. The Israelis were necessary if the boats were ever to be completed; after all, it was the Israelis who had designed them.

Because the most natural reaction of the Israelis in such circumstances (in which they had been refused the right to boats which they had commissioned) would have been to pull out every last man from Cherbourg and refuse any further cooperation, Admiral Limon had a delicate path to tread. He did not want to appear too eager to permit Israeli technicians to remain; nor did he wish to seem so intransigent that the French themselves would suggest that the Israelis go. Fortunately, the question of compensation was a complex one, and Limon agreed that the technicians could remain until it had been settled, and then made certain that the Israeli side quibbled over the very smallest details for as long as possible.

Admiral Limon himself and a senior naval officer, Brigadier General David Kimhi, were in charge of the operation on the ground. Kimhi, short, moustachioed, a man known for his keen sense of humor but, as his nickname "the Shark" implied, also for his ferocity, had already seen "action" in Cherbourg by slipping the sixth boat to Israel. At the beginning of September, he was told from HQ in Haifa to get the seventh boat out of Cherbourg as well. Though it was not quite ready for the long voyage, Kimhi made sure that it was fully provisioned and overflowing with fuel, ready to make the dash to Gibraltar where the sixth boat would be waiting. Kimhi told the French naval command—already under attack from Paris for letting the sixth boat go—that he needed twenty hours of sea trials for the vessel and asked to see weather maps. It was a Saturday, when there was little activity on the dock—an ideal time to go. At 2:00 P.M., the crew were instructed to be on board. At the same time, every single car attached to the French mission arrived at the dockside filled with supplies, so that loading could be carried out quickly, drawing as little attention to themselves as was humanly possible. At the last moment, he called to get a quick clearance.

The only additional problem was a road bridge which crossed the harbor and served as a barrier to the military arsenal, but which had to be raised for each sailing. Kimhi coolly called the French Naval command and asked that the bridge be opened for him at 4:30 P.M. and again at 5:00 P.M., when he would return after a short sail. With that minimal assurance, the boat was allowed on its way and made the dash to Gibraltar to meet up with its sister ship.

Kimhi returned from Gibraltar to Cherbourg immediately. The French Naval command then made a second mistake. Angry and humiliated by the way Kimhi had outsmarted them, they informed him that he had not acted "correctly" toward his hosts. Accordingly, the other five boats inside the arsenal could no longer receive assistance from the French Navy, and he and his crew would no longer be welcome in the navy mess. Furthermore, the boats themselves would have to leave the arsenal immediately and berth in the civilian harbor.

Kimhi hugged himself with delight. Because of the sheer petulance of the French Navy, he and his boats were being expelled from the harbor and thereby removed from military surveillance. The commercial harbor was unguarded, there were no checks on movements, and there was no way that the entrance to the harbor could be locked.

Operation Noah's Ark was officially operational from August 1969. The actual details as to how to smuggle the boats out were still not finally worked out, but, as in the best of all espionage operations, preparations on the ground had to be completed long in advance to ensure that whatever plan was finally decided upon in Tel Aviv, the operational ability would be there to mount it. On the engineering and technical side, this meant that the design specifications had to be so altered as to ensure that the time gap between commissioning and sailing could be very short indeed. It also meant that all ancillary equipment (which the shipyard would not normally be expected to supply) had to be on hand in Cherbourg and kept in tiptop condition. For this purpose, the Israelis rented a large flat, which became a storeroom for all manner of naval equipment purchased all over Europe. Most of all, there had to be a much larger contingent of Israeli sailors in the port than would normally be necessary.

Dayan had laid down one difficult condition. The boats could not be removed from France illegally. Yariv had to come up with a plan which gave the boats the *legal right* to leave the harbor, even though their final destination might surprise the French government. So the first phase of the operation had to be conducted elsewhere.

In early November 1969, a London firm of solicitors specializing in maritime affairs was asked by a representative of Israel's biggest shipping company, Maritime Fruit, to help set up a Panama registration for an off-shoot of the firm. The lawyer contacted the Panama firm of Arias, Fabrega & Fabrega. The new Panamanian firm was quickly registered under the name Starboat, which if one were looking for an Israeli connection, might not have been difficult to find, given the fact that the Star of David is internationally known as the Israeli emblem. A little more investigation would have established that connection with no room left for argument: one of the principal shareholders of Starboat was a Mr. Mila Brenner, a director of Maritime Fruit, the major Israeli shipping firm.

It was Mila Brenner, with his connections in the international shipping world, who called upon Ole Martin Siem, a Norwegian industrialist and one of the most dynamic businessmen in Scandinavia, who after graduating as a civil engineer had worked his way up to become managing director of the Aker shipyard and Aker group of companies, one of the biggest industrial enterprises in Norway. Siem's shipyard had already done a great deal of work for Maritime Fruit, and he agreed to act as front man for Starboat.

The Israeli plan was to use Starboat, with the very respectable Ole Siem at its head, as the official purchaser of the boats from the French government. The Israelis knew that President de Gaulle had established a very high-powered committee to examine all arms exports, and this would be a major hurdle if the sale to Starboat was to go through. The chairman of that committee was General Bernard Cazelet, the fifty-nine-year-old Secretary General of National Defense and one of France's most intelligent senior officers, and one of the members was General Louis Bonté, director of international affairs at the Defense

Ministry's Army Department and France's chief arms salesman.

One of the weaknesses of the committee was that it was never quite clear to whom it was responsible. Under the 1958 Constitution the committee was directly answerable to the Prime Minister and this held good while first Pompidou and then Couve de Murville held that office. But after Pompidou became president and appointed for political reasons the arch-Gaullist Michel Debré as Minister of the Forces rather than Minister of Defense, Debré had insisted that the committee and its staff should be responsible directly to him.

It was this confusion the Israelis had observed, and upon which they felt they could play. On the one hand, General Bonté was the chief salesman for French armaments abroad; on the other hand, he sat on General Cazelet's committee, which was required to monitor such sales for any political implications they might have. The committee itself was answerable to two masters.

Subsequent events can only properly be explained if one assumes that General Yariv had at least one senior official within the French government service acting on behalf of Israel and who was able to control the presentation of the sales of the boats to the government. Events moved quickly.

At the beginning of November 1969, Admiral Limon informed the French government that Israel was at last ready to settle the question of compensation. Only a few days later, the shipyard heard from Ole Siem that he would be prepared to purchase the boats on behalf of Starboat. Immediately Siem's offer was put into the hands of General Bonté's office. The Israelis now had to get action before anyone could think too carefully. Their cover was, in fact, so thin that it was almost ludicrous. The arms committee was supposed to examine all potential purchases carefully, and a minute's examination would have made the Siem offer look as threadbare as it was.

According to Siem, Starboat wanted these thoroughbred vessels, built for speed and maneuverability, for oil exploration—as unlikely a tale as a French farmer insisting that he was buying a Lamborghini in order to haul his chickens to market. But there was nothing the Israelis could think of which would make more sense. These were missile boats, and there was no way that fact could be disguised.

Nevertheless, seeing a way of getting rid of these embarrassing boats quickly and at the same time recouping for France and for the Cherbourg shipyards the money which was going to have to be repaid to Israel—and more besides—the French raised no real questions about this remarkable deal, which had so fortuitously materialized apparently from nowhere.

At the meeting Bonté simply informed General Cazelet that he had an offer for the boats from Norway. Cazelet and other members of the committee assumed from this that he meant the Norwegian government and asked only two questions: first, whether Israel had entirely dropped any interest it might have have felt it still retained in these boats, and, second, whether there was a clause in the agreement guaranteeing that the boats would not be reexported. General Bonté, in his capacity as France's chief arms salesman, received an unqualified affirmative to both questions, and the matter was concluded. Cazelet then sent an account of the meeting to President Pompidou, the Prime Minister and the Ministers of Finance, Defense and Foreign Affairs; their experts, each already primed, not by Cazelet but by others, to the effect that speed was of the essence, signified their approval.*

In theory, the Israelis could have sailed out then and there. The boats had been legally sold to an Israeli dummy company; on the surface there was no reason at all why they could not go through the normal formalities, sail out of the harbor, and on emerging from the channel

---

* Interestingly, when the affair became a major political scandal in France, Debré, the man in the government who would perhaps be most hostile to the boats' going to Israel, went on record as saying that he had known nothing about the sale to Norwegian interests until after the boats had sailed. If this was the case, then the matter was deliberately kept from him by his own staff. Generals Montplanet and Bonté went to see Debré's *Chef de cabinet* before the ministerial committee and told him of the sale of the boats. It seems very odd that he did not pass this information along to his minister. Equally, it seems very odd that the experts on Debré's staff, having been officially informed by Cazelet about the impending sale after the meeting, would not have passed on this information to Debré as well.

turn to port instead of starboard. But the moment the new Norwegian owners announced an intention to sail, there was likely to be mention of it in the French press, perhaps prompting some last-minute inquiries. The legal cover was painfully thin, and the Israelis knew that any official doing a morning's work would have no difficulty in piercing it. The stakes were simply too high. The Israelis had in their possession the official documents permitting them to clear Cherbourg. But the actual sailing had to be under conditions of secrecy; the boats had to get out onto the high seas before anyone began asking the first questions.

Admiral Limon and Brigadier General Kimhi advised sailing around Christmas—preferably on Christmas Eve night, when all of France would be celebrating with their families in their homes.

Kimhi arrived in Cherbourg on December 18th to make the final preparations. The tides were such that the boats would be able to sail either over Christmas or on New Year's Eve.

Two problems still existed. First, the shipyard had had delays in delivery and supply of all the equipment it needed. In some cases, these items, though small, were crucial. General Yariv was called in to help, and he asked for the assistance of Mossad. Mossad agents are used to handling unexpected requests, but even veteran agents found the order they subsequently received from Tel Aviv puzzling. Agents in every European country were told to go to particular manufacturers and try to buy —on the spot, with cash—arcane pieces of naval equipment. Some pretended to be owners of oil tankers, holed up in some distant harbor for lack of a crucial part; others claimed they needed some equipment in order to evaluate it against a rival manufacturer's for a vast order for an unspecified country. Only a few were permitted to say they represented the C.C.M. Shipyards on this extraordinary shopping spree. But it worked, and to the astonishment of the buying office at C.C.M., the stuff actually began arriving.

There was another problem. The sixty sailors already in Cherbourg would not be enough to take the five boats 3,000 miles to Tel Aviv. At least another sixty would be required. If Israel was not exactly trying to smuggle a whole navy into France, it was trying to bring in a sufficient number of sailors quickly in a way which would not alert the French security services to the fact that an operation of some kind was under way on French soil. So a careful timetable of travel for each of the men was worked out by Military Intelligence in Tel Aviv. No more than two men would be permittted to travel together on the same plane. Some were to travel early, by ship to Marseilles and then by train to Paris and Cherbourg. Where hotel accommodations were needed, no more than three would be permitted to stay in any hotel together for more than a single night, so that no register would record a sudden influx of young Israelis. Every plane from Israel and every train from Paris to Cherbourg was utilized to bring in the chain of men. In fact, an initial plan to fly them all into Italy and then send them by train to Paris and Cherboug fell by the wayside because of a rail strike in Italy at the time.

The selection of men was made by Military Intelligence, who then carefully briefed each sailor individually on what some intelligence officers mordantly referred to as "the Invasion of France." Care had to be taken about passports; no one traveled on false documentation (that would have been too risky), but some were told to use civilian passports. The men were divided into six groups of ten individuals each, with an officer in charge, and each group broken down into subgroups of two each.

They were briefed over and over again, because, though Mossad men would be meeting them, these were not trained agents but young servicemen going abroad on what amounted to a clandestine mission. In each man's pocket were two slips of paper: one was the name and address of a contact officer at the Israeli Ministry of Defense's purchasing mission in Paris, the other carried details of travel arrangements and the address he should make for once in Cherbourg. There was much argument about those slips of paper. To most men inside Military Intelligence, the thought of sending an agent out into the field with a carefully typed itinerary in his pocket was (as one man expressed it at the time) as bizarre as it would be for a rabbi to take a pork chop on a picnic. The risk was clearly immense: it just needed one of the sixty to be picked up by French customs or police and searched, and the whole plan could have been revealed. Against that was what was finally regarded as the greater risk: young Israelis getting lost in France, confused about where they were going, and eventually drawing attention to themselves. The slips of paper were the lesser of the two evils.

By December 22nd, all but two of the group had arrived in Cherbourg and been tucked away, either on the boat or in Israeli "safe houses," which had been established over the months. The missing two gave rise to immense alarm, not least when a rumor was picked up by a Mossad agent that they had been arrested in Paris and that the French had got wind of Operation Noah's Ark. For several hours, the Israeli contingent in Cherbourg, the Paris office of the Israeli purchasing mission, and the authorities in Tel Aviv were at fever pitch. No move had yet been made against the other Israelis in Cherbourg by the authorities, but clearly anything could happen. The two men, a naval officer and a doctor, arrived shamefaced on the morning of the 23rd. Neither will ever forget the roasting they received from the Shark. Their explanation was simple and very human. They had arrived in Paris on schedule and had a few hours to kill before catching the train to Cherbourg. Why not use the time by doing some shopping for their families at the Galeries Lafayette? What neither of them knew was quite how awesome a thing a Paris Christmas traffic jam can be and in their case was. In theory leaving themselves plenty of time, they missed the train, stayed put at the station all night, and caught the first train in the morning.

In Cherbourg itself the big problem was one of housekeeping. The boats had to be provisioned for eight days at sea with enough food for 120 people. Clearly, the supply officer could not go to one store and make all his purchases at once. That would almost certainly have caused the kind of comment which the Israelis were most anxious to avoid. So, laboriously, he toured the town over a period of three days with his enormous shopping list, buying bits and pieces from here and there, until, by literally visiting every provision store in Cherbourg, he had collected all he needed.

The fuel problem had already been taken care of. (They would need a quarter of a million liters of petrol —without the luxury of having a tanker come alongside and simply pump it aboard.) What Kimhi had done was consistently to over-order the petrol he had taken on for the sea trials, which had been conducted during the previous three weeks.

The final hurdle was the weather. These boats had not been designed for winter conditions in the Bay of Biscay, and it was clear that they would be in severe trouble if conditions didn't suit them. A meteorologist was brought in from Tel Aviv to set up a weather station in one of the boats. Over a period of ten days, every weather forecast, whether in French, English, or Spanish—broadcasts intended for commercial ships, planes or farmers—was monitored and recorded, and the information fed onto the weather charts the meteorologist had prepared.

Early on the morning of Christmas Eve, Admiral Limon arrived from Paris and booked into the Sofitel Hotel and immediately called a war council of all his senior officers. Rain was gusting down, and the report from the meteorologist was far from reassuring. The strong southwest wind meant that the boats would make slow progress out of French waters, but nevertheless a provisional departure was fixed for 8:30 that night—precisely the time when it was expected most French families in Cherbourg would be sitting down to their Christmas meal.

Orders were immediately given to load the boats with the food and other provisions, but, as always, the totally unexpected managed to upset the timing of a beautifully organized operation. One of the sailors, staying at a safe house where the food was stored and not knowing anything about the plan to sail to Israel that day, had, as Commander Kimhi ironically told Limon, "taken unto himself a French teacher," and the French lesson was taking place in the room just above where the stores were packed. It didn't help anyone's nerves, either, when it was discovered that the French teacher was a journalist. When that was at last over, the slow process of loading could begin, a process which was to continue all day.

In an attempt to cover some of this activity, Limon instructed several of his officers to book a table at the Café du Théâtre, one of the best restaurants in Cherbourg, for a Christmas Eve party that night just to give the impression that nobody was going anywhere.

At 7:30 P.M., the boats were ready to sail, but the weather, still blowing a strong sou'wester, was against them. Seldom can a fleet officer have ever been under as much pressure as was the Shark during those next few hours. By 8:30 P.M., there was still no shift of direction in the wind. At 10:30 P.M., which was to be the next scheduled point of departure, with everything tied down, ready for sea, and the crew at their stations, the weather forced him to abort once again. By now, Tel Aviv was all but hysterical, and instructions flowed from HQ to Kimhi's command vessel ordering him to sail. But he kept his nerve. In those conditions, to go would risk at best being forced to seek shelter in French, Portuguese or British harbors or at worst receiving such a battering that they'd be forced to limp ignominiously back to Cherbourg. The hours ticked by as the small boats wallowed uncomfortably in the harbor.

The BBC weather forecast just before 2:00 A.M. on Christmas Day morning removed, as Kimhi has said, "a stone from my heart." The winds had turned northerly. Though still strong, they would now come from behind as the boats made their way down the French coast. It was enough . . .

At exactly 2:30 A.M. by the stopwatch—so that there would be one vast roar rather than a series of five smaller ones—Commander Kimhi's captains started their engines. The noise was earth-shattering as twenty engines—four to each boat with a combined sixty-five-thousand horsepower—opened up. Within moments, all the boats had cast off and headed for the open sea, with three in a row leading off, the other two taking up the rear. It was only then that Commander Kimhi acknowledged something which he had known in his heart of hearts all along. Whatever the French government may have thought was going on, the people of Cherbourg involved with the building of the boats and those who had worked in the harbor had never had any doubts. One of the owners of the shipyard had even come down that evening, despite his Christmas Eve feast, to wish them all well. Workers who had put so much craftsmanship into the boats, on hearing the noise of the engines, rushed out and waved shyly from the quay as the boats they had built left for their destination. All around the harbor where the houses abut onto the waterfront, people came to their windows and signaled *shalom* with their lights. No one called the French authorities—the people of Cherbourg went back to sleep content to keep to themselves the knowledge that the boats they had built for Israel with the aid of Israeli technicians were going home.

For the small Israeli contingent left in Cherbourg, little else remained to be done. A man who called himself Haim Sharak went around to each of the small hotels in which the Israelis had stayed and scrupulously paid all the bills. Admiral Limon woke up the concierge at his hotel, said he wasn't staying the night after all, paid his bill, climbed into his Jaguar, and drove to Paris. On Christmas Day, when Cherbourg awoke to discover that the boats had gone, every Israeli in town was gone as well. When the news got out, it caused almost as great an international sensation as did the Entebbe raid six years later.

From time to time, the boats were spotted as they made the journey to Tel Aviv, although no one outside the operation actually witnessed the tankers of Maritime Fruit, standing by in the Mediterranean at prearranged spots, refueling the boats and speeding them on their way. At 6:40 P.M. on December 31st, the first of the boats nosed its way into Haifa Harbor. It was over. If there is such a thing as perfection in an undercover operation—where all of the objectives are achieved cleanly, without anyone getting hurt—then Operation Noah's Ark was it.*

The Israelis would have wished for less publicity during that final incredible dash down the coast of Europe and across the Mediterranean. But as it was, they were ready with their own cover story. The boats would be used, they told the international press, for oil exploration off the coast of Israel. No one believed it, but that didn't matter much. If the world had grasped the shadow of what the Israelis had achieved, they had missed the substance: that these missile boats (always referred to in the press as gunboats) would represent in any future war with the Arabs the main offensive weapon of the Israeli Navy.

The two French officers, General Bernard Cazelet and General Louis Bonté, at the heart of the affair were the scapegoats; they were suspended, never to be brought back.

* Some Frenchmen were, of course, hurt by the affair, and experienced a certain amount of mental anguish. President Pompidou declared to his Cabinet at the height of the crisis: "We have been made to look complete fools because of the incredible casualness and intellectual complicity of our civil servants."

An inquiry was completed by a senior French civil servant, Jacques Labarraque, but only three copies were made of his report, which went to Pompidou, to Chaban-Delmas, the Prime Minister, and to Debré, the Minister of Defense. Neither Cazelet nor Bonté was permitted to see it. General Cazelet, who had authorized the sale to Starboat, first heard about the Israeli *coup-de-main* over his radio while on holiday. Interestingly, his first reaction was to chuckle to himself at how clever the French government had been in getting the boats to Israel after all.

PART VI

Palestinian Terrorism

Chapter 21

THE DIPLOMATIC PROBLEMS caused by the Six-Day War were of major concern to the country. But to the ordinary people of Israel, these appeared unimportant compared with the specter which now rose to haunt the nation —the Palestinians on the rampage.

Ever since the mid-fifties, before the Suez war, the Palestinian cause had been allowed to fester in the refugee camps surrounding Israel. The Arab governments had made no attempt to resettle these people, preferring to keep them as a constant and public reminder to the rest of the world of the injustices done to the Palestinian people by the creation of the State of Israel. The Palestinians themselves, not unnaturally, had sunken into a state of torpor and inactivity. There was much talk, of course, especially among the young, of "revenge," of "armed resistance," and of "the forthcoming battle for the homeland." The Israeli intelligence community through its agents both in Military Intelligence and Mossad, kept a careful watch on all this and had rooms literally stuffed with agents' reports of "revolutionaries" who were unable to carry their fight beyond the doors of the coffeehouses in which they planned and plotted their great coups.

Nevertheless, they all had to be watched—as did an organization known as Al Fatah, founded in the mid-fifties by Palestinians at the universities of Cairo and Alexandria and headed by an (on the surface at least) unattractive leader named Yasser Arafat. Arafat preached a return to the homeland, through violence if necessary, and he was attracting more and more support in the refugee camps. He succeeded where others before him had failed because he made it clear, both in his manner and appearance, that he drew his constituency from the poor inhabitants of the refugee camps, not from the cultural elite who had made it out of the camps and were now prospering in Beirut.

The "Palestinian Entity," as it was known, became a reality in 1959, when it began to be regularly discussed by the Arab League. In 1963, under the patronage of President Nasser, the Palestine Liberation Organization, which was to be the political arm of a movement, was formed. Beirut intellectuals mistrusted the PLO from the very beginning as being far too reliant upon the rest of the Arab world. The Palestine the intellectuals wanted was not merely another Arab state but a modern Marxist revolutionary nation, which would be in the vanguard of a Marxist revolution involving every Arab nation. The "Arab Nationalist Movement," under a spellbinding ex-dentist named Dr. George Habash, was formed to give voice to this attitude, harder and more vigorous in opposition to the Israeli presence but at the same time demanding vast social and economic changes throughout the Middle East.* It was not until 1965 that the modern battle began between the Palestinians and the Israelis, the bloody battle which over the years has become so careless of human life.

It was on January 3, 1965, that Ayre Chizik, an Israeli water engineer employed by the national water utility, noticed a sack floating down a canal he was inspecting. He bent down and picked it out of the water and found that it contained a detonator and an explosive charge. Immediately, he called in the Security Service; he was well aware of the much-trumpeted boast of Al Fatah † that they would sabotage Israel's intricate water network (on the grounds that the water which ran into the canals was

---

* There were, of course, several other Palestinian organizations and political groupings around at the time, but, by and large, whatever differences may have existed between them, by the early sixties they were forced to seek a loose alliance with either George Habash or Yasser Arafat. These alliances down the years ebbed and flowed according to the political and military situation. In theory, at least, all these groups came to be represented on the Central Committee of the Palestine Liberation Organization, but were not necessarily beholden to it or it to them. I do not attempt in this book to chart these movements, not because they are not of immense importance, but because it would require a whole book to do them justice.

† *Al Fatah* is Arabic for "the victorious," and is the main guerrilla organization of the PLO.

stolen from Syria), and that it might now have become a reality.

The Israeli Security Service established that the sack had been put into the canal near the Nefuta Valley in northern Israel by saboteurs who had come on horseback from Jordan. The operation had been bungled and inept. The tools were primitive, to say the least, and the method somewhat hazardous. Nevertheless, though the government took the matter lightly enough, both Meir Amit and Aharon Yariv were sufficiently concerned to make certain that water installations throughout the country were put under heavy guard. They tried to hush up the incident, but Al Fatah issued a communiqué in Damascus proclaiming that battle had been joined.

Right up to the Six-Day War similar attacks were launched by Al Fatah, mainly from Jordan but sometimes from Syria and Lebanon. But they were only pin pricks. Many of the terrorists, far from being committed young Palestinians prepared to risk their lives for their homeland, were actually criminals released from Jordanian prisons and given what was then the prevailing rate of fifteen dinars (about $42) to carry out an act of sabotage within Israel. It is hardly surprising that the damage done by these mercenaries was minimal. More often than not the explosives were placed against telephone poles or remote and isolated installations, old army bunkers long since fallen into disuse. The Palestinians, most Israelis believed, were a problem they could live with in comparative comfort.

The Six-Day War at first changed little. Despite the fact that Israel now held the areas where Palestinian terrorists had largely been based, the extraordinary feat of arms which permitted the Israeli Army to demolish the Syrians, the Egyptians and the Jordanians in six days had a shattering effect upon the whole of the Palestinian resistance movement. In the towns and villages of the West Bank, now in Israeli hands, many Palestinians who had once given support to the terrorists decided that the Israelis could never be defeated. Nor—initially at least— did the Israelis on close inspection seem to be the monsters the Palestinians had believed. If they were occupied, that occupation was comparatively benevolent. Teams of Israelis were even touring the country showing local farmers how they would prosper if they used Israeli technology and Israeli marketing techniques.

Wanting, above all, a quiet life, believing that the Palestinian cause had been lost, and, having sometimes suffered in the past from bullying members of Al Fatah, now under Israeli protection the West Bankers turned on Al Fatah and the Popular Front for the Liberation of Palestine (PFLP), as Habash's organization was now known. If the Israelis had believed that they would have constant security problems in the occupied territories, they soon discovered to their astonishment that not only was this not the case, but the flow of hard information about terrorists from the Palestinians themselves reached a remarkable peak. After about three months, the PLO had been all but eliminated on the West Bank and, demoralized and dispirited, was forced to regroup in Jordan.

The first suggestion that this victory over the Palestinians was only temporary came from one of the most successful agents Israel has ever employed. Perhaps only half a dozen people in the country know his real name. I shall call him David Shaul. Very early, David Shaul, an Iraqi Jew and a lieutenant in the Israeli Army, was asked by Fatti Harkabi to infiltrate Al Fatah, and he became one of its first recruits. He had risen through the ranks to become a company commander and, in order to maintain his cover, had fought heroically against the Israelis on the West Bank during the Six-Day War. Of all the agents the Israelis had in Al Fatah, Shaul was the most effective. He was of sufficient rank to be privy to some of Al Fatah's most vital secrets, which he had passed to the Israelis, along with a long list of Al Fatah and PFLP sympathizers on the West Bank, when he was "arrested" by the Israelis after the war.

Shaul was an important enough agent to be serviced by a back-up team; they were not permitted to know his identity and their prime function was to collect his information from various dead-letter boxes in the Jordanian capital. Arrangements had been made years before to get him out from wherever he happened to be if he felt threatened or had information of such importance that a letter would not suffice. In 1968 he believed he possessed such information. After sending a coded message, he received a letter in Amman a few days later from his "family" in Lebanon telling him that his father was desperately ill and asking him to come to Beirut immediately. Three days later, he was in the Lebanese capital, where, in a safe house established by the Israelis, he met his control, who had flown in via Cyprus.

Shaul's report was indeed worth the journey. For some time, Shaul said, there had been rumors that the Russians were going to give concrete assistance to the Palestinians, and he had heard, though he could not vouch for its authenticity, that Yasser Arafat, George Habash and others had secretly flown to Moscow for top-level talks with the Soviet leadership.

He himself had been ordered, suddenly and unexpectedly, to crack down hard on any criticism of the Soviet Union he heard among his troops. Such criticism was then endemic in the Arab world, for many believed that one of the reasons why the Arab armies had collapsed was because, while American aid to Israel had been unstinting, the Russians had been slow and ineffective in providing the Arab armies with weaponry, which in any case was no match for what the Israelis possessed. Shortly after this, a small group of Russians, together with senior officials of the PLO, turned up unexpectedly at the camp where he was stationed on the outskirts of Amman. Senior PLO officers, including Shaul, were called to a meeting, ostensibly because the Russians wanted to explain the Soviet role during the war. The meeting lasted all day. In the morning, the Russians detailed the immense contribution they had made both in terms of matériel before and during the war and diplomatically after it was all over.

Then, subtly at first, the mood changed. There was no overt criticism of the Arab armies, but the Russians left no one in any doubt that it was the view of the Russian military machine that Russia had been let down by the Arabs rather than the other way around. The Arabs had all the weaponry they needed; their failure had been a failure of leadership. Swiftly, the Russian spokesman changed tack once again. It would take a long time to build up the Arab arsenal to a position where it could once again threaten the Israelis, and it would take even longer to train the Arab armies so that they could match their enemy on the battlefield. But the war had to go on if the Israelis and the imperialists were to be defeated. In that war, the Palestinians would have to fight, just as the Viet Cong were fighting.

From there, he moved swiftly into what Shaul was convinced was the real purpose of the meeting. Al Fatah had been no more successful against the Israelis

than had the Arab states. The damage they had done
internally to Israel was inconsequential. This was not their
fault, said the Russian. It was because they were inadequately armed and trained, and faced a foe which possessed a highly professional and superbly equipped
counter-intelligence apparatus. The Palestinians could
no longer rely upon others to do their fighting for them—
the Six-Day War had shown the truth of that. Now the
Palestinians themselves had to take the offensive, inside
Israel and out, and the Russians were prepared to help.

This statement was met with general applause and the
meeting broke up. Subsequently came another gathering,
this time addressed by one of Arafat's principal lieutenants, who made it plain that the Russians had come not
merely to give a "pep talk." The Soviet government, he
said, was in earnest, and already certain members of
Habash's organization, the Popular Front for the Liberation of Palestine, had sent men to Russia for training.

As Shaul* returned to Amman "from his father's bedside," Meir Amit called the Security Committee (made up
of himself, Yariv, the head of Shin Bet, and the chief of
police, along with their principal advisers) into emergency session. The Israelis had fought the KGB directly in
Israel and indirectly abroad from almost the first days of
independence, and everyone sitting around the table
knew what Shaul's discovery meant for Israel. KGB-
trained (and possibly even KGB-officered) Palestinians
would now have all the experience of the world's most
powerful and most ruthless espionage agency to call upon.
Operational units would operate as cells; discipline would
be imposed; modern techniques of explosives and communications would be brought into play; targets would
be carefully defined both for their political and military

---

* Shaul was active in Al Fatah, then in the PFLP until he
retired two years ago. His appearance has been subtly altered,
and he now lives in Israel and works for Military Intelligence.
He is one of those fascinating men who spent most of his life
fighting Israel in order to prove his operational virility to the
organization into which he had been infiltrated. He operated in
Europe for a period and, under one of his many Arab
pseudonyms, appeared on the Interpol wanted list. The Arabs
gained one benefit from his presence among them for so many
years: he is today vocal in his support and understanding of
the Palestinian cause.

signficance; propaganda would be skillfully used to get the maximum effect out of both defeat and victory; and rigid security would be evoked to make attempts by the Israelis to infiltrate that much more difficult.

Fear is not something which men like Meir Amit admit to; yet the entire Israeli intelligence community, preparing for the crucial battle, was in a state of high tension, awaiting the first attack. No one knew where or when it would come.

On July 22, 1968, an Indian priest called at El Al's ticket office in the center of Rome and asked for three tickets on the following day's El Al flight to Israel. He showed his Indian passport and produced two Iranian passports for his colleagues. He gave his address as the Imperial Hotel, Rome.

On the following day, thirty-eight passengers and twelve crew boarded El Al Flight 426, a Boeing 707, from Rome's Fiumicino airport for Lod, Tel Aviv. Twenty minutes after take-off, three men got to their feet and walked toward the cockpit door. Maoz Proaz, the first officer, looked up as the door opened, tried to block the intruders' way, and was immediately shot in the face. Within a few minutes, Captain Oded Abarbanel accepted the terrible logic of his position, obeyed instructions, and altered course for Algeria. The PFLP had struck at Israel's most vulnerable spot—El Al. And for the first time hijackers were demanding the release of convicted prisoners (in this case Arab terrorists, held in Israeli prisons) as the price for the lives of the hostages they held.

George Habash's PFLP immediately claimed credit for the hijacking, and not only did the Algerian government agree to help the hijackers, but it permitted the official newspapers to praise their actions. For forty days the Israeli passengers were held in the plane, until, finally, after failing to get any real international support, Israel traded fifteen terrorists for the passengers on what was described as "humanitarian grounds." It was a bitter defeat for Israel, made all the more terrible by the certain knowledge that, thus encouraged, the Palestinians would try again.

The post-mortem in Israel was as savage as any the country had experienced. A nation which had just won one of the greatest military victories in modern history found itself brought humiliatingly low by three armed men operating on the orders of a dentist in Beirut. It was hard for anyone to understand how Israel's much-vaunted intelligence community had so utterly failed. If the Israeli public had known that, in fact, its intelligence services had received hints that the PFLP's "spectacular" might well be a hijacking, that anger might have been even greater, but it would have been misplaced.

Certainly Mossad would try to get advance warnings of terrorist activity: certain means needed to be found to combat hijacking attempts when they occurred or to try to frustrate them before they did, but, inevitably, there would be more—and some would be successful. The only approach was to take an extended view—this was Meir Amit's belief—to set out to defeat the Palestinians and their KGB mentors in the long term.

That meant that Mossad, Military Intelligence and Shin Bet had to declare total war on the Palestinians. It meant that Israel, with the cooperation of its army and air force, had to be prepared to punish transgressors with a ruthlessness which up to then the politicians had forbidden them to display. The enemy was more clearly defined than it had ever been, and yet, because that enemy was an undercover terrorist organization, trained by the KGB in the arts of subterfuge, it would be more difficult to grasp than ever before.

Meir Amit's acceptance of the fact that the Palestinians would have many more successes was not a message which found its way into the Israeli press. What did get into the papers and was eagerly snapped up by the international press were the stories of ex-paratroopers and soldiers around the country who had believed their active service days were over being invited to run shotgun on El Al flights (a crash training course was prepared for them by Military Intelligence) and their remarkable ability to shoot a man between the eyes across the length of an aircraft cabin. Cabin doors were reinforced with steel and kept permanently locked. But the electronic gadgetry that was publicized as being aboard each aircraft (capable of sniffing out explosives and the like) only existed in the imagination of the engineers, inventors and scientists hard at work looking for solutions.

Attempts by Foreign Minister Abba Eban on the diplomatic net and Meir Amit on the security net to get some

form of international agreement to combat terrorism in
the air failed abysmally. The rest of the world saw this as
an Israeli problem—unfortunate, even lamentable, but
nothing anyone else wanted to be involved in for fear that
if they were, they, too, would draw fire. The world's
ability to deny its own nightmares was never shown to
better advantage.

Five months after the Rome hijack, the PFLP struck
again. On December 26, 1968, at Athens airport, two
terrorists, armed with guns and hand grenades, attacked
an El Al flight still on the tarmac, with forty-one passengers and a crew of ten aboard. Miraculously, only one
passenger was killed and two stewardesses wounded, for
there could be no doubt that the purpose of the assail-
ants was to blow up the plane and every man, woman
and child inside. It was, by any standards, a cruel and
barbarous assault. Near the El Al flight, an Olympic Air-
ways Comet was refueling, and two other aircraft were not
far away. It was only chance, said Colonel Patroklus
Nikos, head of the Athens airport police, that 300 tons of
fuel had not been ignited by the terrorists and the whole
airport blown up. Screaming "We want to kill Jews!" the
Arabs were perilously close to killing hundreds of non-
Jews as well.

This time the Israelis were prepared. For months, Meir
Amit's agents had carefully mapped out Beirut's international airport as the site for Israeli revenge. On December 30th, two helicopters swept in from the sea and
disgorged Israeli paratroopers, who, in full sight of hundreds in the aircraft terminals, methodically destroyed
every Arab aircraft on the ground. It was as smooth an
operation as the Israeli Army had ever mounted. Not a
single person was hurt. Passengers already on board a
Middle East Airlines flight to Jeddah were politely ordered
out of the plane and into the airport building before the
plane itself was blown up. No non-Arab airliner was
touched, though many stood on the tarmac. All in all,
thirteen Arab aircraft went up in flames. The commander
of the ground operation, then described only as "the best
soldier Israel has," is today Israeli Chief of Staff, General
Rafael Eytan. So cool was he that as his troops blew up
the planes, he went to the bar in the final departure
lounge and—to the total astonishment of staff and pas-

sengers—asked for a cup of coffee. He drank it, paid in Lebanese currency and left.

But the attack on Beirut had little effect upon the Palestinians. In February 1969, at Kloten airport in Zurich, four terrorists moved in to attack another El Al flight taxiing on its way to the runway. They were spotted by a young Israeli security officer, Mordechai Rachamim, who shot one of them dead; the other three were arrested.

It was in August of that year that a somewhat complacent world outside Israel suddenly realized it was not to be immune. A group who called themselves the Che Guevara Command Unit of the PLO hijacked a TWA flight en route for Lydda airport and ordered the captain to fly to Syria. The Syrians held two of the Israeli passengers, then finally swapped them for two Syrian pilots who had been held in Israel when they were shot down after straying over Israeli air space a few months previously. All over Europe, the terrorists moved to attack Israeli installations.

On and on it went: August 29th, a time bomb at the ZIM offices in London; September 8th, bombs at the Israeli embassies in The Hague and Bonn; November 27th, a hand grenade thrown into a crowded El Al office in Athens, killing a two-year-old Greek boy and injuring dozens of others, none of whom happened to be Jewish.

On February 10, 1970, an Israeli security guard challenged an Arab in the lounge at Munich airport. Immediately, he and two accomplices let loose with pistols and hand grenades, killing one Israeli and injuring eleven others. A Caravelle of Austrian Airlines managed to land safely after an inboard explosion, but a Swiss airliner on the same day, a quarter of an hour out of Zurich with thirty-eight passengers and a crew of nine aboard, wasn't so lucky. The last words of the captain were: "Suspect explosion in aft compartment of aircraft . . . fire on board . . . nothing more we can do . . . goodbye."

An investigation of both incidents showed that sophisticated explosive devices, set to an altitude meter designed to go off at 10,000 feet, had been placed in parcels addressed to recipients in Israel. The PFLP, realizing world opinion would turn against them, denied that they had been involved in either incident, but most western agencies and Mossad established PFLP's guilt without question when they each independently obtained information on a secret inquiry into the whole affair held by George Habash in Beirut.*

Habash's people had bungled: no one realized that mail for Israel would be shipped by other carriers than El Al. The method had proved only too effective. It was the target that was wrong. Israel's feelings of being cut off and alone were only intensified by the reaction of the airlines: the lesson they chose to learn from this affair was to refuse to carry Israeli mail. Certainly, for the first time, airports other than Israeli imposed massive security, and passengers and their baggage were subjected to painstaking searches. Yet the result was that the terrorists had, temporarily at least, succeeded in making travel to and from Israel for people and for goods incredibly more difficult. That was an important victory, both in real and in psychological terms.†

And still the war waged by the Palestinians using the map of the world as their battleground went on. On May 2, 1970, terrorists broke into the Israeli Embassy in Paraguay and killed thirty-six-year-old Mrs. Edna Peer, wife of the first secretary and a mother of three, and seriously wounded a woman secretary. On July 22nd came a new twist. This time the PFLP hijacked a plane in order to free terrorists who had been arrested through their involvement in previous hijack attempts. Six Palestinians

---

* Because in this book I have not dealt with internal security and the activities of Shin Bet, the Israeli equivalent to the FBI, I have not gone into the huge increase of internal sabotage in Israel and the occupied territories during this period. Dayan told the Knesset on January 1, 1970, that up to that time there had been 999 acts of sabotage by Palestinians since the Six-Day War in Israel or Israeli-held territory.

† This was the first occasion that the PFLP employed the technique (taught them by the KGB) of using front organizations which could take the blame for any incident that went embarrassingly wrong. On this occasion, the PFLP let it be known that a breakaway group led by a hitherto unknown Palestinian called Ahmad Jibril was responsible. Most Western intelligence agencies, on this and other occasions, chose to believe this fiction and rejected Israeli information that the so-called breakaway groups were part and parcel of the same organization. This information was too inconvenient to accept, for to do so would mean that Western powers would be forced to condemn the Palestine resistance movement wholesale. They preferred to blame so-called extremists.

hijacked an Olympic Airlines flight, and threatened to blow it and its fifty-five passengers sky high, unless terrorists held by the Greek government were released. The agreement between the Greeks and the Palestinians also pledged that "Arab commandos" would never again operate on Greek soil. If Greece thus received a dubious immunity from further trouble, the rest of the world and particularly Israel became even more vulnerable.

In September of that year, the Western world received the reward due to it for the supine manner in which it had dealt with these appalling acts of terrorism. In that month, the PFLP finally broke loose from any restraints as to targets and organized a massive hijacking on a scale and ferocity no one could possibly have imagined.

At 11:50 A.M. on September 6, 1970, a TWA Boeing 747 carrying 145 passengers and crew en route from Frankfurt to New York was hijacked over Belgium and diverted to a desert airfield north of Amman called Dawson's Field after Air Marshal Sir Walter Dawson, A.O.C., Levant, who built it in 1948 for the operational use of the RAF.

Eighty-four minutes later, at 1:14 P.M., a Swissair DC-8 flying from Zurich to New York, carrying 143 passengers and a crew of 12, was hijacked over central the control of the PFLP, who had set up an entire military base to receive the aircraft. With the world of aviation still in deep shock, thirty-six minutes later, at 1:50 P.M., two hijackers, one of whom was Leila Khaled, who had already hijacked a TWA flight to Damascus in February 1969, attempted to seize an El Al Boeing 707 on a flight from Tel Aviv to New York via Amsterdam. While the airliner was over Clacton, Essex, the two hijackers, brandishing pistols and grenades, ran down the aisle and tried to force themselves into the pilot's cabin. An Israeli security guard shot the male terrorist dead, but a steward was shot in the stomach in the melee. Thanks to the great courage of an American passenger, who flung himself on Leila Khaled, greater tragedy was averted. Though a grenade rolled across the floor with its firing pin removed, there was something wrong with its mechanism and it failed to explode. The plane made an emergency landing at London Heathrow, and Leila Khaled was handed over to the authorities.

At 4:00 P.M., a Pan American 747 Jumbo, also bound

from Amsterdam to New York, with 158 passengers and a crew of 18 aboard, was hijacked shortly after it left Amsterdam and diverted to Beirut. There the PFLP had taken over the control tower and threatened to blow up the jet and everyone aboard if a rescue attempt was made.

The Jumbo had been destined for Dawson's Field, too, but the hijackers were persuaded by the crew that the runway there simply wasn't long enough to handle a plane of that size. So it was flown to Beirut, where the crew and its passengers were ordered to "get out fast" by the emergency exits. As the last of the passengers scrambled clear, a time bomb went off and engulfed the plane in a ball of flames.

In the meantime, at Dawson's Field—renamed "Revolution Airfield" for the occasion—over three hundred passengers of the U.S. and Swiss airliners spent the night in the desert as prisoners of the PFLP, who were dug in around the planes with mortars, machine guns and bazookas. In temperatures of over 100°F., the passengers had to sit out in the stifling hot aircraft awaiting the result of negotiations with the Jordanian authorities.

The PFLP demands were straightforward. All non-Israeli passengers would be released in exchange for: three PFLP guerrillas serving sentences in Switzerland for the attack on an Israeli airliner in Zurich; the release by Britain within seventy-two hours of Leila Khaled; and the immediate release by the West German government of three Arabs held since the Munich airport attack in which an Israeli passenger was killed and a well-known Israeli actress had to have her leg amputated as a result of the injuries she received. Israeli passengers would be released in exchange for an unspecified number of guerrillas held in Israeli prisons.

On September 9th, two days after the original hijackings, just to rub salt into the world's wounds the Palestinians successfully hijacked another airliner, this time a British VC-10 en route from Bombay to London via Dubai and Bahrein. It was diverted to Dawson's Field via Beirut for refueling, where once again the Lebanese authorities were unable to intervene.

The Israeli response to the situation was hard-headed. Throughout the West Bank about 450 prominent Palestinians, among them lawyers, doctors and teachers, and including 80 women, were arrested for suspected PFLP sympathies. It was now a question of hostage against hostage.

The PFLP had at last overreached themselves. They were expelled from the PLO as the world's outrage at what had occurred vented itself on the whole Palestinian movement. But worse was to follow.

In a final act of carnage, the terrorists blew up all three planes before the hostages were finally released. This proved too much for King Hussein, who had been forced to stand by, helpless and humiliated, as the Palestinians used his country as if it were their own. For months his Bedouin officers had been urging him to drive the Palestinians out. Now he ordered his troops into action. On Tuesday, September 15th, King Hussein's Arab Legion swept down on the Palestinian camps. It was to be a massacre as the Jordanian Army, finally unleashed from its political shackles, drove the Palestinians out of their land with a ruthless, cold-blooded savagery.

Israel's part in what became known to Palestinians as Black September was small. It intervened only to warn the Syrians that if they moved in to help the Palestinians, then Israel would be bound to move against them. That was enough to ensure that the King's victory was complete. Ironically, the Palestinian resistance movement, which had grown fat on its war against Israel, was temporarily destroyed in battle by another Arab state. Several years later, in Lebanon, history was to repeat itself.

Yet, if the Jordanians had done Israel's work for her, there was no cause for rejoicing in Tel Aviv. No one believed that the Palestinians were finished.

Chapter 22

GENERAL MEIR AMIT had retired in 1969 to become president of the largest industrial conglomerate in Israel, Koor Industries (owned by the trade union movement), when the Jordanian civil war ended the first phase of Israel's present-day war with the Palestinian resistance movement. The Palestinian cause was running rampant. Politically, the PLO had become respectable. The PFLP were roaming far and wide, leaving a blood-stained trail in their wake. Yet, though this was not something which could be boasted about too openly, under Amit, Mossad felt it had won the opening rounds rather than lost them.

Unquestionably, Mossad had defeated the Palestinians in achieving their prime objectives: to make it almost impossible to fly El Al and to cut Israel off from the rest of the world. For what began to be apparent was a remarkable fact: during this quite extraordinary period, from July 23, 1968, when the El Al Boeing was hijacked to Algeria, right through to September 9, 1970, when a British VC-10 joined two other aircraft on the ground at Dawson's Field, there had been 115 hijackings throughout the world, but El Al, though attacked on the ground, remained otherwise untouched. Far from having people frightened off, El Al was carrying more and more passengers and flying more and more miles as it gradually began to dawn upon everyone that only El Al could guarantee getting them to their destination, despite all initial Israeli fears that they would never efficiently counter this new terrorist weapon.

In 1968, Dr. Habash, being interviewed by Oriana Fallaci, the well-known Italian journalist, asked rhetorically: "Would you really want to fly El Al?" The answer to that was given by the world's airline passengers. In 1967-68, the annual turnover of the airline was $52 million; in 1972-73, this had risen to $135 million. By then El Al had the highest load factor of any airline on the North Atlantic route. This was unquestionably a major achievement—and it was directly attributable to Meir Amit, who before his retirement not only personally instituted the extraordinary security precautions which precede every El Al flight and organized the sky marshal program, but also put a Mossad team into every El Al office in the world. It was one last, unpublicized measure which probably had the most significant effect. The name of every passenger was checked through computers, and all last-minute bookings were treated with the greatest caution. Sometimes the results of this vetting process were spectacular.

In the spring of 1969, a young man traveling on an Italian passport presented himself at the El Al ticket desk in Frankfurt and asked for a ticket for the following day's flight to Tel Aviv. One of the Mossad men in the office was instinctively suspicious of him. He seemed unnaturally nervous and hesitant. An Italian-speaking clerk was asked to deal with him, and she reported that, though he spoke fluently, there was a trace of an accent which might be regional but did jar a little.

As a direct result of Meir Amit's patient negotiation with governments around the world, the airlines had perfected a system whereby dubious passports could be quickly checked out with the country of origin. A telex message to Rome, however, produced no results. The Italians were prepared to cooperate, of course, but this was Saturday, and the Italian weekend was sacred. One of the things which made the Mossad operative wary was that the man gave his address as the Frankfurter-Hof, probably the best and certainly one of the most expensive hotels in town. He didn't seem the type of man who would stay in that kind of establishment, and it had become very much part of PFLP operating practice to put their young volunteers into first-class hotels on the night before a mission and to give them a night out on the town.

The Israelis simply could not risk waiting until the following day (when the young man would check in for his flight) to establish the truth. Obviously, if he was a terrorist, then at least two or perhaps three others had also managed to check onto the flight without arousing any suspicion. It was possible that only one of them would be carrying arms, and he might not be the "Italian." Even if he was, and was picked up, the others might decide to go for their weapons there and then. The Mossad man telexed his disquiet to Amit, who immediately put six Mossad operatives in Germany at his disposal. It was decided to search "the Italian's" room at the Frankfurter-Hof while he was lured to the lobby on some pretext. It didn't take long to establish that he was indeed a hijacker. They found plastic explosives concealed in a body corset (which would have got through any metal detector test and probably would have escaped a body search as well), and a copy of the speech he intended to

make over the aircraft intercom once he had hijacked
the plane was lying in full view on the hotel blotter.

The list of passengers was once again put through the
computer, but this time knowing that hijackers would
be on it, it was not too difficult to isolate two other probable culprits. Fortunately, they gave themselves away,
when right under the noses of the Mossad men tailing
"the Italian," they met on the pavement outside the
Frankfurter-Hof to go off to their "last supper."

The three young people—two men and a girl—were
well into their second course when suddenly and unexpectedly a very large, smartly suited gentleman sat down
at their table and motioned them to be quiet. In his hand
he had a napkin, which he flicked up for a moment to
reveal a small handgun, before smilingly covering it up
again.

Conversationally and courteously, he explained that
he was a colonel in the Israeli Army. With a sweep of his
hand, he pointed out other diners (in reality, perfectly
ordinary local citizens) whom he assigned various ranks
in various branches of the Israeli Army. Outside—and
this was no fiction—were well-armed Israeli agents. He
wished the youngsters no harm; he regarded them as being misled naughty children, who had simply fallen into
bad company. As soon as they had finished their meal
(and he would keep them company while they did), he
would take them back to their hotel, remove from them
all their weaponry and explosives, and any documents
they might possess, ask them a few questions, and put
them on the first flight to Beirut the following morning.
Refusing to hurry and with the utmost urbanity, the Israeli insisted that they eat their meal, suggesting courses
and liquors, which the three, totally hypnotized by
him, somehow forced down as all the while he talked
about the problems of Israel and the Middle East. Back at
the hotel, the three young Arabs were photograhed,
fingerprinted, debriefed, and told that if ever they came to
Europe again, they would receive a somewhat different
reception. The following morning they were taken to the
airport and given tickets to Beirut, paid for out of the
money they had handed over for tickets to Tel Aviv, then
waved on their way. A fortnight later, the parents of
two of the Arabs received letters, delivered by hand,
warning what would happen to their children if they ever

tried such a thing again. Their career as terrorists was over.

The world was not permitted to learn of many of the hijacking alerts which from time to time were flashed to the big international airports around the globe because of a Mossad tip. On at least two occasions, passengers whom local security had isolated as being potentially dangerous didn't appear for their flights, presumably because of sudden evidence of heavy security.

On Meir Amit's retirement, the chiefs of most of the Western intelligence agencies wrote expressing their unanimous view that it was Meir Amit and Mossad which had managed—if not to halt—at least to check international terrorism, giving the world the chance to organize its defenses. No one could doubt that Meir Amit laid down the operational principles which made that possible.

Meir Amit doubled the size of Mossad, began the program to incorporate the latest technological equipment (carried on and broadened by his successor), set forth new operating principles still in effect today, and, most important of all, ended the long-running feud between Mossad and Military Intelligence.

Isser Harel's Mossad had been a troubleshooter, a role it handled with considerable success; working closely with the Prime Minister's office, Harel ran major operations when the need arose. Meir Amit, without the dominating figure of David Ben-Gurion looming over him, fashioned Mossad along completely different lines. Big, expensive and glamorous special operations still had their parts to play, but it was the continuity of intelligence that in the end would be most significant.

Though Meir Amit had won the respect of Mossad, many hoped that when he retired the agency would return to having a civilian at its head. There was (and remains today) a respectable argument for Mossad's being a completely nonmilitary establishment. The military voice in matters of national security has never been muted. The role of the general staff in Israeli public life is enormous, and the Six-Day War exaggerated this tendency greatly. Suddenly, the Israeli Army, which had gloried in its spartan tradition, sprouted generals who adopted life styles to match the personality cults they encouraged around them. As General Ezer Weizmann said mockingly of this new breed of officer turning up at Palmach reunions: "They don't wear ties, but they wear eighty-dollar shirts." David Ben-Gurion put it even more neatly just before he died: "It's a tragedy that Israeli generals are beginning to think of themselves as *generals!*"

With generals not only in the military, but also in politics, in industry, in the universities and foundations, a free-masonry of retired general-staff officers developed whose influence ran deep in the ruling establishment. Mossad would have been an ideal place for a counterweight; yet, realistically, it was supremely doubtful that any civilian head of Mossad would be able to provide it. The military were simply too strong. A civilian chief would have either had to go along with the Army or be swamped by it. Better, therefore, to pick a general who knew his way around the back corridors of the Ministry of Defense than have a civilian locked in perpetual and ultimately dangerous conflict with it. Isser Harel had managed for a while, but he had David Ben-Gurion at his elbow. Those were different times and a different army.

The only realistic candidate for those who wanted a civilian *Memuneh* of Mossad was Ehud Avriel, still only fifty, a man with great experience both in government (he had headed the private offices of David Ben-Gurion when he was Prime Minister and for Levi Eshkol when he was at the Treasury, and was in charge of African Affairs and International Cooperation when Golda Meir was at the Foreign Ministry) and in intelligence.

An attempt had been made to bring Avriel into the intelligence community at a high level much earlier. When Isser Harel quit for the last time (leaving his post as personal assistant to the Prime Minister on intelligence affairs), some sought to replace him with Avriel. But Meir Amit, who was by then well established, would not hear of the appointment, and Avriel didn't get the job.

Before his retirement, Meir Amit tried to use his influence again, not only to keep Avriel from replacing him (on the grounds that the appointment should go to an army man) but to extend his own period of appointment. Amit and Prime Minister Levi Eshkol had never got on, especially after the Ben Barka affair. Amit was contemptuous of what he regarded as Eshkol's inability to make a decision, while Eshkol always feared that Amit would involve the government in what he described as "entan-

gled situations." To be fair to Eshkol, his whole period of
office was dominated by the Lavon and Ben Barka affairs,
and he knew only too well what could happen if a chief
of intelligence got out of hand. Amit was simply too sure
of himself, too much of a personality in his own right for
Eshkol to feel that he could easily be controlled. It had
been agreed when Harel left that no head of Mossad
should remain longer than five years. Meir Amit argued
that his term of office should be extended on the
grounds that there was no obvious successor. Eshkol's
decision-making powers didn't desert him this time, and
he rejected the request out of hand. That seemed to leave
Ehud Avriel a clear field, even though the Army was insisting that one of its officers should take over. But Avriel's supporters were soon complaining justifiably that he
wasn't making a fight of it. For all his many talents, Ehud
Avriel, as one of his friends has said, is simply too nice
a man to fight dirty in order to secure his own advantage.

In the end, Eshkol produced, apparently out of thin
air, one of his well-known compromises. He appointed a
general as head of Mossad, a man on the verge of retirement, who had never been involved in intelligence work
of any kind and whose whole career was the antithesis of
the concept of the fighting general upon which Israel
prided itself.

Zwi Zamir—known as Zwicka—was born in Poland in
1924, but his family emigrated to Israel that same year.
He joined the Palmach in 1942 and became a divisional
commander at the age of twenty in 1944. He was imprisoned by the British for work on the illegal immigration
program and, on independence, fought actively as a battalion commander in and around Jerusalem.

In 1950 he became an instructor of an advanced course
for senior officers, and in 1953 attended a course for
senior British officers in England. He was appointed
commander of the infantry school on his return, and
in 1956 was promoted to a senior job in training
command at the Ministry of Defense. He took a study
leave in 1957 to get a B.A. in humanities at the Hebrew
University and on completing that was promoted to the
rank of brigadier and took charge of Training Command.
In 1962 he took over Southern Command during a period
of very little tension, and on July 15, 1966, was appointed
military attaché in London; this meant, of course, that he

didn't fight in the Six-Day War, which in the Israeli Army was a lapse roughly akin (as it was unkindly put at the time) to a man failing to consummate his marriage.

Zwicka Zamir, the least glamorous, then, of Israeli generals, was as astonished as anyone by his appointment. Instead of gently moving out to pasture, he was taking on one of the most demanding jobs in Israel, with no background experience at all to help him handle it. The Army, though inclined to grumble, had been neatly outflanked by Eshkol. They had demanded a general and they'd got one, and now could hardly complain. But Mossad professionals were appalled.

When asked how such an inexperienced man could be expected to handle such a sensitive job, Eshkol replied breezily: "It's all right. In a year or two, he'll learn." It was an extraordinarily complacent statement, and yet events were to prove the Prime Minister right. It took Zamir all of two years before he began to feel and understand the real dimensions of his job, but he did it. By sheer industry—working day and night, studying and listening —he became one of the great masters. His methods were different from any of his predecessors. His reports were voluminous. He never tried to conceal anything from the government. He took responsibility for both successes and failures, and he always took the latter much to heart. Golda Meir, when she became Prime Minister, used to console him: "When trees are felled, the chips will fly." Her trust in him was absolute.

In the beginning, however privately disappointed the staff might have been, Zwicka Zamir was permitted to assume office without having to deal with the enormous internal turmoil which had occurred in varying degrees with the appointment of every one of his predecessors. If Zwicka Zamir was not an inspired choice, he was nevertheless the kind of man who was able to draw the best out of people working for him. Amit had been very much the boss; Zamir was more like the chairman of the committee. Once they had got used to his way of working, many senior executives came to appreciate the Zamir style. All of them, after all, were professionals, with years of experience in the field. This professionalism was now given a fuller rein than it had ever had before.

In 1969, Zwicka Zamir took over the *Memuneh*'s chair at Mossad when the war against Palestinian terrorism was at its height, and, to the outside observer at least, terrorism still seemed almost totally unchecked. In actuality, by the time Zamir took office, the patient groundwork initiated by Meir Amit to achieve a "long-term solution" was beginning to pay off.

Zamir's first significant success owed everything to Amit and to a young intelligence operative Amit had sent into Europe months before. His name was Baruch Cohen. Baruch came from one of the oldest and most distinguished families in Israel. He himself, like so many other sabras of his generation, had been brought up cheek by jowl with local Arab boys, played with them as a child, and learned to understand and respect their langue and customs. One of his brothers, Yehuda, was killed in the 1948 War of Independence, a brother whom he loved deeply. It was enough of an incentive to make him want to fight. He did his military training in intelligence and was one of the many Military Intelligence officers whom Meir Amit took across with him to Mossad on his appointment as chief.

In July 1970, at the age of thirty-five, Baruch Cohen was sent, together with wife and two children, to Brussels, where Baruch held down a minor diplomatic job at the embassy under the name of Moshe Hanan Yishai. His real job as a Mossad station chief was to coordinate the activities in Europe of other Mossad men, who with increasing success were infiltrating agents into proliferating Palestinian cells all over the Continent. It was Baruch Cohen's job to meet and make an assessment of these agents in an attempt to weed out double agents.

Paris was the real hotbed of Palestinian activity. De Gaulle's pro-Arab policies meant that they could move about virtually unmolested, especially as the presence of a large Arab-Algerian population gave them the opportunity to fade into the local scene without attracting too much attention. Mossad quickly established names and addresses of many of the "foot soldiers" of the movement, as well as the hiding places of arms caches and the like, all of which information could be called upon by French security whenever a hijacking attempt appeared imminent. This was high-level intelligence indeed, but what Mossad couldn't get and desperately needed were the names and addresses of the chief PFLP operations officers in Europe, the men who employed the small army with whom Mossad agents mingled so freely. The leadership had been well taught. The system of cut-outs and the use of dead-letter boxes meant that few rank-and-file Palestinians knew who the real chiefs were—and these were the men Israel wanted.

It is a truism that the secrets of any underground organization are most vulnerable when it goes operational —when it temporarily leaves the shadows. At the end of March 1971, Baruch Cohen picked up some information from one of his Palestinian agents that an operation was planned in Israel itself to prove to the Jews once and for all that they would never be masters in their own house. Two pretty girls had been recruited as couriers. They had no previous connection with the Palestinian movement, and would never be suspected by the Israelis. They would fly into Tel Aviv, deliver explosives to a team already in position, and that would be that. All this would happen soon.

It was little enough to go on, apart from the fact that no one could be sure how reliable the information was. Nevertheless, it could hardly be ignored. El Al ticket offices were warned, though the chances of the girls traveling on the Israeli national airline seemed remote, and security was tightened up at Lod airport. For the next few days a number of young women passengers arriving from Europe and even from the United States suffered the indignity of body searches when they arrived in Israel, but nothing was found. Then on April 11, 1971, an Air France flight arriving from Paris carried two extremely beautiful mini-skirted passengers, who not only looked as if they were dressed from the same shop but were very similar in appearance. An alert Mossad agent noticed them in the line waiting to get through customs. What interested the agent most was that, though in appearance they could easily have been sisters, they behaved as though they did not know each other. Customs was tipped off in time to stop one of them; the other got through. But she returned to see why the "friend" she had been so careful to ignore was being held up. The passport of one showed her to be Danielle Rivet, a twenty-six-year-old secretary employed in Paris. The other, also a secretary, gave her age as twenty-one and her name as Martine Ellen Garcier. Their suitcases, when examined, were found to be packed with high explosives, and more explosive material was strapped to their bodies. These were the girls Baruch Cohen had heard about.

The girls turned out to be sisters, Marlene and Nadia Bardeli, from a wealthy Moroccan family. So deep in over their heads were they that, once caught, they talked so much that one exhausted Mossad interrogator told his superior: "They're even too fast for the tape recorder." The two girls had been told to meet an older couple called Pierre and Edith Bourghalter at an arranged point near Dizengoff Street in the center of Tel Aviv. These two were quickly picked up that day. From them, Mossad traced the leader of the operation: a fifth woman, traveling under a passport in the name of Francine Adeleine Maria but in reality the twenty-six-year-old Evelyn Baradj, a Marxist intellectual, with strong links to the Baader-Meinhof gang in Germany and known to have been involved with numerous hijackings and terrorist activities in Europe.

Evelyn Baradj was picked up and eventually admitted that her strange team had intended to attack the big hotels in the country in the hope of discouraging tourism (a major source of income of the nation).

However important it was for Mossad to frustrate this operation, of far greater importance was the further, extraordinarily valuable information the Bardeli sisters possessed and which with very little prompting they now revealed. The two girls had got into left-wing politics at the Sorbonne. On leaving the university, both got jobs as secretaries, but Nadia's ambition was to be a journalist—she had once done some work on a paper in Casablanca—and Marlene wanted to become an actress. One day they had met an Algerian, Mohammed Boudia, manager of a small but artistically prestigious theater in Paris, the Théâtre de l'Ouest. He had been charm itself, had promised to help them in their careers, and, after a liaison of a few weeks, asked them to do a job for him: to take some packages to Tel Aviv in order to further the revolution. Naively, they had agreed to help and with childish excitement had gone through various rehearsals as to how they should behave at Lod airport before setting off with their false passports on what they regarded as being no more than an adventure.

Mossad in Paris quickly provided a file on Boudia. In the fifties, he had been a reasonably well-known actor in Paris, very much involved politically with the left. But when the war in Algeria broke out into the open in the mid-fifties, he went back home and fought against the French with the FLN, establishing a reputation as a cold and ruthless killer. In 1959 he was caught by the French and only released in 1962 on Algerian independence. Immediately, he was appointed manager of the Algerian National Theatre, but, as a protégé of Ben Bella, he had to flee Algeria once again, when, on June 20, 1965, Houari Boumedienne, one of Ben Bella's closest friends, staged his *coup d'état*. Presumably afraid of Boumedienne's men getting to him, Boudia went all the way to Buenos Aires, where, it is now believed, a Soviet agent made his acquaintance and persuaded him to take a scholarship at the Patrice Lumumba University in Moscow. He accepted the invitation and there learned the arts of revolution.

He returned to Paris straight from Moscow and resumed the career he had given up ten years earlier. He was a man of unquestioned talent, and he appreciated and was appreciated by avant-garde writers, who looked to him and his theatre for help and support.

What was immediately clear was that Boudia would never agree to be a mere infantryman of Palestinian terrorism. Obviously, he was one of the movement's senior, if not *the* senior, operational commanders in Europe, and he used the Théâtre de l'Ouest as his cover. It was clear, too, that his contacts spread to Baader-Meinhof, and probably to other international terrorist organizations as well. Certainly, he was tied in with the KGB.

Through a single piece of carelessness—by using amateurs who could easily be traced to him (presumably because he believed they themselves would never be suspected)—Boudia had exposed not only himself but the whole network built up around him. That network proved to be of international significance.

Since de Gaulle's breach with Israel, Mossad headquarters in Paris, once the center of its whole European operation, had been allowed to run down and was divided up between Brussels and Amsterdam. Now, despite the fact that the French government was likely not to be helpful, it was clear to Zwicka Zamir that the Israelis had to return in force if they were to carry on their battle effectively and establish the connections that existed between the world's terrorist organizations.

Though journalists toyed with phrases like "Terror International," conjuring up images straight out of a James Bond book of some dark and mysterious Blofeld-type character intent upon world domination, the truth was a good deal simpler, though not necessarily less sinister. Organizations like the Angry Brigade or the Provisional IRA in Britain, the Baader-Meinhof gang in Germany or the Japanese Red Army all had in common with the PFLP a nihilistic doctrine: the belief that before society could be rebuilt, it first had to be destroyed. So it was that while relations between the Israeli government and the French government became increasingly more bitter, relations between Mossad and the French secret service flowered as never before. Nevertheless, the burden of proof of the links between international terrorists, the KGB and the Palestinian movement was on the Israelis. It was their thesis, and they were obliged to justify it. The Israelis found themselves monitoring the activities and subsequently doing battle with European terrorist groups which, on the surface at least, had no connection whatsoever with Israel. The doctrine Meir Amit had enunciated, that the Israel Intelligence Community should only concern itself with those matters which had a direct application to the continuing war with the Arabs, had not changed—it was only that the perimeters of that battlefield had widened to a remarkable and frightening extent.

No army and no intelligence service in the world can work successfully if luck is not on its side, and it was luck which helped turn the tide Israel's way and permit the West German Government to get on top of the Baader-Meinhof gang and expose its international links.

At the beginning of 1971, a thirty-one-year-old extremely left-wing lecturer at a German university who was involved with Baader-Meinhof and one of the leaders of the Berlin Free University riots in 1967 and 1968 returned to the home he had left several years earlier to go through the effects of his parents, who had been killed in an autobahn accident a few days previously. His mind, as he subsequently admitted, was in a turmoil. He had not been in touch with his father or mother for years; they disapproved of his ultra-left politics and he of their bourgeois way of life. Yet now they were dead, he regretted the estrangement.

His entire world was turned upside down when he found a particular set of documents in his father's safe. The first paper was an agreement signed in 1940 between his father and a Jewish family in which the father promised to bring up their child as his own. The second made evident that as soon as the war was over, his foster father had searched far and wide for the boy's real parents, only to discover that they had died in a concentration camp. To Albert Schmidt (a pseudonym), the shock was mindbending. It was not merely that the parents who had brought him up were not his real parents; it was not even that he was Jewish, though that was shock enough. It was the realization of how cruelly he had behaved toward them.

The documents revealed that his real parents and his foster parents had been firm friends. Once his foster parents had agreed to take him, they had had to disrupt their own lives, move away from the area in which they had always lived to somewhere where they were not known and could register the child with no difficulty. For weeks, Albert Schmidt grappled with the crisis which had enveloped his life. How often, he wondered, during the bitter quarrels he had had with them, how often must it have been on the lips of his father or his mother to justify themselves to him by telling him the truth, to present themselves to him not as those who had given him birth, but as those who had permitted him to live. They had not done so; they had been more prepared to accept his angry rejection of them than to permit him to suffer the crisis of identity which the truth would be bound to create. Albert Schmidt had no doubt that if they had not died together so unexpectedly in a crash, he would never have known the truth.

Three months later, Schmidt made his decision. He was Jewish, and there was only one place for him as a Jew —that was in Israel. He had told no one about his discovery—there was no one to tell. His mind full of the Jewish history which he had in the intervening period, swallowed whole, he approached the Israeli Embassy in Frankfurt, told them his story and his intention under the Law of Return of emigrating to Israel. The story was an extraordinary one, and he was not at first believed. The local Mossad resident was approached by a nervous consul: Schmidt's application could be a clever ruse by the Palestinians to introduce a Baader-Meinhof operative into Israel. A check was run on Schmidt's story, and he himself was interviewed on several occasions. There could be no doubt that he was telling the truth or that he was completely sincere. It was then that the idea hit the resident. He flew to Tel Aviv to put it to Zwi Zamir. Schmidt was, in a sense, on ideological as well as emotional grounds, a defector from the extreme left. Attempts by German security and others to infiltrate Baader-Meinhof and similar organizations had been notoriously ineffective. It was a closed little world; friendships struck up at university or at school were what mattered. New recruits, though welcomed, seldom, if ever, got into the inner circle. But Schmidt was there already. Zwicka Zamir agreed immediately, and Schmidt was approached.

It didn't take long to convince Schmidt that he was in a unique position to do a great service for his newly adopted country. He applied for and received permission to take a sabbatical from his university post and he used it for perhaps the strangest purpose an academic ever had: to travel to Israel to take a crash course in clandestine techniques. He proved to be an apt and willing pupil, as fanatical an Israeli as he'd once been a Marxist. Just before he returned to Germany, at a private and emotional ceremony attended only by those few people responsible for his training and including the man who would become his control in Europe, Schmidt entered into the Jewish religion. A rabbi had been found who was prepared to accept that, for good and proper reasons, the act of circumcision would be symbolic until such time as it could be properly performed and that Albert Schmidt, having been born of a Jewish mother, was automatically entitled to be accepted as a Jew. Security was broken briefly on that day so that he could go to the Holy Wall in Jerusalem, where he stood and prayed for his two sets of parents. He was then put on a flight to Europe to begin a career which was to ensure that virtually the entire leadership of Baader-Meinhof was rounded up in a matter of months.

In order to carry this out, the West German authorities were totally reliant upon information given to Mossad by Schmidt. But though they were told that the Mossad source came from within Baader-Meinhof they were never told that it was being provided by an Israeli agent. That was a secret kept to a very small elite within Mossad. As the Baader-Meinhof gang began first to wilt and finally to crack, other European terrorist groups were crumbling, too. International terror was gradually on the retreat.

But there was still to be much bloodshed and tears before Israel was to start winning the ugliest war it has ever had to fight.

In November 1971, the Jordanian Prime Minister, Wasfi Tal, was shot down and killed outside the Sheraton Hotel in Cairo by an organization which called itself "the Hand of Black September" (subsequently shortened to Black September), a breakaway group of Palestinians who, it was said, were taking their revenge for the September war of 1970, when the Jordanian Army had expelled the Palestinians with such brutality from the country. Within hours of the killing, from information gathered from within Al Fatah, Israel was able to tell the world's intelligence agencies that Black September was simply a front for the KGB-trained "revolutionary surveillance system," or Fatah Intelligence, headed by Salaf Halaf, better known throughout the Arab world and in revolutionary circles as "Abu Iyad."*

The birth of Black September represented the final and unqualified capitulation to terror tactics of the PLO

---

* It is one of the more humbling experiences in one's life to be present when history is being made and not recognize it. By chance, I happened to be in Cairo, staying at the Sheraton Hotel, on the day of Wasfi Tal's assassination. That morning, as my wife and I walked through the lobby of the hotel, Wasfi Tal, who was standing talking to some of his officials, recognized me (I had met him for a long conversation a few months before) and called me over. We had a pleasant chat for a few moments and agreed to meet that evening to talk about the Jordanian situation. My car arrived first to take me on a tour of the canal zone. I returned from Suez that night to find Cairo in an uproar. Two or three minutes after I had left the hotel Wasfi Tal had been shot. I saw no more significance in the shooting than yet another killing in the long sad history of fratricidal dispute between Arab and Arab. Yet here was the birth of an organization which was to become a byword of unbridled terror throughout the world.

—and thus of the official leadership of the Palestinian people. In a sense, this had been forced on Yasser Arafat and his people by the success of the PFLP and its leader, George Habash. It was to take the initiative away from him that the PLO, to satisfy the demands of the young aggressive elements within the Palestinian movement who had joined the PFLP in droves, formed its own organization, called Black September, from which it could publicly disassociate itself whenever necessary, but which was to be used as the strong arm of the movement all over the world. No sooner had it been formed than Yasser Arafat lost control of it.

Black September was soon active—with a spectacular demonstration of its determination to be at least as ruthless as the PFLP. On May 8, 1972, a Black September group headed by Ali Shafic Ahmed Taha ("Captain Rafat"), who had already carried out at least one hijacking on behalf of the PFLP and who was responsible for the bomb attack on El Al's offices in Brussels, diverted a Sabena 707 shortly after take-off from Vienna and ordered the captain to fly to Lod airport, Tel Aviv. There, on the ground, inside the Israeli fortress their commandos had so frequently tried to infiltrate, Black September demanded that Israel release a hundred Arab guerrillas held in prison or face the consequence that the terrorists would blow up the plane with its crew and passengers. It was an audacious plan. The Palestinians knew that the Israelis had vowed they would never again (as they had at the time of the first El Al hijacking) give way to blackmail. But Black September believed that faced with the prospect of mass slaughter of foreign nationals on Israeli soil, the government would have no alternative.

Never for a moment did the Israeli government consider giving in. The plane was immobilized on landing, and after long negotiations, designed merely to give the Israeli security authorities time to plan and execute their assault, the plane was attacked by a handpicked team of paratroopers, disguised as mechanics, who stormed the emergency exit doors, killing two terrorists, injuring one woman hijacker and capturing another after she pleaded for her life. One passenger, a woman married to a Norwegian, was wounded, and she later died of her injuries.

While the world was still congratulating Israel on the way it had dealt with the hijackers, the PFLP was organizing "Palestine's Revenge." It was to be the most bizarre and bloody incident yet.

Three weeks later, on May 30, 1972, three young Japanese who had arrived at Lod with many other passengers on an Air France plane from Rome suddenly flung hand grenades and with automatic weapons opened fire indiscriminately on scores of passengers in the packed arrival hall. Twenty-four people were killed on the spot —among them sixteen Roman Catholics from Puerto Rico on a pilgrimage to the Holy Land and seven Israelis, including Professor Aharon Katzir, a scientist of international repute. Seventy-eight other passengers were wounded, many seriously, and another subsequently died.

The gunmen proved to be members of the Sekigun, popularly known as the Japanese Red Army. The Israelis had long known about the connection between this terrorist group and the Palestinians, who had recruited them for this suicide mission, but as a tired Zwi Zamir told the Cabinet, only if Israel cut herself off from the rest of the world could she be protected from incidents such as these, and cutting herself off was exactly what her enemies wanted.

This extraordinary act of terrorism left a gaping wound. Somewhat unfairly—for who could possibly have foreseen an act of such brutal insanity—the intelligence services were, in the public mind, held responsible.

Suddenly, the terrorists seemed to be getting the upper hand. In August, Black September struck again. Two young British girls traveling on to Tel Aviv via El Al were given a tape recorder as a going-away present by two young Arabs they had met in Rome. The tape recorder was a cleverly concealed bomb, triggered to detonate at 25,000 feet. Fortunately, it had been stowed in the baggage compartment, which on all El Al flights for some time had been lined with armor plating. The bomb exploded, and the captain, a Skyhawk pilot, dived his Boeing as if it were a fighter plane and made a successful emergency landing.

All the while, of course, reports were coming into Mossad of some kind of Black September demonstration to coincide with the Munich Olympics. Precisely what the nature of this demonstration would be no one could say, but in August 1972 a two-man team from Mossad traveled to West Germany to meet the security authorities there and go over their plans to safeguard the Israeli team. On one point the West Germans were adamant: there must be no overt signs of heavy security. These were to be the Games of Peace. But the West Germans did agree that two Mossad men could work with them to help plan the security of the games. Every Arab coming into the country would be carefully vetted. Nothing would be left to chance.

There have been several books on the Munich massacre, in which nine Israeli athletes were killed in the full glare of the TV cameras by a group from Black September, and there is little to be gained by repeating that story here.

Zwicka Zamir himself flew to Munich too late to be able to influence events, and became merely an eyewitness to the terrible battle which raged so briefly and so bloodily at the military airport where the terrorists took their prisoners. Indeed, when Zamir arrived, the Germans didn't want to know him; to Zamir's great humiliation the Israeli ambassador, Elisha Ben Horin, literally thrust him physically into the car of Dietrich Gunsher, the West German Minister of the Interior, as it was leaving the athletes' village to go to the showdown at the airport.

A commission of inquiry found three officials of medium rank to have been negligent in their duties. One was a security officer in the Israeli Embassy in Bonn, one a Mossad employee who had been due to retire much earlier, but had been kept on because of a personal situation, and a third a clerk in the Foreign Ministry.

Zamir had to face much criticism, too. Mossad had believed that the Palestinians would not dare attack the Israeli team. Once satisfied that the West Germans were taking their obligations seriously, Mossad's people were withdrawn. The team itself was not armed or prepared in any way for a terrorist attack. There was no security man with the Israeli delegation, and, perhaps most curious of all, the member of the delegation whose duty it was to keep in contact with local security was simply the team doctor.

Hindsight could make obvious certain mistakes and omissions in security at Munich and in the attack three months later by Black September on the Israeli Embassy in Bangkok (the hostages were subsequently released, thanks to the firm intervention of the Thai government, who conducted the negotiations). But as Zwi Zamir told the Israeli government, short of surrounding a country with a high wall and pulling up the drawbridge, no security service in the world could guarantee that, given a determined and ruthless opponent, it could always protect its citizens against terrorism.

Nevertheless, Mossad was under something of a cloud, and Mrs. Golda Meir reacted by appointing a "Special Assistant for Terrorist Affairs" and taking away from Zamir some of his control. The man who got the job—a personal favorite of Mrs. Meir—was General Aharon Yariv, who was due to leave his job as chief of Military Intelligence after nine brilliant years to become an assistant to Defense Minister Moshe Dayan.

Aharon Yariv and Zwicka Zamir established a slightly uneasy partnership. Yariv's appointment was, after all, a direct challenge to the *Memuneh*, undercutting his authority considerably in the most important intelligence battle now in process.

But the Black September disasters did have one immediate effect upon Mossad. Overnight its budget was almost doubled. Beaten and humiliated at Lod and Munich, Ahrele Yariv and Zwicka Zamir ("We can't lose," joked an insider, "we've got them covered from A to Z"), with the full backing of the government, changed policy. From then on, the Prime Minister's adviser on terrorism and the Israeli Secret Service decreed, Israel would go on the offensive in the bitter, savage, and merciless war being fought in the back streets of Europe and the Middle East.

Golda Meir asked prophetically: "What happens if things go wrong?" She was told: "Things have gone wrong already." Israel could not afford a repetition of Lod or Munich. The morale of the nation could take no more.

Chapter 23

IT WAS NOT REVENGE that Ahrele Yariv and Zwicka Zamir were after, though that was undoubtedly part of it. What motivated them in their actions at this point was the awareness that they were now fighting what had become a superbly professional organization.

While the ordinary Israeli wondered why no attempt was made to assassinate Yasser Arafat, Mossad's main concern was to keep him alive.* Politicians like Arafat are expendable. Remove one and another, perhaps even more extreme, will spring up in his place. To an intelligence organization which knows its business, there is every advantage in maintaining in office the political leader of the other side, unless one can be sure that by removing him, one has made room for opponents of his whose friendliness is guaranteed. Obviously, that condition would never apply in the case of the Palestinians. To Mossad, Arafat represented some kind of continuity. They had learned his thought processes and could, with some confidence, predict his future actions. All this valuable research, so vital to an understanding of the PLO, would count for nothing the day that Arafat died.

But the men who actually ran the terrorists—they were another matter. These were the technicians, carefully trained, experienced, resourceful and imaginative. Their ability would always be at a premium; remove *them,* and a gap would appear which might not be able to be filled.

In the immediate aftermath of the Lod massacre, Zwi Zamir had, in fact, with the approval of the Israeli government, already used the ultimate weapon of assassination, the first time since the fifties that such extreme measures had been countenanced. (Then, two men who

* Arafat has frequently said that he's on the Israeli assassination list. This is sheer fantasy.

had organized the Fedayeen were killed on the orders of Fatti Harkabi of Israeli Military Intelligence.) What so angered the Israeli government about Lod was not so much the killings—though these were terrible enough—but the exultant triumph of the Palestinians in Beirut, who behaved as if Arabs had scored an extraordinary victory on the battlefield and had not merely bought the services of three foreign terrorists to murder in cold blood innocent civilians, most of whom were not only not Israeli, but were not Jewish either.

There were many who sought to justify Lod, but the first of these was Ghassan Kanafani, a thirty-six-year-old Palestinian intellectual, poet and novelist. An apparently gentle, sophisticated man, a friend of many Western journalists who had visited Beirut and found him to be a moderate and compassionate spokesman for his people's cause, he was not quite all he seemed. What few people knew was that he was a member of the PFLP Central Command, and had helped plan the killings.

The fact that he was so well known in Lebanon and beyond gave him, he believed, a peculiar kind of protection; any attempt to assassinate him would have extraordinary repercussions from which the Israelis might never recover. What he didn't know was that his real persona, beneath the mask of intellectual apologist for moderate Palestinians, had long since been established by the Israelis and documentary evidence of it passed on to the American, British, French and, perhaps most important of all, the Lebanese secret services.

The Lebanese, already in deep trouble just as the Jordanians had been before them because of the activities of the Palestinians on their soil, had every reason not to protest too vigorously the death of Kanafani, and the Americans, British and French, recognizing at last that the war against the PFLP was not a uniquely Israeli concern, could be relied upon not to turn an attack on Kanafani into an international *cause célèbre*.

Two days after Lod, the Israelis had moved. Kanafani's car was booby-trapped; he, and tragically his seventeen-year-old niece, who was unexpectedly traveling with him, were blown up. Six weeks later, on July 25, 1972, Bassam Abou Sharif, a twenty-nine-year-old member of Kanafani's staff and his natural successor as information officer of the PFLP, opened a parcel at his home in Beirut. The explosion, triggered when he ripped open the wrapping, blinded him in one eye and seriously damaged the other. The long arm of Israel had stretched out, pinpointed its target and struck home—ample demonstration to members of the PFLP that if they persisted in their terror attacks they would not be immune from Israel's revenge. Nevertheless, the murder of Kanafani and the attempted murder of Bassam Sharif were regarded only as isolated hits, not a policy of reprisal.

Munich was to change everything. Israeli policy had always been to meet fire with fire. When Palestinians raided across the border from Lebanon, and in earlier years from Jordan, Israel had sent in its air force or army to smash the camps from which the terrorists had come. Genuine attempts were made to avoid unnecessary civilian casualties, but the terrorist practice of building their headquarters or arsenals right next to schools or hospitals in order to seek some kind of immunity from the proximity made this all but impossible. Inevitably, too, the the Israelis sometimes hit the wrong target; civilians did die and civilian installations were attacked. The PLO made much of these incidents, inviting in the international press in order to show them bombed hospitals or schools and dying women and children.

More relevant to the real task were the detailed dossiers Mossad now possessed (thanks to the work of men like Baruch Cohen) on those men who were behind Munich, Lod and other hijackings. These men, of course, were never seen in the front line, facing the hideous dangers with which the young people they sent into battle, motivated either by money, glory or psychosis, always had to grapple. Yariv and Zamir now decided, as Harkabi had done before them, to take up arms against the real leaders of Palestinian terrorism. Until these men were eradicated, there would be no let up. The time had come to strike back—but this time the technique would be different. Instead of saturation bombing of refugee camps, individuals, those in command, would be assassinated. With cool clinical precision. Mossad would seek out the real enemy and remove him.

It was not an easy decision to take. It was not the moral question which worried either Yariv or Zamir. The men who planned Lod or Munich had already, in the Israeli view, forfeited the right to live. What did concern them were the operational problems such a program would involve.

Golda Meir's intuitive sense that things could go wrong was more than a pertinent consideration. A great many of the assassinations would have to be committed in Western Europe, where the Palestinians ran many of their operations. In the eyes of any European police authority, the Israelis, whatever their motive, would be committing murder. If the Heidi Goerke case had proved an embarrassment to Mossad, it would be nothing compared with the effect if a member of an Israeli hit team ever came to be arrested.

There was also a more complex problem. Mossad—despite what the Arab countries may believe to the contrary—has always been careful about the kind of men it employs. Any applicant, for example, who expresses what Mossad psychologists regard as an unreasoning hatred of the Arab people is automatically excluded. Any applicant who can kill easily will never get past the first interview. What Mossad looks for, as Zamir once put it, are men trained to kill who have a deep aversion to killing.

Under Mossad's head of special operations, a special unit was established to organize a series of assassinations throughout Europe and the Middle East. Not only did the operations have to be planned down to the smallest detail, but the director of these operations had to try to ensure that they did not leave a psychological scar on the operatives involved.*

---

* In 1976 a book entitled *The Hit Team*, by David B. Tinnin (Little Brown & Co., Boston), claimed that, as its title suggests, a single unit was responsible for carrying out the assassinations. The basic premise of the book was totally incorrect. There is no "hit team" as such, moving around like a traveling circus picking off one Arab leader after another, though there was an office inside Mossad HQ set up as control of these operations. Each operation, using in every case a fresh team, was an entity of its own. In terms of sheer operational logic, this had to be so. Because there could be no room for error, each killing took weeks to plan. Each team needed to establish its cover, set up its safe houses, and plot down to the smallest detail the movements, the life style and the security of the target. Only then were they in a position to pick a *modus operandi* which would be sent to

The file on every Arab terrorist leader was now reviewed. Baruch Cohen in Europe returned to Tel Aviv to help in the evaluation of the Arabs on the list. One basic difficulty emerged from the very start: every Palestinian in Europe and Beirut liked to give the impression of being on the inside of Black September or the PFLP and was inclined to turn the most mundane task into something immeasurably grander than it was. It would have been easy if the Israelis could have gone by the maxim that those with most to say had the least to do, but it never quite worked out that way. The boastfulness of the real leaders was, in many cases, as indiscreet as that of their foot soldiers. Zwi Zamir could not afford any mistakes. If Palestinians were to be killed, they had to be the right Palestinians.

But the most wanted men of all, the prime targets, were clear: Mohammed Yussuf El-Najjar, the head of the whole Black September movement; Kemal Adwan, his deputy; and Ali Hassan Salameh, the Black September's chief of operations. In a way, the last was the most interesting of the three. Given a free hand by Najjar, he had personally planned and supervised the Munich massacre and Lod, and was responsible for turning Black September into an organization whose sense of barbarism surpassed even that of the PFLP.

Ali Hassan Salameh was born in Ramle between Tel Aviv and Jerusalem, where his father, Sheik Salameh, was the leader of one of the many marauding Arab gangs which terrorized Jewish settlements in the thirties and early forties. He was killed in the War of Independence when a bomb planted by a Haganah demolition team went off at the headquarters from which he controlled the road to Jerusalem. Ali Salameh rose quickly through the ranks of Fatah, showing the same ruthlessness of purpose as his father and the same implacable resolve to "drive the Jews into the sea." From the very beginning, he was urging within Fatah the view that Israel could only be defeated if the Palestinians conducted a violent

---

Tel Aviv for approval. The head of Mossad's special operations and on at least one occasion Zamir would fly in to inspect the operational plan on the ground, suggest amendments where necessary, and give final approval. They would always be well away when the assassins struck.

and relentless war of terror against them. When his view finally prevailed, he was a natural choice to head all of Black September's operations.

Mossad knew that if Salameh was the most important target, he was also likely to be the most difficult. He was both intelligent and cunning—a man who never stayed in the same place for long. He had a string of diplomatic passports, which he used whenever he traveled. He carefully cultivated a life style with little pattern. He lived well, but not ostentatiously, and never moved far without a well-trained guard conveniently at hand.

Much more vulnerable were Salameh's top aides in Europe. Thanks to the initial breakthrough which had established Mohammed Boudia as head of PFLP operations in Europe, Mossad now had an impressive dossier on the entire PFLP and Black September network. Carefully, Zwi Zamir's operational office sorted out the names —going back for more information whenever necessary —until they had a dozen or so verified case histories of men they knew were the organizing brains behind Palestinian terrorism. No name went on that list lightly. A great many Palestinians are walking around today who were considered for inclusion but were not ever put on the list, either because they were not, in the last analysis, considered important enough or because the evidence against them was regarded as insufficient. Those few who remained had become targets for assassination.

Target No. 1 in this bitter war was to be Wadal Adel Zwaiter, a Palestinian intellectual who had lived in Rome for sixteen years. Mossad had long since marked Zwaiter down as Black September's operational chief in Italy. His most ambitious and most imaginative project had been the August 1972 tape-recorder bomb designed to blow an El Al Boeing 707 and all its passengers out of the sky. Officially, he worked as a translator at the Libyan Embassy in Rome, a useful address no doubt from which to conduct his operations. Likeable, perennially short of money, he lived modestly, giving not the slightest hint to any of his acquaintances of the other life he lived deep in the shadows of international terrorism.

At 10:30 P.M., on October 16, 1972, Zwaiter returned home from a visit to an Italian friend. Minutes later he was dead—with twelve .22 bullets in his body. Witnesses outside the flats testified that before the shooting they had noticed what appeared to be a courting couple in a green Fiat 125 parked outside. Suddenly, two men burst from the front entrance of the building, dived into the back seat of the Fiat, which roared off into the night, almost colliding with a small minibus as it went. The getaway car was found, parked some three hundred yards away, where another car had been waiting to take the assassination squad to a safe house in an elegant district of Rome. The killers returned to Israel several days later to receive handsome awards. For while they had been Mossad-trained and recruited, neither were fulltime intelligence officers. The whole team at the actual hit were trained for this one specific assignment. If caught, all they would know would be the details of their training and the pseudonyms of their case officers.

Target No. 2 was to be Mahmud Hamshari. He was Black September's man in Paris, much further up in the hierarchy than Zwaiter, very different in manner and style, with a long history of PFLP involvement. He had managed to establish for himself an extremely comfortable life style through his involvement with the PFLP —an involvement which had become as far as he was concerned a well-paid profession. Initial surveillance was discouraging, to say the least. Wherever he went, he was surrounded by bodyguards. They were posted outside his flat, at his front door and in the street below. He never traveled anywhere without his men first "sweeping" the ground before him. That security had increased still further since the death of Zwaiter. He and his boss, Mohammed Boudia, were taking no chances.

It was obvious to Mossad's chief of special operations ("Mike") that conventional methods of disposing of Hamshari had too high a risk of failure. "Mike" wanted to avoid, at all costs, a shoot-out in which some of his men could be killed or captured. Hamshari's death had to be arranged more subtly. It was to the Mossad "armorers" that "Mike" now went for help.

The armorers of a secret service agency are among the most skilled employees on the staff. They are experts on every imaginable form of gun or explosive, but are as well men of great technical skill and—the best of them —imaginative inventors. These were the men in Mossad who had decided that the semiautomatic weapon for Israeli assassination teams should be a Beretta .22 fitted with West German shells, deadly at close range, yet making very little noise. This gun was originally used by El Al sky marshals on the advice of the armorers on the grounds that if they missed their target, the bullet would not necessarily puncture the skin of the aircraft. They were adapted for use by assassination squads principally because they discouraged "long shots"—handguns are notoriously inaccurate at anything but the closest range —and also because of their deadly precision. The guns had been especially adapted by the armorers so that the very light gunpowder in the cartridge of the special bullets they perfected was still sufficient to push the next round into the chamber. Now these armorers were asked to find a method to kill Hamshari.

Shortly after Zwaiter's death, a plumber turned up in the building alongside Hamshari's and began work on the pipes. No one took much notice of him as slowly he worked his way into the courtyard housing Hamshari's apartment. The plumber was, in fact, an engineer—a Mossad armorer, a trained and skilled man who was more interested in the telephone cables running alongside the pipes than he was in the pipes themselves.

Soon Hamshari's telephone began to give him trouble and continued to do so for several days until, angrily, he called the exchange to have it fixed. What Hamshari didn't know was that he now had his own personal exchange, a truck parked nearby into which his telephone line had been fed. There the engineer had been cutting in and out of Hamshari's calls until he picked up the inevitable request for professional attention.

Hamshari was told that an engineer would be round the following day. On schedule, driving up in an official-looking van the following morning, a man reported to Hamshari's flat. In full sight of Hamshari for most of the time and of his bodyguards for the rest, the engineer began fixing the telephone. What no one realized was that, in its base, he had concealed sufficient explosives to blow the flat apart. Two days previously, Hamshari had received a telephone call from an Italian journalist seeking an interview. Hamshari, as a spokesman for the PLO, was quite used to such requests and, at the journalist's suggestion, agreed that they should meet at a nearby café two days later. The journalist said he would telephone Hamshari's flat as soon as he arrived in the morning.

At 9:25 A.M., after his wife and daughter had left the apartment (as the Mossad team from close observation knew they would), the phone rang in Hamshari's flat. He picked it up—it was the Italian. "Are you Dr. Hamshari?" the Italian asked. "Yes," replied Hamshari. He lived long enough to tell the police about the Italian and the high-pitched buzz he had heard before the explosion. A few hours later, he died. The telephone had been turned into a lethal bomb. The high-pitched signal transmitted by the caller was all that was needed to detonate it.

As far as the outside world was concerned, Victim No. 3 surfaced in an unexpected place—Cyprus. Cyprus, the halfway house between the warring parties of the Middle East, had become the center of the KGB operation in the area, which was based in the Soviet Embassy. It was a perfect setup for the Russians, who were not diplomatically represented in Israel but from Cyprus could get close enough to listen in to their signal traffic and yet not too close to their Arab customers to become too uncomfortably embroiled. The local Palestinian contact with the KGB was a man who had a passport under the name of Hussein Abad Al Chir. On January 24, Abad Al Chir went into his room at the Olympic Hotel, climbed into bed, read awhile, and then turned off the light. At a distance, a Mossad agent pressed the button of his ultrasonic radio transmitter and Abad Al Chir and his room were blown to pieces.

Dr. Basil Al Kubaissi, an Iraqi professor at the American University of Beirut, was the next to go—Victim No. 4. Al Kubaissi, on his frequent trips to Europe, was responsible for maintaining at a proper state of preparedness Black September's arsenal in Europe, arranging for new arms where appropriate, maintaining and overseeing the communications system, and supervising safe houses and the like. On April 6th, Dr. Al Kubaissi had come from a meeting with Black September men in Paris and was passing the beautiful Eglise de la Madeleine at the top of the Rue Royale near to Maxim's. Suddenly, two men emerged from the shadows and at pointblank range killed him with their Berettas. Twenty-four hours later Zaiad Muchasi, the replacement man for Black September's contact with the KGB in Cyprus, ended his short career in the same manner as had his predecessor. He switched off the bedside lamp in his hotel and was killed outright by the explosion that followed. This time the Palestinians were ready to take their revenge, and on April 9th three Palestinians sought to blow up the Israeli ambassador in his home. Almost simultaneously, another group of Arabs, traveling in two vehicles, burst through the barrier at Cyprus airport and opened fire on an El Al airliner standing on the tarmac. Both attacks proved abortive. The explosion at the ambassador's apartment caused damage to the ground-floor flats but not to the ambassador's residence on the second floor, and in any case he was not in. At the airport, an El Al security guard returned the fire, killing one Arab and wounding two others. The Israelis had the right to feel some sense of triumph; a bungled operation of this kind could only be the result of panic. Black September was on the run.

But all the Israeli "hits" were only a prelude to the daring operation Yariv and Zamir had planned from the very outset—a commando raid into central Beirut in order to kill the leaders of Black September in the homes where they felt most safe. For months, their addresses and their movements had been accurately pinpointed and monitored, and at the beginning of 1973, conditions were ideal.

On April 6th, five men and one woman arrived at Beirut airport on separate flights from London, Rome and Paris. All of them had been to Beirut before, and, while they had been instructed to behave like ordinary tourists, they were to make sure that they knew the streets and beaches of the city as well as any local taxi driver.

No resident Mossad agents could be actively involved because of the risk of blowing their cover. In any case, their job had been done long before. The markers had been laid down for others to pick up. These markers led to Mohammed El-Najjar, Kemal Adwan, Ali Salameh, Mohammed Boudia (visiting Beirut from Paris) and other Black September council members. The six Mossad agents—three traveling on British passports—rented cars from Hertz and Avis (Mercedes, Buicks, Plymouths and a Renault) on their American Express cards, inspected the four safe houses which had previously been rented for the raid, to be occupied by any member of the raiding party who for some reason had to be left behind and then, in an ordinary commercial telegram sent from the Beirut central post office to an address in France, they confirmed that all was ready.

At 1:30 A.M. on the morning of April 9th, six rubber Zodiac landing craft, with their engines cut, wallowed into shore at Dove beach, a small out-of-the-way cove that visitors to the Beirut beaches came to to get away from the crowds. Two members of the advance party, a woman and a man behaving like a courting couple, signaled the boats in.*

Apart from the crew, the boats carried thirty men all dressed in civilian clothes, many looking very "hippie" indeed. Mostly they were experienced paratroopers, with a sprinkling of officers from Military Intelligence. As the boats came in, the soldiers broke into units of five and piled into the large cars (previously hired by Mossad at the airport) which pulled up at the beach at intervals of three minutes, so that in fifteen minutes everyone had been taken care of. The Israelis were off to war in hired limousines.

The cars drove through the city's nightclub district and headed out to the inner ring of suburbs and an intersection of streets called Khaled Ben Al Wald and Rue 68. There were two main objectives as the cars stopped in the car park of an unfinished apartment block previously mapped out by the markers. The first was a seven-story building, standing between two others under construction, which was solely occupied by members of the PFLP, and the second was a three-story house on the Rue El-Khartoum where Arafat's deputy Mohammed Yussuf El-Najjar, the head of Black September and the No. 3 man in the PLO, Kamal Nasser, chief spokesman

---

* Every secret-service agency in the world has a signature that trained counterintelligence agents can pick out. From the very first days of the *Lino* affair, the technique of using a woman agent as part of the cover for its operations has frequently been employed by the Israelis. The Israelis believe that two men sitting in a car or, as on this occasion, hanging around a deserted beach attract attention and suspicion, but every policeman in the world respects the right of two people of the opposite sex to enjoy an uninterrupted liaison.

for the PLO, and Kemal Adwan, El-Najjar's deputy, were to be found.

All three men were in their apartments when the Israelis arrived. There was not much time for subtlety. The markers had done their jobs brilliantly, and the soldiers knew precisely where to go. The sentries at the doors of the building were killed instantly by a burst of machine-gun fire. The men ran up to the second floor and simply shot off the locks of El-Najjar's door. He died instantly in a fusillade of machine-gun bullets and Beretta slugs. As his children watched, his screaming wife, who tried to interpose herself between her husband and the assassins, was cut down, too, and fell across his body. A woman from the next apartment who heard the noise poked her nose out through her front door and met her death instantly.

Kamal Nasser was the next to go. He was writing a speech at his desk and was shot dead as the Israelis burst into his apartment.

In the meantime, at street level, PLO soldiers, shooting wildly in all directions, were responding to the attacking forces, who were now holding their position in the foyer. One of the Mossad men now telephoned the police chief responsible for maintaining some semblance of order in the Palestinian community and reported that the Palestinians were fighting among themselves, and that a lot of people were getting hurt. He knew what the reaction would be. The police chief, with a shrug, called off the Lebanese policemen from the local station who had got momentarily involved. If the Palestinains wanted to kill themselves, then why should the Lebanese be involved?

An area around the first building was now secure for Israeli doctors to tend to the wounded, while demolition men began laying their charges against the building. Inside, four Mossad experts were going through the papers in the safes of all three men they had killed and sorting out those files which would be useful. They had exactly half an hour before the building in which they were working was due to be blown up.

At the second building, a battle was raging, but it appeared to be terribly one-sided. There was something almost obscene in the way the Arabs were being mowed down. The PLO was using the elevators to reach street level in order to engage the enemy. As each elevator reached street level, the attacking force killed all the occupants, pulled out the bodies, and sent the cars up again for the next batch.

Eventually, that building, too, was secure, and, after a fast sweep of safes and the like for documents, the demolition charges were placed in position and then set off. Slowly at first, and then with a sickening momentum, the building began to disintegrate on its foundations, killing a great many people trapped inside. There was still more work for the paratroopers. Leaving this area they sped north to a group of warehouses where the terrorists stored their arms and equipment. After a brief gun battle this, too, was blown up.

With the raid now into the first hour, the Mossad team broke radio silence and called in helicopters stationed offshore to help lift off the wounded. Simultaneously, Beirut's police chief received a telephone call, ostensibly from the Lebanese Army, saying that they were putting helicopters in the air to pinpoint the center of the trouble, while Beirut's coastal command received similar telephone calls supposedly from the police advising that they were putting helicopters in the air for the same reason. Such was the incredible confusion that no one bothered to check with anyone else. Surprise had been total.

Two of the attacking force had been killed and one seriously wounded. Only one of the original Mossad men had been hurt—his hand crushed by a car door. In just over two hours, it was all over.

The commando force, accompanied this time by the six Mossad agents, left the way they had come, by boat.

Back in Beirut, all that the Lebanese authorities found were the cars neatly parked on the promenade with the keys in the ignition. (The rental bills were subsequently paid through American Express.) More than a hundred Palestinians, all terrorists, lost their lives in the action. Of the main targets, only Mohammed Boudia and Ali Hassan Salameh were still alive; by chance they were out of Beirut when the Israelis struck.

In one comparatively minor detail, the raid was not a total success. The Israelis had hoped to deny any involvement at all and had prepared a cover story which would have cast sufficient doubt on Palestinian claims to make it impossible for anyone ever to have got at the real truth. The Israelis hoped it would appear that the battle had been fought out between rival groups of Palestinians jockeying for supremacy. But the fact that the helicopters had had to be called in made that impossible. The following morning, Israeli chief of staff General David Elazar told journalists: "Israel will not play by the rules of limited warfare. You can't win a war by defense. If we cannot prevent war, we will bring about a quick and decisive victory as we have in the past."

A victory it certainly was. The two top leaders of Black September had been eliminated, their headquarters destroyed, and documentation of quite extraordinary value was now being pored over by the experts. Within hours intelligence chiefs of all the Western intelligence services were invited to send experts to Tel Aviv to examine these documents themselves and take what copies they liked. No longer open to doubt were the links Black September had not only with the KGB but with urban terrorist groups all over the world. The documents revealed the extent of the money available to these groups, pinpointed contact men, and made clear the plans they had for the future. If anyone—as some had—still believed that Black September was a grass-roots movement that grew spontaneously out of the wretched plight of so many Palestinian families, these documents, whose authenticity could not be questioned, dispelled that illusion once and for all.

The documents were as useful to Arab governments as they were to Western powers. The CIA undertook to present the relevant material to the kings and presidents of the Arab countries in order to show how Black September was actively engaged in subverting their governments in a great revolutionary drive which its leaders hoped would eventually sweep the whole Arab world before it. Even as the impressive memorial services for those who had died in the raid were being held in Cairo and Beirut, security police everywhere in the region had started operations—by grace of the Israelis—to round up dissidents whose real mission turned out to be considerably more sinister than anyone had thought possible. There were bonuses all round—not least for one Israeli agent who had been planted with the PLO years before. It was clear from one document that he was under suspicion because he always seemed to have more money than his normal circumstances would have allowed. Black

September thought that he was working for the Lebanese. He was moved out of Beirut and back home to Tel Aviv within twenty-four hours.

Zamir and Yariv were still not quite satisfied. Mohammed Boudia and Salameh were still at large. Boudia was finally dispatched on June 28th when a bomb placed under his white Renault, parked in the Rue des Fossés-St.-Bernard, was set off by a remote-control device as soon as he got into it, killing him instantly. Now only Salameh remained. Apart from him, the top Palestinian terrorists had been wiped out. Of course, they would be replaced by men perhaps even more fanatical in their determination. But, as Zamir told the Prime Minister, the Palestinian resistance had been as effective as it was internationally because these were men of unusual intelligence and ability. Intellectuals are not notoriously courageous men. Every Palestinian leader now knew without any room for doubt that the moment his hand rested on the trigger he, too, would become an instant target.

Not that this was the end of the PFLP, Black September, or international terror. There would be many more incidents to hold the world fascinated and appalled. Jews would be hijacked at an Austrian transit camp set up for Russians leaving the Soviet Union; the OPEC ministers themselves would be hijacked from the building in Vienna; Mossad would lead the Italian police to a group of Palestinians with Soviet-built missiles and a rocket launcher of advanced design in their possession with which they proposed to attack El Al flights on landing or take-off from the Rome airport; and at Orly, bazookas would actually be fired from the public gallery against aircraft on the ground, missing an El Al Boeing and hitting a Yugoslav Airlines DC-9. Boudia himself would be replaced in Europe by a Venezuelan, Carlos Sanchez, who was to wreak great havoc.

What cannot be doubted, however, is that where the security services of the Western world once had the ability only to *react* to events, they were now in the driving seat and the terrorists were on the run.

Gradually, inexorably, the terrorists were being squeezed and with them the anarchist groups in Europe who had been such a powerful mainstay for terrorism.

In Britain, France, Germany, and even in the Arab countries, the extreme terrorist factions were either being arrested or were forced to burrow so deeply underground that they had little air to breathe; they and the ideas they represented were slowly being asphyxiated.

There is no security service in the West which does not today have direct ties with the Israeli service. Israelis worked with the Germans to crack the Baader-Meinhof gang. Israelis worked with MI-5, provided vital information which pointed to the members of the Angry Brigade who had been planting bombs in London, and helped break the increasingly worrying connection between the Provisional IRA and the Arabs, especially the Libyans. When a boatload of arms destined for Belfast was on its way from Libya, it was an Israeli agent who first heard about the shipment, and it was Israeli information which helped the British Navy shadow its prey all the way to its destination.

In the late sixties, it looked for a period as if all of Europe was to be engulfed in violent forms of urban terrorism. That this threat gradually faded is due in no small measure to a small intelligence service in the Mediterranean which had the gall to tackle this menace head on. By any standards, this was indeed an astonishing achievement.

PART VII

Into the Eighties

Chapter 24

MOSSAD SUFFERED ONE GRIEVOUS BLOW during its war
with the Palestinians: the death of the incomparable
Baruch Cohen, gunned down in the streets of Madrid on
January 26, 1973, the only Mossad case officer ever to
lose his life while on active service in the history of the
agency.

To this day, no one but Black September knows who
or what it was that gave Baruch Cohen away. But it was
clear, at least in retrospect, that the Palestinians did
know by September 1972 that one of Mossad's prime operational centers, set up to do battle with them, was the
Israeli Embassy in Brussels out of which Cohen operated.
On September 10th, Ophir Zadok, a Mossad employee
working undercover as a member of the embassy staff,
was telephoned by an informant promising information
about planned attacks by Arabs on Jewish property in
Belgium. Zadok went to a local café, where a twenty-
nine-year-old unbalanced Moroccan with a police record
shot him at point-blank range. Zadok survived the attack.
It had been amateurish in the extreme and a throw-
back to the days when the Palestinians regularly employed prison fodder on their really dangerous missions.
Apart from a personal concern for Zadok, no one at the
Brussels center worried too much about this attack.
Zadok himself was not under particularly deep cover; it
required no feat of great ingenuity to have established
that he was involved in security work. So, apart from increasing precautions at all of Israel's diplomatic posts
around the globe, no lessons were drawn from this episode at all. More worrying perhaps was the death of a
Syrian journalist, killed at close quarters in his flat in
Paris on November 13th. Khader Kano was a low-level
Israeli informant, employed by Radio Damascus as their

Paris stringer. His tastes had long outgrown his ability to pay for them, and a year or so earlier he had begun volunteering information to the Israelis about Palestinian activity in Paris in return for money. Mossad never wholly trusted him. What information he had was accepted and paid for, but no one was entirely satisfied that he was not a Black September plant. Accordingly, no one (certainly not Baruch Cohen or anyone Kano could possibly identify) ever got close to him. On September 10th, his body was found in his apartment with three 9-mm. bullets through the heart. He had been executed by the Palestinians.

At the time Kano's death did not disturb Mossad unduly. The information he possessed was never of the highest quality, even accepting (as the Israelis now had to) that he had been on the level all the time. But it didn't seem surprising that the Palestinians had got on to him. It was indeed possible that he told them himself of his Israeli connection, hoping to do a deal as a double. In that way, he would have signed his own death warrant, because he would have had to reveal that he had made unauthorized approaches to the Israelis previously.

So when, in January 1973, Baruch Cohen received word from one of his most reliable informants that he wanted to see him in Madrid, Baruch Cohen didn't hesitate for a moment. They had often arranged their meetings in the Spanish capital, well away from prying eyes. Everything was quite normal. Precisely what happened on the morning of Cohen's death is not clear. Cohen himself was not covered by a Mossad agent—the meeting was regarded as being too routine for any elaborate security precautions—and so Zwi Zamir had to rely on the reports of the Spanish police, themselves muddled and confused, and make what he could of them. All that was certain was that Baruch Cohen had been shot several times by an unknown assailant; some eyewitnesses had seen two men who could have been Arabs near the Unidia José Antonio, one of the biggest and smartest streets of the capital, hurrying away after the shooting.

It is very rare for an intelligence organization to be able to analyze its mistakes precisely—particularly when these mistakes have led to the death of one of its officers. There could be no doubt about the fact that Cohen had felt totally secure; otherwise he would not have gone to Madrid or he would not have gone alone.

It was obvious, however, in retrospect that the attempted murder of Ophir Zadok and the killing of Khader Kano were more serious matters than they had appeared at the time. Clearly, Black September, as Cohen's killing finally proved, had penetrated Mossad's European operation—and through an Arab agent Israeli intelligence had grown to trust. Zwicka Zamir had to take immediate protective action and dismantle existing networks in Europe and wherever else there were interlinked informers—many of whom had proved to be of immense value. These informers had to be paid off in case they were contaminated. Senior Mossad officers who, like Cohen, had successfully run a wide variety of agents were recalled to Tel Aviv in case they, too, had been fingered. Almost overnight the Mossad operation in Europe ground to a halt; a certain amount of time would have to elapse before new men, working out of new headquarters, with different covers, could be activated once again. Only the operations long since planned were kept alive, among them the murders of Dr. Basil Al Kubaissi and of Boudia in Paris. But they had been operational long before Cohen's death, and could not be affected by it. The process of "renewal" took a few months, but it was precisely during that period that the Israeli Secret Service suffered its worst public humiliation. The fiasco came about not because the men who replaced Baruch Cohen and the others were amateurs, but because they simply lacked the incredible degree of experience and knowledge their predecessors had built up over the years. In time they would become equally as effective, but it was during that dangerous interim period when they were still treading water that disaster struck.

At 10:40 P.M. on July 21, 1973, in Lillehammer in Norway, an Israeli assassination team killed a man whom they believed to be the notorious Ali Hassan Salameh. Not only did they get the wrong man, but Norwegian police managed to apprehend some members of the back-up team, interrogate them and put them on trial. The nightmare question—What happens if things go wrong?—had finally become reality.

No doubt the inexperience of Baruch Cohen's successors was primarily to blame, and, of course, no one should have permitted them to go operational until they were securely established. They acted on information which was of an abysmally low grade without having the background to realize it. This does not, however, quite explain how it was that a nation which boasted one of the most sophisticated intelligence agencies in the world went quite so disastrously wrong as it did.

It all began when Mossad HQ in Tel Aviv received "hard" information that Black September was planning a major hijacking spectacular out of Norway. Since Palestinian terrorists had launched their campaign against the airlines of the world, most countries had set up special antiterrorist departments which kept trained men at airports specifically to watch out for trouble. Only the Scandinavian countries, despite the hijacking of an SAS plane by Croatian terrorists in 1972, had kept comparatively aloof from all this activity. They relied upon their neutralism and their non-involvement in Middle East affairs to see them through. This expectation in the view of Mossad had always been, at best, naive. The Palestinians didn't really care whom they attacked, provided the headlines it produced were big enough to justify the expenditure.

This is not necessarily a cynical view. Most Palestinians do believe absolutely that people only began talking about the plight of the Palestinians after the wave of hijackings—a crude form of advertising which had its desired effect.

Scandinavia also seemed a fairly logical place for the Palestinians, defeated elsewhere in Europe, to regroup. Already, Sweden had become a center for Europe's new left, attracted by the liberality of the government, the social-security system, and even the overly baroque reputation of Swedish girls.

Mossad's information out of Beirut was immediately passed on to the security services of Denmark, Norway and Sweden, and permission was sought for Mossad operatives, now widely recognized as the best anti-hijacking precaution any country could invest in, to operate on Scandinavian soil. It was this agreement which was subsequently to cause problems between the Norwegian and the Israeli governments.

Almost as soon as this agreement was obtained, new information came in which turned what would otherwise have been a fairly routine intelligence sweep into an operation given the highest priority. This was that Ali Hassan Salameh would be operating out of a temporary base in Norway to set up a Black September network which would cover the whole of Scandinavia. Since their failure to corner him in Beirut, Salameh had successfully gone to ground, and this was the first hard piece of intelligence Mossad had had about him since. It was an opportunity not to be missed.

It was quickly established that a Palestinian living in Geneva called Kemal Benamane would be Salameh's liaison officer and would be leaving shortly for Norway. Benamane's past has always proved difficult to check out, but it seems fairly certain that he did fight for a brief period with the FLN during the Algerian war.

With every one of Benamane's movements covered, an assassination squad was hurriedly assembled. But while the logistics were being speedily arranged, the quality of information was being inadequately assessed. The Israelis badly wanted Salameh and began cutting corners to get him.

"Mike," Mossad's head of operations, brought together a team consisting of fourteen people to do the job—a two-man assassination squad (the action team), a two-man cover team, a two-man logistics team, one communications officer and six operatives, and the team leader, who on this occasion was Mike himself, so much importance did he attach to the operation.

Mike traveled as a Frenchman, Edouard Stanislas Laskier; the Mossad man in charge of the operatives, Abraham Gehmer, who had served as first secretary of the Israeli Embassy in Paris for Mossad, traveled on a passport which showed him to be Leslie Orbaum, a schoolmaster from Leeds in England.

The operatives were a curious collection. When the Palestinian problem first broke in a major way in Europe, it was clear to the Israelis that Mossad simply did not have the staff that the massive task of tailing a man or watching his apartment requires. So Zwi Zamir expanded enormously a policy which had already been under way, though in a very limited way, in Isser Harel's day: to recruit help from Israelis living out of the country, and whose military service indicated that they were reliable, for limited operations. Most frequently, these were people who approached their local embassy first, offering their services while abroad should this ever be required.*

These part-time agents, well trained in Israel, provide the back-up work for the main assault, though they rarely know the purpose behind the surveillance they are required to do. Britain's Special Branch estimates that it needs twenty men to maintain a twenty-four-hour watch on one individual. If the Israelis feel it can be done with fewer, this is only because they are prepared to put greater demands upon their operatives, but even then a twenty-four-hour watch is a boring and soul-destroying task, and needs a minimum of ten people. It is the part-time agents' job to provide that service.

The *modus operandi* of all the assassinations so far had followed a strict pattern. The "casuals" kept watch

---

* In his book *Night Watch* (Atheneum: New York, 1977), the ex-CIA executive David Atlee Phillips puts the Israeli Secret Service at the top of the rankings of all international secret services because they have "learned to be tough enough to operate in pitch-black alleys." He adds: "While the Israeli service deserves the first ranking on my or any other list, it has a built-in advantage that all other intelligence operators envy. The first phases of recruiting a spy are the essential ones of approach and cultivation before the pitch is made. The Israelis have ready access in nearly every country in the world to persons prominent in political, scientific and economic areas: the indigenous Jews who are unlikely to resent a proposal that they cooperate with their chief homeland." As indicated previously, in the early fifties a firm decision of principle was made that indigenous Jews should never be recruited by Mossad. Despite what other intelligence agencies may imagine, that policy has been rigidly adhered to ever since. Israelis who have gone abroad, or in some cases Jews who have moved away from their own country and are living as foreigners elsewhere, are in a different category. But basically the rule is a simple one: a Frenchman who moves to Israel and becomes an Israeli citizen could well work for Mossad in France. A French Jew who is a non-Israeli citizen would never be invited to help the Israeli Secret Service, however pro-Israeli he may be in France. If, however, he were working in England, circumstances might arise where he could be called upon—or if he offered, his services accepted— to work against the interests of the country in which he was temporarily living.

on the target and were removed well before the actual "hit," not only so that they would not be involved, but so they would not be in the way of the main squads making their getaway. That system was strictly adhered to in Lillehammer. What went wrong was that Lillehammer was a small town, a long way from anywhere. The casuals were simply not given sufficient time to break away before the road blocks began operating. The casuals, under their Mossad commander Abraham Gehmer, picked up Kemal Benamane the moment he arrived in Norway. The team included an attractive South African Jewess called Sylvia Rafael, who worked as a photographer in Paris under the name of Patricia Roxburgh. A Canadian citizen, she was the only other Mossad operative in the party. By and large, she had not been used on active service missions, but through her wide press contacts in Paris and elsewhere in Europe had provided Mossad with a constant and steady flow of information about the activities of the European left and their Palestinian friends.

Others in the party included Dan Aerbel, a Danish-born Israeli, and Marianne Gladnikoff, of Swedish origin, both specifically recruited for this job because they spoke the language, understood local customs, and knew the geography. Neither was told the real purpose of the journey to Norway. Their only function was to follow Benamane when he arrived and establish whom he was contacting. Zwi Steinberg, a thirty-six-year-old Brazilian Israeli, was the baggage master on this, his first real trip abroad as a Mossad operative. It was his job to look after equipment and to organize the hiring of the cars the team would need, as well as to arrange their getaways. Michael Dorf, aged twenty-seven, whose last job before he had been recruited by Mossad two years earlier had been at the Tel Aviv telephone exchange, was the group's communications officer. Little or nothing is known about the killer. He traveled to Norway under the name of Jonathan Ingleby, an Englishman from Manchester. According to eyewitnesses, he was tall and blond, very Scandinavian in appearance. Benamane arrived in Oslo on schedule, checked into a local hotel, and then took a train to Lillehammer.

From an operational point of view, everything was wrong with Lillehammer that could be wrong. Unlike great cities like Paris or Rome, where Mossad was used to operating, this was a small sleepy holiday town of 20,000 on Lake Mjøsa, where everyone knew everyone else and where a group of strangers was bound to draw attention to themselves if they behaved in the slightest way out of the ordinary. On July 19th, most of the team were in Lillehammer and had Benamane under observation. He had checked into the Skotte, a small tourist home. That night as he sat in the TV lounge of the hotel briefly watching a Norwegian fishing saga on television, two of the cover team were there, too. The following morning, he rose and went for a walk, with the Israeli agents keeping what is known as a "loose trail"—that is to say that the subject is not actually followed for long, but that all possible routes he could take are checked off to permit him to be picked up at any point along the way. Lillehammer's small size made such a procedure not only possible but necessary. Only by keeping a loose trail on him would Benamane not realize that he was being followed.

He was picked up at the Karoline Café, a coffeehouse in a small square near the town hall and the police station. With him were an Arab and a European. It was the Arab whom Marianne Gladnikoff now concentrated upon. Marianne had been issued a small picture of Salameh, and now, cupping it in her hand and comparing it to the man who sat so close to her, she was left in no doubt. They had found Salameh.

Benemane left Lillehammer on the 2:08 train that afternoon to Oslo, where Sylvia Rafael, Abraham Gehmer and Dan Aerbel were waiting for him. Mike had originally doubted that Lillehammer could possibly be the site for Benamane's "meet" with Salameh, and so had held most of his team back in the capital. Benemane was tracked to the Stephen Hotel in central Oslo and was heard making preparations to return to Geneva the following day, which indeed he did. Gehmer and Aerbel then returned to Lillehammer.

By now, of course, Mike had heard from his people in Lillehammer, who had supplied him with a full report of Benamane's meeting at the Karoline. The fact that the man believed to be Salameh had ridden off on a bicycle might have alerted Mike to the inherent improbability that this was the man they were after. Yet Salameh, though he certainly liked the good life, was also clever enough in the view of the Israelis to adopt various profiles that would permit him to wander around Europe and the Middle East almost at will. If he was not actually the archetype "Man of a Thousand Faces" beloved by writers of newspaper headlines, it was known that he had in the past slipped through security nets by adopting unexpected identities.

On the next day, July 21, 1973, the Mossad first team checked into the Victoria Hotel, Lillehammer, believing that they were at last on the track of the man they had been seeking for years. At 11:15 A.M., "Salameh" was spotted entering the municipal swimming pool, and Marianne, rapidly renting a bathing suit, followed him in. There, he met a European with a beard with whom he spoke French, none of which could be picked up by Marianne. He then left with an obviously local girl who was visibly pregnant. This time he was closely trailed.

The Arab and the girl boarded a bus and traveled to a new housing estate on the outskirts of the town and entered an address, Rugdeveien 21A. Mike had had the chance of a good look and was convinced. Benamane had come all the way from Geneva to meet him. He must be the man they were after.

At 2:00 P.M., the assassination squad arrived. The three men, driving a dark-green Mercedes, booked themselves into the Oppland Tourist Hotel, all using false documentation and false identities. Jonathan Ingleby's British passport had never been issued by the Passport Office in London. Rolf Baehr's German passport number 408948L had one too few digits, and Gerard-Emile Lafond's passport number 996262 was also later discovered to be a forgery. At about the same time, still another agent, called Tahl, checked into the Esso Olrud Hotel on the Autostrat. The team was in position and ready to go.

That same day, at 3:42 P.M., a Japan Airlines flight from Amsterdam to Tokyo was hijacked by a team of Arab and Japanese terrorists who in their customary way announced that there would be a change of call-sign for the plane; it was now to be called Operation Mount Carmel. The name had a particularly ominous ring to the Israeli authorities. Mossad knew that Black September had been talking in terms of a colossal outrage against Israel, whereby a suicide squad—one of whose members would be a trained pilot, probably Japanese—would make a kamikaze run over Israel and crash on an Israeli city. It was the Israeli fear of this which had led to a terrible tragedy five months earlier, when the French pilot of a Libyan Boeing 727 lost his way on his approach to Cairo airport and flew into Israeli air space. He mistook the signals of Israeli planes sent up to intercept him, and when he didn't respond to their order to land immediately, his plane was shot down, causing the death of 106 people. Now Operation Mount Carmel appeared to be en route to Israel. This could be the kamikaze raid—the revenge for Beirut.

As a result, Zwicka Zamir and the whole of his senior hierarchy were caught up in the various contingency plans being made to deal with Operation Mount Carmel. It would be ludicrous to suggest that the team assembled in Lillehammer was forgotten during the drama, but it is certainly true that the usual, very tight, top-echelon executive control over an operation of this kind was temporarily diverted. So when, at 6:00 P.M., the Lillehammer team signaled home for the "Go" instruction, it was given with rather less attention to detail than had characterized these operations in the past.

The rest was comparatively straightforward. At 8:00 P.M., the man believed to be Salameh, with the same woman at his side the team had seen previously, entered the local cinema to see *Where Eagles Dare,* featuring Richard Burton. They left at 10:35 P.M. At 10:40 P.M., the couple got off their bus and began the short walk to their flat. At first they didn't notice the Mazda coming slowly toward them. When they did, it was too late. Two men—one specifically identified as Jonathan Ingleby—jumped from the car and began pumping bullets from their Berettas into the Arab. All he managed to say was "No!" before, mortally wounded, staggering desperately in the attempt to get away, clawing at his stomach, he collapsed in a bleeding mess on the pavement with the screaming woman huddled over him. At 10:50 P.M., the police were notified, and within minutes of the shooting were at the scene of the crime. The Israelis knew that they had little time. The Mazda was ditched, and the team in their various cars, the green Mercedes and a white Peugeot filled with agents, made its way to the road to

Oslo. They were almost literally in the middle of nowhere, and it would take some time to reach the safety and anonymity of a big city.

One can't be sure when they and Zwicka Zamir realized that the wrong man had been killed. The most that could be said of Ahmed Bouchiki, the unfortunate man gunned down so recklessly, a Moroccan-born waiter who lived and worked in Lillehammer and was married to the girl the execution squad had seen him with, was that he had loose links with Black September, though almost certainly he had never taken any part in any operation or shown much inclination to do so. If Benamane was doing anything in Lillehammer, he was on a recruiting mission —perhaps hoping to use Bouchiki in future operations in Scandinavia, where his knowledge of the language would be invaluable. Whether he agreed or not, no one save Benamane, and certainly not Mossad, could know. Whatever dark hints were subsequently dropped in the Israeli press by Mossad propagandists, the fact is that, to all intents and purposes, a totally innocent man had been brutally slain.

As far as Mossad was concerned, worse was to come. Though the Norwegian police were remarkably slow in setting up road blocks, the Peugeot, No. DA-97943, rented from Scandinavian Rent-a-Car in Oslo by Patricia Roxburgh, was spotted by police on the road from Lillehammer.

On Sunday morning, twenty-four hours after the shooting, the car was seen again at Oslo airport by an alert ticket clerk who, like other employees at the airport, had been asked to keep a lookout for the vehicle. Quickly, he informed the police, and within minutes Marianne Gladnikoff and Dan Aerbel were in custody and, to use that splendid British phrase, "helping the police with their inquiries."

Oddly, perhaps because she panicked, Marianne, asked by the police for her address in Oslo, gave that of the safe house to which she and her party had gone from Lillehammer. There, the police found Sylvia Rafael and Abraham Gehmer, who were also arrested. It was Marianne who first cracked under questioning. The police already had a shrewd ideas as to who had killed Bouchiki and why. It was Marianne who confirmed it. "I was asked if I were willing to perform a service for the State of Israel," she said in her interrogation, "and I felt obliged to do so because I had not done military service."

But it was Dan Aerbel who was most careless. On the back page of his passport, investigators found a phone number: 14-15-80. A check with the telephone company found that it was an unlisted number; the subscriber was a man called Eyal who was on record as working for El Al.* The police timed their raid perfectly. A woman opened the door when the police rang. They pushed their way past her and into the living room, where three men were sitting. They were ordered against the wall with their hands up while the police searched the flat and found a pistol. It was the owner of the flat who made the first move. He introduced himself not as Eyal—obviously a cover name for the purpose of getting the telephone—but as Yigal Zigal, a senior "security officer" at the Israeli Embassy with full diplomatic immunity.

He produced his credentials and ordered the police to leave what was technically Israeli diplomatic territory. But the police would have none of it, and the two men, identified as Zwi Steinberg and Michael Dorf, were arrested then and there.

The police now had six people out of the original assassination squad. The Mercedes was discovered in Denmark, obviously taken on the ferry which runs from Oslo to Copenhagen. Others of the team simply took normal commercial flights, probably in some cases using different passports from the ones they had operated under in Norway.

The two professionals, Dorf and Steinberg, had little to say to the police, but their possessions were a giveaway. Steinberg had two keys, each attached to a blue name tag, which opened an apartment in Paris. There, French investigators found more keys, similarly marked, which opened virtually every Mossad safe house in Paris, and they also discovered clues to the fact that some members of the Lillehammer team had been involved in earlier assassinations of prominent Palestinians.

---

* Mossad had been fairly careless, too. Aerbel proved to be a cooperative witness because he found that he suffered from the most appalling claustrophobia. Simply being shut in a cell proved to be unbearable to him. For all of Mossad's much vaunted psychological screening, it had never discovered this crippling weakness.

In Dorf's possession was a telex message from the Amsterdam Mossad headquarters, which ran the whole European operation.

1. Get away from Norway's capital by rail.
2. Depart as soon as you are in possession of an Israeli passport.
3. From Denmark's capital, you are to proceed to Amsterdam and get in touch with CNT [the code name for the Mossad Amsterdam HQ].
4. You must not bring along any controversial material or any document. Just the mentioned documentation.
5. Mikki is to stay behind in the embassy in Norway's capital, in hiding for the time being, to establish with KHT [code for Mossad's special-operations department in Tel Aviv] to track traffic until KHT lifts the contract.*
6. Mikki is to report to base special news of the topic.

The Israeli government sought to put immense pressure on the Norwegians to cover up the fiasco. The Israeli attorney, Meir Rosenne, with a special commission from Prime Minister Golda Meir, flew into Norway in an attempt to intercede. He pointed out to the Norwegians that the Israeli team had the tacit approval of Norwegian security to operate in their country, but he was told, in turn, that this authority did not include the right to kill, certainly not the right to kill an apparently completely innocent Morrocan waiter.

Eventually, the six Israelis had to face the indignity of a full-scale public trial as accessories to the murder of Ahmed Bouchiki. On February 1, 1974, Sylvia Rafael was sentenced to five-and-one-half-years' imprisonment, Marianne Gladnikoff to two-and-one-half-years, Abraham Gehmer to five-and-one-half years, and Dan Aerbel to five years. Ironically perhaps, Zwi Sternberg, who was probably more important than all of them, received only one year for espionage, and Michael Dorf was acquitted.

It was a bitter pill for Mossad to have to swallow, made worse by the fact that Mossad's hands would be very much tied from now on. Zwi Zamir knew only too well, without needing the Foreign Ministry to tell him (which

* "Mikki" is almost certainly "Mike," the unit commander.

it did *ad nauseam*), that any other killings in Europe would now be pinned directly to Israel, would get maximum publicity, and what's more, with the court records of the Lillehammer case to go by, permit newspapers as well as security organizations to reach conclusions with regard to the Israeli methodology that would be dangerous for Mossad in the extreme.

The problem for Israel was, as it was succinctly put at one staff meeting, that if one Palestinian should get hit by a Parisian bus, the whole world would accuse Israel of his murder. That most valuable, most necessary and most fundamental of all intelligence weapons, "deniability," had, because of Lillehammer, been temporarily taken away from Mossad. This was such a major defeat that there were some in Mossad who believed the Israelis had been deliberately "set up" by Benamane and the Palestinians, and an investigation was conducted to see whether this was possible.

It was finally decided that this could not have been the case, although Benamane himself continued to play a somewhat curious role in the whole affair by surfacing in Geneva and demanding of the Israelis an explanation as to how he had been dragged into a business he knew nothing about. Everybody tried to find the reason that things had gone so wrong. There were those on the operations staff who argued that operations of this kind are inherently fragile, inevitably vulnerable to disaster. This was not a view which Zwicka Zamir was prepared to accept. The operation had gone wrong because the analysis had been bad and operational procedures had been ignored. Israel was being forced to pay the price for incompetence. The fact that the operation took place in Norway was perhaps its greatest inherent weakness. There were enough people within the Israeli intelligence community who knew every town and city in Italy, Germany, France or Britain to ensure that Mossad could never be defeated by geography, but Scandinavia was virgin territory, for which the experts simply did not exist.

It was only two years later that Mossad, through a Palestinian informant, learned the truth of the Lillehammer operation. Contrary to what was thought, Salameh *had* been in Lillehammer at the time. By some incredible mischance, the assassination squad had gone to the right town, at the right time, but had killed the wrong man.

The upshot of this bungled and tragic operation was that Mossad's assassination option was virtually eliminated, save for in Arab territory; as a result, Israeli intelligence felt itself to be hamstrung. This was clearly indicated in the Carlos affair. The son of a Venezuelan Communist, Carlos Ilich Ramirez Sanchez (who, like the now deceased Mohammed Boudia, had learned his trade at the Patrice Lumumba University in Moscow, where he had been plucked out by the KGB and given a complete grounding in the arts of underground warfare), had taken over from Boudia as the European head of Palestinian terrorist organizations.

The Israelis were on Carlos' trail fairly quickly, but in the aftermath of Norway, were forced to play by the rules. A leading Palestinian courier who traveled extensively back and forth between Beirut and Europe had been "turned" by a Mossad operative in Paris. A weak man, he was cornered by Israeli agents and offered a choice of death or cooperation. He chose the latter, at which point large sums of money were made available to him to ensure his loyalty. No one, of course, could ever take him seriously. The chance that he was playing both ends against the middle was better than even, yet his contacts as a courier were so extensive that he became one of those men familiar to all intelligence agencies, people who are helpful even when they lie.

It was this man, Michel Murkabal, who led the Israelis to Carlos and the address he was living at in Paris. Murkabal was turned over to the French DST, with whom Mossad had always enjoyed the best of relations, and it was with two DST officers that Murkabal went to Carlos' address at 9 Rue Toullier so that he could aid in identification. Unfortunately, the French security services only theoretically accepted the Israelis' thesis that men like Carlos were not simply bored middle-class kids who had become terrorists because it afforded them excitement and glamour, but were highly skilled, highly trained professionals taught by the best school in the world, the KGB.

As a result, the two DST officers and Murkabal were all shot dead by Carlos as they tried to make the arrest. These killings of a team of officers from an intelligence service experienced in countries like Algeria and Indochina, some of the roughest of them all, were a remarkable demonstration of Carlos' training and ability. He would never be taken lightly again.

Carlos made his getaway, leaving the Israelis determined to add one more name to an assassination list they had not entirely scrapped. Well protected by the Libyans and the Algerians, Carlos still, at the time of this writing, goes free.

The hunt for Salameh continued as well. Six years were to elapse before the Israelis finally caught up with the elusive "Red Prince." After Lillehammer, Salameh began making the mistake of believing his own propaganda. What had always saved him in the past was a perfect, almost instinctive feel for conspiracy—a "sense of place" which ensured that his enemies could never predict his movements accurately enough to bring together an assassination team that could catch him unprepared. Now he was beginning to believe that he was fireproof, so much so that he moved out of the shadows sufficiently to become the intermediary between the U.S. and the PLO to secure safe passage for nearly a thousand Americans and Europeans caught in Beirut at the time of the civil war and to oversee their safe transfer to landing craft sent in to rescue them. During the war itself, enjoying the life of an ambassador at large in the war-torn streets of Beirut between all of the rival factions, the man who once described himself as "a ghost who haunts the Israelis" became flesh and blood, a constant presence, a man whose life style had suddenly become predictable. No doubt because he had escaped so often, he believed he was invincible, but perhaps the fact that he was nearing forty, a time when the attractions of his peripatetic life had begun to pale, and the vague thought that, having tried so often and failed, the Israelis would give up on him, persuaded Salameh that he could enjoy a normal life. But it was when, on June 29, 1978, he took a second wife, the beautiful Lebanese girl Georgina Rizk who had become Miss Universe in Miami Beach in 1971, that he sealed his own doom. He bought a flat for her in Beirut's Rue Verdun and, though still keeping close contact with his first wife and his two sons, spent more and more time with Georgina. Salameh now had a routine, and it was that routine which permitted the Israelis to kill him.

Toward the end of 1978, a middle-aged woman called Erika Mary Chambers, traveling on a British passport, moved into an apartment opposite the new Mrs. Salameh on the Rue Verdun. She soon became well known in the area, insisted upon being called Penelope, collected stray cats, and spent a lot of her time at the window of her apartment painting certainly naive but nevertheless tellingly accurate cityscapes of the street below her.

In January 1979, Peter Scriver, bearing British Passport No. 260896, arrived at Beirut International Airport. He gave his occupation as technical consultant and was in every way the model British businessman. He checked in at the Méditerranée Hotel, where he rented a Volkswagen. A day or so later, Ronald Kolberg, carrying Canadian Passport No. DS 104277, arrived in Beirut, checked in at the Royal Garden Hotel and rented a grey Simca. It was only when investigators began checking immigration records that it was realized that both passports were forgeries, and that Regent Sheffield Limited of New York, of whom Kolberg claimed he was a representative, had never heard of him.

It was almost certainly Erika Mary "Penelope" Chambers, well enough known now not to rouse the slightest suspicion, who slipped a tiny radio transmitter, emitting a specific short-range signal, under the fender of Salameh's Chevrolet station wagon. It would only have taken a second or so—perhaps as she bent down to tie a shoe lace—to fit the magnetic device into place.

Scriver's job was to fill the Volkswagen with plastic explosives (though how he got hold of them still remains a secret), leave the keys with Kolberg, and on a different passport fly out of the country. Kolberg now took the car and parked it near Salameh's flat along a route which he took almost daily.

On January 22, at 3:35 P.M., Salameh passed the Volkswagen in his Chevrolet. With him were four bodyguards. Another four rode in a car at the rear. As the station wagon drew level with the Volkswagen, the radio signal implanted on Salameh's car set off a highly sophisticated detonator in the Volkswagen. With an almighty roar, the car bomb exploded. The carnage was fearful.

Salameh and his bodyguards were dead, along with four passers-by. Kolberg and Penelope had disappeared. The Simca was found abandoned. They had almost certainly, like Scriver, exchanged passports and calmly left the country hours before the actual remote-controlled assassination. The message that day from Mossad HQ to the Prime Minister's office did not need to be more explicit. It simply said: "Munich has been avenged."

Today, the Israelis still regard assassination as a legitimate weapon in the war they wage against the Palestinians. But they have gone back to first principles, as laid down by Fatti Harkabi in the middle fifties. Any top Palestinian leader who organizes acts of terror against Israel knows that he must always go well guarded and that his life—as well as the lives of the young men he sends out on missions—is always on the line.

Probably sixty percent of Mossad activity is today directed against the Palestinian movement. There are varying estimates as to how successful the Israelis have been in the underground war they have been forced to fight so unrelentingly for nearly twenty years. Israel's intelligence chiefs claim that all they have done, and all they can possibly be expected to do, is to control the situation. They won't lose the war, but they can't win it, either; at least in the foreseeable future, there will be terrorist outrages in Israel itself, against Israeli installations abroad and against "softer" targets in those countries which the Palestinians believe support Israel or are in a position to put pressure upon Israel.

CIA analysts pitch the Israeli achievements a good deal higher. Major acts of international terrorism which had the Palestinian camps as their breeding ground have fallen off remarkably since their high point in the late sixties and early seventies. There are economic, social and political reasons why this is so. But there are professional reasons, too. The terrorists declared war on society and lost, and they lost principally, the CIA believes, because of the outstanding qualities of the Israeli intelligence community, which was the first service in the world—out of its own unique historic experience—properly to recognize the threat these people posed to democracy everywhere and the first to learn to combat the threat which they represented.

The war had been a ruthless one—but, as the Israelis would say, their enemy would have it no other way.

Chapter 25

ON THE EVENING of Saturday, October 6, 1973, the Prime Minister, Mrs. Golda Meir, went on television to address the nation. "For a number of days," she said, "our intelligence services have known that the armies of Egypt and Syria were deployed for a coordinated attack on Israel . . . our forces were deployed, according to plan, to meet the impending danger."

As she was speaking, soldiers on the Golan Heights were fighting a desperate battle which she knew well could decide the continued existence of the State of Israel. Grossly outnumbered, completely unprepared, the Israeli Army sought to stem a ferocious Syrian assault, which if the Israelis could not hold would leave the whole of northern Israel at the mercy of the Syrian Army. Meanwhile, in the Sinai, the Egyptian Army, having made an almost unopposed crossing of the Suez Canal, had taken the Bar Lev Line, that marvel of electronic fortification, and were digging in preparatory perhaps to a frontal assault on the Sinai passes and then on Israel itself. The Israeli Air Force, which had so convincingly won the Six-Day War in two hours, now found that it could not give air support to its beleaguered troops because of a Russian missile barrier which the Air Force knew existed but the extraordinary effectiveness of which it had underestimated.

For thirty-six hours Israel was on the edge of defeat. It is an article of faith of ninety-nine percent of the Israeli population that the first war Israel loses will also be her last. Defeat would bring a new holocaust.

Miraculously, the Israeli Army, fighting at quarter strength, held the Arabs during those first few terrible hours and then finally, with all its forces in the field, drove them back to win a famous victory. Only then, at the moment of triumph, did most Israelis come to realize what a close thing it had been. Mrs. Golda Meir could well have been excused for misleading the country on that Yom Kippur Day, for to have told the truth might well have destroyed the morale of the Israeli people at a point when for those few hours only spirit and pathetically few tanks kept the country from certain defeat.

But the Israelis do not forgive easily, and Golda Meir, who for so many years personified the indomitable will and courage of the Jewish people, was, along with her Minister of Defense, Moshe Dayan, who is perhaps the most celebrated soldier of modern times, cruelly vilified by the press and public alike for their roles in the tragedy in which nearly three thousand Israeli officers and men lost their lives, a huge casualty list in a nation of 2.5 million people. The question everyone wanted answered was why was the Israeli Army not prepared? That it was not was quickly made clear by the soldiers when they returned from the front. The reserve had not been mobilized; tanks were still in their parks when the Arabs struck. The Bar Lev Line was in the hands of some five hundred men, mostly inexperienced reserves, drafted to let regular army men spend Yom Kippur with their families and against whom the Egyptians launched 8,000 men in the first wave. In the Golan, soldiers spoke of individual Israeli tanks being forced to take on whole Syrian squadrons until reinforcements arrived. Not since Operation Barbarossa in 1941, when the German armies attacked the Soviet Union, has a nation been caught so supremely unawares as Israel was on Yom Kippur 1973.

There are other parallels with Barbarossa, too. Stalin possessed the intelligence, including the date and time of the impending assault, but refused to believe it. The Israelis, too, were informed from a variety of sources a good week before Yom Kippur of Arab intentions, but disregarded it entirely.

Gradually, the country became aware that Israeli intelligence, that proud and magnificent edifice which had served the nation so splendidly, had failed at the moment of greatest peril.

The truth could not be avoided. Twenty-four hours before the attack at 1405 hours on Saturday, October 6th, when 4,000 rocket launchers, guns and mortars opened up upon the Egyptian front and 1,500 on the Syrian front, Military Intelligence had officially estimated that the probability of war was "low." Mrs. Meir was not lying when she said that the intelligence services had known that the Arab arms "were deployed for a coordinated attack on Israel." What she failed to say was that, knowing this, General Eli Zeira, the chief of Military Intelligence, had, nevertheless, not merely discounted the possibility of attack, but had taken the whole Israeli government with him in this prognosis. So enormous was the prestige of Military Intelligence within the Israeli establishment that though everyone could see what was happening, when Eli Zeira told them not to believe it, they obediently shut their eyes.

When, a year earlier, in 1972, General Eli Zeira was appointed head of Military Intelligence, an Israeli general whose identity we can only guess but could easily have been General Ahrele Yariv, one of Zeira's most brilliant predecessors, declared: "Now we are heading for catastrophe, because the system is headed by three men who do not know the meaning of fear."

It was one of those astute judgments which, in time, would take on the mantle of prophecy. The three were Moshe Dayan, the Minister of Defense, Chief of Staff David "Dado" Elazar, and Eli Zeira, the chief of Intelligence, "the hierarchy of heroes," as they have been ironically described.

Of the three, only Moshe Dayan had an intelligence officer's mind. During his period as Chief of Staff and even as minister, Dayan insisted on seeing raw intelligence, discussed and quarreled with his senior intelligence men, and always reserved the right to form his own independent assessments, which often differed from those of his intelligence chiefs.

The Chief of Staff, David "Dado" Elazar, was never Moshe Dayan's first choice for the job. Though Elazar was a great tank commander, with the ability to make fast decisions on the spot, he nevertheless lacked that extra reserve of astuteness which a nation like Israel, always on the edge of war, so desperately requires. When, at the beginning of 1973, a Libyan Boeing 727 strayed over Israeli air space, the pilot having made a serious navigational error, it was Dado Elazar who made the decision to shoot it down.

Mossad had known for years of a PFLP plan to employ kamikaze Japanese to take a passenger plane crammed with high explosives and crash-land it on an Israeli city. When the Libyan aircraft refused to take notice of the Israeli jets sent up to intercept it (the pilot believed he was in Egypt and the planes were MiGs), there seemed to be an operational justification to shoot it out of the skies. But, as was shown by an internal inquiry later, Elazar had acted precipitously. He had not used all the time he had at his disposal. He acted in fact very much in character—like a decisive tank commander, not the Chief of Staff of a sovereign power.

If David Elazar had not been Dayan's first choice as Chief of Staff, Major General Eli Zeira was not Elazar's first choice as chief of Intelligence, either. Yet, when Ahrele Yariv retired to go into politics, there didn't seem to be a better qualified candidate for the job.

Eli Zeira was without question one of the brightest and ablest officers in the Israeli Army. He had been a military attaché in Washington, had served as Yariv's deputy at Military Intelligence, and had distinguished himself as a front-line commander of great bravery and resourcefulness. Few senior officers in the Israeli Army had Zeira's air of effortless brilliance; it seemed even to those who didn't much like him that to refuse him this promotion would be putting personal considerations above professional ones. Those who doubted his professional competence for this most specialized of all army jobs numbered very few indeed. Not many then realized that of the many shortcomings which a chief of Intelligence could afford to possess, arrogance was certainly not one of them.

Zeira quickly established himself. Bursting with self-confidence, he impressed both the government and the army with the forcefulness of his intelligence presentations. He was one of the architects of what was known as "the concept." Simply stated, the concept laid down first that the Arabs were not ready for an all-out war with Israel. Though they had the ability to mount a limited war, they knew perfectly well that Israel would not feel itself bound by the rules of that game, and a limited war would quickly escalate into a general one. Second, Zeira's concept laid down, if there was to be a war, it would be a short one.

The third assumption was that in an overall war, the Arabs would be quickly defeated. The Israelis would break through to the other side of the Suez Canal, with options to advance toward Cairo, the Nile Valley and Upper Egypt. On the Syrian front, the only real question that would face Israel would be whether to take Damascus or not.

"The concept" was a doctrine to which most officers inside Military Intelligence ardently subscribed. The whole organization became rather like a newspaper office with a strong proprietor or editor where journalists only seek and file those stories which fit in with the party line. Zeira's intelligence officers, almost certainly unconsciously, began ignoring any information which appeared to contradict any part of "the concept." Zeira himself set the example from the top. Anything at all which contradicted his thesis was firmly buried.

After the war, he defended his actions. "Most of my years in the Israeli Army," he said, "I served as a commander, not a staff officer, and my nature . . . does not lead me to refer responsibility upwards . . . matters within my scope of responsibility, I generally do not pass on to my superior officers."

He then went on: "The best help a head of intelligence can provide the Chief of Staff . . . is to give him as clear and as sharp an assessment as possible. It is also true that the clearer and sharper this assessment, the clearer and sharper the error, if it is erroneous—but this is a risk the head of intelligence must take."

It was, to say the least, a curious notion of the functions of a chief of intelligence. This desire for "clear and sharp assessments" in a region where reality is notoriously vague and uncertain led to the fundamental error of assuming that all of the apparent indices of Egyptian and Syrian preparedness for war were either preparations for military exercises or saber rattling. The idea that it was the head of intelligence who took risks when he made his assessments gave the task an almost sporting quality, a betting game in which Zeira's concept was obliged to do battle with the rest. At the end of the war, Chief of Staff Elazar claimed that "some two hundred cables" from Israeli agents around the world indicating that war was imminent never reached him. If they had done, he implied, then perhaps he would have taken a different view than the one he did when he accepted Zeira's evaluations. While it may be perfectly true that a chief of intelligence cannot flood his commanding officers with every cable that comes in, those relating to a probability of war, however unlikely, clearly need to be examined not merely by the chief of intelligence but also by the Chief of Staff and his political masters. At meetings between Elazar and Zeira and their assistants, the opposite occurred. Zeira was so intent on establishing his "concept" that any information which ran counter to it was suppressed. Zeira's motives were not dishonorable—merely wrongheaded. To him, the issue was clear—the Arabs would not go to war. Thus any information which went against that thesis could only serve to confuse the elegant clarity of this evaluation.

Such was Zeira's confidence that he was able to convince the entire Israeli political establishment. Moshe Dayan, in the face of this barrage, reversed his own personal views dramatically. Throughout 1971 and 1972 Dayan was telling his staff that he "could not understand how the Egyptians could avoid war." In May 1973, he issued guidelines to the generals to the effect that "a renewal of war in the second half of summer must be taken into account." But then, in the summer of that year, he predicted there would be no war for ten years.

All the signs, in fact, were there. During that month the Egyptians had moved ground units to the canal; some sixty-five ramparts had been built, while the main one was made higher so that the Egyptians could look down upon the Israeli troops on the other side of the canal, as well as providing new openings with new descents to the water. The Egyptian civil defense was mobilized, blackouts were declared in the cities, and an appeal went out for blood donors, while President Sadat spoke of a "phase of total confrontation."

In the face of all this, Zeira maintained adamantly that Sadat would not go to war. Chief of Staff Elazar disagreed and ordered a partial mobilization, at a cost to the Israeli economy (as reservists were pulled out of industry and into the army) of several million pounds. Then the Arabs backed down. Zeira had been dramatically vindicated. From that time on, few dared quarrel with "the concept." Moshe Dayan himself was so completely converted that in August 1973 he told senior officials at the Defense Ministry that there would be no war for "several years," and then added jokingly that if he was proved wrong, he would gather them all together again to explain why.*

* Ironically, Eli Zeira had been wrong on that occasion. Sadat *had* intended to go to war that May, but had pulled back from the brink at the last moment when the Russians set the date for the second summit conference with Nixon in Washington for the same month. Politically, Sadat believed that it would be wrong to go to war at that time. This was a consideration which Zeira could not and did not know about. Apart from this incident, the Egyptians were cleverly playing on Israeli nerves and deliberately fanning opinion in Israel which held that all the Arabs were capable of was making rude noises. There had been a partial Egyptian mobilization in April and September, followed by an immediate stand down. Knowing that since the Six-Day War, the Israelis had grown contemptuous of the Arabs, Sadat's intelligence officers played beautifully upon Israeli psychology. The Egyptian and the Syrian deception operation, of which Sadat's apparent vacillation was a part, was so brilliantly organized that most experts believe that it was run by the Russians who have long proved themselves to be the masters of "disinformation" techniques. From the winter of 1972, the world's press was full of reports underlining Arab inefficiency and incompetence. On December 26, 1972, a *Financial Times* man, after a short visit to Castro wrote: "The Egyptian Army isn't at all prepared to fight, though some elements want war with Israel." *La Stampa* in Cairo wrote on January 27, 1973: "Corruption spreads. The Egyptian Army had only enough ammunition for one week." In February, the *Corriere della Sera* said: "Egyptian military sources openly acknowledge a shortage of gasoline and spare parts. There is one pilot for every two planes. New supersonic aircraft lie like unturned stones. Thirty supersonic aircraft have crashed in exercises over the past five months." *Figaro* reported in February: ". . . a foreign attaché told me, 'There's never been a more beaten army. They have neither Nasser nor Soviet advisers. The army lacks spirit.'" Jim Hogland wrote from Cairo in the Washington *Post* in March that Egypt's air-defense network was vulnerable to Israeli attack, and he quoted Cairo stories of two Israeli jets that had approached within thirty miles of Cairo without the Egyptians' launching missiles. The examples abound. But not only the press were treated to these nuggets of pure disinformation. In July 1973, military attachés in Cairo were invited to an exercise outside Cairo to observe Egypt's latest ground-attack equipment being put to the test. It was, said one attaché, rather like watching the early Keystone Cops. Everything that could go wrong did go wrong. Only after the war

By late September and the beginning of October, it was clear to everyone with eyes to see that the Egyptians were preparing for something or, as one senior Israeli officer caustically put it, no army in the history of warfare was doing so much to go nowhere.

On October 1st, the order-of-battle officer of Southern Command intelligence, Lieutenant Benjamin Siman-Tov, submitted a report to his chief, Lieutenant Colonel David Gedaliah, intelligence officer of Southern Command, with a brilliant analysis of the deployment of the Egyptian forces along the Suez Canal. "War," he said, "by any possible reading of the signs is inevitable."

It was not merely the huge quantities of armor and amphibious equipment which were being brought up and the hundreds of vehicles moving back and forth along the lines, but the methodology of those movements which caught Siman-Tov's attention. On October 1st, too, the intelligence agencies received from totally reliable, albeit clandestine, channels, reports of massive and unprecedented movements of Soviet arms into Syria. Everybody seemed to know what was going on—even the Lebanese press was reporting Egyptian movements up to army strength, from Cairo to Suez.

By October 2nd, this incredible activity began to percolate down, and some Israeli leaders in the Army and outside began to feel the nervous pinch of expectation. On that day, tough Major General Samuel Gonen, General

---

did they realize that they had observed a splendid piece of pantomime designed to impress them with Egyptian incompetence, a message which undoubtedly got back to the Israelis. On the Syrian front, too, the disinformation campaign was expertly handled. Stories of the "rift between Syria and the Soviet Union" began appearing, especially in Beirut newspapers. Indeed, while the Russians were busily setting up the most sophisticated missile screen the world had ever seen, both in Egypt and Syria, the press was led to believe that the Russians had finally become so irritated by the incompetence of their Arab clients that they were pulling out altogether. A classic disinformation program relies upon feeding the opposition with material which they half believe already and wish to believe entirely. The Israelis, still celebrating their utter triumph in the Six-Day War, were quite ready to accept the veracity of any report which cast doubts upon the competence of the Arabs to wage another war.

Officer Commanding (G.O.C.) Southern Command, made an inspection tour of the canal area. What he saw, he didn't like, and he put his forces on a higher state of alert. Some leaves were canceled and other precautionary measures were taken, but when he asked the Chief of Staff for permission to move to full alert, he was turned down. Major General Abraham "Albert" Mandler, commanding officer of the armored division, Suez, followed suit and put his 280 tanks on alert. But Israeli Military Intelligence remained unimpressed. They missed nothing. They saw the ships unloading vast quantities of arms and ammunition at Port Fuad; they saw the SAM missiles moving into their operational pods on the Damascus Plains; the mine fields being cleared from the canal and stakes being driven into the water, apparently to assist bridge building. There was nothing very impressive about that. Sadat was once again playing his games to keep his army happy.

On October 3rd, a critical meeting took place in Jerusalem between ministers, army generals, and Military Intelligence under the chairmanship of Golda Meir. The Syrian line was noticeably thickening and several generals, including General Yitzhak Hofi, the G.O.C. Northern Command, were expressing grave anxiety about the rapid and obvious escalation they could see by merely observing enemy lines without the need for any intelligence evaluations at all. General Zeira himself was unwell and could not attend; he sent his deputy, the able Brigadier General Aryeh Shalev in his place. Zwi Zamir of Mossad was not invited and neither was anyone from the Foreign Ministry including the Foreign Minister. This, the only serious meeting between the Prime Minister and her senior intelligence advisers before the outbreak of fighting, was the one opportunity to put Zeira's concept up to critical examination at the highest level. Of those present, only General Dayan had the experience and the knowledge to do so, and for a moment at least under Dayan's pressure Aryeh Shalev, as wedded to the "concept" as Zeira himself, began to wilt.

In front of him were reports that the Syrians had transferred to the front line most of their antiaircraft missiles. The Syrians, Dayan argued, would only do this if they intended to go to war, or if they themselves were convinced that Israel was about to attack them. But Israel had not even mobilized, so they could not seriously imagine that an Israeli attack was imminent. Accordingly, they themselves must be preparing an assault.

Shalev agreed that the Syrians' movements were mysterious. But, he said, every piece of intelligence they had ever received had indicated that the Syrians would not and could not go to war without the Egyptians, and the Egyptians were simply not prepared to fight. It was a decisive argument, and the intelligence evaluation that the "probability of war is low" was formally entered into the records.

In retrospect, one can see why Dayan accepted that situation. Oddly enough, though well informed about what was happening on the northern front, which he had personally inspected, he had virtually no information about Egyptian preparations. Not a man normally accustomed to accepting things at face value, he nevertheless accepted without demur Shalev's assurance that, however warlike the Syrian preparations appeared, the Egyptian front indicated that nothing out of the ordinary was going on. Two telephone calls to General Samuel Gonen and General Mandler would have changed everything. But no longer a fighting general, Dayan was now inclined to go along with the general view prevalent in the Cabinet and the country that Israeli Intelligence could never be wrong.

Having said that, it is hard, even with the benefit of hindsight, to understand why no independent analysis was conducted or even called for of Zeira's evaluation. The Israeli Army has always relied upon its intelligence to give it at least twenty-four hours' notice of attack. Everything, from basic training through to the deployment of its weaponry, depends absolutely upon the armed forces getting this minimum period. The country is too small to be able to afford, as the Russians in World War II could do, to absorb an enemy within its sovereign territory, suck it in, and finally go back on the offensive to spit it out. Israel's wars need to be fought on its borders or outside its borders. Not to understand that basic point, dug deep into the consciousness of every Israeli, is not to understand its diplomatic or political posture on almost any issue affecting its relations with the Arabs.

In any case, views which ran counter to Zeira's—by now the officially accepted wisdom—were quashed at source. Zwi Zamir at Mossad was certainly a very worried man. His people were reporting disturbing trends from inside the Arab countries and from Europe as well, but his information never went further than Golda Meir's military secretary, who filed it away.

Intelligence officers in Southern Command were reporting with increasing alarm Egyptian activities, but these reports never even got to Tel Aviv. Even the CIA was persuaded to change its own evaluations. For years, of course, the Americans had relied heavily upon the Israelis to provide battle intelligence in the Middle East, and though the CIA was always careful to provide its own analysis, this would invariably be heavily colored by Israeli reporting. The CIA's initial evaluation that "war is imminent," made in early October and passed on to Yitzhak Rabin, then Israeli ambassador in Washington, who, in turn, passed it on to Golda Meir, so infuriated Zeira that though the normal conduit to the CIA was through Mossad, he himself saw to it that the CIA became fully aware of the very different interpretation which his service was placing on events in the area.

Indeed, on October 4th, Henry Kissinger met Israeli Foreign Minister Abba Eban in Washington. They disposed of the question of an early war in five minutes, both agreeing that the latest intelligence was of a reassuring character. What neither seemed to realize was that they were speaking to each other on the basis of the same brief, prepared by the same people. Each was, in effect, having a conversation with his mirror.

On the following day, the Soviets launched a Cosmos-596 spy satellite, which went into orbit over Israeli lines, and reports from battlefield commanders to HQ were now becoming almost hysterical as they watched the preparations before them.

On Friday, October 5th, Golda Meir convened what was later to become known as the "War Cabinet" to look at the latest reports flowing in. The Chief of Staff had already put into effect a "C Alert," the highest state of preparedness the Israeli Standing Army had employed since the war of attrition. But the move came too late; by then virtually the whole of the Army had already left their positions, were on their way to their families for Atonement Day Leave, and could not be recalled.

Though the situation was worrying, no great sense of urgency was expressed by anyone. The Deputy Prime

Minister, Yigal Allon, was at his kibbutz, and, though he was once a distinguished soldier, it wasn't thought necessary to bring him all the way back for the Cabinet meeting. The Treasury Minister, Pinchas Sapir, wasn't asked to attend and was told later that this was because he couldn't be found. He observed acidly after the war: "They couldn't find me because I'm such a small man!"

In the meantime, Mossad had been shut out completely. The brilliance of Yariv had had the unexpected effect of downgrading Mossad, which, in any case, had been so involved with the Palestinian problem that its intelligence networks in the confrontation states had been given a lower priority by Zamir than ever in the past.

Nevertheless, at least two Mossad agents in Cairo knew of Operation Badr—the Egyptian cover name for the attack—and had informed Tel Aviv. They backed their information with detailed reports of Egyptian troop movements, which proved to Mossad at least that there could be no doubt about Sadat's intentions. An extraordinary breach of Egyptian security was also picked up by Mossad. On October 2nd, the Middle East News Agency put out a message that the Egyptian Second and Third Armies —which would be used to cross the Suez Canal—had been put on a state of alert. The message was supposed to have gone out only on restricted circulation to a small number of senior Egyptian government officials, but the operator made a mistake and put it out on general service.

But Military Intelligence, still clinging to "the concept," preferred to believe items in *Al Ahram,* the official government newspaper, which Mohammed Heikal subsequently revealed were deliberately planted pieces of disinformation. One was a small item which said the commander in chief was opening up a list of officers who wished to go on a pilgrimage to Mecca. Another set a date for the Minister of Defense to visit Rumania on October 8th. And yet another designed to cover the gaffe on the Middle East News Agency report warned Israel in rather over-blown language of the consequences if it persisted in escalating the situation on the northern front. Cleverly, the Egyptians were playing upon their own predilection to bombast in the past, issuing a typically bombastic statement in the hope that the effect upon the Israelis would be to make them laugh. It did just that.

Mossad, however, was deeply concerned. It seemed to

men like Zamir that, whatever else Sadat and the Syrians might decide to do, they would surely not seek deliberately to create a war neurosis in Israel which might lead to an actual war and permit the Israelis once again the luxury of a first strike. Eli Zeira's answer to that was that the Arabs knew full well that Israel's international position was now such that she couldn't go to war unless either she was physically attacked or the Arab provocation was so extreme that the whole world would be aware of it.

This didn't seem, in the light of the information he was receiving, very convincing to Zamir, who sought every opportunity to press home his point. But Zeira was adamant. There would and could be no war. On October 4th, a Mossad duty officer had received information from an agent in Cairo supplying the date and time of the attack, and he rang up one of Zeira's deputies at home. Furious at being woken up in the middle of the night by yet another Mossad panic, he told his caller that if he ever dared call him again with such a ridiculous story at such an hour he, personally, would make sure that he never worked in the government service of Israel ever again.

But it was at such an hour, at 3:00 A.M., on the night of October 5th, that Zeira finally knew he had been desperately wrong. An agent—an Egyptian Jew in the canal zone—radioed to headquarters that orders had come down the line to launch an attack over the Suez Canal at 1800 hours on the following day, Yom Kippur. Special equipment was being issued, including special chemicals to spray on clothes against napalm. This is never issued on an exercise because once used on uniforms they have to be discarded. At that very moment, final operational orders were being prepared for the units at the ramparts. There could no longer be any doubt.

The most important question now was not if the attack would come, but whether Military Intelligence information that it would come at 1800 hours could be believed. The Israeli Army needed the answer to that one badly. How much time they had would determine how they would deploy. Zeira, who had been so adamant a few hours earlier that there would be no war, was now adamant about the time that war would come. More information had come in which he accepted unquestioningly. The Arabs, he said, would strike at 1800 hours. To young field intelligence officers, it hardly squared with the fact that by ten o'clock in the morning the Arabs were already maintaining radio silence. This is one of the eeriest and, in a strange kind of way, most frightening times of war— the silence which precedes a battle. An attacking army will always clear its radio transmissions before zero hour in order to ensure that commanding generals have total access to all units. These days, there is a new dimension to a military practice observed since World War II. Once, all one could hear was the silence. Now, it is possible to detect that enemy radios are switched on, ready to receive.

This is what was happening all that morning, and few could accept that any army would be put on stand-by for as long as was now being suggested. Higher up, too, there were doubts. Deputy Prime Minister Yigal Allon, himself a distinguished Israeli general from the War of Independence, expressed the view that no army in the world would attack just before sunset, giving its own air force time for only two strikes at the defending lines before night set in.

But Zeira once again was believed. In a backhanded kind of way, that was his finest hour. Golda Meir decided that Washington must be told immediately what was known of the Arabs' intentions and asked to do what it could, through the Russians and through the Arabs themselves, to stop the attack before it was too late. Henry Kissinger actually told the Arabs that the Israelis knew of their plans to launch an attack at 6:00 P.M. Already astonished at the total lack of reaction from the Israeli side, the Arabs now knew they would descend like wolves unto the fold.

At 2:00 P.M. that afternoon, Zeira was briefing military correspondents, telling them that whatever advice had been given them in the past few days, war was now imminent and would be likely to start that day. As he was talking, a junior officer walked in and handed him a card. He looked at it briefly and said gravely: "They tell me that war may be starting at any minute." A few minutes later, another card was brought in. He looked at it again and this time left the room without a word. Seconds later he returned. "Gentlemen," he said, "the meeting is over." And so was the career of General Zeira. His was the ultimate failure. He had promised the general staff and the government that he would always be able to deliver forty-eight hours' notice of an Arab attack. In fact, all he gave was ten . . . and then he got the time wrong.

After the war, Military Intelligence had to pay. Four officers lost their jobs. A commission was set up to examine the failure of intelligence to give adequate warning of the Arab attack. Their verdict on Zeira was that "in view of his grave failure, he could not continue in his post as chief of Military Intelligence." Zeira's deputy, Brigadier General Aryeh Shalev, Lieutenant Colonel Yona Bendman, in charge of the Egyptian desk, and Lieutenant Colonel David Gedaliah, chief intelligence officer of Southern Command, were also dismissed.

Before that happened, of course, the Israeli war machine had won a famous victory, but at great expense and only because it showed once again its genius for improvisation on the battlefield. Nothing and nobody had warned the Israeli Army what to expect. Military Intelligence knew that the Egyptian infantry had antitank missiles, capable of knocking out an enemy tank without the tank commander ever even knowing that he was under observation. But the Israelis didn't believe that this weapon would turn out to be an effective force in the hands of an Egyptian soldier. They knew that this would be an electronic war, but totally underestimated the capacity of the Arabs to wage it. Above all, for all their information on the Egyptian Army, down to the names of company commanders, nobody in Israeli intelligence had realized that out of a standing army of 800,000, 110,000 were graduates of universities or institutes of higher education, and that, by the standards of any army, is an impressive statistic.

As one bewildered and battered Israeli tank commander declared: "They hit us with weapons we didn't even know existed." He was, of course, wrong. Israeli Military Intelligence services did know, but either didn't pass that information on or did so in such a way that the potential importance of this equipment was never fully appreciated in an army which also suffered from the delusion that it had nothing to fear from the Arabs.

Intelligence, for example, knew perfectly well that for about a year the Egyptians had been experimenting with something they called "Tank-Hunter Units," but hadn't realized that, equipped with new-technology weapons, these would be quite the destructive force they proved to be in battle. Intelligence knew of the Arabs' new antiaircraft missiles, but had taken no cognizance of the indirect effect these would have upon the land battle. The intelligence was always there: the evaluations were bogged down by "the concept."

"The quality of information one receives," said Meir Amit, the ex-head of both Military Intelligence and Mossad, "satisfies the recipient who is willing to be satisfied by it—according to his needs at the time. When the need doesn't exist, lesser data may be considered as sufficient information." Though Meir Amit may have been engaging in a piece of special pleading for the profession, the relationship between any powerful intelligence community and its customers, its government and its military would, if one could ever get at it, make perhaps the most fascinating field study of all.

Eli Zeira, who had inherited perhaps the greatest military-intelligence operation in the world, must take—and did take—considerable responsibility for what occurred. Again, in his defense, it may be said that the Arabs themselves had learned a great deal. If the Israelis today are, in the view of many, unnecessarily suspicious of Arab intentions, then Mohammed Heikal's description of the deception plan laid down by Sadat before the war gives their suspicion some point. Heikal wrote: "Egyptian and Syrian representatives at non-aligned conferences, the United Nations and similar gatherings spoke in pacific terms (without, it must be added, knowing the purpose of the directive from which they spoke), while the press and radio were encouraged to play up the concern of Egypt and Syria over the search for a peaceful solution to the Middle East conflict, and to refer with disapproval to the belligerent speeches and actions of the Palestinian Fedayeen."

Unlike his predecessors, Zeira was dealing with Arab countries who had learned to respect the high caliber of Israeli intelligence. Cairo used to be a city where every taxi driver knew what had occurred at that morning's Cabinet. All this had changed. As few Egyptians as possible were brought into the secret attack plan. A survey carried out among the 8,000 prisoners who fell into Israeli hands during the war showed that only one knew on October 3rd that preparations were for a real war, and ninety-five percent only knew on the morning of October 6th that they would be in action that day. The platoon commander of twenty assault boats in the 16th Brigade of the 16th Egyptian Infantry Division realized it was war only minutes before H Hour, when his men took their boats out of their crates and carried them down to the canal still believing they were engaged in an exercise. Of the eighteen Egyptian colonels and lieutenant colonels in Israeli captivity, four knew about the war on October 4th, one was informed on October 5th, and the rest only on the morning of the actual day. One colonel described how at two o'clock on October 6th he was standing watching the Egyptian planes flying over the Third Army headquarters toward the Israeli lines. He turned to his brigadier and asked him: "What's all this about?" The reply was: "Ask the general." He turned to where the general had been standing and saw him on his knees praying toward Mecca. This was his first intimation of war.

Yet if Israeli intelligence owed its reputation solely to the ease with which it was able to penetrate a target which up to Yom Kippur 1973 had always been wide open, then its achievements would hardly be noteworthy. But this was not the case. When the files were opened after the war, the material the intelligence community had collected was found to be of as high a grade as it had ever been. The trouble was that Zeira had failed to grasp its significance.

When he finally said goobye to his officers in April 1974, General Zeira observed sadly: "Intelligence work is very hard. You are called upon to prophesy."

Aluf Hareven, once one of Yariv's closest aides, remarked: "Zeira was wrong. Prophecy is a gift of the gods and not the will of man. Only very few are blessed with it. . . . Intelligence is not required to prophesy, but to *know* about the enemy and his intentions as much as possible. Since one cannot know everything, one should also state where the domains of ignorance, uncertainty and doubt exist. This is exactly what Zeira refused to admit. In law, one is acquitted on the grounds of doubt, and there is always room for appeal. Intelligence, on the eve of the Yom Kippur War, dealt with the life and death of people, but the voice of doubt and the right of appeal were silenced until after its outbreak."

The Agranat Commission, set up to investigate the intelligence disaster, said that Zeira took upon himself to be "the sole arbiter of all intelligence matters in Israel."

The fact is that Zeira, if he had not accepted the appointment of chief of Military Intelligence, might well have ended up as the Israeli Chief of Staff. But as Israel learned to its cost, you need to be more than a brilliant soldier to be a chief of intelligence.

The fascination of intelligence, which Yariv described as being as potent as opium, lies in its lack of precision. The great intelligence officer, as Amit says, is the man who "can admit, 'I don't know,' and who understands he is always dealing with options."

Zeira was impatient with that approach. He wanted facts in a world where facts, as such, rarely exist.

The perimeters of intelligence never possess hard edges. There can be no boundaries to knowledge. An intelligence man needs to be a free and not a fixed thinker. Zeira didn't fail—he was simply the wrong man for the job—and several of his colleagues knew it when he was first appointed.

When General Shlomo Gazit took over Military Intelligence upon the dismissal of General Zeira, he called all the department heads together and said: "Improbability is not a dirty word." It was a brave declaration, underlying the dilemma which now faced a badly bruised and shellshocked intelligence community. Gazit inherited a seat which was perhaps the hottest in Israel. Only ten senior officers of the Israeli Army had ever been dismissed from their posts. But during the history of Military Intelligence, there had been seven commanders, of whom four had been sacked. After the Yom Kippur War, not only Zeira went, but, as we have seen, three other officers were forced out with him. Gazit could be forgiven for feeling himself to be in a no-win situation. It is part of the function of intelligence not only to predict the likelihood of war but to determine when it is not likely as well. To have an intelligence establishment fearful of ever again going out on a limb or of challenging the unscientifically based beliefs of front-line commanders or of setting forth clearcut intelligence estimates would spell disaster not only for Israel but for the whole Middle East. If every time the Egyptians held a military exercise a little more ambitious than expected, the Israeli reserves mobilized, not only would the Israeli economy be shattered, but the whole region would be permanently psychologically and physically on the brink of war. To avoid that, the whole system required review; it was not sufficient merely to sack the men who had failed, for it had also to be acknowledged that the system had permitted them to fail.

Some Israeli senior officers, in fact, were beginning to take the view that the Israeli intelligence community needed the Yom Kippur War in order to discover how it had become morally corrupted by fame and adulation. The casualty list might have been a high price to pay but better an intelligence defeat at a time when Israel could be sure it would win the ensuing war than later when the Israelis could not be so confident.

What had happened to Israeli intelligence is what happens to any organization which owes its success to the personality and genius of outstanding individuals. Practices which worked when men with an intuitive grasp of affairs like Ahrele Yariv or Meir Amit were in charge could not work when less gifted men wielded the same power, using the same tools.

Isser Harel's departure from Mossad way back in the early sixties had ended the virtual state of war which had existed between Mossad and Military Intelligence. Only now was it seen that the peace treaty between the two agencies had proved a very expensive purchase indeed. It had been achieved by each side informally agreeing to keep out of each other's territory. The effect of that was that Military Intelligence, given the task of preparing the intelligence estimate, rose in importance at the expense of Mossad, which clearly declined. Mossad became a mere collecting agency, brilliant at what it did, but imperceptibly ceasing to have any real influence or power upon decisions made in Tel Aviv.

When the Israelis raided Beirut, it was Military Intelligence which set out for the government in advance the military plan as well as the likely political repercussions. Of course, Mossad was involved in the planning and had its own people along, but in the last analysis it was Yariv's operation and not Zamir's, though this was Zamir's territory.

Mossad's own Research Department, less and less required to help formulate policy, received inevitably less and less money to do so until it ceased to have the capability. But if Mossad had opted out, so, more seriously, had the Foreign Ministry, whose Research Department had been specifically set up by David Ben-Gurion to produce independent political evaluations for the military. But at the time of the Yom Kippur War, the department had virtually ceased to function. Successive economy cuts had resulted in a situation where it did not even get every main Arab newspaper. As a serious center for political analysis, it was a joke.

Since Moshe Sharett, the only Israeli Foreign Minister who regarded his Research Department as being of value, left the Foreign Ministry in the fifties, the decline had been steady. By 1973, there were only twenty people in the department, half of whom were secretaries. One man and one alone dealt with the whole of Egypt—even if he had got all of the newspapers he would never have been able to read them, never mind the stream of cables, coming in from all over the world, involving Israeli-Egyptian relations.

Without research backing, successive Foreign Ministers were also imperceptibly weakened in their relations with the military until they, too, lost out, not merely in status, for that would not have mattered too much, but in the ability to mount a well-constructed argument against the evaluations of the military. When Yitzhak Rabin, ex-Chief of Staff of the Israeli Army, was the ambassador in Washington, he fell out with the Israeli Foreign Minister Abba Eban and refused to have dealings with him. His cables went directly to Golda Meir, who, whatever her private feelings may have been, was perfectly prepared to accept that her Foreign Minister should not have first access to information coming from Israel's only diplomatic post which really mattered. Though perhaps not terribly important in itself, it was indicative of the decline of Israel's Foreign Service, an extraordinary situation for a country whose very existence depended upon its ability to maintain proper relations with the outside world.

None of this, naturally, came as a surprise to the man who predicted it all in the late forties, the forgotten man of Israeli intelligence, Boris Guriel, the head of the Political Department of the Foreign Ministry, the organization which was the forerunner of Mossad. He had been laughed out of office because he had insisted that the only intelligence that really mattered was that intelligence which read the political intentions of one's opponents. These ideas had seemed peculiarly arcane and impractical for a country facing the real and terrible problems Israel then did. But Guriel was vindicated by results, and his critics—men like Isser Harel, who regarded political intelligence as being the airy-fairy talk of intellectuals—were proved wrong. As it was, what political intelligence was gathered, much of it acute and sophisticated, was put into the hands of men who by their very nature were least able to understand it, the military. The intelligence community had become a monolith, and its evaluations were not open to challenge from any quarter.

What had clearly gone wrong, therefore, derived not so much from the ability of the people who had risen to the surface of the intelligence community but from the structure of that community itself. The great intelligence chiefs like Yariv, Amit or Harel had by virtue of their genius been able to operate successfully despite the structure rather than because of it. But by so doing they had actually, and ironically, distorted it still further. When Harkabi built his great edifice, the research and evaluation department of Military Intelligence, it had not been his intention that this should be the sole such depository in Israel, but almost inevitably as his department grew in size, importance and status, research and evaluation elsewhere declined.

The question is this: How far should intelligence services, with their very special expertise, be permitted to draw operational or political conclusions from their own analyses? The easy and classic answer is that it is up to the intelligence community merely to provide the information, letting others decide what conclusions should be drawn and what actions taken. Yet intelligence today requires the consideration and refinement of so much detailed material that the intelligence community and the intelligence community alone has all the relevant material at its fingertips to reach appropriate conclusions. There has to be a process of editing—that is, political leaders must get a package which has already been predigested by the machine or else they would do nothing but read intelligence reports.

Meir Amit sees the problem clearly. He says that since political leaders don't have much time to sift through raw intelligence, they would prefer clearcut analysis to be put to them. When this does not happen and they are provided with a great deal of raw intelligence, they tend to pick out the dramatic or the "spicy" bits, as Amit puts it, draw conclusions from that, and cannot subsequently be budged. The fact is that raw intelligence—and the Israelis, with a comparatively small service compared to the CIA, estimate that they receive twenty or thirty thousand pieces of raw intelligence a day—has to be sifted by someone. That process of editing must inevitably imply a process of subjective judgment.

Whatever the theory, an intelligence service does make political and military decisions, even when it is careful to parade alternative scenarios to its political and military masters. Chaim Herzog remembers a lecture given by Kenneth Strong, Eisenhower's head of intelligence during World War II. Strong said that intelligence agencies have always been targets for attack and criticism. If an agency is afraid of criticism, it will always give pessimistic assessments. For if an agency makes an optimistic assessment which proves correct, it is forgotten; if it is not correct, the agency is castigated. But if the assessment is pessimistic and proves wrong, a feeling of relief follows, and the agency is forgiven. It was Zeira's optimism which proved to be his undoing.

Thoughts very much akin to that must have gone through the minds of the men who sat at the top of the Israeli intelligence community when, at the end of a meeting of ministers on June 29, 1976, they were asked for an analysis, from the intelligence point of view, of the chances of success of an Israeli raiding party flying to Entebbe airport in Uganda to rescue 105 men, women and children, passengers of Air France Flight 139, which had been hijacked to Uganda, where they were under the malign patronage of President Amin.

Zwi Zamir, who became a favorite of Golda Meir, had retired from Mossad after seven years' service, two more than the five years laid down as a maximum tenure of office when Harel resigned, and his place had been taken by Major General Yitzhak ("Hacka") Hofi, who had been General Officer Commanding Northern Command during the Yom Kippur War. Hacka Hofi had been a thorn in the side of General Zeira before Yom Kippur. He was convinced that an attack was imminent and bombarded HQ with every disturbing report produced by his

own intelligence officers. Hofi was the only general who
risked making himself permanently unpopular by insisting
at the highest level that Military Intelligence was being
dangerously complacent. In many ways, Hacka Hofi, still
head of Mossad up to the time of writing, was a curious
choice to head Israel's political-intelligence agency. He
had had little, if any, direct involvement with intelligence
and seemed, on the face of it at least, anything but the
kind of man who could be a ruminative thinker, capable of the sophistication so essential to intelligence work.
Squat, quiet to the point of being almost dour, he was
popular with his men by virtue of his straightforwardness
and his obvious courage, but in an army brimming with
thinkers no one would have put him in among the first
dozen. But this was very much a shallow judgment. For
forty-eight hours at the start of the Yom Kippur War, almost nothing lay between the Syrian Army and the destruction of Israel. Hofi first fought a brilliant holding
action and then counterattacked to smash the pride of
the Syrian Army in one of the great armor battles in the
history of warfare. In modern warfare, no one without a
first-rate mind can be a first-rate tank commander, but
Hacka Hofi also brought to Mossad all the prestige and
luster of his name as well as his reputation of speaking
out when he believed things were going wrong. It is doubtful that Hofi would even permit himself to be quite so
easily shunted to one side as Zwi Zamir was before the
Yom Kippur War when Zamir was convinced that Military Intelligence was leading Israel to disaster.

The new chief of Military Intelligence, Major General
Shlomo Gazit, was one of the most outstanding and experienced staff officers in the Israeli Army. Gazit had
been A.D.C. to General Mordechai Maklef when, in December 1953, Dayan took over as Chief of Staff. Normally, officers taking up new appointments brought their
own A.D.C.s with them, and Gazit had expected that
Dayan would do likewise—particularly since Gazit could
legitimately be regarded as a member of the Maklef faction who resented Dayan's rapid promotion. But Dayan
kept him on, recognizing that Gazit possessed remarkable
administrative abilities while Dayan had almost none.

The Israeli intelligence community now had a third
arm, operating out of the Prime Minister's office, a special adviser on intelligence. This was designed to ensure

that assessments from the various branches were kept as fluid as possible when presented to the Cabinet, that there should not be a repetition of what had occurred before Yom Kippur when the government found itself being forced to rely upon a single source for its information. That appointment went to a third general, Major General Rehavam Zeevi, known throughout the Israeli Army as "Gandhi" since the occasion when as a young officer he had wrapped himself in a bed sheet and, dragging a goat behind him, had appeared in company lines after a mess party dressed like the Mahatma. Gandhi's appointment was an imaginative one. He had been talked of in the past as a possible head of Mossad or Military Intelligence, but was too unconventional a figure, too little a desk man and too much of a loner to be regarded as an effective head of what is inevitably a bureaucracy as well as an intelligence operation.

In the long years between the Six-Day War and the Yom Kippur War he was Commanding General of Central Command and so dealt on a daily basis with the problems of terrorist infiltration, sabotage and the like. He had taken part in more than 120 raids into enemy territory after terrorists had effectively sealed the Jordanian frontier against infiltrators, and through his own intelligence network had caught hundreds in the occupied areas under his jurisdiction. He had traveled frequently abroad, in Africa and Europe and the United States on missions connected with intelligence, and had acquired in the process a lasting relish for cloak-and-dagger operations. Gandhi is the kind of unconventional figure who thrives in a country like Israel which is in a state of semipermanent war, but he would have little chance of promotion or preferment in any peacetime army almost anywhere in the world.

It was to these three men of the intelligence community —Hofi, Gazit and Gandhi—that the Israeli government would logically turn for advice when the terrorists hijacked the Air France flight in June 1976. Unfortunately, Gandhi was still in Canada, where he had been engaged in talks with local security officials concerning the forthcoming Olympic Games. That left only Hofi and Gazit in a position to assess the possibility of a rescue mission. The Chief of Staff Lieutenant General Mordechai ("Mota") Gur had already canvassed his senior officers and had been impressed by their eagerness to go to Kampala. Backed by Defense Minister Shimon Peres, Gur was anxious to go, too. Hofi, in particular, but also Gazit, were asked what resistance a raiding party was likely to meet on the ground, what refueling facilities if any could be provided en route, and what chances the raiding party had of hitting the terminals at Entebbe before the terrorists were aware of what had happened and had time to kill the hostages.

Hofi's blunt answer to the government was that he didn't know, but that he would find out. Luckily, one of those unpublicized undercover alliances which Israel from time to time enjoys existed then between Tel Aviv and Nairobi. At the same time, two Mossad undercover men were attending the Organization of African Unity meeting in Mauritius, and they, as well as half a dozen other Mossad men who knew Africa well, were flown in for a meeting in Nairobi.

The local Nairobi Israeli "resident"—I will call him Motta—was put in charge of that operation; he was not the most senior man present, but he knew Africa better than anyone else in the room. Kenyan Security had already been approached about landing rights at Nairobi, and had agreed that an El Al plane could land on "humanitarian grounds." There could be no question, however, of Nairobi's being used as a jumping-off point to attack Entebbe. The problem was Uganda itself.

Motta already had a small though not particularly active network in Uganda, principally because the PLO had used Uganda more and more as its center for operations in Africa under the direction of Haled el-Sid, who, with a touch of nice malice, had been given 17 Mackinon Road, the old private residence of the Israeli ambassador in Kampala before diplomatic relations were broken off in March 1972 by Amin, to serve as his home and headquarters. With little time to spare, four Israelis and two Kenyans who had been used by Motta before made their way across Lake Victoria in a fast Kenyan police boat to land near Entebbe.

Kampala airport was sealed off, but the Israelis quickly established that, apart from the Palestinians, Amin's troops were thin on the ground. Obviously the last thing anyone was expecting was a rescue mission. Every operation requires a little bit of luck, and it had come for the

Israelis when it was discovered that a member of the Mossad network in Uganda, a Ugandan citizen, was friendly with one of the officers mounting guard over the hostages. He had asked to go and see "the Jews," and was allowed into the airport building itself. He reported that the terrorists were obviously nervous, but that, at least while he was there, only half a dozen or so Ugandan troops were anywhere in the vicinity.

At the same time, other Mossad men hired two twin-engined planes from Wilson airport in Nairobi while filing a flight plan which showed their destination to be Kisumu on the Kenyan shore of Lake Victoria. The planes strayed from their course and flew high above the lake until Uganda and Entebbe airport were in sight. The photographic equipment they had was fairly primitive, but they were able to take good enough pictures of the airport not to require the Israelis to have to ask the Americans to take satellite pictures of the target zone.

An ambitious plan to bug 17 Mackinon Road came to nothing. Haled el-Sid was well protected by his own Palestinians, and Motta's orders had been clear. The raiding party must take no risks and do nothing to expose themselves for fear that the Ugandans would become aware of their presence.

Meanwhile, in Paris, Gandhi, who had flown back from Canada as quickly as possible, called in every Mossad man in Western Europe to meet the non-Jewish passengers who had been released by the terrorists and were flying back directly to Orly airport. As each ex-hostage arrived, he was pressed for any detail he could remember about the terrorists, about Kampala airport, about the state of hostages, and the attitude of the Ugandan military. The information thus gleaned plus the information from his men in Uganda permitted Hofi to send a full memorandum to the Prime Minister. The gist of that message was that from the intelligence point of view Kampala airport was wide open. The mission was on.

Gandhi used "open" telephone lines, which he was sure would be tapped, to "reveal" that the Israeli government was on the point of surrender. A "neutral" diplomat whom everyone knew passed every bit of information he received to the PLO was told that the only thing holding up immediate negotiation was Rabin's difficulty in drafting a statement that would be politically acceptable in

Israel. Meanwhile, President Amin's ego was boosted when he was told by another well-primed diplomat that the Israelis had been saying that this time he had them in the palm of his hand.

Nairobi was clear. A Boeing 707, to be used as a flying hospital, had landed. What is not generally known is that it also unloaded fifty Israeli paratroopers, who were immediately put into boats and ordered to the center of Lake Victoria, ready to move in fast if anything went wrong.

The six Mossad men on the ground in Uganda went into position armed principally with high-frequency radios tuned in to the command plane which would circle Kampala throughout the raid. Their function was to monitor activity, to signal any changes in the local security pattern, which could indicate right up to the moment of landing that either the terrorists or the Ugandans had been alerted. The Mossad men carried with them an electronic device which jammed the radar of the control tower. It was probably the first time this remarkable piece of modern electronics was used anywhere in the world. Similar devices were later used by the American Special Forces Unit that flew aircraft and helicopters into Iran, undetected by radar, in the abortive attempt to rescue the hostages. These devices—which come under the generic description of counter-electronic measures—rank among the most secret equipment of the armies of all the world's major powers.

The full story of the raid on Entebbe has been told too often to bear repetition now, but the part Mossad played has not been revealed elsewhere. Yet the men who watched through their night binoculars the action at the airport, saw the hostages embark and take off before they themselves made their way back to Lake Victoria to be picked up by launch and returned to the safety of Kenya were as crucial to the success of the mission as the soldiers who fought the action on the airstrip.

A great intelligence operation is one which is neither seen nor heard and leaves no trace behind. But after the Entebbe raid, the then Israeli Prime Minister Yitzhak Rabin spoke of his admiration for those involved and said: "This tribute is the least we can do for the anonymous soldiers of the intelligence community, the stouthearted paratroopers, the brave infantrymen of the Golani

Brigade, the air-force pilots and all the others who made
the impossible come true."

It was no slip of the pen that the intelligence community headed that list. It was the acknowledgment of a remarkable intelligence operation and an accolade designed
to tell the Israeli intelligence community that the shadow
which had hung over it since the Yom Kippur War had
at last been lifted. Just as Israel itself needed Entebbe to
restore its own self-confidence, so did the intelligence
community need to have restored its self-respect so badly
dented by the Yom Kippur War.

What Yom Kippur did do for the intelligence services
was to require them, in the face of this most terrible
trauma, to re-examine every detail of the way they conducted their operations, their relations with the government and military commanders, their own hierarchical
structures and their relationships with parallel services.
Many thought that the Israeli intelligence services might
be irretrievably weakened by this process of destructive
patch analysis. "Intelligence," said one Mossad desk man
angrily, "is so busily examining itself that it has no time
left to examine the enemy." But Entebbe proved that the
intelligence community had emerged on the other side of
the tunnel, its ability to act with speed, daring and precision unimpaired.

As one great ex-intelligence chief has written: "Israel
was marked by two deep traumas since its establishment."
The first was the Lavon affair and the second the Yom
Kippur War. Both deeply involved the intelligence community, which, while capable of acting with a burst of
brilliance unmatched by any country in the world, always
appeared ultimately flawed because of a seeming inability
to monitor its own performance.

There are some Israelis who believe that by virtue of
its sheer secretiveness, the Israeli intelligence community
is prey to a kind of corporate insanity—in retrospect in-
comprehensible and out of character—which may go unchecked when any group is not immediately accountable
to others. (In fact, whatever many radical Israelis believe
to the contrary, there is as much if not more democratic
control of their intelligence community than exists in almost any other country in the world with an intelligence
service of significance.) Both the Lavon affair and the
Yom Kippur War shared the common link that in each

case chiefs of intelligence deliberately bypassed the controls. In the former, documents were forged in order to protect the service from political attack. In the latter, documents were withheld in order that there would be no real debate within the government as to the correctness of Military Intelligence's position.

The real trouble in Israel was that the hierarchical structure within which the intelligence community existed gradually broke down. Chaim Herzog, who was twice chief of Military Intelligence under David Ben-Gurion, says that when Ben-Gurion headed the country he regarded himself as being ultimately responsible for all intelligence matters. It was he, therefore, who presented intelligence analysis to the Cabinet and to the Defense and Foreign Affairs Committee of the Knesset. He studied the issues, argued with his intelligence chiefs, and then, having taken responsibility for them, set forth the conclusions to the appropriate political body for debate. Intelligence performed its classic function—as adviser rather than policymaker. The fact that this system broke down was partly due to the fact that the community drew to itself individuals who were so outstanding that in many ways they towered, intellectually and even politically, above the politicians whom they were called upon to serve, and partly due to the increasing complexity of the issues they had to face. But whatever the reason, the Israeli intelligence community gradually became a body answerable only to its peers, a state within a state.

Yet having said that, it should also be acknowledged that Mossad and Military Intelligence have tried to maintain civilized standards for the world in which they have been obliged to operate. Of course, Israeli intelligence has resorted to assassination, but it did so because it believed terrorism had to be met with terrorism. The morality of those operations in the seventies severely exercised the minds of many Israelis, including the entire intelligence community. In the end, Israel felt itself justified, and given the circumstances of those days it is difficult to gainsay it.

After a stumbling start in the forties, when a state had to be created by a bunch of argumentative, largely undisciplined amateurs, an ethic for the profession was quickly established. Save for the inevitable black sheep who fell by the wayside, that ethic survives today. It was

David Ben-Gurion, so frequently hawkish in his response to any Arab provocation, who first laid down the principle that Jewish history, if it means anything at all, means that there are certain things that Jews cannot do.

Propositions advanced from time to time to kill a Nasser or an Arafat have been rejected out of hand. The assassination of political leaders is not thought consistent with the dignity of the State of Israel. Psychological testing of new recruits to Mossad or Military Intelligence is stringent, and a full-time psychiatric department exists within Mossad to maintain surveillance of career officers throughout their service. During the spate of assassinations of leading Palestinian terrorist leaders, one senior Mossad man spoke in somewhat intemperate terms at a planning session about the "vermin" which it was Mossad's task to eliminate. He was politely retired, even though a case was made for him, pointing out that this did not represent his real feelings at all. A gentle man, distressed by what was going on, he justified the killings to himself by loudly expressed contempt for the victims. But he failed the psychiatrists' criteria. Rather, they said, a man who suffers nightmares than a man who justifies himself by calling his victims "vermin." Today that might not represent his true feelings; tomorrow it will.

The function of intelligence has been described as "hearing voices through the noise." Before World War I, the French Deuxième Bureau warned that the Germans would attack, giving precise details as to how the assault would come. The French government didn't believe it because political and diplomatic "noises" suggested the opposite. Stalin was deceived by the Germans, even though his intelligence service warned him about Operation Barbarossa, and, in more recent times, the West was completely fooled by the Soviets before they invaded Czechoslovakia in 1968, an eventuality which the United States, British, French and German secret services had all dismissed as too improbable a course to be considered seriously. Jack Kennedy involved himself in the Bay of Pigs fiasco because off-stage "noises" convinced him and the entire CIA that the Cuban people would rise up as one man the moment outside help arrived to throw off the shackles of Fidel Castro.

The Israeli intelligence community has always been faced with the problem that the "noises" through which it

must listen for "voices" are peculiarly acute. Arab leaders
are adept at the grandiose boast; have perfected to a fine
art that most infuriating characteristic of states which are
not pure democracies—of making two statements, one for
home consumption and the other for abroad. Arabs are
traditionally both a pragmatic people and a people for
whom concepts of honor and dignity mean a great deal.
Their relations with Israel have been a long and, to them,
painful attempt to reconcile these quite irreconcilable
characteristics, which have led inevitably to irrational
choices of options and have made intelligence assessments
based upon rational considerations particularly difficult.

To add to the problem, many of the "noises" Israeli
intelligence has been forced to try to filter out come from
within Israel itself. Intelligence will always be influenced
by the prevailing wisdom. As Yehoshaphat Harkabi has
said: "One cannot have good intelligence in a society of
fools."

Israel is a society inclined to hysteria. Its victories are
greeted with extraordinary jubilation and its defeats with
massive national gloom. The Israelis are a people whose
currency is exaggeration. They either underestimate the
capabilities of their enemies or overestimate them. They
treat their heroes with shameless adulation and those who
have failed with noisy brutality. The Israeli intelligence
community has been much influenced by this atmosphere.
Yet it is to the credit of the men who have led it, men like
Isser Harel, Meir Amit, Zwicka Zamir and Yehoshaphat
Harkabi, that it is the one place in the country where
coolness of judgment has been an honored and respected
virtue.

From the very beginning, Israel set out to establish an
intelligence community which followed the same high-
minded principles of the State itself. Alas, like the State,
it has often fallen short of this ideal. But, as "Abraham,"
a Mossad executive for many years and the man mentioned in the Preface of this book, once told me: "I am a
Jew. This means more to me than that I work for Mossad.
If ever I found that being a Jew and working for Israel's
secret service were irreconcilable, if ever my personal
ethic and the ethic of the state collided, I would pack my
bags and leave. This has not happened, and it has not
happened because I and people like me would not let it

happen. I am convinced that there will always be enough of us to ensure that continues to be so."

Today, the Israeli intelligence community, a little less romantic and dashing than perhaps it once was, a little more bureaucratic, somewhat more thorough, still ranks as one of the greatest intelligence services in the world.

With all its faults, with all the scandals which have rocked it, with all the mistakes, it still remains, somehow, a remarkably human service.

"Remember," Amit said once at a briefing, "people count—and people are people whether they are Jews, Moslems, Christians, Hottentots, or whatever."

Sometimes that message has been forgotten. But it has been forgotten fewer times, I believe, than the world has the right to expect from the intelligence community and the armed forces of this small and beleaguered nation.

Bibliography

ALLON, YIGAL, *The Making of Israel's Army*. London: Vallentine Mitchell, 1970.

ALLON, YIGAL, *Shield of David*. London: Weidenfeld & Nicolson, 1970.

AVRIEL, EHUD, *Open the Gates*. New York: Atheneum, 1975.

BAR-ZOHAR, MICHEL, *Ben-Gurion, A Biography*. London: Weidenfeld & Nicolson, 1977.

BAR-ZOHAR, MICHEL, *La Chasse aux Savants Allemands*. Paris: Libraire Arthème Fayard, 1965.

BAR-ZOHAR, MICHEL, *Spies in the Promised Land*. London: Davis-Poynter, 1972.

BAUER, YEHUDA, *From Diplomacy to Resistance*. New York: Atheneum, 1970.

BEN DAN, E., *L'Espion qui venait d'Israël*. Paris: Librairie Arthème Fayard, 1967.

BEN-GURION, DAVID, *Israel, A Personal History*. Tel Aviv: Sabra Books, 1972.

BEN-HANAN, ELIE, *Our Man in Damascus*. Tel Aviv: A.D.M., 1969.

BEN-PORAT, YESHAYAHU, and others, *Entebbe Rescue*. New York: Delacorte Press, 1977.

BEN-PORAT, YESHAYAHU, and others, *Kippur*. Tel Aviv: Special Edition, 1973.

BEN SHAUL, MOSHE (ed.), *Generals of Israel*. Tel Aviv: Hadar, 1968.

COLLINS, LARRY, and DOMINIQUE LAPIERRE, *O Jerusalem*. New York: Simon & Schuster, 1972.

COOKRIDGE, E. H., *Gehlen, Spy of the Century*. New York: Random House, 1971.

COPELAND, MILES, *The Real Spy World*. London: Weidenfeld & Nicolson, 1974.

CORSON, WILLIAM R., *The Armies of Ignorance*. New York: The Dial Press/James Wade Books, 1977.

DAWIDOWICZ, LUCY S., *The War Against the Jews, 1939-1945*. New York: Holt, Rinehart and Winston, 1975.

DAYAN, MOSHE, *Story of My Life*. London: Weidenfeld & Nicolson, 1976.

DEKEL, EFRAIM, *Shai: The Exploits of Hagana Intelligence*. Tel Aviv: Yoseleff, 1959.

EISENBERG, DENNIS, and ELI LANDAU, *Carlos: Terror International*. London: Corgi Books, 1976.

EL-AD, AVRI, *Decline of Honour*. Chicago: Henry Regnery, 1976.

ELON, AMOS, *The Israelis: Founders & Sons*. London: Weidenfeld & Nicolson, 1971.

ENGLE, ANITA, *The Nili Spies*. London: Hogarth, 1959.

FARAGO, LADISLAS, *Aftermath*. New York: Simon & Schuster, 1974.

FRIEDMAN, TUVIA, *The Hunter*. London: Gibbs & Phillips, 1961.

GILBERT, MARTIN, *The Arab-Israeli Conflict*. London: Weidenfeld & Nicolson, 1974.

GOLAN, AVIEZER, and DANNY PINKAS, *Shula, Code Name the Pearl*. New York: Delacorte Press, 1980.

GOLAN, MATTI, *The Secret Conversations of Henry Kissinger*. New York: Quadrangle, 1976.

GROUSSARD, SERGE, *The Blood of Israel*. New York: William Morrow & Co., 1973.

HAREL, ISSER, *The House on Garibaldi Street*. London: Andre Deutsch, 1975.

HEIKAL, MOHAMED, *The Road to Ramadan*. London: William Collins, 1975.

HERZOG, MAJOR GENERAL CHAIM, *The War of Atonement*. London: Weidenfeld & Nicolson, 1975.

LAQUEUR, WALTER (ed.), *The Israeli-Arab Reader*. New York: Bantam, 1969.

LAQUEUR, WALTER, *The Struggle for the Middle East: The Soviet Union & the Middle East 1948-68*. London: Routledge & Kegan Paul, 1969.

LARTEGUY, JEAN, *The Walls of Israel*. New York: M. Evans, 1969.

LITVINOFF, BARNET, *Weizmann*. London: Hodder & Stoughton, 1976.

LOTZ, WOLFGANG, *The Champagne Spy*. London: Vallentine Mitchell, 1972.

LOVE, KENNETT, *Suez, the Twice Fought War*. London: Longman Group Ltd., 1970.

MARDOR, MUNYA, *Strictly Illegal.* London: Robert Hale Ltd., 1964.

MASTER, ANTHONY, *The Summer That Bled.* New York: St. Martin's Press, 1973.

MEIR, GOLDA, *My Life.* London: Weidenfeld & Nicolson, 1975.

MONROE, ELIZABETH, *Adelphi Papers, No. III, The Arab-Israeli War, October 1973: Background and Events.* International Institute of Strategic Studies, London, 1975.

NINIO, MARCELLE (and others), *Operation Susannah.* New York: Harper & Row, 1978.

OFFER, YEHUDA, *Operation Thunder: The Entebbe Raid, the Israelis' Own Story.* Harmondsworth, England: Penguin Books, 1976.

PEARLMAN, MOSHE, *The Capture of Adolf Eichmann.* London: Weidenfeld & Nicolson, 1961.

PIEKALKIEWICZ, JANUSZ, *Israels Langer Arm.* Frankfurt: Goverts Verlag im S Fischer Verlag, 1975.

RABIN, YITZHAK, *The Rabin Memoirs.* London: Weidenfeld & Nicolson, 1979.

SCHIFF, ZEEV, *October Earthquake.* Tel Aviv: University Publishing Projects Ltd., 1974.

SLATER, LEONARD, *The Pledge.* New York: Simon & Schuster, 1970.

SMITH, COLIN, *Portrait of a Terrorist.* New York: Holt, Rinehart and Winston, 1976.

STEVENSON, WILLIAM, *90 Minutes at Entebbe.* London: Bantam Books, 1976.

TEVETH, SHABTAI, *Moshe Dayan.* London: Weidenfeld & Nicolson, 1972.

THAYER, GEORGE, *The War Business.* New York: Simon & Schuster, 1969.

TINNIN, DAVID B., *The Hit Team.* Boston: Little, Brown and Company, 1976.

TULLY, ANDREW, *The Super Spies.* New York: William Morrow & Co., 1969.

WIESENTHAL, SIMON, *The Murderers Among Us.* London: William Heinemann, 1967.

WISE, DAVID, and THOMAS B. ROSS, *The Espionage Establishment.* New York: Random House, 1967.

Index

391

ABOUT THE AUTHOR

Stewart Steven, a longtime international journalist and student of Israeli intelligence, is now Deputy Editor of the *London Daily Mail*. For THE SPY-MASTERS OF ISRAEL, the author conducted well over one hundred interviews and spoke to virtually every figure of significance who has emerged in either political or military intelligence since the founding of the state of Israel.

Stewart Steven is also the author of OPERATION SPLINTER FACTOR, and he is currently at work on a nonfiction book about Poland.

Go undercover with the CIA, the KGB and...

The Ballantine Espionage/Intelligence Library

True stories of international espionage that read like the best espionage thrillers...

FOR YOUR EYES ONLY!